1

Book Of Dreams
And Dream
Interpretations
By
Douglas Hensley

No one is better at interpreting your dreams than yourself. Interpreting your own dreams can be a powerful tool. To guide you with your interpretation, I have spent months compiling dream interpretations. These meanings will hopefully inspire you to explore and understand your own dreams.

Every detail in your dream is important and must be considered when analyzing your dreams. This book, along with your own personal experiences, will serve to guide you through a meaningful and personalized interpretation. If you spend some time practicing interpreting your dreams you can gain an understanding of the hidden secrets your dreams are trying to tell you. For your convenience I have placed all interpretation in alphabetical order.

A

To see the letter "A" in your dream, represents superiority. You are moving on to something new and grand. Alternatively, it may indicate the name or initial of a person.

Abandonment

To dream that you are abandoned, suggests that it is time to leave behind past feelings and characteristics that are hindering your own growth. Let go of your old attitudes. A more direct and literal interpretation of this dream is that you have a fear of being deserted, abandoned, or even betrayed. Do you feel that people are neglecting your feelings?

Dreaming that you are abandoned, may stem from a recent loss or a fear of losing a loved one. The fear of abandonment may manifest itself into your dream and is part of the healing process of dealing with losing a loved one. It may also stem from unresolved feelings or problems from childhood.

To abandon others in your dream, suggests that you are overwhelmed by the problems and decisions in your life.

Abbey

To see an abbey in your dream, signifies spirituality, peace of mind and freedom from anxiety. You are in a state of contentment and satisfaction. Help for you is always around the corner.

To see an abbey in ruins, foretells that your hopes and schemes will fall into failure and incompletion.

Abdomen

To see your abdomen in a dream, refers to your natural instincts and repressed emotions. This symbol may also have a strictly physiological factor where you may be experiencing constipation or indigestion. Emotionally, seeing your abdomen in your dream may imply something in your real life that you "cannot stomach" or have difficulties accepting You want to get it out of your system.

To dream that you abdomen is exposed, signifies trust and vulnerability. You may be expressing a desire to express your primal emotions/instincts

Abduction

To dream of being abducted, indicates that you are being controlled by your circumstances or by someone.

To dream about witnessing an abduction, foretells of unexpected news.

Abhorrence

To dream that you abhor a person, suggests your waking dislike for some person. You feel that this person has been acting in a less than honorable way.

To dream that you are being abhorred by others, symbolizes that your good intentions to others will subside into selfishness.

Abject

To dream of being abject, signifies financial changes. If the abjectness altered at some point in the dream, then the consequences will only be temporary. However, if during your dream, you respond amicably to an abject situation, then you will experience substantial financial benefits.

Abnormal

To dream of abnormal things, indicates that you will soon come to a sound solution to problems that you have been preoccupied with in your mind. Anything appearing abnormal draws attention to that particular aspect.

Abode

To dream that you can't find your abode, symbolizes your loss of faith in the integrity of others.

To dream that you have no abode in your dreams, signifies misfortune and loss.

Abominable Snowman

Aborigine

To see an Aborigine in your dream, represents both your untamed, natural self and your innocent side, It also suggests that you are being overindulgent or overly emotional. You may be harming yourself and jeopardizing your well-being due to your unrestraint.

Abortion

To dream that you have an abortion, suggests that you are hindering and blocking your own growth. You may be hesitant in pursuing a new direction in your life. The dream may also be a reflection of your own real-life abortion. And thus serve as a way of healing from the trauma and working towards self-acceptance.

This dream may also be a message for you to take care and look after your health.

Above

To see something above you in your dream, suggests that you need to set your goals higher.

Abroad

To dream of going abroad via ship, foretells that you befriend a powerful and influential person.

To dream of being abroad in a foreign land, indicates an unbalance and chaos to your current situation and condition. Consequently, you may seek for a change in scenery.

Abscess

To dream that you have an abscess, suggests that something need to be expressed.

Abscond

For a man to dream of absconding, indicates fraud and possible deceit from co-workers.

For a woman to dream of absconding, forewarns that she should be careful of falling in love to quickly. Be cautious of whom and where you devote your affections.

Abstinence

To dream that you practice abstinence from drinking, sex or any other sort of sensual temptation, is a warning against being over confidant.

Abundance

To dream of having a great abundance of a certain item, is a warning to conserve your resources and energies.

To dream of having a great abundance of a wide variety of things, foretells a future of comfort, happiness, and success.

Abuse

To dream you are abusing someone, foretells that you will suffer repercussions from friends toward whom you have acted less than honorable.

To dream you are being verbally or physically abused, forewarns that you will fall into the hands of an enemy.

Abyss

To dream of an abyss, signifies an obstacle that you need to overcome in your life. It may be creating anxiety for you. You are afraid and/or uncertain as to what you will discover about yourself and your hidden feelings and fears.

To dream that you are falling into an abyss, symbolizes the depths of your unconscious. The abyss may also represent your primal fears and feelings of "falling into the pit of despair" or fear of "taking the plunge".

Academy

To dream of an academy, signifies new friendships and opportunities.

Accelerator

To see an accelerator in your dream, indicates that you will achieve your goals through you own efforts.

To dream that the accelerator is jammed or broken, indicates a loss of control.

Acceptance

To dream about acceptance, indicates issues of self-esteem and measuring up to the expectations of others. There is a waking situation where you are seeking acceptance and wanting to be a part of.

Accident

To dream that you are in an accident, signifies pent up guilt and you are sub-consciously punishing yourself over it.

To dream of a car accident, symbolizes your emotional state. You may be harboring deep anxieties and fears. Are you "driving" yourself too hard? This dream may tell you to slow down before you hit disaster. You need to rethink or re-plan your course of actions and set yourself on a better path.

To dream that a loved one dies in an accident, indicates that something in your own Self that is no longer functional and is "dead". It is also symbolic of your own relationship with that person. Perhaps you need to let go of this relationship.

Accident dreams may also represent your straightforward fears of being an actual, physical accident. You may be simply nervous about getting behind the wheel. This dream may be a clear warning to cautious of approaching vehicles.

Accordion

To hear the music of an accordion, signifies that some amusement and joy will take your mind off a saddening and depressing matter.

To dream that you play the accordion, denotes intense emotions that are causing you some physical strain and body weariness.

Accountant

To see or dream that you are an accountant, represents your objectivity toward some situation. You are taking a step back and looking carefully at the facts.

Accounts

To dream that accounts are presented to you for payment, forewarns that you will be in a dangerous position or possibly be entangled in a lawsuit. You should also be careful in who you lend your money to.

To dream that you hold accounts against others, signifies of a rocky road in the management of your business.

Accuse

To dream that you are being accused of something, indicates that you are feeling guilty. It may also mean that you are having some doubts about yourself and the choices you are making

To dream that you accuse others, signifies that you will have arguments with those around you.

Aches

To dream that you have aches, signifies that you are showing too much hesitation in pursuit of your business deals and someone else will profit from your ideas.

Achievement

To dream of an achievement, denotes that you will be greatly satisfied with the outcome of a situation or project. The bigger the achievement, the greater the satisfaction.

Acid

To see poisonous acid in your dream, represents feelings of hatred, rage, and/or revenge.

To dream that you drink acid, indicates that you are emotionally paralyzed and need to learn how to express yourself.

Acorn

To see acorns in your dream, symbolizes strength and durability. It is indicative of small beginnings and minor goals which have great potential for growth.

To dream that you are picking acorn from the ground, signifies that you will receive much success after your long and hard work.

To dream that you are eating acorn, denotes that your hard work will pay off in the future where you will enjoy a life of ease and pleasure.

To dream that you are shaking acorns from a tree, indicates that you have significant influence on others.

Acquaintance

To see an acquaintance in your dream, signifies positive affairs in business and harmony in your home life. It also foretells that you will see or hear from them shortly after this dream.

To dream that you are in a dispute with an acquaintance, denotes that you will soon find yourself in a humiliating situation.

Acquit

To dream that you are acquitted of a crime, denotes the threat of a lawsuit pertaining to acquiring some valuable property.

To see others acquitted in your dream, signifies that your friends will balance your hard work and labors with fun and pleasure.

Acrobat

To see acrobats in your dream, signifies that you will be hindered and prevented to carry out your tasks as a result of the fears of others.

To dream that you are performing acrobats, denotes that the scheming of your rivals will be growing quite unbearable.

Actor/Actress

To see an actor or actress in your dream, represents your pursuit for pleasure. Your admiration of a particular celebrity may lead to a desire to have some of their physical or personality traits. Consider also who this actor/actress is and what characteristics your associate him/her with. These may be the same characteristics that you need to acknowledge or incorporate into yourself. The dream may also be a pun on his or her name.

To dream that you are an actor, denotes that your hard work and labor will be well worth it in the end. It also indicates your strong desires to be recognized and acknowledge. This may also be an indication of a role that you are playing in your real life, whether it be the role of a parent, sibling, co-worker, etc. Or perhaps you are putting on an act or a facade.

Adam And Eve

To see Adam and Eve in your dream, signifies an occurrence in your life that will cause you to lose your hopes and chances of success.

Adamant

To dream that you are adamant, signifies that you will be thwarted in some desire that you held ever so highly in your life.

Adder

To see an adder in your dream, signifies that a deceitful person will cause a lot of trouble for you.

Addict

To dream that you are an addict, indicates that you are no longer in control of a situation. You have surrendered your power and denied responsibility in your actions. The dream is also representative of fear, low self-esteem issues, and insecurities.

Addition

To dream that you are solving an addition problem, signifies that you will struggle to overcome adversaries and other formidable situations.

To dream that there is a mistake in an addition problem, denotes that you will successfully outwit your rivals by discovering their plans before they have a chance to execute it.

Adieu

To dream that you are bidding cheerful adieus to someone, signifies much pleasant festivities and enjoyable visits.

To dream that you are bidding sad adieus, signifies grief and loss.

Admire

To dream that you are the object of admiration, signifies that although you will rise above your circle of associates, you will not be resented. You will remain much regarded and well- loved.

Adolescent

Adopted

To dream that you or others are adopting a child, indicates that you are taking on something new and different. Ask yourself what is missing in your life that would make you happy.

To dream that you are adopted, suggests that you are longing for the child within you.

Adultery

To dream that you commit adultery or have an affair, is an expression of sexual urges or self-betrayal from your subconscious. It also indicates that you will be entangled in a situation that is not in your best interest, perhaps even illegal.

To dream that your mate, spouse, or significant other is cheating on you, indicates your fears of being abandoned. You may feel some lack of attention in the relationship. Alternatively, you may feel that you are not measuring up to the expectations of others.

To dream that you are committing adultery with your spouse's friend, denotes that you are feeling neglected by your spouse.

Adulation

To dream that you seek adulation, signifies that you will arrogantly step up to undeserved position of honor.

To dream that you are offering adulation, denotes that you are willing to part with something near and dear to you in the hopes of material advancement.

Advancement

To dream that you are advancing any some situation, signifies your rapid rise to success and honor. Affairs of the heart will also be in your favor.

To see others advancing ahead of you, denotes that friends will hold important and favorable positions.

Adversary

To dream that you are confronted by an adversary, signifies that you will defend any attacks against your interest.

To dream that you overcome an adversary, denotes that you will escape the effects of some serious disaster.

Adventurer

To dream that you are an adventurer, signifies that you are too absorbed in your conduct that you do not realize your fall from grace and honor.

Adversity

To dream that you are met with adversity, signifies failures and continued bad fortune.

To dream that others are in adversity, denotes gloomy surroundings and that someone near you will be stricken with some illness.

Advertisement

To dream that you are looking through advertisements, suggests that a message is being conveyed to you via your unconscious.

To dream that you are putting out an advertisement, indicates hard work is needed to achieve your goals.

Advice

To dream that you are receive some advice, signifies your high level of integrity and morality.

To dream that you seek legal advice, denotes that you will be involved in some doubtful activity in which its merits and legality will be called into question.

Advocate

To dream that you are an advocate for a cause, signifies your faithfulness towards your interest and your loyalty to your friends.

Affection

To dream that you are showing your affections for someone, suggests your contentment and happiness with a current relationship. It may also indicate your need to be more affectionate to the ones you love and care about.

Afraid

To dream that you are afraid to continue on some situation, signifies trouble in the home and failure in business.

To see others afraid in your dream, signifies that some friend will be too wrapped up in his or her own problems then to help you out with some favor.

Afternoon

To see a cloudy and rainy afternoon in your dream, signifies disappointment and gloom.

To see a warm and pleasant afternoon in your dream, foretells of long-lasting friendships.

Affliction

To dream that you have an affliction, signifies the coming of disaster.

To dream others afflicted in your dream, denotes that you will find yourself surrounded by grief and misfortune.

Affrighted

To dream that you are affrighted, forewarns that you will be injured as a result of some accident.

To see others affrighted in your dream, denotes that you will be unexpectedly confronted with a miserable and distressing situation.

Affront

To dream that you are affronted, signifies that some malicious person will take advantage of your ignorance and may even put you in a compromising situation.

Affluence

To dream that you have affluence, signifies fortunate endeavors and that you will be associated with people of wealth.

African American

To see an African American in your dream, signifies your roots and heritage. You may need to discover the soul within your own self. Additionally, you are ready to be more expressive and creative.

Agate

To see agate in your dream, denotes a small advancement in your business affairs.

Age

To dream of your age, signifies you anxiety and concern of growing older. It may also represent some regrets or failure in your endeavors.

To dream that you are accused of being older that you really are, signifies that you will fall into negative companionship.

Aggression

To dream that you exhibit aggression in your dream, denotes repressed sexual needs. It is also a reflection of conflict in your waking life.

Agony

To dream that you are in agony, signifies that pleasure will be interrupted with much worry.

Agreement

To dream of an agreement, indicates resolution to a conflict or problem. Your unconscious is working in accordance with your conscious.

Ague

To dream that you are shivering with an ague, forewarns that you will suffer from a physical disorder.

To see others affected with ague in your dream, signifies that you will offend some people through your indifference.

AIDS

To dream that you have AIDS, indicates that your psychological integrity is being attacked. You are unable to defend your position in some matter.

To dream that your mate has AIDS, suggests that the relationship may be a destructive one.

Air

To feel cold air in your dream, signifies discordance in your domestic relations and setbacks in your business affairs. You may be in danger of losing touch with reality.

To dream that you are breathing hot air, signifies the influence of evil around you.

Air Conditioner

To dream that the air conditioner is not working, suggests that you are not able to relax and breathe freely. You may be overly worried about a situation.

To see or feel the air conditioner in your dream, represents purification and relief. You have cooled off from some heated argument.

Air Force

To dream that you are in the air force, suggests that you need to be more spiritually disciplined.

Airplane

To see an airplane in your dream, indicates that you will overcome your obstacles and rise above to a new level of prominence and status. You may experience a higher consciousness, new-found freedom and greater awareness.

To dream that you transfer planes, implies an important transitional phase in your life which will take you away from your intended path. Changes will occur in your life which will take you to new directions and new heights of status and recognition.

To dream that a plane crashes, suggests that you have set overly high and unrealistic goals for yourself. Your goals may be too high and are impossible to realize. You are in danger of having it come crashing down. Alternatively, your lack of confidence, self-defeating attitude and self-doubt toward the goals you have set for yourself is represented by the crashing airplane; you do not believe in your ability to attain those goals. Loss of power and uncertainty in achieving your goals are also signified.

To dream that an airplane is hijacked, signifies disturbing feelings and past emotions in your unconscious mind.

To see a busy airport in your dream, signifies the desire for freedom, high ideals, ambition, and hopes. It is an indication that you are approaching a new departure in your life. Some new idea is taking off or is ready to take off. You may be experiencing a new relationship, new career path or new adventure.

To dream of a deserted airport, indicates that your travel plans will be changed or delayed.

Alabaster

To see alabaster in your dream, foretells of success in love and marriage.

To dream that you break a alabaster figurine, signifies grief and sorrowful regrets.

Alarm

To hear or pull an alarm in your dream, suggests that you are experiencing a conflict in a relationship or situation. You may be questioning the decisions you have made.

Alarm Bell

To hear an alarm bell in your sleep, signifies a situation that is giving you much anxiety. This situation may arise unexpectedly where you are then required to spring into action.

Albatross

To see an albatross in your dream, represents freedom.

To see a dying or dead albatross in your dream, symbolizes bad luck and harsh, vulnerable times.

Albino

To see an albino in your dream, represents purity or eternal life. You need to be more accepting and tolerant.

To dream that you are afraid of the albino figure, suggests that you are irrationally concerned about the well-being of a loved one. It may also mean denial.

Album

To see an album in your dream, indicates that you are surrounded by true friends.

To dream that you are looking through a photo album, suggests that you are unwilling to let go of your memories and the past. You are idealizing about the past.

Alchemy

To dream of alchemy, signifies that you are going through a period of turmoil, inner transformation, and self-renewal. Although these may be tough and difficult times, it will have a positive outcome.

Alcohol

To dream that you are enjoying alcohol in moderation, denotes contentment and satisfaction in the decisions that you have made. Chances for success is likely.

To dream that you are consuming alcohol in excess, signifies feelings of inadequacy and regrets. You harbor fears of being discovered for who you really are. Alcohol may serve as a way for your to escape or an excuse for something you did.

Aliens

To dream that you are an alien, symbolizes the undiscovered part of yourself. Your manifestation as an alien may be your way of 'escaping' from reality. Dreams of this nature also symbolizes your outlandish ideas and your wild imagination.

To dream that you are being abducted by aliens, indicates your fears of your changing surroundings or your fear of losing your home and family. You feel that your space and/or privacy is being invaded.

To see aliens in your dream , signifies that you are having difficulties adapting and adjusting to your new surroundings. You are feeling "alienated" and invaded. You are also having difficulties in how to handle or deal with a certain situation or person. On a psychological level, seeing aliens may represent an encounter with an unfamiliar or neglected aspect of your own self.

Alimony

To dream that you are paying alimony, suggests that you are now paying for your past actions and mistakes.

Allergy

To dream that you have allergies, signifies your sensitively to some situation. You may feel that you are physically or emotionally restrained from doing something.

Alley

To see an alley in you dream, suggests that you have limited options. Alternatively, it indicates that you may be sidetracked due to domestic duties and find yourself in a dilemma.

To dream that you are walking through an alley, represents that you may be walking into a dead-end or that you have taken a short cut in life. It also may denote that your reputation is in jeopardy.

Alligator

To see an alligator in your dream, symbolizes treachery, deceit, and hidden instincts. It may be a signal for you to take a new perspective on a situation. It may also represent your ability to move between the material world of waking life and the emotional, repressed world of the unconscious. Alternatively, the alligator represents healing powers and qualities.

To dream that you are running away from the alligator, indicates that you are unwilling to confront some painful and disturbing aspect of your unconscious. There is some potentially destructive emotion that you are refusing to acknowledge and owning up to.

According to biblical interpretations, an alligator suggests that leviathan is king over the children of pride. (Psa 74:14, Job 41:1,Isa 27:1)

Alloy

To see an alloy in your dream, signifies that your business will be full of complications.

Almanac

To see an almanac in your dream, denotes inconstant fortune and illusive pleasures.

Almonds

To see almonds in your dream, signifies that after a short period of sorrow and grief, you will experience great wealth. You will have time for reflection and leisure.

To dream of eating fresh almonds, foretells that you will have much success and financial gains.

To see an almond tree in your dream, signifies happiness. Wedded bliss is also in your near future.

Alms

To dream that you are giving alms, is a good omen. To dream that you are giving alms unwillingly, signifies the coming of evil.

Alone

To dream that you are alone, indicates feelings of rejection. You may be feeling that no one understand you.

Alphabet

Please see Letters.

Altar

To see the altar in your dream, symbolizes that you are making a great personal sacrifice. You may also be expressing concerns about your spirituality.

To see a priest at the altar in your dream, signifies strife and disharmony in both your work and home.

Alum

To see alum in your dream, signifies frustrations on plans that you have set for yourself.

To dream that you taste alum, denotes that you have feelings of regret and remorse over the evil you have done onto an innocent person.

Aluminum

To see aluminum in your dream, signifies your ability to retain what is valuable to you. It indicates contentment in your fortunes, no matter how small.

Amber

To see amber in your dream, indicates something in your life that is rigid and inflexible. Something in your life that was once lively, has now ceased to exist. Or that something in your past will prove to be extremely important to your future. Alternatively, it represents an outdated way of thinking or old ideas.

Ambulance

To see an ambulance in your dream, indicates that your careless activities and indiscretion may lead to major problems and complications. This dream may also stem from your own fears of declining health or that you have contracted a disease. Alternatively, it suggests that you need to stop and pay close attention to some waking situation.

To see an ambulance full of wounded passengers, signifies a fear of letting of your old Self and making space for the new you. You are projecting your emotional wounds and painful experiences onto others. Alternatively, it may also mean that you are hanging around the wrong crowd and are doing yourself more harm than good.

To dream that someone is hit by an ambulance, suggests that some aspect of your psyche is injured and needs immediate care and attention.

Ambush

To dream that you are attacked from ambush, forewarns of a danger lurking near you. Your situation has taken an unanticipated turn for the worse or that you have been prevented or blocked in reaching your goals or destination.

To dream that you are lying in ambush, signifies that you will ruthlessly work to defraud your own friends.

Amethyst

To see an amethyst in your dream, signifies contentment and satisfaction in business and love. It does not take much to make you happy. Although you may not be rich, you are completely satisfied with a modest income.

To dream that you lose an amethyst, foretells of broken engagements and disappointments in love.

Ammonia

To see ammonia in your dream, signifies that you will experience some distress over the behavior of a friend which will result in a strain or separation of the friendship.

Ammunition

To see ammunition in your dream, suggests that you are utilizing your power to persuade or protect. Alternatively, it may indicates that you are trying to get your way via destructive means.

Adversary

To dream that you are confronted by an adversary, signifies that you will defend any attacks against your interest.

To dream that you overcome an adversary, denotes that you will escape the effects of some serious disaster.

Adventurer

To dream that you are an adventurer, signifies that you are too absorbed in your conduct that you do not realize your fall from grace and honor.

Adversity

To dream that you are met with adversity, signifies failures and continued bad fortune.

To dream that others are in adversity, denotes gloomy surroundings and that someone near you will be stricken with some illness.

Advertisement

To dream that you are looking through advertisements, suggests that a message is being conveyed to you via your unconscious.

To dream that you are putting out an advertisement, indicates hard work is needed to achieve your goals.

Advice

To dream that you are receive some advice, signifies your high level of integrity and morality.

To dream that you seek legal advice, denotes that you will be involved in some doubtful activity in which its merits and legality will be called into question.

Advisor

Please See Counselor.

Advocate

To dream that you are an advocate for a cause, signifies your faithfulness towards your interest and your loyalty to your friends.

Affair

Please see Adultery.

Affection

To dream that you are showing your affections for someone, suggests your contentment and happiness with a current relationship. It may also indicate your need to be more affectionate to the ones you love and care about.

Afraid

To dream that you are afraid to continue on some situation, signifies trouble in the home and failure in business.

To see others afraid in your dream, signifies that some friend will be too wrapped up in his or her own problems then to help you out with some favor.

Afternoon

To see a cloudy and rainy afternoon in your dream, signifies disappointment and gloom.

To see a warm and pleasant afternoon in your dream, foretells of long-lasting friendships.

Affliction

To dream that you have an affliction, signifies the coming of disaster.

To dream others afflicted in your dream, denotes that you will find yourself surrounded by grief and misfortune.

Affrighted

To dream that you are affrighted, forewarns that you will be injured as a result of some accident.

To see others affrighted in your dream, denotes that you will be unexpectedly confronted with a miserable and distressing situation.

Affront

To dream that you are affronted, signifies that some malicious person will take advantage of your ignorance and may even put you in a compromising situation.

Affluence

To dream that you have affluence, signifies fortunate endeavors and that you will be associated with people of wealth.

African American

To see an African American in your dream, signifies your roots and heritage. You may need to discover the soul within your own self. Additionally, you are ready to be more expressive and creative.

Agate

To see agate in your dream, denotes a small advancement in your business affairs.

Age

To dream of your age, signifies you anxiety and concern of growing older. It may also represent some regrets or failure in your endeavors.

To dream that you are accused of being older that you really are, signifies that you will fall into negative companionship.

Aggression

To dream that you exhibit aggression in your dream, denotes repressed sexual needs. It is also a reflection of conflict in your waking life.

Agony

To dream that you are in agony, signifies that pleasure will be interrupted with much worry.

Agreement

To dream of an agreement, indicates resolution to a conflict or problem. Your unconscious is working in accordance with your conscious.

Ague

To dream that you are shivering with an ague, forewarns that you will suffer from a physical disorder.

To see others affected with ague in your dream, signifies that you will offend some people through your indifference.

AIDS

To dream that you have AIDS, indicates that your psychological integrity is being attacked. You are unable to defend your position in some matter.

To dream that your mate has AIDS, suggests that the relationship may be a destructive one.

Air

To feel cold air in your dream, signifies discordance in your domestic relations and setbacks in your business affairs. You may be in danger of losing touch with reality.

To dream that you are breathing hot air, signifies the influence of evil around you.

Air Conditioner

To dream that the air conditioner is not working, suggests that you are not able to relax and breathe freely. You may be overly worried about a situation.

To see or feel the air conditioner in your dream, represents purification and relief. You have cooled off from some heated argument.

Air Force

To dream that you are in the air force, suggests that you need to be more spiritually disciplined.

Airplane

To see an airplane in your dream, indicates that you will overcome your obstacles and rise above to a new level of prominence and status. You may experience a higher consciousness, new-found freedom and greater awareness.

To dream that you transfer planes, implies an important transitional phase in your life which will take you away from your intended path. Changes will occur in your life which will take you to new directions and new heights of status and recognition.

To dream that a plane crashes, suggests that you have set overly high and unrealistic goals for yourself. Your goals may be too high and are impossible to realize. You are in danger of having it come crashing down. Alternatively, your lack of confidence, self-defeating attitude and self-doubt toward the goals you have set for yourself is represented by the crashing airplane; you do not believe in your ability to attain those goals. Loss of power and uncertainty in achieving your goals are also signified.

To dream that an airplane is hijacked, signifies disturbing feelings and past emotions in your unconscious mind.

See The Meaning In Action: "*On The Airplane*" & "*Plane Crash*"

Airport

To see a busy airport in your dream, signifies the desire for freedom, high ideals, ambition, and hopes. It is an indication that you are approaching a new departure in your life. Some new idea is taking off or is ready to take off. You may be experiencing a new relationship, new career path or new adventure.

To dream of a deserted airport, indicates that your travel plans will be changed or delayed.

See The Meaning In Action: "*Online Encounter*"

Alabaster

To see alabaster in your dream, foretells of success in love and marriage.

To dream that you break a alabaster figurine, signifies grief and sorrowful regrets.

Alarm

To hear or pull an alarm in your dream, suggests that you are experiencing a conflict in a relationship or situation. You may be questioning the decisions you have made.

Alarm Bell

To hear an alarm bell in your sleep, signifies a situation that is giving you much anxiety. This situation may arise unexpectedly where you are then required to spring into action.

Albatross

To see an albatross in your dream, represents freedom.

To see a dying or dead albatross in your dream, symbolizes bad luck and harsh, vulnerable times.

Albino

To see an albino in your dream, represents purity or eternal life. You need to be more accepting and tolerant.

To dream that you are afraid of the albino figure, suggests that you are irrationally concerned about the well-being of a loved one. It may also mean denial.

Album

To see an album in your dream, indicates that you are surrounded by true friends.

To dream that you are looking through a photo album, suggests that you are unwilling to let go of your memories and the past. You are idealizing about the past.

Alchemy

To dream of alchemy, signifies that you are going through a period of turmoil, inner transformation, and self-renewal. Although these may be tough and difficult times, it will have a positive outcome.

Alcohol

To dream that you are enjoying alcohol in moderation, denotes contentment and satisfaction in the decisions that you have made. Chances for success is likely.

To dream that you are consuming alcohol in excess, signifies feelings of inadequacy and regrets. You harbor fears of being discovered for who you really are. Alcohol may serve as a way for your to escape or an excuse for something you did.

Aliens

To dream that you are an alien, symbolizes the undiscovered part of yourself. Your manifestation as an alien may be your way of 'escaping' from reality. Dreams of this nature also symbolizes your outlandish ideas and your wild imagination.

To dream that you are being abducted by aliens, indicates your fears of your changing surroundings or your fear of losing your home and family. You feel that your space and/or privacy is being invaded.

To see aliens in your dream , signifies that you are having difficulties adapting and adjusting to your new surroundings. You are feeling "alienated" and invaded. You are also having difficulties in how to handle or deal with a certain situation or person. On a psychological level, seeing aliens may represent an encounter with an unfamiliar or neglected aspect of your own self.

**See The Meaning In Action: "Kidnapped By Aliens"*

Alimony

To dream that you are paying alimony, suggests that you are now paying for your past actions and mistakes.

Allergy

To dream that you have allergies, signifies your sensitively to some situation. You may feel that you are physically or emotionally restrained from doing something.

Alley

To see an alley in you dream, suggests that you have limited options. Alternatively, it indicates that you may be sidetracked due to domestic duties and find yourself in a dilemma.

To dream that you are walking through an alley, represents that you may be walking into a dead-end or that you have taken a short cut in life. It also may denote that your reputation is in jeopardy.

Alligator

To see an alligator in your dream, symbolizes treachery, deceit, and hidden instincts. It may be a signal for you to take a new perspective on a situation. It may also represent your ability to move between the material world of waking life and the emotional, repressed world of the unconscious. Alternatively, the alligator represents healing powers and qualities.

To dream that you are running away from the alligator, indicates that you are unwilling to confront some painful and disturbing aspect of your unconscious. There is some potentially destructive emotion that you are refusing to acknowledge and owning up to.

According to biblical interpretations, an alligator suggests that leviathan is king over the children of pride. (Psa 74:14, Job 41:1,Isa 27:1)

*See The Meaning In Action: "Alligator In Ostrich Suit"

Alloy

To see an alloy in your dream, signifies that your business will be full of complications.

Almanac

To see an almanac in your dream, denotes inconstant fortune and illusive pleasures.

Almonds

To see almonds in your dream, signifies that after a short period of sorrow and grief, you will experience great wealth. You will have time for reflection and leisure.

To dream of eating fresh almonds, foretells that you will have much success and financial gains.

To see an almond tree in your dream, signifies happiness. Wedded bliss is also in your near future.

Alms

To dream that you are giving alms, is a good omen. To dream that you are giving alms unwillingly, signifies the coming of evil.

Alone

To dream that you are alone, indicates feelings of rejection. You may be feeling that no one understand you.

Alphabet

*Please see Letters.

Altar

To see the altar in your dream, symbolizes that you are making a great personal sacrifice. You may also be expressing concerns about your spirituality.

To see a priest at the altar in your dream, signifies strife and disharmony in both your work and home.

Alum

To see alum in your dream, signifies frustrations on plans that you have set for yourself.

To dream that you taste alum, denotes that you have feelings of regret and remorse over the evil you have done onto an innocent person.

Aluminum

To see aluminum in your dream, signifies your ability to retain what is valuable to you. It indicates contentment in your fortunes, no matter how small.

Amber

To see amber in your dream, indicates something in your life that is rigid and inflexible. Something in your life that was once lively, has now ceased to exist. Or that something in your past will prove to be extremely important to your future. Alternatively, it represents an outdated way of thinking or old ideas.

Ambulance

To see an ambulance in your dream, indicates that your careless activities and indiscretion may lead to major problems and complications. This dream may also stem from your own fears of declining health or that you have contracted a disease. Alternatively, it suggests that you need to stop and pay close attention to some waking situation.

To see an ambulance full of wounded passengers, signifies a fear of letting of your old Self and making space for the new you. You are projecting your emotional wounds and painful experiences onto others. Alternatively, it may also mean that you are hanging around the wrong crowd and are doing yourself more harm than good.

To dream that someone is hit by an ambulance, suggests that some aspect of your psyche is injured and needs immediate care and attention.

Ambush

To dream that you are attacked from ambush, forewarns of a danger lurking near you. Your situation has taken an unanticipated turn for the worse or that you have been prevented or blocked in reaching your goals or destination.

To dream that you are lying in ambush, signifies that you will ruthlessly work to defraud your own friends.

Amethyst

To see an amethyst in your dream, signifies contentment and satisfaction in business and love. It does not take much to make you happy. Although you may not be rich, you are completely satisfied with a modest income.

To dream that you lose an amethyst, foretells of broken engagements and disappointments in love.

Ammonia

To see ammonia in your dream, signifies that you will experience some distress over the behavior of a friend which will result in a strain or separation of the friendship.

Ammunition

To see ammunition in your dream, suggests that you are utilizing your power to persuade or protect. Alternatively, it may indicates that you are trying to get your way via destructive means.

Asparagus

To see asparagus in your dream, denotes prosperous times.

Aspen

To see an aspen in your dream, indicates loneliness.

Ass

To see an ass in your dream, signifies a lack of understanding. It also suggests that you will come upon many annoyances.

To see an ass carrying burdens in your dream, signifies that after much patience and hard work, you will succeed in business and in love.

Please also see Donkey.

Assassin

To dream that you have been assassinated, represents a hopeless situation which need your immediate attention and action.

To dream that you are a witness to an assassin, indicates that you need to pay more attention to every little detail. Do not overlook the seemingly insignificant things in life.

Assistance

To dream that you are giving assistance to someone, suggests that you are being called on for support, either emotional support or physical support.

To dream that you are being assisted, denotes your helplessness in a situation.

Asteroid

To see an asteroid in your dream, represents a spiritual message from above. You are about to be enlightened with some knowledge. Alternatively, it signifies a brainstorming of ideas and thoughts. If the asteroid hits the earth, then it indicates that your idealistic notions are deteriorating are being shattered apart.

Asters

To see asters in your dream, symbolize your hopes, wishes, and your dreams.

Asthma

To dream that you have asthma, refers to insecurity and emotional instability. There is a lot of stress and tension around you.

Astral Projection

To dream of astral projection, suggests that you are looking at things from a whole new perspective. You may be feeling liberated and free. Alternatively, it may indicate that you are physically or emotionally disconnected from those around you.

Astrology

To dream about astrology, suggests that you are concerned about your future. Your dream astrological forecast may offers a significant message which should be analyzed closely and how it relates to your life.

Astronaut

To see or dream that you are an astronaut, indicates that you are expanding your awareness and consciousness. You are utilizing the information you have and making the best of it.

Asylum

To dream that you are at an asylum, signifies sickness and ill luck in store for you. You will undergo some mental strain.

Athlete

To dream that you are an athlete, suggests that you have pushed yourself to the limits. You have achieved something which you thought you could not do.

Atlas

To dream that you are looking at an atlas, signifies that you will carefully draw out your plans before undertaking any changes or journey.

Atomic Bomb

Please see Nuclear Bomb.

Attack

To dream that you attack someone, indicates that your ill-mood and temper may cause harm to another. You are releasing some pent-up frustration and anger. You feel that you have been wronged. Such feelings may be easier and safer for you to express in your dream.

To dream that you are being attacked by someone, signifies questions on your character and the need for you to defend yourself. You are feeling stressed, vulnerable and helpless. You may also be faced with difficult changed in your waking life.

To dream that you are being attacked by an animal, is a warning to be careful with those around you. Take notice on who you know in your waking like that shares and exhibits the same qualities of the animal that attacked you in your dream.

To dream that you kill an attacking animal, signifies that your life will be saved by a stranger.

Attic

To see an attic in your dream, represents hidden memories or repressed thoughts that is being revealed. It also symbolize your mind, spirituality, and your connection to the higher Self. Alternatively, it signifies difficulties in your life that will hinder you from attaining your goals and aspirations. However, in the end, after a long period of struggle, you will overcome them.

To see a cluttered attic, is a sign to organize your mind and thoughts.

Attorney

To see an attorney in your dream, suggests that you are seeking guidance and advise.

Auction

To dream that you are at an auction, indicates that you may be undervaluing or overvaluing something or some relationship. It may also mean that you have learned from your past experiences and are ready to move on.

Audience

To dream that you are in front of an audience, represents the world around you and it is paying close attention to your actions. Alternatively, it suggests your fears of having your personal feelings and private thoughts discovered or revealed.

Audition

To dream that you are at an audition, indicates feelings of insecurity and trouble with expressing yourself. You feel that you are being put to a test and are put in a vulnerable situation. The attitude and behavior of the audience will also guide you in how you think others perceive you.

August

To dream of the month of August, signifies misunderstanding in love affairs and unfortunate deals.

Auger

To see an auger in your dream, signifies hard labor and struggle.

Aunt

To see your aunt in your dream, represents family characteristics and values. It is a connection to your own heritage. The aunt may also represent aspects of yourself that you like or dislike. She can also be seen as a substitute mother.

Aura

To see an aura around you or someone else, suggests that some important information is being relayed to you in the dream and you need to pay close attention to the message. You need to draw on this energy for strength.

Aurora Borealis

To see the aurora borealis in your dream, signifies a positive spiritual experience filled with warmth and love.

Australia

To dream about or that you are in Australia, suggests that you feel that you are being pulled toward opposite directions. The dream may also indicate self-exploration into your natural and uninhibited self. Often referred to as the land down under, the dream may be a metaphor to represent your unconscious and your underlying thoughts.

Author

To see an author at work in your dream, signifies that your mind is preoccupied over some literary work that you or your associates is working on.

Autograph

To dream that you are asking for an autograph, indicates your desire to be like the person whose autograph you seek. You may be seeking some form of approval.

To dream that someone is asking for your autograph, suggests that you are giving your consent or approval to someone.

Autopsy

To see an autopsy in your dream, suggests that you are disconnected from your feelings or devoid of emotions. You need to carefully evaluate the consequences of your actions.

Autumn

To dream of autumn, denotes that you will obtain some property from the hard work and struggle of others.

Automobile

To dream that you are riding in an automobile, signifies that even in pleasant situations, you will still be restless and uneasy.

To dream that you nearly escape from the impact of an automobile, denotes that you will successfully overcome any rivalry.

Please Also See Car.

Avalanche

To see an avalanche in your dream, signifies your raging emotions which have been held back and repressed for a long time. You may not have been dealing with them in a productive manner and now your emotions are about to erupt in violent anger. Alternatively, it symbolizes the inescapable stresses and pressures in our life.

Avoid

To dream that you are avoiding a person in your dream, suggest that you are not confronting some aspect of yourself. Consider what aspects and characteristics of the person you are avoiding which you are not recognizing in yourself. Alternatively, this word may also be a pun for "a void" in your life that you have been unable to fill.

Awaken

To awaken in your dream, represents a spiritual rebirth. You may be acknowledging and embracing both your feminine and masculine aspects of Self.

You are utilizing your fullest potential. Consider also who or what awakened you. This is an indication of what is lacking or missing in your life.

To dream that you awaken someone up, suggests that you are acknowledging core aspects of that person within your own self.

Awakening

To dream that you have an awakening, signifies that new ideas will be realized. You are experiencing new awareness that is unfolding in your life.

You may also be on the verge of lucid dreaming.

Award

To dream that you receive an award, indicates that you feel you deserve some recognition or some acknowledgment of your work.

Ax

To see an ax in your dream, indicates that you are overly controlling. It is symbolic of destruction, hostility, and the frustrations that you are experiencing. Perhaps you "have an ax to grind" with someone.

To dream that you are chopping wood in your dream, suggests that you need to divide your problem into smaller, more manageable sizes. Break down your problems into parts that you can handle. Alternatively, it may indicates that your strength and power has been cut down to size.

B

Baboon

To see a baboon in your dream, suggests that you need to be more expressive in your feelings. You need to be more direct in telling others how you feel. On the hand, it could be saying that you are expressing yourself in an inappropriate manner.

Baby

To see a baby in your dream, signifies innocence, warmth and new beginnings. Babies may symbolize something in your own inner nature which is pure, vulnerable, and/or uncorrupted. Babies may represent an aspect of yourself that is vulnerable and helpless. If you dream that you forgot you had a baby, then it suggests that you are trying hide your own vulnerabilities; You do not want to let others know of your weaknesses.

If you dream that you are on your way to the hospital to have a baby, then it signifies your issues of dependency and your desire to be completely care for. Perhaps you are trying to get out of some responsibility. If you are pregnant, then a more direct interpretation may simply mean that you are experiencing some anxieties of making it to the hospital when the time comes.

To dream of a crying baby, is indicative of a part of yourself that is deprived of attention and needs some nurturing. Alternatively, it represents your unfulfilled goals and a sense of lacking in your life.

To dream about a starving baby, represents your dependence on others. You are experiencing some deficiency in your life that needs immediate attention and gratification.

To dream of an extremely small baby, symbolizes your helplessness and your fears of letting others become aware of your vulnerabilities and incompetence. You may be afraid to ask for help and as a result tend to take matters into your own hands.

To see a dead baby in your dream, symbolizes the ending of something that is part of you.

To dream that you are dipping a baby in and out of water, signifies regression. You are regressing to a time where you had no worries and responsibilities. Alternatively, it is reminisce of when the baby is in the fetus and in its comfort zone. In fact, some expectant mothers even give birth in a pool, because the environment in the water mimics the environment in the uterus. It is less traumatic for the baby as it emerges into the world. So perhaps, the dream your search for your own comfort zone.

Baby Carriage

To dream of a baby carriage, denotes that you will soon be pleasantly surprised by a good friend.

Baby Clothes

To see baby clothes in your dream, suggests that you are expressing yourself in a more subtle way. Alternatively, baby clothes represent your former ways of thinking. You may refer to old habits or former notions which you have outgrown.

Baby Shower

To dream of a baby shower, suggests that you are welcoming a new start. You are given a chance to start over again and do things differently this time around. You have a new found faith in life itself.

Babysitter

To dream that you are babysitting, suggests that you need to care for the child within yourself.

To see or call for a babysitter in your dream, indicates that you need to acknowledge and work on your inner child.

Bachelor

For a man to dream that he is a bachelor, is a warning for him to keep clear of women. His honor and dignity will decline was well.

For a woman to dream of a bachelor, denotes forbidden love and loss of purity and innocence.

Back

To dream of your back, represents your attitudes, strengths, burdens and stance in the world. It may also relate to stress and pressure that someone is putting on you.

To see a naked back in your dream, symbolizes secrets that you may have kept from others or aspects of yourself that you have kept hidden and shielded away. Consider the pun, "watch your back!"; this dream may be telling you to do just that. Traditionally, seeing a back in your dream, forewarns that you should not lend money to anyone. In particular, lending money to friends will cause a rift in your relationship.

To see a person turn their back on you, signifies that you will be deeply hurt as a result of envy and jealousy.

Back-biting

To dream of back-biting about someone, warns that you will cause harm to someone if you do not stop whatever you may be doing. Think twice over your actions and its consequences.

To dream that someone is back-biting you, signifies that you will have some family problems.

Backflips

To dream that you are doing backflips, suggests that you are going out of your way to help or please someone. You may feel under-appreciated or that your work is going unnoticed.

Please see also Cartwheels.

Backgammon

To see a backgammon game in your dream, signifies that you will have an unwelcome guest in the near future.

To dream that you are playing a losing game of backgammon, symbolizes misfortune and unlucky in love. You seem to seek out the wrong type of people and your pursuit for love will be a rocky path.

Backpack

To see or carry a backpack in your dream, represents the decisions and responsibilities that are weighing your down.

Backpacking

To dream that you are backpacking, symbolizes your self-sufficiency and survival skills. You may be reflecting on all the obstacles and adversities that you have overcame.

Backstroke

To dream that you are doing the backstroke, suggests that although you are acknowledging your emotions, you are not confronting them head on.

Backward

To dream that you are walking or moving backward, signifies that what you are doing may be counter-productive. What you are seeking in life appears to be moving away from you. Thus you may be feeling a sense of failure or believe that you are unable to achieve your goals and aspirations. On the other hand, moving backward in your dream may symbolize that you should back off or retreat in a situation you may be facing in your waking life.

Backyard

To dream about your backyard, represents your childhood memories or your unconscious. Things in the backyard are things you want to keep hidden and out of the view of others. The condition of the yard is also symbolic of how well you maintain and balance aspects of your life.

Bacon

To see bacon in your dream, symbolizes essentials, staples, and life's supply. It may also be a play on the common phase "being home the bacon" to refer earning a living.

To see bacon that has gone rancid in your dream, suggests a forbidden situation.

Backyard

To see the backyard in your dream, refers to the secrets your are keeping. There are some aspects of your life which remain hidden from view. Alternatively, it represents poverty.

Badge

To see or flash a badge in your dream, represents your position of stature, honor and status. You regard yourself highly.

Badger

To see a badger in your dream, signifies your persistence and final victory over your opponents. The dream may also be a pun on badgering and aggravating others.

Badminton

To play or watch a badminton game in your dream, indicates that you need to make a decision quickly or else opportunities will pass you by. You need to learn to keep up.

Bag

To see a bag in your dream, represents the responsibilities that you carry. If the bag is ripped or torn, then it indicates that you are carrying a lot of burden.

To dream of a bag full of junk, symbolizes that you are burdened with worries and problems; you have to find a way on unloading some of this load.

Bagel

To see or eat a bagel in your dream, suggests that there is key element missing from your life. You are not completely whole. Alternatively, it refers to sexual urges.

Baggage

To see or carry baggage in your dream, refers to the problems and things that you are carrying on your shoulders and weighing your down. It may also be symbolic of your identity.

Bagpipe

To hear pleasing music from a bagpipe, signifies good fortune and contentment.

To hear unpleasing music from a bagpipe, signifies that misfortune will head your way.

Bail

To dream that you are making bail, symbolizes your need to accept help in your business dealings. This dream is trying to make you acknowledge that it is perfectly all right to accept a helping hand.

Bailiff

To see a bailiff in your dream, signifies that your hard work and diligence will be means for you to elevate your standard of living and possible promotion at your work.

To dream that a bailiff is arresting you, signifies your need to improve your business ethics. Your integrity is being called into question.

Bait

To see bait in your dream, denotes that you may be fishing for a deal or a compliment. It may also indicate your desire to lure or entice someone.

Baking

To dream that you are baking, represents your creative self and you ability to make things happen. If you are mixing ingredients together that you normally would not combine, then it suggests that you need to find a connection between two seemingly different things. Perhaps these things that seem incompatible may yield surprising but positive results.

Bake-house

To see a bake-house in your dream, signifies danger and pitfalls that you may be run into.

Bakery

To see a bakery in your dream, signifies richness and success. Your future will be an enjoyable, pleasant and filled with satisfaction.

Balcony

To see or dream that you are on a balcony, refers to your desire to be seen and noticed. It may also mean that you are on your way up the social ladder.

Bald

To dream that you are going bald, suggests a lack of self-esteem or worries about getting older. Alternatively, baldness symbolizes humility, purity, and personal sacrifice. You are at a stage in your life where you are confident in fully exposing yourself.

Please see also Hair.

Ball

To see or play with a ball in your dream, symbolizes completeness and wholeness. It may also indicate that you need to be more in tune with the inner child within.

To dream that you are watching a ball game, indicates that you need to take more of an initiative. Your lack of action may stem from your shyness which you must overcome. Perhaps you are too over self-conscious.

Ballet

To dream that you are watching a ballet, symbolizes balance, cooperation, and harmony.

To see or wear ballet slippers in your dream, represents your understanding of the principles of balance and grace. You carry yourself with much poise and get along well with others.

Ballerina

To dream that you are a ballerina, suggests that you are moving through the obstacles of your life effortlessly. You feel unrestricted. It is also a symbol of innocence, frailty, and vulnerability. Alternatively, you may feel unable to attain and measure up to society's ideals of beauty.

Balloon

To see balloons in your dream, indicates declining hopes in your search for love. A situation in your life will take a turn downward. Balloons also represent arrogance and an inflated opinion of yourself.

To see black balloons in your dream, symbolizes depression, especially if the balloons are descending.

To see an ascending balloon in your dream, signifies frustrating conditions in your life in which you are seeking to rise above. On a positive note, balloons symbolize celebration and festivities. You need to acknowledge your inner child.

To see a balloon pop in your dream, symbolizes an unrealized goal or dream. It may also represent the stresses in your life. The pressure may be starting to be too great for you to bear.

To see or dream that you are in a hot air balloon, suggests that it is time to overcome your depression. The dream may be a metaphor indicating that you are losing your ground or your foothold on some situation/problem. Alternatively, it represents the process of individuation and your quest to fulfill some spiritual needs. You feel the need to be elevated in someone's eyes.

Bamboo

To see bamboo in your dream, symbolizes trustworthiness, strength and resilience. You easily bounce back from setbacks and disappointments in your life. Alternatively, it refers to strong ties/bonds and fair dealings.

Bananas

To see bananas in your dream, may be a metaphor for repressed sexual urges and desires.

To dream that you are eating bananas, denotes that you hard work will be met with little reward and gains.

Band

To see a band in your dream, represents a sense of community and belonging. The dream may also be a pun on banding together and need for cooperation/unity.

Bandages

To dream that you have bandages, indicates your need to heal. You may be feeling emotionally wounded and are trying to cover/shield your hurt from others. Consider where on the body was the bandage for more additional clues.

Banjo

To dream that you are playing a banjo, symbolizes that your time spent with friends will be most cherished and enjoyable.

To see someone playing a banjo in your dream, foretells of an escapade. You will meet an exciting new love and will be drawn into a wonderful affair.

Bank

To see a bank in your dream, denotes your desires for financial security. You dream may serve to reassure you that your fears of financial instability are unfounded.

To dream that you are robbing a bank, signifies that you are expending too much energy and are in danger of depleting your inner resources.

Please see also Vault.

Bankrupt

To dream that you are bankrupt, indicates that you need to start take measures in protecting yourself and your resources. You may be feeling insecure.

Banquet

To dream that you are at a banquet, indicates that you are emotionally malnourished. You are seeking emotional stimulation.

Baptism

To see a baby being baptized in your dream, represents renewal and a new way of being, a new attitude toward life, or a new approach toward others. Immersion in water represents death, whereas emergence signifies resurrection and a new life. You have let go of your old negative you and this new you will likely be successful.

On a spiritual note, this dream signifies your renewed faith in God and that you are coming closer to self-realization and spiritual fulfillment.

Bar

To dream that you are at a bar, signifies your desire to escape from the stresses of your daily life and retreat into a light-hearted environment where pleasure abounds. Alternatively, you are seeking for acceptance in some aspect of your daily life.

Bar Mitzvah

To dream that you are at a bar mitzvah ceremony, represents a transitional phase into adulthood. It indicates your social responsibilities, sense of morality, mental reasoning, and hopes.

Barbarian

To see a barbarian in your dream, represents the savage and instinctual aspect of your character.

Barbecue

To dream of a barbecue, refers to a minor problem that is affecting your social life.

Barbed Wire

To see barbed wire in your dream, represents difficulty in breaking through or getting your point across to someone.

To dream that you are caught in barbed wire, suggests that you are feeling trapped and restricted in some relationship. You find yourself confined to specific boundaries.

Barbie Doll

To see a Barbie doll in your dream, represents society's ideals. You may feel that you are unable to meet the expectations of others. Alternatively, the Barbie doll refers to the desire to escape from daily responsibilities.

Barefoot

To dream that you are barefoot, represents your playful attitudes and relaxed, carefree attitude. You have a firm grasp and good understanding on a situation. Alternatively, it mean indicate poverty, lack of mobility, or misunderstanding.

Bargain

To dream that you got something for a bargain, indicates that you are being undervalued. Perhaps you are not putting in as much effort into a project or relationship as you should be. Consider the symbolism of the item and how you feel about it in your dream.

Bark

To hear barking in your dream, represents your tendency of barking orders at people instead of asking or talking kindly. It may also indicate that you are annoying others, grumpiness, or fussiness.

To see a happily barking dog in your dream, symbolizes pleasures and much social activity. If the dog is barking ferociously, then it represents your habit of unnecessary barking at people and the situations around you. It could also mean unfriendly companions.

Barn

To see a barn in your dream, signifies feelings kept in your unconscious. There is a possibility that you may be holding back your instinctual action or natural urges.

Barricade

Please See Barrier

Barrier

To see a barrier in your dream , represents an obstacle to emotional growth. You may feel hindered in fully expressing yourself. The dream may also indicate your resistance to change.

Baseball

To dream that you are attending a baseball game, represents contentment and peace of mind.

To dream that you are playing a game of baseball, denotes your need to set goals and achieve them. It is time for you to stop goofing around and set your sights for the long term. Consider how baseball is often used as an analogy to sexual foreplay as in getting to first, second, or third base on a date. Baseball can have sexual innuendos where the masculine aspects is depicted by the bat and the feminine aspects is depicted in the form of the ball or the ballpark.

To see a baseball field under construction, refers to unresolved sexual issues.

Baseball Bat

To see or hold a baseball bat in your dream, represents your motivating and driving forces. The dream may also be a pun on an "old bat" or old woman. Alternatively the baseball may be a phallic symbol and thus have sexual connotations.

Basement

To dream that you are in a basement, symbolizes your unconscious mind and intuition. The appearance of the basement is an indication of your unconscious state of mind and level of satisfaction.

To dream that the basement is in disarray and messy, signifies some confusion in which you need to sort out. It may also represent your perceived faults and shortcomings.

Basil

To see, smell, or taste basil in your dream, refers to kindness, sweetness, and deep love.

Basket

To see a basket in your dream, symbolizes the material body. It also represents the things that you are holding onto.

Basketball

To dream that you are playing basketball, indicates that you will need the cooperation and assistance of others in order to achieve your goals. Perhaps you are standing in the way of your own progress and need to ask for help.

To see a basketball in your dream, suggests that you need to make the first move. You also need to concentrate and be more focused in your goals.

Bath

To dream that you are taking a bath, signifies a cleansing of your outer and inner self and a washing away of difficult times. This dream may also be symbolic of ridding yourself of old ideas, notions, opinions, and other negativities. Your dream may be pointing toward forgiveness and letting go.

Bathrobe

To see or wear a bathrobe in your dream, represents personal needs or privacy issues. It also relates to sexual/intimate situations and your need to confront and deal with them.

Bathroom

To dream that you are in the bathroom, relates to your instinctual urges. You may be experiencing some burdens/feelings and need to "relieve yourself". Alternatively, it may symbolize purification and self-renewal. You need to cleanse yourself, both emotionally and psychologically.

To dream that you are in a public restroom with no stalls, signifies your frustrations about getting enough privacy. It may also indicate that you are having difficulties letting go of old emotions. If you reveal these feelings, you are afraid that others around you will judge and criticize you.

To dream that you can not find the bathroom, signifies that you are have difficulties in releasing and expressing your emotions.

Please also see Urination. See The Meaning In Action: "Restroom Maze" , "Sitting On The Toilet", " Filthy Stalls" & "Dogs In The Bathroom"

Bathtubs

To see or be in a bathtub in your dream, suggests a need for self-renewal and escape from everyday problems. You need to rid yourself of the burdens that you have been carrying. Alternatively, it indicates your mood for love and pursuit of pleasure and relaxation.

To dream that you or someone has drowned in a bathtub, indicates that you are not as ready as you had thought you were in facing your fears and emotions. You are feeling overwhelmed in confronting your repressed emotions. You need to take things more slowly, instead of trying to dive right in.

Bats

To see bats in your dream, symbolizes uncleanness, demons, and annoyances. Alternatively, bats also represent your need to let go of old habits for your current way of life no longer suits your new growth and outlook. It is symbolic of a rebirth. It may also mean that you are entering blindly into a situation. You need to evaluate the facts more carefully The dream may also been a pun on feeling "batty" or feeling crazy.

To dream of a white bat, signifies death of a family member. To dream of a black bat, signifies personal disaster.

To see a vampire bat in your dream, represents that a person in your life may be draining your of self-confidence and/or your resources.

Battery

To see a battery in your dream, symbolizes life energy. If the battery is dead, then it suggests that you are emotionally exhausted or feeling low.

Battle

To be in or see a battle in your dream, suggests that you are overworked. You need to give yourself a break. There is a conflict between your rational thinking and your irrational impulses. Alternatively, it represents eroticism. You may be overly stimulated or you are trying to suppress your instinctual urges.

Battlefield

To dream that you are on a battlefield, represents some major conflict occurring in your waking life. It may indicate a new situation, new problem or new relationship which you need to solve and conquer.

Bay

To see a bay in your dream, represents understanding. Something is become clearer to you. The dream may also suggest that you are keeping someone at a distance and not let them get too close to you.

Bay Tree

To see a bay tree in your dream, symbolizes immortality, longevity, success and/or victory.

Beach

To see the beach in your dream, symbolizes the meeting between your two states of mind. The sand is symbolic of the rational and mental processes while the water signifies the irrational, unsteady, and emotional aspects of yourself. It is a place of transition between the physical/material and the spiritual.

To dream that you are on the beach and looking out toward the ocean, indicates unknown and major changes that are occurring in your life. Consider the state of the ocean, whether it is calm, pleasant, forbidding, etc.

To dream that you are looking toward the beach, suggests that you are returning to what is familiar to you. Alternatively, you may be adapting or accepting to the changes and circumstances in your life.

To dream that you are relaxing on a beach, signifies that the coming weeks will be calm and tranquil for you. Your stress will be alleviated and you will find peace of mind.

To dream that you are working on the beach, signifies a business project that will consume most of your time.

Beads

To see beads in your dream, indicates your tendency to please others and put their needs in front of your own.

To dream that you are stringing beads, suggests that you have laid the groundwork for your success. You will be recognized and/or rewarded for your achievements.

To dream that you are counting beads, symbolizes pleasure and joy.

Beans

To see or eat beans in your dream, signifies your connection to your roots and to humanity. Consider what binds you to your community. Alternatively, beans are symbolic of the soul and of immortality. They also relate to fertility.

Bear

To dream that you are being pursued or attacked by a bear, denotes aggression, overwhelming obstacles and competition. You may find yourself in a threatening situation. Alternatively, bears symbolize the cycle of life and death and renewal. It may signal of period of introspection and thinking. The dream may also be a pun on "bare". Perhaps you need to bare your soul and let everything out into the open.

To see a polar bear in your dream, signifies a reawakening.

**See The Meaning In Action: "Polar Bears" & "Bear In A Field"*

Beard

To see a long beard in your dream, is representative of old age and insight, and wisdom.

If you are a woman and you dream of growing a beard, signifies your masculine aspect of your personality. You want to be more assertive and wield more power.

Beast

To see a beast in your dream, signifies foolishness and ignorance.

To see faceless beasts in your dream, indicates a situation you are refusing to see or confront, but are aware of it in some passive way. This dream also suggests that something in your life is bringing up feelings of fear and insecurities.

According to the bible, a beast symbolizes men in honor without understanding. (Psa: 73:22)

Beating

To dream that you are beaten, indicates that you need to make some fundamental changes to yourself. You need to make some conscious adjustments and evaluations.

To see others being beaten, suggests that some part of your life is out of balance.

Beauty Contest

Please See Pageant.

Beauty Parlor

Please see Salon.

Beaver

To see a beaver building a dam, symbolizes ambition and that hard work is necessary to achieve your own goals. It is time to put your ideas into action and settle any differences with fellow coworkers and friends. In isolating yourself from these people, you will find it difficult to attain your goals. The support of people around you are important.

Bed

To see your bed in your dream, represents you intimate self and discovery of your sexuality. If you are sleeping in your own bed, then it denotes security and restoration of your mind. You are looking for domestic bliss and peace. If you are waking up in different and/or unknown beds, then it represents the consequences of the decisions you have made.

To dream that you are searching for a bed, suggests that you are having difficulties acknowledging your intimate self. You may be feeling inhibited in expressing your sexuality. Alternatively, it may also mean that you are looking for domestic security and happiness.

To dream that you are going to bed with a stranger, suggests that you are making friends too fast. You need to be more cautious.

To dream that you are floating or lifting up into the air from your bed, suggests that you are feeling helpless and disconnected from those around you. Your ideas may be alienating people. You might need to tone down your personality a bit.

Bedroom

To dream that you are in the bedroom, signifies aspects of your self that you keep private. It is also indicative of your sexual nature and intimate relations.

Bedspread

To notice or buy bedspread in your dream, represents your open sexuality and outward beauty. The design and look of the bedspread may be a clue as to what you are looking for sexually.

Beehive

To see a beehive in your dream, denotes that there are many opportunities for you to get ahead in life and to not let them escape from your grasp. It symbolizes hard work and the importance of teamwork. A promotion may be in store for you.

To see an empty beehive, signifies sorrow over love affairs and loss in income.

To dream of destroying a beehive, symbolizes losses and temporary poverty.

Beeper

*Please See Pager.

Beer

To see or drink beer in your dream, represents happiness, fogginess, or inspiration. It also indicates that you have quite a social life.

*Please also see Alcohol.

Bees

To see bees in your dream, symbolizes good luck, harmony, and bliss. Bees are also symbolic of work and industry as represented by the common phrase "busy as a bee."

To dream that you are stung by a bee, signifies unexpected misfortune. You will be surrounded by trouble and severely reprimanded.

Beetle

To see a beetle in your dream, indicates that some destructive influences may be at work in your waking life. You may also feel that your values and beliefs are being compromised.

Beggar

To see or dream that you are a beggar, represents your sense of insecurity and lack of self-worth. You feel that you are undeserving.

Begin

To dream about beginning something in your dream, indicates that valuable time has been wasted through procrastination. You need to get on with life and put your plans into motion.

Behead

To dream that you or someone else is being beheaded, signifies poor judgment or a bad decision that you have made and regretted.

Please see also Decapitation.

Behind

To dream that you are behind someone, suggests that you are offering your support and encouragement for someone. Alternatively, it refers to emerging unconscious thoughts and feelings.

To dream that you are left behind, indicates your fear of not being able to keep up. You are questioning your abilities and/or may not be utilizing your full potential.

Belch

Please See Burp.

Bells

To hear a bell in your dream, represents a warning or a call to order. It may also be a signal from your unconscious to prepare you for whatever is happening next. If the bell rings and never stops, then it suggests that you are experiencing extreme anxiety.

Belly

To see your belly in your dream, indicates that your are processing and integrating your ideas and feelings from the unconscious to the conscious level. The belly symbolically holds repressed emotions and unexpressed feelings. Your dream may also be telling you to trust your gut feeling and intuition.

To see a pregnant belly, represents emotions that are due to come to the surface. They can no longer remain suppressed.

To dream that you are stroking or touching a belly, indicates that you are coming to terms with certain feelings. You are slowly confronting and acknowledging your repressed emotions.

Belly Button

Please See Navel.

Belt

To see a belt in your dream, signifies a constricted flow of life energy and issues of morality. You may be feeling conflicted between what you think (your intellectual reasoning) and what you feel (your instinctual nature). Alternatively, a belt may symbolize punishment and discipline.

Bench

To see or sit on a bench, signifies your tendency to procrastinate and put things aside. It also suggests that you often take on a passive role instead taking initiative.

Bending

To dream that you are bending signifies your ability to adapt to new situations. In particular, bending backward may represent how you are going out of your way to please, while bending forward, implies your eagerness to do something.

Betrayal

To dream that you have been betrayed, represents your suspicions about a particular person, relationship or situation. This dream often occurs when you are having feelings of insecurity and are faced with major commitments in your life at the same time.

Bewilderment

To dream that you are bewildered, indicates that you are stuck in the middle between two opposing views. It represents your indecision and your inability to make up your mind. Such dreams often reflect your waking state of confusion and shock.

Bible

To see or read the bible in your dream, symbolizes truth, belief, inspiration and knowledge. You are seeking some form of comfort. The bible may also refer to your fundamental belief system. Perhaps you need to turn to the bible more.

Bicycle

To dream that you are riding a bicycle, signifies your desires to attain a balance in your life. You need to balance work and pleasure in order to succeed in your current undertakings. If you have difficulties riding the bicycle, then it suggests that you are experiencing anxieties about making it on your own.

To see a bicycle in your dream, indicates that you need to devote time to leisurely pursuits and recreation.

Big

To dream that someone or something is bigger than normal, indicates that you either have an inflated opinion of yourself or of someone. You may be expressing a desire to be more dominant in some situation or relationship.

To see a big figure in your dream, represents authority and power.

Billboard

To see a billboard in your dream, is a sign or message that you need to take note of in your path toward your goals. Consider what advise the billboard is trying to convey to you.

Billiards

To dream that you are playing billiards, represents your competitive nature. You need to learn to win or lose gracefully. Alternatively, it may mean that you need to concentrate harder on a problem in your waking life.

Bikini

To dream that you are wearing a bikini, suggests that you are feeling exposed. You may feel unprotected emotionally. It may also signal a return to innocence or youth. Alternatively, it indicates superficial desires.

Binoculars

To dream that you are looking through a pair of binoculars, suggests that you need to take a long and close look at a situation. You need to carefully evaluate your choices and decision.

Bird

To dream of a chirping and/or flying birds, represents joy, harmony, ecstasy, balance, and love. It denotes a sunny outlook in life. You will experience spiritual freedom and psychological liberation. It is almost as if a weight has been lifted off your shoulders.

To dream of dead or dying birds, foretells a period of coming disappointments. You will find yourself worrying over problems that are constantly on your mind.

To see bird eggs in your dream, symbolizes money.

To see birds hatching in your dream, symbolizes delayed success.

To see a bird nest in your dream, symbolizes independence, refuge and security. You need something to fall back on. Alternatively, it may signify a prosperous endeavor, new opportunities, and fortune.

Birdcage

To see a birdcage in your dream, represents a loss of freedom. You are feeling locked up and unable to fully express yourself.

Birdhouse

To see a birdhouse in your dream, suggests that you see your home as your own spiritual haven. You may need to pay more attention to your spiritual side and work on developing it. Alternatively, it symbolizes the season of spring.

Birdseed

To dream of feeding birds with birdseed, suggests that you are nourishing your higher, spiritual qualities. Alternatively, it many indicate insufficient rewards for your efforts.

To dream that you are spreading birdseed on the ground, signifies minor growth in your business endeavors.

Birth

To dream of giving birth or see someone else giving birth, suggests that you are giving birth to a new idea or project. It also represents a new attitude, fresh beginnings or a major upcoming event. Alternatively, the dream may be calling attention to your inner child and the potential for your to grow. A more direct interpretation of this dream, may represent your desires/ anxieties of giving birth or the anticipation for such an event to occur.

To dream that you are giving birth to a non-human creature, signifies you overwhelming (an unfounded) fear in the health of your baby. You are overly concerned that your baby may have birth defects. This type of dream is common in expectant mothers in their second trimester. If you are not expecting, then it refers to your fear in the outcome of some decision or project. You are trying to overcome difficulties in your life and achieve inner development.

In particular, if you dream that you are giving birth to a monster, then it implies that your inner creative energy has yet to differentiate itself and grow into expression. You may hold some hesitation in releasing this "monster" for fear that others will judge your or that they will not accept your ideals.

To dream that the mother dies during birth, represents transformation. The dream represents the ending of one thing (death) and the new beginning of another thing (birth). You may be making life changes or getting rid of your old habits and ways.

*Please see also Pregnant

Birth Control

*Please See Contraceptive.

Birthday

To dream about your birthday, denotes acceptance of yourself. You are celebrating who you are and coming to terms with who you are as a person.

Birthmark

To dream that you have a birthmark, serves as a reminder that something you must do or never do again. It represents a stain on your soul.

Birthday Cake

To see a birthday cake in your dream, indicates that the best of your wishes will be realized. It also represents your willingness to let people in and share your life with others.

Bisexual

If you are not bisexual and dream that you are, then it may indicate some sexual repression. You may be trying to compensate for your lack of sexual expression. Alternatively, it may represent general sexual confusion.

Bison

Please see Buffalo.

Bites

To see bites in your dream, forewarns of danger from someone who has wished you harm, either physical or monetary. Be careful of people who surround you.

To dream that you are being bitten, represents your vulnerability regarding your unresolved issues emotions. You may be pestered by a problem or obstacle.

To dream that you are being bitten by a vampire, signifies your need to shut out a person in your life who has been using you. It is time to open your eyes and stand up for your self. Do not let yourself be manipulated and played for a fool.

To dream of biting someone in your dream, signifies the pressure you are putting on some people causing them great distress. You may have unexpressed, perhaps even childish, feelings of anger or resentment that need to be recognized. This dream is a message for you to lighten up and alleviate the stress that you are putting on others.

Bitter

To dream that something is or tastes bitter, suggests that a certain aspect or condition in your life is becoming difficult to swallow/tolerate. You may also be experiencing some guilt.

Black Widow

To see a black widow in your dream, suggests fear or uncertainty regarding a relationship. You may feel confined, trapped, or suffocated in this relationship. You may even have some hostility toward your mate.

Because the female black widow has the reputation of devouring its mate, it thus also symbolizes feminine power and domination over men.

Blackberries

To see or eat blackberries in your dream, suggests that you are becoming careless. It is also an expression of your hidden sexual desires.

Blackbird

To see a blackbird in your dream, is a bad omen, bringing about misfortune for you in the coming weeks. It also signifies your lack of motivation and that you are not utilizing your full potential.

To see a flying blackbird in your dream, signifies good fortune.

Blackboard

*Please See Chalkboard.

Blackmail

To dream that you are blackmailing someone, indicates your issues with power and domination. You may be letting your competitive nature get the best of you.

To dream that you are being blackmailed, represents inner weaknesses and helplessness. You may not have confidence in your own ability. It may also be a pun on a "black male" you may know in your life.

Blacksmith

To see a blacksmith in your dream, represents inner strength and endurance.

Blade

To see a blade in your dream, suggests that you are making some difficult and important decisions. You need to be able to make clear distinctions between your choices. It also indicates that you are walking on a thin line and need to balance aspects of your life carefully.

Blanket

To see a blanket in your dream, symbolizes warmth, love, security and protection. You may be seeking for some form of shelter from the outside world. Consider also how your dream may be calling attention to a "cover-up" in some situation or circumstance in your waking life.

To dream that you are wrapped in a blanket, indicates your fear of the unknown. You may feel some sort of threat/chaos or sense some coldness from those around you.

To dream that you are covering or wrapping someone in a blanket, suggests you desire to care for that person.

Bleach

To see or use bleach in your dream, signifies a time of healing and cleansing. You are ready to mend past hurts and resolve any unexpressed emotions.

Bleachers

To see or sit on bleachers in your dream, indicates that you are are reflecting on your progress in achieving your goals. The appearance of bleachers can also serve to bring you back in time to the high school gym or track field and the feelings you experienced at the time.

Blender

To see a blender in your dream, symbolizes your ability to blend various ideas into a harmonious whole.

Blind

To dream that you are blind, represents your refusal to see the truth or your lack of awareness to a problem. Perhaps you are rejecting something about yourself or your situation. Are you refusing to see any other point of view except your own? Consider the pun, "turning a blind eye".

Blinds

To see or dream that you are shutting the blinds, suggests that you are in denial about a situation or problem. The dream may also be a pun on being blind and refusing to see something. Perhaps you are hiding something.

To dream that you are opening the blinds, indicates that you are ready to reveal something significant and/or personal that was previously unknown.

Blinking

To dream that you are blinking, indicates that there is something you fear in seeing. You are refusing to see the obvious.

Blister

To dream that you have a blister, indicates that some minor annoyance or problem is draining your energy and time. Consider how you may have gotten the blister. To dream that you got the blister from manual and hard labor, indicates that you need to put forth more effort in order to overcome your little problems. To dream that you got the blister from a burn, suggests an emotional or relational problem.

Where the blister is located is also significant. If the blister is on you hand, then it suggests that you are having issues related to power and competency. If the blister is on your face, then it indicates issues related to your identity, self-image, and self-identity.

Blizzard

To dream about a blizzard, suggests that you are feeling emotionally cold and frigid. You are feeling excluded and left out. It may indicate a lack of love and the absence of warmth within your own family circle.

Blond

To see a blond person in your dream, suggests that you need to enjoy life and live it up. Be a little glamorous.

To dream that you dye your hair blond, indicates that you literally need to lighten up and quit being so serious all the time. Try to be more upbeat.

Blood

To see blood in your dream, represents life, love, and passion as well as disappointments. If you see the word "blood" written in your dream, then it may refer to some situation in your life that is permanent and cannot be changed.

To dream that you are bleeding or losing blood, signifies that you are suffering from exhaustion or that you are feeling emotionally drained. It may also denote bitter confrontations between you and your friends. Your past actions has come back to haunt you. Women often dream of blood or of someone bleeding shortly before or during their periods and when they are pregnant.

To dream that something is written in blood, represents the energy you have put into a project. You have invested so much effort into something that you are not willing to give it up.

To dream that you are drinking blood, indicates that you have a fresh burst of vitality and power.

**See The Meaning In Action: "Menstruation"*

Blossom

To see a blossom in your dream, represents the beauty within your Self. It may also mean that your hard work will pay off in the end.

Blow Dry

To dream that you are blow drying your hair, suggests that you are clearing out your thoughts and getting some fresh ideas. It may also be a pun on something that blows your mind.

Blue Jay

To see a blue jay in your dream, indicates that you are over-confident and being too arrogant. Alternatively, a blue jay may be trying to call attention to something which you have overlooked.

Blueberries

To see blueberries in your dream, represents your youth and the desire to recapture aspects of your youth. It is a symbol of eternity and optimism of the future. Alternatively, it may depict your depressed mood and sadden state of mind.

Bluebird

To see a bluebird in your dream, symbolizes both happiness and sadness. It is also an indication of purification and resolution to the opposing conflicts/paradoxes in your life.

Blueprint

To see a blueprint in your dream, indicates that you need to pay closer attention at the details before proceeding forward with some plan or relationship. It may also mean that you are in the process of going through some inner changes in your life. You are working on expanding your way of thinking.

Blurry

To have a blurry dream, indicates that there is something you are not confronting or refusing to see. It also represents secrets and confusion. Perhaps you think that someone is trying to keep something from you.

Blush

To dream that you are wearing blush, indicates that you want to be more expressive and loving.

Boar

To see a boar in your dream, signifies that you need to look inside to find the answers and secrets about yourself and the people around you. Consider the pun, "they are such a bore".

Boat

To dream that you are in or see a boat, signifies you ability to cope and express your emotions. Pay particular attention to the condition and state of the waters, whether is is calm or violent, clear or murky, etc. Are you "smooth sailing"? Alternatively, you may be ready to confront your unconscious and unknown aspects of yourself.

To dream that you are trying to jump off a boat, suggests that you want to dive directly in and confront those difficult emotions and approach your problems head on.

Bobcat

To see a bobcat in your dream, suggests that you need to pay close attention to what you see and hear in your daily life.

Please see also Cat.

Body

To dream about your own body, signifies your level of self-worth and self-esteem. Often times, these qualities are dependent on your physical appearance or how your perceive yourself. The dream body also reflects your conscious identity. The body is also representative of your state of health.

Boiling

To dream that something is boiling, represents transformation and/or sacrifice. There is something that you need to get down to the heart of. In particular to dream that water is boiling, suggests that you are expressing some emotional turmoil. It also may mean that feelings from your unconscious are surfacing and ready to be acknowledged.

Bolt

To see a bolt in your dream, suggests that you are protecting yourself from difficult emotions and experiences. The dream may also be a pun on your tendency or desire to flee from a situation.

Bomb

To see a bomb in your dream, signifies that you may be going through a potentially explosive and trying situation in your waking life. The bomb could represent repressed desires and unexpressed emotions that are likely to explode or burst if not dealt with soon. It could be something within yourself, such as the desire to explode with anger over an issue that's affecting you.

To dream of a bomb threat, suggests that you are experiencing some inner anger and/or pressures which are on the verge of exploding into violence.

Bondage

To dream that you are in bondage, signifies that aspects of your emotions and/or character are too tightly controlled or that are repressed. You may be restricting your need for self-expression or feel that you are a prisoner of your circumstances.

In a sexual sense, dreams of bondage represents your desires to be more sexually submissive or that you have unacknowledged sexual passions.

Bones

To see bones in your dream, suggests the discovery of your personal, family, or cultural secrets. It is also symbolic of your underlying strengths that you have not yet recognized.

To dream of broken bones, signifies that you have discovered or realized that there is a weakness in your plans or in your thinking. Your dream may call for you immediate attention to a particular situation or relationship.

Bonfire

To see a bonfire in your dream, suggests that you need to find a new path and set forth toward a different goal.

Bonnet

To see or wear a bonnet in your dream, represents your sheltered ideals and old-fashioned beliefs. Your close-mindedness is restricting your vision and plans.

Bonsai Tree

To see a bonsai tree in your dream, indicates the limitations of your own conscious mind. You need to consider what your instincts is telling you.

Boogie Board

To see or ride a boogie board in your dream, indicates that you are riding out the difficulties and take each day one day at a time.

Booing

To hear booing or dream that you are being booed, indicates that you are seeking approval. Alternatively, you may find yourself in an embarrassing or shameful situation.

Books

To see books in your dream, indicates calmness. You will advance toward your goals at a slow and steady pace. Books also symbolize knowledge, intellect, information and wisdom. Consider the type of book. It may represent a significant calling into a specific field of work.

To see dusty books in your dream, denotes forgotten knowledge or previous "chapters" of your life.

To see children's books in your dream, memories and a collection of personal memories from your own childhood. It may also suggest your desire to escape from reality and retreat into some fantasy world.

To see a satanic book in your dream, symbolizes your one-sided way of thinking and looking at things. You are trying to denounce any responsibility in your actions and are putting forth a little effort as possible.

Book Bag

Please See Knapsack.

Bookkeeper

To dream that you are a bookkeeper, represents a need to keep you life in balance and in harmony. Alternatively, it may indicate that you should be held accountable for some condition or circumstance.

Bookshelf

To see a bookshelf in your dream, represents the various levels of your mind where ideas, concepts, and memories are kept. It also suggests your need to acquire some information or knowledge in a situation before making your decision.

Boomerang

To see or throw a boomerang in your dream, indicates that what you do to others will come back to you, whether it is positive or negative.

Boots

To see or dream that you are wearing boots, refers to the power in your movement and the boldness of your position. You are taking a firm stance.

Border

To see or cross the border in your dream, indicates that you are entering a new phase or transition in your life. You are encountering new territory. Alternatively, it represents the conversion of two states of mind or attitudes.

Boss

To see your boss in your dream, represents the bossy or authoritative side of your own personality. Your boss may reveal self-confidence and the assertive aspect of yourself. It is telling of your issues of control and authority. Alternatively, to see your boss in your dream may indicate your over-involvement or obsession with your work. Negatively, the boss in your dream may symbolize your limitations and lack of freedom/originality.

To dream that you are afraid of your boss, indicates your fear of authority. You may feel that someone else is running your life or dictating what you can and can not do.

Consider also the relationship you have with your boss. This may provide clues to work-related issues that need to be resolved.

Bottle

To see a bottle in your dream, signifies how you may be pushing your feelings back inside rather than expressing them. The contents of the bottle indicate the nature of the emotions. A bottle of champagne shows your need to socialize, while a bottle of poison signifies evil thoughts.

To see an empty bottle, denotes that you have exhausted your inner resources. You may be feeling drained and empty inside.

Boulder

To see a boulder in your dream, symbolizes a major obstacle and problem in some component of your life.

Boundary

To see a boundary in your dream, indicates that something is restricting your growth and hindering your goals. You are being limited.

Bouquet

To dream that you receive or give a floral bouquet, signifies respect, affection, approval, graciousness, admiration, and love. It is indicative of some healing energy.

Bow

To bow in your dream, represents respect. You are acknowledging a greater and larger power.

To see an archer's bow in your dream, refers to the pursuit and accomplishment of your goals.

Bowel Movement

To dream that you have a bowel movement, signifies that you are successfully getting rid of your old habits/ways and thinking patterns. It is usually analogous to the release of strong emotions, such as anger and anger.

*See Constipation. or Diarrhea.

Bow And Arrow

To see a bow and arrow in your dream, represents a combination of female and male energies. It may refer to your libido or some sexual energy/desire. Alternatively, it symbolizes anger, aggression, or tension. This dream symbol may also be a metaphor that you are aiming for perfection.

Bowing

To dream that you are bowing, symbolizes respect, honor, humility, and reverence. You need to be more submissive to another's wishes.

Bowl

To see a bowl in your dream, symbolizes the womb and sense of security. Consider the condition of the bowl and how it is treated or handled in the dream. This may offer clues as to how you feel you are being treated in a particular relationship.

Bowling

To dream that you are bowling, refers to the strikes, hits, and misses in your life. Perhaps you are expressing some regrets if you are bowling a bad game. And if you are bowling strike after strike, then it suggests that you are on your way toward a successful future. It may also be a pun on your striking performance and/or stellar ability.

To dream that you bowl a gutter ball, suggests that you are stuck in a rut and need to make some changes of where your life is headed.

Alternatively, bowling and bowling alleys may also be a metaphor for sexual conquest. Consider all the sexual innuendos that are at play in the bowling alley. The pin deck is symbolic of the womb or vagina (as is with with any dark receptacle like caves, bowls, containers, etc.) The pins and bowling balls, can be viewed as masculine symbols.

Box

To see a box in your dream, signifies your instinctual nature and destructive impulses. Alternatively, you may be trying to preserve and protect some aspect of yourself. The box may also symbolize your limitations and restrictions.

To dream that you are opening a box, denotes that things are being revealed about yourself that were once hidden. Consider your feelings as you open the box. If opening the box fills you will fear, you may be uncovering aspects of yourself that make you feel anxious. Also consider the pun, "being boxed in".

Boxcar

To see a boxcar or a cable car in your dream, signifies that you will make an adequate income to support your lifestyle.

Boxing

To dream that you are boxing, suggests that you are experiencing some internal struggle or conflict. The dream may also be a pun on "boxing" things us. It suggests that you are limiting yourself and your goals/ideas. It may also indicate that you keep your emotions inside.

Boy

If you are female and dream that you see or are a boy, then it indicates that you are developing the masculine aspects of character. Alternatively, it may represent your feelings about a real-life boy who is important and significant to you. You may have a crush on this boy and your waking thoughts of him has carried over into the dream world. Your motherly instincts may be taking over.

If you are an adult male and dream that you see or are a boy, then it suggests your playful, innocent, childlike nature. Alternatively, it can symbolize the immature aspects of yourself that still needs to grow. Your inner child may be trying to draw your attention to parts of yourself that you need to recognize and acknowledge.

Boy Scout

Your own experience as a boy scout will definitely affect this dream symbol. If you were never a boy scout and dream that you are, then it signifies your commitment and discipline toward some task. The dream may emphasize a sense of community, belonging, and helpfulness.

To see a boy scout in your dream, denotes that you or someone else has displayed exemplary behavior. You will gain the ranks necessary to achieve your goals and success.

Boyfriend

To see your boyfriend in your dream, represents your waking relationship with him and how you feel about him.

To dream that your boyfriend is dead, indicates that something in your own Self that is no longer functional and is "dead". You are not being allowed to fully express yourself. It is also symbolic of your own relationship with that person. Perhaps you need to let go of this relationship.

If your boyfriend is away and your dreams of him involve a lot of touching, signify how much you miss his presence and have him being nearby. The dream is telling you not to take the day to day things for granted. Learn to cherish the smaller things in life.

To dream that your boyfriend tells you that he is gay or that he doesn't love your anymore, represents your own insecurities with the relationship. It may also mean that the relationship is moving to a new level to which you are expressing some anxiety and fears about the changing situation. You may feel left out it in his life or that you are unable to share in all his experiences. It boils down to trust and communication.

Bra

To dream that you are wearing a bra, signifies support and protection. Perhaps you need to have your spirits uplifted. Alternatively, it may represent your nurturing side and maternal feelings.

To dream that you are not wearing a bra, indicates that you have no discipline or control. Alternative, it may reflect your sexual nature.

Bracelet

To see or wear a bracelet in your dream, refers to an expression of deep passion and fire. The dream also highlights your need to reach out to others. It is a sign that you need to rekindle old friendships and to call up an old friend that you haven't heard from in awhile.

To see a broken bracelet in your dream, suggests that you tend to sacrifice your own comfort and happiness for others.

Braces

To dream that you have braces, indicates that you should not be so quick to criticize. You should stop talking too much and listen to what others have to say. It may also indicate your brashness. The dream may also be a pun on "brace yourself"

**See The Meaning In Action: "Braces"*

Bragging

To dream that you are bragging, indicates that you are feeling insecure about yourself. You are trying to overcompensate for your shortcomings.

Braids

To dream that you hair is in braids, represents your neat and orderly way of thinking. It symbolizes your determination and a strong mindset.

Brain

To dream of your brain, suggests that you are under severe intellectual stress. It may also symbolize your problem-solving abilities and that you need to put those abilities to use. Alternatively, it may imply that your ideas are not receiving enough attention and validation. You are concerned that your knowledge and teachings are not be transmitted clearly.

Brakes

To dream that you are applying your brakes, signifies that you should slow down in your business and/or personal affairs. You have been living on the fast lane and you need to take it easy.

To dream that your brakes failed, forewarns that you lack any sort of stability in your life. Your life is out of control. Any agreements that you entertain or engage yourself into will prove risky.

Branches

To see branches in your dream, is a symbol of good luck, growth, and new life. Alternatively, branches represent the relationships and communication between you and your family/relatives.

To see broken branches in your dream, indicates some personal or work-related problem.

See The Meaning In Action: "Scissors In The Forest"

Brass

To see brass in your dream, indicates deception, falsehood and deceitfulness. It may also refer to your boldness.

Bread

To see bread in your dream, represents the basic needs of life. Bread may signify the positive qualities and great things you have learned on your journey of life.

Break

To dream that you break something, indicates that changes are ahead for you. You want to change the direction that your life is headed. Alternatively, it suggests that you need to take things slower.

Break-Up

To dream that you break up with your significant other, indicates that there is something in your life that you need to let go no matter how hard it may be.

To dream that you did not break up with your boyfriend or girlfriend, suggests that you are still in denial about the break-up. Your mind many not have accepted the notion that the relationship is over.

Breakdown

To dream that your vehicle breaks down, suggests that you may be pushing yourself too hard and going beyond your limits. You are in danger of driving yourself toward physical difficulties, hardships, and even illness. You need to take better care of yourself or reevaluate your choices and alternatives.

Breakfast

To dream about breakfast, indicates the start of a new project or the beginning of a new stage in your life. Alternatively, your mind may already be thinking ahead on what to make for breakfast in the morning. It is not uncommon for your fleeting thoughts to be incorporated into your dream.

Breast Feeding

To dream that you are breast feeding, symbolizes tenderness, love, nurturance, and motherly love. Good things will be at your grasp.

Please see also Nursing.

Breasts

To see breasts in your dream, symbolizes primal nourishment and your need to be nursed and care for. It represent motherhood, nurturance, and infantile dependency. Alternatively, breasts represents sexual arousal and raw energy.

Seeing naked breasts can also denote a feeling of exposure and invasion of privacy. In particular, for a woman, the dream may indicate anxieties about becoming a woman/mother.

Breathe

To dream that you are breathing rapidly, indicates that you are experiencing some anxiety, tension, or fear concerning a new situation in your waking life.

To dream that you are breathing underwater, represents a retreat back into the womb. You want to return to a state where you were dependent and free from responsibilities. Perhaps you are feeling helpless, unable to fulfill your own needs and caring for yourself. Alternatively, you may be submerged in your emotions.

To dream that you are holding your breath, indicates your stubborn state of mind. Your views may be one-sided and the dream is telling you to be open to the opinions of others.

To dream that you cannot breathe, indicates that you are feeling exhausted.

To dream that you have bad breath, suggests that you are misleading others.

Breeze

To feel a breeze in your dream, represents the movement of ideas and minor changes.

Bribery

To dream that you are being bribed, suggests that you are easily influenced. Perhaps you are letting others persuade you into doing something you don't really want to. Gather your strength and stand up for yourself.

To dream that you are bribing someone, indicates that you expect too much of others. You may be too demanding. In particular, if you dream that you are bribing a policeman, then you believe that you are above the law or rules. You think you can get away with being dishonest and deceitful.

Brick

To see a brick in your dream, represents your individual ideas and thoughts. Experience and/or heartbreak may have hardened you.

To dream that you are building a brick wall, signifies a wall that you are putting up to protect yourself against hurt. It may also indicate that you may be hard on the outside but still sensitive on the inside.

Bride

To see a bride in your dream, signifies the most feminine qualities about you. A bride may also symbolize a union or partnership or some sort.

To dream that the bride is shot at her wedding, suggests that a feminine aspect of yourself has come to an abrupt end.

Bridge

To dream that you are crossing a bridge, signifies an important decision or a critical junction in your life. This decision will prove to be a positive change with prosperity and wealth in the horizon. Bridges represent a transitional period in your life where you will be moving on to a new stage.

To dream of a run-down bridge, indicates that you should not contemplate any major changes in your life at this time.

To see a bridge collapse in your dream, denotes that you have let a great opportunity pass you by.

**See the Meaning In Action: "God Is Dead"

Briefcase

To see or carry a briefcase in your dream, represents your level or preparedness in some situation or circumstance. It also refers to your concerns and worries about work and travel.

Bright

To dream that something is bright, represents divinity, a higher consciousness, and spirituality. You need to honor an admirable person or situation. The dream may also be a metaphor for intellect and someone who is smart.

If the brightness is blinding, then it suggests that you are not paying attention to some new insights.

Bronze

To see bronze in your dream, suggests that you need to provide more care to something. It indicates maintenance of beauty and health.

Broom

To see a broom in your dream, denotes that it is time to clean up your act and resolve your past issues. You need to discard what is no longer useful to you. Alternatively, brooms symbolize domesticity and the establishment of a household. Also, brooms are sometimes associated with witches and thus broomsticks may refer to the female shadow aspect of yourself.

Brothel

To dream that you are in a brothel, indicates dissatisfaction and deprivation in your emotional or sexual relationship. Your physical urges need attention.

Brother

To see your brother in your dream, may symbolize some aspect of your relationship with him. It can also serve to remind you that someone in your waking life has certain characteristics/behavior similar to your brother's.

If you do not have a brother and dream that you have one, then he may symbolize characteristics that you need to acknowledge within yourself. The brother in your dream can also be synonymous with a close friend or buddy. Brother also has religious implications and thus represents spiritual issues. Consider also the familiar phrase "big brother is watching you" which indicate that your dream has to deal with issues of authority and oppression.

To dream that you are mad or angry at your brother, signifies repressed anger that you are feeling but afraid to express in your waking life.

Bruise

To dream that you have a bruise, represents stress and mounting pressure that you are dealing with in your waking life. It may also refer to a reawakening of old, family wounds. Alternatively, you need to accept the consequences of your actions. Consider the symbolism of the specific part of your body that is bruised.

Brunette

To see or dream that you are a brunette, indicates that you need to be more down to earth. It may also be symbolic of your sultriness and smoldering sexuality.

Brush

To see a brush in your dream, symbolizes your desire to brush away problems or something in your life that needs to be cleaned up. Perhaps you are taking a nonchalant attitude to circumstances that need serious consideration.

If you lose or can't find your brush, then suggests that you are unable to sort our your problems.

Bubble

To see bubbles in your dreams, represent merriment, fun, and childhood joys. It may also symbolize wishes or unrealistic expectations. In deciphering this dream symbol, consider also the phrase of "bursting one's bubble".

Bubble Bath

To dream that you or someone is taking a bubble bath, represents ultimate relaxation. You have rid yourself of your worries/difficulties and release all the negative emotions you have been keeping inside.

Bucket

To see or carry a bucket in your dream, indicates an improvement in your current situation. If the bucket is filled, then it signifies abundance, love and wealth. If the bucket is empty, then it signifies that you will overcome some loss or conflict.

Buddha

To see Buddha in your dream, symbolizes wisdom, insight, compassion, and inner spirituality.

Budgie

Please See Parakeets.

Buffalo

To see a buffalo in your dream, symbolizes survival. The dream may warn that you are go off your life path.

To see an injured or killed buffalo, forewarns that you must not accept any new ventures.

To see a herd of buffalo in your dream, signifies tranquility and plentitude.

Bug

To see a bug in your dream, suggests that you are worried about something. It is symbolic of your anxieties and/or fears. What is literally bugging you? Consider also the popular phrase "bitten by the bug" to imply your strong emotional ties or involvement to some activity/interest/hobby. Alternatively, the bug may be representative of your sexual thoughts.

Building

To see a building in your dream, represents the self and the body. How high you are in the building indicates a rising level of understanding or awareness. If you are in the lower levels of the building, then it refers to more primal attitudes and/or sexuality.

To see a building in ruins or damaged, indicates that your approach toward a situation or relationship is all wrong. You need to change. Your own self-image may have suffered and taken some blow.

To dream that you or someone fall off a building, suggests that you are descending into the realm of unconscious. You are learning about and acknowledging aspects of your unconscious. Alternatively, it symbolizes your fear of not being able to complete or succeeding in a task. See also Falling in our Common Dream Themes section.

Bulb

To see a plant bulb in your dream, represents your spiritual, physical, and intellectual potential. It refers to the growth of some project, relationship, or situation. Alternatively, it symbolizes your genetic heritage, family tradition or fertility.

Bull

To see a bull in your dream, symbolizes stubbornness, strong will, strength, and power. It is time to take some action and be more assertive. Alternatively, it indicates rich, prosperous, and abundant life. Consider the pun, "being bull-headed". May you need to have a little compromise in a situation.

Bulls are also symbolic of repressed sexual energies, fertility and virility. To see an untamed, raging bull represents that your passions may be out of control. The bull may also represent a person in your life who is born under the Taurus sign.

*Please See Also Steer.

Bulldozer

To see a bulldozer in your dream, suggests that you are feeling pushed away from what you want. Or you are being diverted away from the path to your goals. You may be feeling helpless and bullied. Alternatively, it may indicate that you need to organize and clear away the clutter in your life.

Bullets

To see a bullet or bullets in your dream, indicates anger and aggression directed at you or someone else. You need to be cautious on what you say and do. Your actions and words may easily be misinterpreted.

To dream of being hit by a bullet, suggests that you need to persevere and endure the difficult times.

Bullfight

To dream that you are watching a bullfight, symbolizes the struggle between your animalistic desire and your spiritual side.

Bully

To dream that you are a bully, indicates your tendency to dominate a conversation, relationship or situation. You have difficulties in recognizing your weaknesses and asking for help when you need it.

To see a bully in your dream, signifies repressed rage. The bully may be seen as your shadow Self which you have rejected.

Bum

To dream that you are a bum, indicates that you are feeling like failure or an outcast. You are losing control of a situation in your life.

To see a bum in your dream, suggests that you are being lazy and need to take more or an initiative.

Bumblebees

To see a bumblebee in your dream, is symbolic of distress and coming problems.

Bunjee Jumping

To dream that you are bunjee jumping, represents your ability to bounce back from adversities and setbacks in your life. The important thing is you took the initial risk.

Bunk Beds

To see bunk beds in your dream, represents childhood and innocence. Alternatively, it may refer to diverging and conflicting views of sexuality. You may have difficulties expressing your needs and desires.

Buoy

To see a buoy in your dream, represents your ability to hold your head up even amidst your emotional distress. It may also indicate a renewed state of mind and emotional calm. Alternatively, it suggests that some of your repressed thoughts or unconscious material has come to the surface and made itself known.

Burglar

To see or dream that you are a burglar, indicates that your energy is being sucked away from you. You are feeling drained. It may also mean that your fears, guilt, and anxiety make it hard for you to say no to others.

Burial

To see a burial in your dream, signifies that you have gotten rid of your bad habits or freed yourself from a negative situation. You are finally letting go of something.

To dream that you are burying a living person, signifies emotional turmoil.

 * Please also see Funeral.

Burning

To see something burning, indicates that you are experiencing some intense emotions and/or passionate sexual feelings. There is some situation or issue that you can no longer avoid and ignore. Alternatively, it may suggests that you need to take time off for yourself and relax.

*Please see also Fire.

Burp

To dream that you burp, indicates that you unconscious is informing you that you are going through some changes and beginning to see things differently as you grow older and gain more experience.

To hear a burp in your dream, signifies a breakthrough in your personal struggles. You have overcame barriers and resistance. You are no longer being held back.

Burst

To dream that something bursts, indicates that you are under a lot of pressure and stress.

Bus

To dream that you are waiting for a bus, indicates a temporary setback in achieving your personal goals.

To dream that you are at the bus station, suggests that you have reached some new level or stage in your emotional or physical life.

To dream that you are riding a bus, implies that you are going along with the crowd. You are lacking originality and are taking no control over where your life is taking.

To dream that you are in a bus accident, signifies that you will find yourself in an embarrassing situation. Your finances will be effected in an adverse way causing your much frustration.

Bus Driver

To see a bus driver in your dream, indicates leadership in some group idea or plan. It is symbolic of collective power. Alternatively, it suggests that you are going around in circles and have showed little progress.

To dream that you are a bus driver, suggests that you are moving forward quickly. You need to show more patience and less force. In particular, if you are a school bus driver, then it signifies that through knowledge and learning you will advance rapidly in life. Your dream may be connected with a new learning situation.

Bush

To see a bush in your dream, symbolizes feminine emotions and desires. It may also be a reference to the female genitalia.

To dream that you are hiding behind a bush, suggests that you are keeping something a secret. You may also be seeking protection. You are not being completely open.

Bustier

*Please See Bra.

Butcher

To see a butcher in your dream, represents your raw emotions or some immoral behavior. You may be testing the limits of your physical strength.

Butter

To see or taste butter in your dream, suggests that you are looking to be gratified in some area of your life. You need to indulge yourself in life's pleasure.

Buttercup

To see buttercups in your dream, refers to your childhood and past memories.

Butterfly

To see a butterfly in your dream, denotes your need to settle down. Butterflies also signifies creativity, romance, joy and spirituality. You may be undergoing a transformation into a new way of thinking.

To see a beautiful colorful butterfly in your dream, denotes the positive impression you will make at a future social gathering.

Buttocks

To see your buttocks in your dream, represents your instincts and urges. It may also indicate feelings of insecurity and reveals your struggles with some situation.

To dream that your buttocks are misshaped, suggests undeveloped or wounded aspects of your psyche.

Buttons

To see button in your dream, indicates wealth and security.

To dream that you are unbuttoning your clothes, denotes that you are opening yourself to others, either on a mental, emotional, or sexual level.

Buying

To dream that you or someone is buying something, represents your acceptance of an idea, condition, or situation. Consider what item you are buying for additional analysis.

Buzzard

To see a buzzard in your dream, symbolizes death and decay. It may represent an ugly aspect of yourself.

C

Cab

To dream of riding in a cab by yourself, denotes pleasantness and satisfaction with what life has to offer.

To dream that you are riding in a cab with others, denotes scandal and gossip.

To dream that you are driving a cab, signifies that you are in a dead-end job will little chance of advancement. It is time to sight your sights on higher goals.

Cabbage

To see or eat cabbage in your dream, suggests that you should not waste time with petty things in your life. You live and thrive on life's challenges.

Cabin

To dream that you are in or see a cabin in your dream, indicates that you succeed via your own means. It suggests that you are self-reliant and independent, yet still remain humble. You prefer the simpler things in life.

Cabinet

To see a cabinet in your dream, symbolizes the female body and/or the womb. Alternatively, you may be hiding some family or personal secret. Consider the contents and condition of the cabinet for more clues.

To dream that someone rearranged your cabinets, suggests that somebody is overstepping your boundaries.

Cable

To see a cable in your dream, represents your stamina and durability. If the cable is frayed or broken, then it signifies a lack of strength.

Cackle

To hear the sound of cackling in your dream, signifies illness and loss.

Cactus

To see a cactus in your dream, suggests that you are feeling invaded. Your space is being crowded into and you feel like you are being suffocated. The prickly spines of the cactus represents your wish to establish a boundary of your personal space and privacy. Perhaps you have found yourself in a sticky situation. Alternatively, a cactus may be symbolic of your need to defend yourself in some way.

To see a cactus in your dream can also signify your need to adapt your existing circumstances instead of trying to change them.

Cafeteria

To dream that you are in a cafeteria, denotes that there may be a lot of issues "eating" you up inside.

Cage

To dream that you are in a cage, denotes that you are experiencing some inhibitions and powerlessness in some areas of your life. You may feel restricted, confined and restrained in a current relationship or business deal. Somebody may be keeping a short leash on you where you are lacking the freedom to act independently.

To dream that you are putting a wild animal into a cage, signifies that you will succeed in overcoming your rivals and fears. It is also symbolic of you being able to control you animalistic rages and anger.

To see a bird in a cage, suggests that you are feeling limited in your expression and a sudden lost of freedom. You may be experiencing frustrations and an inhibited spirituality. The dream may also imply that you are feeling like a "jail bird".

Cake

To see a cake in your dream, indicates that you need to learn to share and allocate your workload instead of trying to do everything yourself. Cakes also symbolize selfishness or the feeling of not getting your fair share. More positively, the dream may represent your accomplishments and achievements. Consider also the metaphor a "piece of cake" or some situation that is easy.

To see a partially eaten cake in your dream, signifies missed and lost opportunities.

To dream that you are buying a cake, suggests that you have accepted the rewards and recognition your are getting for our work. You are learning to be comfortable in the spotlight.

Calculator

To see a calculator in your dream, suggests that you need to thoroughly think through some problem and carefully evaluate your choices. You need to lay out some sort of plan or outline. The symbol may also be a metaphor for someone who is calculating, cunning and scheming.

Calendar

To see a calendar in your dream, denotes that you are well-organized and well-prepared.

Calf

To see a calf in your dream, symbolizes immaturity and inexperience. You need to develop certain qualities.

Calm

To dream that you are calm, denotes a fulfilling life. You will find contentment and satisfaction in what you have.

To dream that someone is trying to calm your down, signifies that you will experience many setbacks if you continue to let your emotions run out of control.

Calomel

To see calomel in your dream, forewarns that a rival will be the main cause of your distress and unhappiness.

To dream that you are drinking calomel tea, signifies that you are being manipulated and used by your lover. It is time to open your eyes and do not allow yourself to be stepped on.

Calves

To see your calves in your dream, symbolizes movement and your ability to jump from situation to situation.

To dream that you are admiring your own calves, foretells that you will soon enter into a love relationship with someone who may be too needy and dependent on you.

Camcorder

Please See Video Camera

Camel

To see a camel in your dream, denotes that you need to be more conservative; you are carrying too many problems on your shoulders. You tend to hold on and cling on to your emotions instead of expressing and releasing them. You need to learn to forgive and forget. Alternatively, it represents you potential for handling big problems, responsibilities, and burdens.

Camera

To see a camera in your dream, signifies your desires to cling on and/or live in the past. Alternatively, it may represent you need to focus on a particular situation. Perhaps you need to get a clearer picture or idea.

Camouflage

To dream that you are in camouflage, suggests that you are hiding your true self and feelings. You are hiding who you really are.

Camper

To dream that you are living in a camper, indicates that you need to move on with regards to some aspect of your life. You may be dwelling on a situation and it is time to move forward. Alternatively, you may be expressing your desire to be more independent and self-sufficient.

Campfire

To start or see a campfire in your dream, represents sharing and your need for companionship. You need to open yourself to others and allow others to get to know you.

Camping

To dream that you are camping, suggests your need for relaxation and a long-deserved break. You may be looking to be more in touch with nature and for a simpler life. Alternatively, it refers to your social circle and support group. You need to have a sense of belonging, but at the same time be self-sufficient and independent.

Campus

To dream that you are on a campus, indicates your need to expand your thinking/knowledge and challenge yourself mentally.

Can

To see a can in your dream, indicates that there is something in your past that you need to hold on to and preserve. The dream may also be a pun on how you "can" do something. Don't underestimate your abilities and talents.

Can Opener

To see a can opener in your dream, indicates you willingness to accept new ideas/concepts. It may also be a symbol of reassurance and way to tell yourself that "I can" do something.

Canary

To see a canary in your dream, represents happiness and harmony.

Cancer

To dream that you have cancer, denotes hopelessness, grief, self-pity, and unforgiveness. You feel you are wasting your life away. This dream also represents areas in your life which are bothering you, disturbing you, and hurting you in some emotional way.

To dream that someone has cancer, indicates that you need to change your negative way of thinking before it creates a cancer in you. Start being more positive.

Candle

To see a burning candle in your dream, signifies that good luck and hope will be coming your way in small and steady amounts. You are in a comfortable stage in your life and may be seeking spiritual enlightenment. Lit candles are also symbolic of intellect, enlightenment, awareness or the search for truth.

To see an unlit candle, denotes that you have feelings or rejection or disappointments. You are not utilizing your fullest potential.

To see a candle blow out in your dream, indicates that you are surrendering a significant aspect of yourself. You are letting go of something that used to be important to you.

To watch the candle burn down to nothing in your dream, signifies your fears of aging and dying or a fear of sexual impotence.

To see a red colored candle in your dream, symbolizes some intimate or romantic relationship. You may not be giving the relationship a fair chance and are dismissing it before you invested time to learn more about the other person. On the other hand, you may just not be feeling any chemistry or passion.

Candle Wax

To see candle wax in your dream indicates that there is too much activity going on in your life. You may need to slow down and take a breather. Alternatively, it may symbolize the passage of time that has long passed.

Candy

To see or eat candy in your dream, symbolizes the joys and special treats in life. It also represents indulgence, sensuality and/or forbidden pleasure.

Cane

To see or use a cane in your dream, suggests that you are in need of some support and advice. The cane may also represent someone you trust and can rely on.

Cannibalism

To see cannibalism in your dream, symbolizes a destructive and forbidden desire or obsession. In a literal sense, cannibals consume people's lives, along with their energy. This dream may then denote an aspect of your life (career, relationship, children...) which is consistently draining your enthusiasm and vitality.

To dream that you are a victim of cannibalism, signifies that you feel that you are being "eating alive" by work, a relationship. or a situation in your waking life.

Cannon

To see a cannon in your dream, suggests that there is something drastic that needs to be done immediately.

Canoe

To see a canoe in your dream, represents serenity, simplicity, and independence. It is also a reflection of your emotional balance. You are moving ahead via your own power and determination.

Canopy

To see a canopy in your dream, symbolizes protection. You may also be elevated to a prominent position.

Canteen

To see or use a canteen in your dream, suggests that you are looking to easily and conveniently satisfy your emotional needs.

Canyon

To see a canyon in your dream, represents your unconscious mind and hidden feelings. It may point to emotions and relationships that you did not recognize.

Cap

To see a cap in your dream, signifies informality and ease. It also suggests that you need to be more tolerant of others.

Cape

To see or dream that you are wearing a cape, indicates that you are trying to shield yourself from being emotionally hurt. It may also mean that you are trying to cover-up or hide something.

Capsize

To dream that your boat has capsized, represents your avoidance in confronting uncomfortable feelings and/or situation.

Captain

To dream that you are a captain, indicates that you are taking charge of your emotions and confronting your feelings and the things that are bothering you.

Car

To dream that you are driving a car, denotes your ambition, your drive and your ability to navigate from one stage of your life to another. Consider how smooth or rough the car ride is. Whether you are driving the car or a passenger, is indicative of of your active role or passive role in your life. If you are in the backseat of the car, then it indicates that you are putting yourself down and are allowing others to take over. This may be a result of low self-esteem or low self-confidence. Overall, this dream symbol is an indication of your dependence and degree of control you have on your life.

To dream that you car has been stolen, indicates that you are being stripped of your identity. This may relate to losing your job, a failed relationship, or some situation which has played a significant role in your identity and who you are as a person.

To dream that your car is overheating, suggests that you are expending too much energy and need to slow down or run the risk of becoming burnt out. You may be taking on more than you can handle. It is time to take a breather.

To see a parked car in your dream, suggests that you need to turn your efforts and energies elsewhere. You may be needlessly spending your energy in a fruitless endeavor. Alternatively, a parked car my symbolize your need to stop and enjoy life. To dream that you cannot find where you parked your car, suggests that you do not know where you want to go in life.

To dream that you are almost hit by a car, suggests that your lifestyle, beliefs or goals may be in conflict with another's. It may also be symbolic of a jolting experience or injured pride.

To dream that you are unable to roll up the windows of your car, suggests that you are showing some hesitation and reservation about the direction that you are taking in life or the path that you have chosen.

Please see Also Automobile.

Carburetor

To see the carburetor in your dream, represents emotional, spiritual and physical balance.

Cardinal

To see a cardinal in your dream, represents vitality and happiness. It also may mean first place or your position in the front.

Cards

To dream that you are playing a game of cards, signifies that you have successfully utilized skills of bluff, strategy, and timing in your everyday life. In particular, diamonds indicates wealth, clubs indicated work, hearts indicate happiness in love, and spades indicate troubling times are in your near future.

Carnation

To see carnations in your dream, symbolizes light-heartedness, vitality and joy. Alternatively, it may represent bachelorhood.

Carnival

To dream that you are at the carnival, represents falsehoods and deception. If you observe freakish sights, then it denotes that there is a lack of harmony in your domestic life. Much sorrow will arise in what were thought to be pleasant times.

To dream that you are on a carnival ride, suggests that you are going in circles. It may also symbolize cheap thrills.

To dream that you run away with the carnival, denotes that you will be involved in or closely connected to the entertainment field.

Carp

To see a carp in your dream, indicates that you need to put aside your pride and ego and not let it get in the way of friendships and relationships.

Carpenter

To see or dream that you are a carpenter, indicates that you are confronting and overcoming your obstacles. Alternatively, it suggests that you need to change your way of thinking and readjust your attitude.

Carpet

To see a carpet in your dream, represents your way of protecting yourself from life's harsh realities. Alternatively, a carpet symbolizes luxury, comfort or richness. Consider the condition and designs of the carpet. Are you hiding something and sweeping it under the carpet?

To dream of a magic carpet, implies your desires and wishes to escape from a situation, relationship, or responsibilities.

Carriage

To see an old-fashioned carriage in your dream, signifies that you must take care in shielding yourself from malicious gossip.

To dream that you are riding in a carriage, denotes that you will be put into an awkward position. Your past relationship may come back to haunt you.

Carrot

To see a carrot in your dream, signifies abundance. It may also symbolize a lure as in the pun "dangle a carrot".

Carry

To dream that you are being carried, suggests that you are feeling like a burden to somebody. You need to be more independent and take on more responsibilities. Alternatively, it may elude to romance.

Cartoon

To dream that your real life is depicted in a cartoon world, signifies that you are perceiving the world in a comical and unserious manner. This dream may also serve as an escape from the stressful realities of your life. It is your way of obtaining moments of lightheartedness and fun. Additionally, you may need to learn to laugh at yourself and at your mistakes.

To dream that you are watching cartoons, indicates that you are not taking life seriously.

*Please see also Cartoon Character.

Cartwheels

To dream that you are doing cartwheels, represents poise and balance in your life or the need to regain balance. You need handle obstacles and stress with more fortitude.

To dream that you have problems doing cartwheels, suggests that you do not have confidence in your own abilities. It may also mean that you lack discipline and are exhibiting some struggles or imbalance in your life.

Carving

To dream that you are carving a piece of wood, symbolizes spiritual and creative energy. Metaphorically, you are transforming unconscious energy into conscious awareness. Consider whether the carving is purely ornamental or utilitarian.

To dream that you are carving a cooked animal, indicates that you are trying to rid yourself of certain feelings. You may be distancing yourself from your emotions and analyzing them from an objective standpoint. Alternatively, some person or situation is violating an aspect of your life.

Cash Register

To see a cash register in your dream, represents financial worries and concerns. On the other hand, you may be expecting monetary gains.

Casino

To dream that you are in a casino, signifies the risk-taker within you. If you are a reserved or passive person, then the dream suggests that you should take a chance. If you are not, then it implies that you need to make a more informed decision instead of relying on fate.

Casket

To see a casket in your dream, indicates that it is time to end a situation or relationship. Additionally, it symbolizes a completion of a project or lifestyle and a beginning of another. In this regards, this symbol may represent new opportunities.

Castle

To see a castle in your dream, signifies reward, honor, recognition, and praise for your achievements. It foretells that your future will be a happy one, surrounded by the love of your children, generosity of neighbors, and comfort of friends. You are destined to a position of power, wealth, and prestige.

To dream that you live in a castle, signifies your need for security and protection to the point where you may be isolating yourself from others.

Castration

To dream of a castration, signifies your overwhelming fears that you have lost your virility or feelings of sexual pressure. Alternatively, it represents a lack of creativity.

Cat

To see a cat in your dream, signifies much misfortune, treachery, and bad luck. However, for the cat lover, cats signifies an independent spirit, feminine sexuality, creativity, and power. If the cat is aggressive, then it suggests that you are having problems with the feminine aspect of yourself. If you see a cat with no tail, then it signifies a lost of independence and lack of autonomy.

To dream that a cat is biting you, symbolizes the devouring female. Perhaps you are taking and taking without giving. You may be expressing some fear or frustration especially when something is not going as planned.

To see a black cat in your dream, indicates that you are experiencing some fear in using your psychic abilities and believing in your intuition. You may erroneously associate the black cat with evil, destruction, and bad luck. If you see a white cat, then it denotes difficult times.

To dream that a cat killed a spider, suggests that you are expressing your femininity in a seductive and cunning manner rather than in an overtly and almost destructive way.

**See The Meaning In Action: ""Black Cat" or Injured Cat"*

Caterpillar

To see a caterpillar in your dream, signifies a stage in your own personal growth and development where you are on your way, but have not yet reached your goal.

Cathedral

Please see Church

Cattle

To see a cattle in your dream, signifies that you need to proceed with caution with some situation or relationship.

To see a herd of cattle in your dream, represents a lack of individuality. You generally go with the flow of things.

Catwalk

To see or dream that you are walking a catwalk, represents your new found confidence. It may also mean that you enjoy being the center of attention. Alternatively, the dream suggests that you are being recognized for your talents or creativity.

Cauldron

To see a cauldron in your dream, implies that you are undergoing some transformation, It also indicates destiny. Consider the symbolism of what is in the cauldron and its importance.

Cauliflower

To see or eat cauliflower in your dream, symbolizes spiritual nourishment, purity and perfection. It also represents sadness and need to be uplifted. You dream indicates that the tough times that you are experiencing will soon be over. Alternatively, the cauliflower represents the brain.

Cave

To dream that you are walking in a dark cave, signifies refuge or the unconscious mind. It also denotes that you experience some unexpected misfortune or disagreement.

Caveman

Please See Barbarian.

CD

To see a compact disc in your dream, represents a need for enjoyment or a distraction. It denotes opportunities and possibilities. Consider the type of music and the title of the compact disc. If you are giving away the CD, you may be trying to convey a message to that person within the songs.

Consider also if the initial "CD" have any additional significance to you. Perhaps it represents a person or may even be a pun on something that is "seedy".

CD Player

To see or use a CD player in your dream, represents the impression that you like to project to others. It may also symbolize inspiration and the pleasure of listening to music.

Ceiling

To see a ceiling in your dream, represents a mental or spiritual perspective.

Celebration

To dream of a celebration, represents your achievement toward a higher level of growth. This dream may also be a self-congratulatory one for the goals you have achieved and for the recognition you have gained. You may be honoring some victory, success, or accomplishment. Alternatively, to dream of a celebration, symbolizes freedom and emotional release. Celebration dreams are common for those who anticipate some upcoming turning points or events in their waking life.

Celebrities

To dream that you are a celebrity, signifies your high aspirations that may be way beyond your reach at the present moment. You may just be setting yourself for a let-down.

To dream that a friend or lover becomes a celebrity, denotes your fear of losing the friendship and loyalty of this person.

To see a celebrity in your dream, represents your beliefs and understanding about him or her. Something in you waking life has triggered these similar beliefs and feelings. It is not uncommon that your obsession with a certain celebrity may carry over onto your dream world. Celebrities are often seen as heroes and all that is mighty. Also consider any puns within the name.

To dream that you are good friends with a celebrity, represents your idealized version of someone you know in your life. Perhaps you hope that a real-life friend can act more like a particular celebrity. Consider the qualities that you see in this celebrity and how you want your friends to have those qualities.

Celery

To see or eat celery, represent your need to be cleansed, either physically or emotionally. The dream may also be a pun on "salary".

Celibacy

To dream that you are celibate, represents your fears of intimacy. You may be trying to block off your sexual energies.

Cell Phone

To see or use a cell phone in your dream, indicates that you are being receptive to new information. It also represents your mobility.

To dream that you lost your cell phone, represents a lack of communication. You have lost touch with some aspect of your feelings or your Self.

*Please see also Telephone

Cellar

To dream that you are in a cellar, represents a part of your subconscious mind where you have kept your fears and problems hidden. To dream that you are going down the cellar, signifies that you are digging deep into your own past and facing your fears.

Cello

To see or hear a cello in your dream, represents sensual or creative achievements. You are exhibiting much strength and stability.

Cement

Please see <u>Concrete.</u>

Cemetery

To dream that you are in a cemetery, signifies sadness and unresolved grief.

Centaur

To see a centaur in your dream, symbolizes the duality of human nature. It indicates that you are trying to balance your intellectual/mental nature with your physical nature. The centaur also represents humanity, wisdom, and compassion.

Centipedes

To see a centipede in your dream, suggests that you are letting your fears and doubts hinder you from making progress and achieving your goals. You need to stop thinking negative thoughts.

Cereal

To dream that you are eating cereal, denotes the start of a new project or new stage in your life. It may also indicate your need to restore yourself in some basic way. Alternatively, your mind may already be thinking ahead to breakfast. It is not uncommon for your fleeting thoughts to be incorporated into your dream.

Ceremony

To dream that you are attending a ceremony, symbolizes the sacrifice and devotion necessary for success. You may be going through a crucial moment in your waking life that requires your commitment. It is a time for introspection, self-discovery, and inner changes.

Certificate

To see a certificate in your dream, suggests that you are seeking some validity and truth to some situation.

Chains

To see chains in your dream, signifies your need to break free from a routine, old idea, or a relationship. If you are being chained, then some part of you is being forcefully head in check.

Chainsaw

To see a chain saw in your dream, indicates that something drastic is about to happen. Success will only come about through willpower. Alternatively, it suggests that you get right to the heart of the matter quickly. The chain saw may be seen as a phallic symbol and can refer to your sexual drives.

Chair

To see a chair in your dream, symbolizes your need to sit down and take time out to contemplate a situation before proceeding.

To dream that someone is offering you a chair, signifies that you need to be open to taking and accepting advice.

Chalice

To see a chalice in your dream, represents your need for spiritual nourishment. You are on a search for your individual self.

Chalk

To see a piece of chalk in your dream, refers to school and learning. Your ability and knowledge is being called into question.

Chalkboard

To see a chalkboard in your dream, represents the classroom and the difficulties you may have experienced in school. There is a lesson to be learned from this dream. You may feel that you are being put to the test. Consider what is being written on the chalkboard. Alternatively, it signifies your debts.

Chameleon

To see a chameleon in your dream, represents your ability to adapt to any situation. You are versatile and are well-rounded. Alternatively, you feel you are being overlooked.

Champagne

To see the opening of a bottle of champagne, is symbolic of a sexual act. It is also representative of a celebration or a personal achievement that you are proud of.

Chandelier

To see a chandelier in your dream, represents grandeur and greatness. You see a bright future ahead.

Charcoal

To dream that you are eating charcoal, symbolizes your burning passion and libido. You are going through some sort of transformation and embracing your sensuality.

Chariots

To dream that you are riding in a chariot, indicates that you need to exercise control in your life.

To dream that you or someone else fall from a chariot, denotes failure.

Charleston

To dream that you are dancing the Charleston, denotes that your success will be substantial and assured.

Charm Bracelet

To see or wear a charm bracelet in your dream, is symbolic of protection from any harm. Consider the symbolism of the specific charm for additional significance.

Chase

To dream that you are being chased, signifies that you are avoiding a situation that you do not think is conquerable. It is often a metaphor for some form of insecurity. In particular, to dream that you are chased by an animal, represents your own unexpressed and unacknowledged anger which is being projected onto that animal. Alternatively, you may be running away from a primal urge or fear.

To dream that you are chasing someone, signifies that you are attempting to overcome a difficult goal or task. You may also be expressing some aggressive feelings toward others.

*For an in depth analysis, click on Common Dreams: Chase.

Cheap

To dream that you or someone is cheap, represents your own feelings of inadequacy. You are not fully acknowledging your own self worth.

To dream that you got something at a cheap price, suggests that you are being undervalued. Or are you cheating somebody of their valuable things? Consider the symbolism of the item and how you feel about it in the dream.

Cheating

To dream that you are cheating on your spouse, mate, fiancé, or significant other, suggests feelings of self-guilt and self-betrayal. You may have compromised your beliefs or integrity and/or wasting your energy and time on fruitless endeavors. Alternatively, it reflects the intensity of your sexual passion and exploring areas of your sexuality. It is actually a reaffirmation of your commitment. Furthermore, it is not uncommon for people approaching a wedding to have dreams about erotic experiences with partners other than their intended spouses. Most likely, such dreams represent the newness of your sexual passion. It may also signify anxieties of changing your identity - that of a spouse.

To dream that your mate, spouse, or significant other is cheating on you, indicates your fears of being abandoned. You may feel a lack of attention in the relationship. Alternatively, you may feel that you are not measuring up to the expectations of others. This notion may stem from issues of trust or self-esteem. The dream could also indicate that you are unconsciously picking up hints and cues that your significant other is not being completely truth or is not fully committed in the relationship.

To dream that you are cheating at a game, suggests that you are not being honest with yourself.

Check

To see a check in your dream, suggests that you may feel indebted to others. The dream may also be a pun on checking things out.

To see a blank check in your dream, symbolizes your unused potential. It may also indicate unclaimed rewards.

To see a check mark in your dream, indicates approval and acceptance. Your hard work has paid off.

Checkerboard

To see a checkerboard in your dream, indicates the many aspects and facets of your personality.

Cheeks

To see your cheeks in your dream, symbolizes commitment, intimacy, and closeness. It also reveals your strength of character and your opinions. Alternatively, cheeks can also be a slang for the buttocks.

To see rosy-colored cheeks in your dream, signifies life energy, enthusiasm and vitality.

To dream that your checks are painted, represents your attitudes of courage and violence/passivity.

Cheerleader

To see a cheerleader in your dream, represents competition and triumph. Your dream may be telling you to offer more praise and encouragement toward others.

To dream that you are a cheerleader, signifies your self-confidence and self-esteem. You need to be more active and more positive in some waking situation in your life.

Cheese

To see cheese in your dream, symbolizes gains and profits.

Cheetah

To see a cheetah in your dream, suggests that you need to get moving and be more active in pursuit of your goals. Perhaps you have been a little lazy and you need to get off from that seat.

Chef

To dream that you are a chef, suggests that you have the ability and talents to choose your course of action and select your path in life. You have learned from your previous life experiences and moving forward in a productive manner.

To see a chef in your dream, represents transformation and changes. Consider what is "cooking" in your life?

Chemicals

To see or use chemicals in your dream, signifies that you are undergoing some transformation and individuation process.

To dream that you are mixing or combining chemicals, represent creativity, manipulation and/or intellectual power.

Cherry

To see cherries in your dream, symbolizes honesty and truthfulness or sweetness and good fortune.

To see a cherry tree in your dream, represents luck, spring, femininity, and youth.

Cherub

To see a cherub in your dream, represents child-like innocence, frailty and mischievousness. You need to take life a little less seriously. Alternatively, you may have been dishonest or manipulative.

Chess

To see or play chess in your dream, indicates that you need to carefully think through the situation before making a decision. The dream may also comment on how you have met your match in love or in business.

Chest

To see your chest in your dream, signifies confidence, conquest and vitality. Alternatively, it represents feelings of being overwhelmed and being dangerously confronted by something. Consider also if the dream is telling you that there is something that you need to "get off your chest".

To dream that you are beating on your chest, indicates triumph and a great accomplishment.

Chew

To dream that you are chewing something, suggests that you are sorting things out and carefully thinking it over.

Chickadee

To see a chickadee in your dream, indicates that you need to pay attention and become aware of something unique and special occurring in your life.

Chickens

To see chickens in your dream, symbolizes cowardliness and a lack of willpower. Chickens also represents excessive chatter and gossip. Listen closely to what people may be saying about you or what you are saying about others.

Chihuahua

To see a Chihuahua in your dream, represents someone around you who is unexpectedly vocal. It may also represent someone who has a small ego.

Childhood

To dream of your childhood, indicates your wish to return to a life where you had little responsibility and worries. It also represents innocence. Alternatively, it suggests that certain aspects of your childhood has not yet been integrated into your adult personality. Or on the other hand, some childhood anxiety has yet to be resolved in your adult life.

Children

To see children in your dream, signifies your own childlike qualities or a retreat back to a childlike state. It is an extension of your inner child during a time of innocence, purity, simplicity, and a carefree attitude. You may be longing for the past and the chance to satisfy repressed desires and unfulfilled hopes. Take some time off and cater to the inner child within. Perhaps there is something that you need to see grow and nurtured.

To dream that your own grown children are still very young, indicates that you still see them as young and dependent. You want to feel needed and significant.

To dream that you are watching children but they do not know you are there, is a metaphor for some hidden knowledge or some latent talent which you have failed to recognize.

To save a child, signifies your attempts to save a part of yourself from being destroyed.

Chili

To see or eat chili in your dream, symbolizes intense passion and raw emotion.

Chimera

To see a chimera in your dream, represents a feeling of confusion. You need to sort out your thoughts and emotions.

Chimney

To see a chimney in your dream, represents warmth, tradition, and family values. Alternatively, a chimney is symbolic of a phallic symbol. Thus, to see the chimney collapse implies impotence.

To dream that you are sweeping the chimney, indicates your need to vent off your frustrations and get things out in the open. You need to release all that negativity and/or guilt that you are holding in.

Chin

To notice your chin in your dream, refers to your resilience and your ability to bounce back from adversity. The chin often symbolizes character, strength, and resolve.

Chiropractor

To see a chiropractor in your dream, suggests that you are seeking support and advise. Don't be afraid to ask for help when you need it; it is not a sign of weakness.

Chocolate

To see chocolate in your dream, signifies self-reward. It also denotes that you may be indulging in too many excesses and need to practice some restraint.

Choir

To dream that you are singing in a choir, symbolizes spiritual harmony and balance. It also refers to your ability to work and cooperate with others.

Choking

To dream that you are choking on an object, suggests that you may find some advice/remarks/situation hard to swallow or difficult to accept. Alternatively, you may feel that you are unable to completely express yourself in a situation. In particular, if you are choking on food, then it may be an expression of self-guilt and unnurtured feelings.

To dream that someone is choking you, indicates that you are suppressing your emotions or that you may have difficulties in expressing your fears, anger, or love. Consider the phrase "being all choked up". Alternatively, you may feel that you are being prevented or restricted from freely expressing yourself.

To dream that you are choking someone, signifies feelings of aggression. You may also be trying to prevent something from being said or revealed.

Choking dreams are often a fearful experience and it is not uncommon for dreamers to awaken from them.

Christ

To see Christ in your dream, represents perfection of the self and spiritual truth. You need to achieve self-fulfillment through love. This symbol has many personal associations for you, depending on your belief.

Christian

To dream of Christianity, relates to your own personal beliefs and religious experiences. It is a sign of inner growth and development of the Self. Alternatively, it may refer to a person in your life whose name is Christian.

Christmas

To dream of Christmas, symbolizes family togetherness, reunions, and celebration. It is also representative of new beginnings and fresh starts. Consider also your own associations with this holiday.

Christmas Card

To see or send a Christmas Card in your dream, indicates that you are reaching out to loved ones and reconnecting with old ties. It is also symbolic of forgiveness. Time to swallow your pride and let the past go.

Christmas Tree

To see a Christmas Tree in your dream, symbolizes family celebrations, gatherings, and familial relationships. You may be experiencing some anxieties and stress in your domestic life. It also signifies a passage of time, self-development, and spiritual enlightenment. Consider also the feelings and emotions you experience during this holiday season to help you decipher this dream symbol.

If your dream of a Christmas Tree occurs in December, it may indicate the expected pleasures, demanding responsibilities, and growing anxieties associated with the holiday season.

Chrome

To see chrome in your dream, suggests that you will experience a surge in energy and vitality. It is time to share your new ideas.

Chrysalis

Please see Cocoon.

Chrysanthemums

To see chrysanthemums in our dream, represents abundance, prosperity, humility, and gratitude. Alternatively, it may suggest that you need to keep silent about some situation.

Church

To see the outside of the church in your dream, signifies sacredness and spiritual nourishment. It is representative of your value system and the things you hold sacred.

To dream that you are in a church, suggests that you are seeking for some spiritual enlightenment and guidance. You are looking to be uplifted in some way. Perhaps you have made some mistakes in the past which have set you back on your path toward your goals. With proper support, you will get on the right track again. Alternatively, it may also mean that you are questioning and debating your life path and where it is leading. You are reevaluating what you want to do.

Cicadas

Please see Locusts.

Cigar

To see or dream that you are smoking a cigar, represents luxury and a relaxed state of mind. You are in control of your own emotions and passions. According to Freud, a cigar is a phallic symbol and is representative of masculinity and raw energy. This dream symbol may also serve as a symbol for someone you know who smokes cigars.

To see dried or shriveled cigars may be a pun on your lack of a sex life.

Cigarettes

To dream that you are smoking or offering a cigarette, signifies your need for a break. It may also points to issues of dependency. However if you are against smoking and have this dream, you must analyze aspects of your waking life and what you are dong that may adversely affect your health.

Cinema

Please see Theater.

Circle

To see a circle in your dream, symbolizes perfection, completeness, immortality and/or wholeness. On a less positive note, it may also mean that you are going around in circles in a particular situation. Or the circle can indicate monotony and endless repetition.

To see circles within circles in your dream, indicate that you are well protected or that you are being overly guarded. You may need to let down your defenses. Alternatively, the dream may highlight the notion that you are going around in a vicious circle. You need to somehow find a way to break this circle.

To see an imperfect circle in your dream, signifies that you will face many obstacles and setbacks in achieving your goals. In the end, you will overcome these obstacles and find that your struggle was well worth it.

To see a circle with a cross, symbolizes earth. It may also serve as guidance toward the center and self-orientation.

Circumcise

To dream that you are being circumcised, suggests that you are getting rid of an essential part of yourself. Alternatively, it may mean that you are regressing and cutting yourself off from feeling emotions.

Circus

To dream that you are having a terrific time at a circus, signifies your satisfaction and contentment with your current surroundings. But to dream that you are just at the circus, denotes that you are being misunderstood in some way. You are giving off the wrong impression to others.

To dream that there is chaos at the circus, signifies that your life is out of control.

Citrine

To see a citrine gemstone in your dream, represents strength and personal power. You need to have more willpower and motivation in pursuing your goals.

City

To see a city in your dream, signifies a sense of community and your social environment. To dream that you are in a deserted city or that you feel alienated from the activity of the city, then it suggests that you feel rejected by those around you.

To see a city in ruins, denotes that you are neglecting your social relationships and allowing them to deteriorate.

Clam

To see a closed clam in your dream, suggests that you are emotionally cold. You may be shutting others out and not letting them in on your problems and what you are feeling.

Clapping

Please See Applause

Class

To dream that you forgot to attend a class you signed up for, indicates your anxieties and fear of failing. You may also be lacking self-confidence in your ability to handle new responsibilities or projects.

Classmates

To see old classmates in your dream, indicates that you need to draw on your old associations with your former classmates to gain insight in some current relationship. It represents a past lesson that you have learned and is applicable in some aspect of your waking life now.

Classroom

To dream that you are in a classroom, symbolizes that you may be learning an important life lesson.

Claustrophobia

To dream that you have claustrophobia, suggests feeling of self-guilt. You fear that you will be punished for your past's actions.

Claws

To see claws in your dream, signifies feelings of vulnerability and/or hostility. You feel a need to defend or protect yourself or your surroundings. You also need to be careful with your words and actions.

Clay

To see or work with clay in your dream, represents creativity and the ability to shape your mind. It may also mean that you are able to manipulate things to your advantage. Alternatively, it indicates your need to set some goals and plans for yourself. You have some growing up to do and need to plan for the future. According to Freudian perspective, clay symbolizes feces.

To see a clay pot in your dream, signifies devotion, virtue or purity. The clay pot is also a healing symbol.

Cleaners

To dream that you are at the cleaners, warns that someone may be taking you to the cleaners. Alternatively, you may need to clear up a matter without any further emotional outbursts.

Cleaning

To dream that you are cleaning, implies that you are removing some negativity in your life and overcoming major obstacles. You are moving ahead toward a new stage in your life. In particular, if you are cleaning your house, then it signifies that you need to clear out your thoughts and get rid of your old ways and habits. You are seeking self-improvement.

To dream that you are cleaning an object, represents an aspect of yourself that is not working or functioning as well as it should. If you are cleaning the refrigerator or oven, then it indicates that you are getting to root of a matter or situation. It may also indicate negative feelings about the female role or that you are feeling inferior or stuck in some area of your life.

To dream that you are cleaning out a desk, suggests that you are getting rid of the burdens that has been weighing you down. You are acknowledging your new choices, decisions, and a new sense of freedom.

Cliff

To dream that you are standing at the edge of a cliff, indicates that you have arrived to an increased level of understanding, new awareness, and a fresh point of view. You may have reached a critical point in your life and may fear losing control.

To dream that you or someone falls off a cliff, suggests that you are go through some difficult times and are afraid of that is ahead for you. You fear that you are not up for the challenge.

Climate

Please See Weather.

Climb

To dream that you are climbing up something (ladder, rope, etc.), signifies that you are trying to or you have overcome a great struggle. It also suggests that your goals are finally within reach. Climbing also means that you have risen to a level of prominence within the social or economic sphere.

To dream that you are climbing down a cliff, indicates that you need to acknowledge and take notice of your unconscious. You are expressing some hesitance and reservation with delving into your more negative feelings. Alternatively, it suggests that you may be feeling low or emotionally drained.

Cloak

To dream that you are wearing a cloak, signifies the need for security, warmth and the feeling of being well protected. It may also mean that you are trying to cover-up or hide something.

If see a torn or ragged cloak in your dream, signifies a separation between you and a friend or lover.

Clock

To see a clock in your dream, signifies the importance of time or that time is running out. You may be feeling some anxiety of not being on top of things. Your mind may be preoccupied with a deadline that you have to meet or some other time-sensitive issue. It is time for you to tread on and speed up your actions. Alternatively, clocks are representative of death, especially if the clock has stopped. This is a common theme for the terminally ill or the dying.

To dream that a clock is moving backwards, parallels the way that your life is going. Instead of moving forward and progressing toward your goals, you feel that you have not made any significant accomplishments. You feel you are stuck in a rut.

A clock seen in your dream may also symbolize the ticking of the human heart and thus is indicative of the emotional side of your life.

Closed

To dream that a door is closed, represents an aspect of your life or and opportunity that is closed off to you. It may also refer to sexual secrets or activities.

To dream that the store is closed, indicates your inability to consider other alternatives and other viewpoints. You may be biased in your judgment and opinion. It also represents feelings of inadequacy and frustration.

Closet

To see a closet in your dream, symbolizes something in your life that you have kept hidden. It may also signify an unveiling of previously hidden aspects of yourself, as in "coming out of the closet".

Cloth

To see cloth in your dream, represents components and various pieces that composes your life. Consider the color for significance in the outlook or how things are going in your life.

Clothesline

To dream that you are hanging out clothing on a clothesline, suggests that you are revealing hidden aspects of yourself, especially if they are underwear. The dream may also signify your hang-ups. In particular, if your are hanging white clothes in the backyard, then it indicates your desire for pureness and to be cleansed. You may also be proclaiming your innocence in some situation.

Clothing

To dream of your clothes, is symbolic of your public self and how you are perceived. It is indicative of the act you put on in front of others. Clothes is also an indication of your condition and status in life.

To dream that your clothes are soiled and you are trying to clean them, signifies your attempts to change something about your character. You may need to change your old habits and old ways of thinking.

To dream that you are wearing brand new clothes, signifies new attitudes and a new persona. You are finding a different way of expressing yourself. If the price tags are still attached to the clothes, then it suggests that you are trying too hard to adapt to this new attitude. Perhaps it is not who you really are and you are not quite fitting in.

To dream that you are constantly changing your clothes, represents the need for change and your need to fit into a new situation or role. You need to establish a new self-image.

To dream that your clothes fit too tightly, denotes that you feel restricted in some way. You may feel constrained in a relationship or held back at work.

To dream that your clothing is torn or ripped, indicates that there is some flaws in your thinking or thought process. Your logic is not making sense. You need to alter your reasoning and make a stronger argument.

To dream that you are shopping for or buying clothes, represents your anxieties about trying to fit in or being "well-suited" for your changing role.

To dream that all your clothes in the closet are white, suggests that you need to lighten up. You may have recently been feeling a little on the depressed side. Perhaps you were going through some crisis. It is time to move on. You need to change your attitude and get a grip of your inner emotions.

Clouds

To see fluffy white clouds in your dream, signify inner peace and spiritual harmony. An issue in your waking life may be clearing up.

To see gray and gloomy clouds in your dream, signify depression or anger. Your decisions may be clouded in some way.

To see menacing or stormy clouds in your dream, indicates an impending eruption of emotions. It also represents a lack of wisdom or confusion in some situation.

Clover

To see a three-leaf clover in your dream, symbolizes the past, present, and future.

To see a four-leaf clover in your dream, represents good luck. You have successfully come to a resolution of some problem.

Clown

To see a clown in you dream, symbolizes absurdity, light-heartedness, and a childish side to your own character. The countenance of the clown is a reflection of your own feelings and emotions. Whether it is a happy clown or a sad clown, that will help guide you through how you may be feeling. The actions of the clown signifies your uninhibited nature. Alternatively, it is an indication of your thoughtless actions.

If you have a fear or phobia of clowns, the clown may represent a mysterious person in your life who mean you harm. Somebody you know may not be who they appear to be. Or somebody may be pretending to be somebody they are not and are hiding under a facade.

*Please see also Jester.

Club

To see a club in your dream, denotes feelings of aggression or submission depending if the club is used by or against you. It is also symbolic of virility and combativeness.

Clumsy

To dream that you or someone is clumsy, suggests that some situation or relationship is not going smoothly in your life. You need to take it easy and not to make things hard on yourself.

Coach

To see or dream that you are a coach, indicates that you need to be more self-disciplined.

Coal

To see a coal in your dream, represents wealth and prosperity. It also points to your unused potential. Alternatively, it may indicate that you have been misbehaving and have caught.

Coast

To see the coast in your dream, suggests that you are on a spiritual quest. The coast symbolizes the meeting between your two states of mind - the rational and the irrational. The dream may be a metaphor for how you are "coasting". through life. You may need to take things more seriously.

Coat

To see or wear a coat in your dream, symbolizes your protectiveness and defensive persona. You may be isolating yourself. Consider also the color, appearance, and type of coat for additional significance.

To dream that a coat is old, worn, or shabby, then it suggests that you are feeling down on yourself.

To see or wear a fur coat in your dream, symbolizes prosperity and luxury. It also indicates your need for attention and your need to be admired.

Coat Of Arms

To see a coat of arms in your dream, represents your familial roots and identity.

Cobra

To see a cobra in your dream, represents creation, and creative energies. Some situation or relationship has you hypnotized.

Please see also Snake.

Cobwebs

To see cobwebs in your dream, suggests that you have not reached your full potential. You are not utilizing your talents.

Cocaine

To dream that you are taking cocaine, indicates that you are feeling empty and devoid of emotions. You are looking to get out of your commitments or denying your responsibilities. You lack ambition. On a more positive note, the dream may be telling you that you need to be more lively and energetic.

Cockroach

To see a cockroach in your dream, signifies your need for renewal, rejuvenation and self-cleansing of your psychological, emotional, or spiritual being. You need to reevaluate major aspects of your life.

Please see also Roaches. See the meaning in action: "Crawling Cockroaches"

Coconuts

To see a coconut in your dream, foretells that you will receive an unexpected gift of money.

Cocoon

To see cocoons on your dream, signifies a place of safety and solitude. It may also represent transformation or healing.

To dream that you are in a cocoon, represents your need to rejuvenate and restore your body, mind and spirit. You may be recreating new paths of expression and perhaps a rebirth.

Coffee

To dream that you are drinking or need your coffee, suggests that you should gain some insight and knowledge before making a decision or tackling some project/relationship. You may be acting too hasty and need to slow down. Alternatively, it may imply a need for you to change your routine.

To dream that you are drinking coffee with someone, indicates that you might have feelings for that person.

To see a coffee pot in your dream, signifies hospitality and sharing of knowledge, hopes, concerns and/or ideas. It may also represent neighborliness, comfort, and companionship.

Coffin

To see a coffin in your dream, symbolizes the womb. If the coffin is empty, then it suggests that you are having some irreconcilable differences.

To see a body in a coffin, signifies that you will be going through a period of depression. You may feel confined, restricted and lack personal freedom. There may be a dead or decaying situation or issue in your life and this dream is calling attention to it. It it time to end this situation or relationship.

Coins

To see coins in your dream, indicates missed or overlooked opportunities that come your way. To see gold coins in your dream, represent success and wealth. Silver coins represents spirituality, values, and your self-worth.

To see coins stacked in your dream, symbolizes masculine power, dominance, and energy.

To dream that you are flipping a coin, represents your casual attitude about making some decision. You may also not be taking responsibility for your decisions. Alternatively, it indicates your irrational thoughts.

Cold

To dream that you are cold, indicates that you are experiencing a breakthrough in some area in your life. Alternatively, you may be feeling isolated. You sense of coldness could reflect your feelings about that person. The dream may also occur as a result of your immediate environment in which you are really feeling cold.

To see the word cold in your dream, suggests that you need to be more neutral or objective in your decision making. You need to remain emotionally detached.

Collapse

To dream that you collapse, indicates that you are pushing yourself too hard. You have lost sight of your goals and what you need to accomplish. You may also be having difficulties trusting your own judgment and decisions.

Collar

To see collars in your dream, signifies confinement and restraint. You may be going through a frustrating work situation or a confining relationship.

Colleague

Please see Coworker.

College

To dream that you are in college, indicates that you are going through some social or cultural changes. You may be wanting to expand your knowledge and awareness. It also suggest that now is a good time for you to experiment and try new things. If you had gone to college in your past, then also consider your personal experiences and memories of your college days. However, if you are currently in college, then it may be a reflection of your current surroundings. It may also represent stress.

Collision

Please See Crash.

Colorless

To have a colorless dream, suggests a depressed mood and a feeling of sadness. You may be shutting yourself off from others.

Colors

Colors in dreams represent energy, emotions, and vibes. First consider what that single color in your dream means to you and your own personal associations and relationship with that color.

To dream in color and then dream in black and white, suggests that you are starting to look at a situation from a more objective perspective instead of from an emotional standpoint. You are subconsciously reacting to events in the dream.

Please see Dream Themes: Colors.

Colt

To see a colt in your dream, suggests that you are feeling awkward and insecure. You are starting to unleash your unused potential.

Column

To see columns in your dream, symbolizes strength and hard work. You may be feeling burdened or drained in some way or that you find yourself needing to support others.

Coma

To dream that you are in a coma, indicates your helplessness and inability to function in some given situation. You are not prepared for the major changes that are happening around you. Alternatively, your dream coma state may reflect what is really happening to you body when you are in the dream stage of sleep. In this stage of sleep, our bodies remain immobile as if it was paralyzed, commonly known as REM paralysis.

Comb

To dream that you combing your hair, suggests your need to organize and sort your thoughts. You need to find or search for some elements that are not clear to you in a situation or relationship.

Please see also Hair:

Comedian

To see a comedian in your dream, suggests that you need to be more carefree. You are feeling overburdened from your daily problems and need an outlet to release all that tension. You need to learn to laugh at yourself and not take yourself so seriously.

Comet

To see a comet in your dream, indicates that you need to move on and free yourself from emotional and physical burdens. Charge forward toward your goals.

Commercials

To dream that you are watching TV commercials, signifies your tendency to jump from one thing to another without completing your initial responsibilities and tasks. You have a tendency to emotionally distance yourself and remain objective about the situations you are faced with.

If the commercials quickly jump from one to another, then is symbolizes your flightiness.

Communion

To dream of communion, symbolizes your conflict with the material world and the spiritual world. You are torn between your values and your feelings. Alternatively, the dream indicates a betrayal. You may also be seeking some form of acceptance.

Compact Disc

To see a compact disc in your dream, represents a need for enjoyment or a distraction. It denotes opportunities and possibilities. Consider the type of music and the title of the compact disc. If you are giving away the CD, you may be trying to convey a message to that person within the songs.

Consider also if the initial "CD" have any additional significance to you. Perhaps it represents a person or may even be a pun on something that is "seedy".

Compass

To see a compass in your dream, is a way of your subconscious to show you the way. It may be an indication for you to reconsider the direction in your life and to rethink the path you are taking.

Competition

To dream that you are in a competition, represents your need to grow and expand. Learn the value of endurance and perseverance. Also be more assertive.

To dream that you win a competition, suggests that you possess the necessary skills to accomplish a goal or solve a problem in your waking life.

Compliment

To dream that you are giving a compliment, suggests that you need to be steadfast and not let others questions your authority and position on things.

To dream that you are being complimented, refers to your desire for romance and love.

Composer

To dream that you are a composer, signifies that you are creating or directing new found energies to a situation or aspect of your life.

Computer

To see a computer in your dream, symbolizes technology, information, and modern life. New areas of opportunities are being opened to you. Alternatively, computers also represent a lack of individuality and non expression of emotions and feelings. Too often you are just going along with the flow, without voicing your own opinions and views. You may also feel a depreciated sense of superiority.

To dream that you computer has a mind of its own, denotes anxiety about technology and loss of control. You are feeling overwhelmed and feel that you are at the mercy of another.

To dream that a computer has a virus, suggests that something in your life that is out of control.

Concentration Camp

To see or live in a concentration camp in your dream, indicates that you are afraid of differences. You are having difficulties accepting others and their differences. Learn to appreciate diversity and the uniqueness in yourself and in others around you. If you actually lived in a concentration camp, the dream may signify a situation in your waking life which is triggering similar feelings felt at the time.

Concern

To dream that you are concerned about something or someone, indicates that you are feeling much anxiety, unhappiness, or uneasiness in some situation of your waking life. The concern you have in your dream may be something you need to pay attention to and acknowledge.

Concert

To dream that you are at a concert, represents harmony and cooperation in a situation or relationship of your waking life. You are experiencing an uplift in your spirits.

Conch Shell

To see a conch shell in your dream, represents sexual inhibitions.

Concussion

To dream that you have a concussion, suggests that you are not utilizing your fullest potential. You need to be more responsive to others, instead of just sitting back and waiting for things to happen.

Concrete

To see concrete in your dream, represents your solid and clear understanding of some situation. The dream may also mean that you are unyielding and inflexible.

To see wet concrete in your dream, suggests that some issue or some aspect of your life still remains unresolved.

Condom

To see a wrapped condom in your dream, represents your one-sided viewpoints and not allowing others to voice their opinions. It also symbolizes sexual possibilities.

To see an unwrapped condom in your dream, indicates sexual frustration. Additionally, it may also indicate that you are experiencing some anxiety about pregnancy or sexually transmitted diseases.

To dream that you or your partner is wearing a condom, suggests that you feel emotionally protected.

Conductor

To see or dream that you are a conductor, represents your abilities to lead and direct yourself toward higher awareness.

Cone

To see a cone in your dream, represents a flow of ideas and feelings.

Confession

To dream that you or someone is confessing, represents feelings of guilt and self-blame. Alternatively, it suggests a form of healing and heralding the new changes in your life.

Confetti

To see or throw confetti in your dream, represents achievement and success. You have achieved a higher level of growth and learning. You have reached a turning point in your life. Alternatively, it symbolizes much festivity and fanfare. You may be expressing joy, victory, and freedom from restraint.

Confusion

To dream that you are confused, may reflect your true confused state of mind and the nonsensical events of your dream. Isolate the single element in your dream that is confusing to you and analyze the meaning of that particular symbol. Alternatively, dreams of confusion signifies that you are being pulled in opposite directions or do not know which viewpoint is right.

Constellation

To see a constellation in your dream, indicates that something in your life is coming together in a complex way. It represents a mental process. Consider what the constellation is depicting.

Constipation

To dream that you have constipation, denotes that you are unwilling to part with your old ways. You are continuing to grasp on to your old ways and failing to let go, forgive, and forget. You may be dwelling on past problems and previous difficulties.

Contact Lens

To see or wear contact lens in your dream, suggests that you need to focus on the task at hand. You need to pay closer attention to a situation before acting on it. The dream may also mean that you need to get in contact with someone.

If you have difficulties putting on your contact lens in your dream, then it indicates that you are having trouble paying attention.

Contraceptive

To see or use contraceptive in your dream, suggests that you are refusing to let your creativity emerge from beneath the surface. You are holding back some aspect of yourself. Alternatively, it signifies your anxieties about pregnancy or sexually transmitted diseases.

Contract

To dream that you are signing a contract, indicates that you are ready to commit to a long term relationship or project.

To dream that you enter into a bad contract, signifies to think twice about committing to a relationship. Carefully examine what you are getting into.

Construction

To see construction in your dream, signifies a new surge of energy, ambition and renewed confidence. It may also represent the rebuilding of your own life.

Contest

To dream that you enter or are in a contest, indicates the need to prove yourself as worthy and deserving. If you win the contest, then it represents your self-confidence, pride, and/or conceit. If you lose the contest, then it indicates a lack of self-esteem. You may not be fully applying yourself to the task at hand.

Convent

To dream that you are at a convent, represents your need for spiritual support and nurturance.

Convention

To dream that you are at a convention, represents your need for contact and communication. You need to keep in mind that the choices you make with effect those around you. Don't be hesitant in getting them involved in your decision making. The dream is also a metaphor for bring various aspects of yourself together. Consider the type of convention for additional clues as to what may be lacking in your life.

Conversion

To dream about a conversion, indicates your hopes that some problem or situation can be changed. This dream also represents your mobility and adaptability to situations in life.

Convertible

To see or dream that you are in a convertible, refers to your glamorous attitude. You are showing off your power and influence.

Conveyer Belt

To see a conveyer belt in your dream, suggests that you are stuck in a rut. Your daily routine has become predictable and unchallenging.

Convict

To dream that you are a convict, suggests that some situation or relationship is making you feel restricted. You may be experiencing a loss of freedom in some area of your life. Alternatively, the dream may represent your feelings of shame and guilt. This dream image is trying to tell you to stop punishing yourself.

To see a convict in your dream, indicates that an aspect of yourself is unable to freely express itself.

Cookies

To dream that you are eating, giving, receiving, or stealing cookies signifies that you will let trivial problems and minor disputes annoy you.

To dream that you are baking cookies, signifies feelings of optimism or an increase in productivity. You may also experience a rise in status.

Cooking

To dream that you are cooking, signifies your desire desire to influence others in such a way that they will like you or become dependent on you. Alternatively, it represents your nurturing side or wanting to be nurtured. You want to be loved.

To dream that you have difficulties cooking, indicates that you are trying too hard.

Cop

Please See <u>Police</u>.

Copier

To see or use a copier in your dream, represents your lack of originality and tendency to copy other's ideas/beliefs. You need to start thinking things through for yourself. Alternatively, it may indicate a desire to spread some idea and circulate the word out.

Copper

To see copper in your dream, represents the power of healing. It also indicates a flow of ideas and information.

Coral

To see coral in your dream, symbolizes the beauty of life. Acknowledging your feelings is the key to a happy and rewarding life. Alternatively, it represents purification and blood.

Cork

To see cork in your dream, represents your versatility and adaptability in different situations. You have the ability to stay afloat in times of turmoil. and rise above your circumstances.

Cormorant

Please See <u>Loon.</u>

Corn

To see corn in your dream, signifies abundance, growth and fertility. Also consider the pun that something is "corny".

Corner

To dream that you are in a corner, signifies feelings of frustration and lack of control in making decisions. You may feel trapped and "cornered".

Cornucopia

To see a cornucopia in your dream, represents abundance, plentitude and prosperity. The dream also highlights the union of the masculine and feminine aspects.

Corpse

To see a corpse in your dream, represents an aspect of yourself that has died. Or it may mean that you are unexpressive. You have shut yourself down and are dead inside.

Corridor

To dream that you are walking through a long corridor, signifies your desperation in trying to escape a repetitive situation or behavior patters. You need to free yourself of this repetition and the corridor is seen as a passage from one phase in your life to another.

Corsage

To see or wear a corsage in your dream, suggests that an aspect of yourself is looking to be acknowledged and recognized. Alternatively, it is a symbol of honor.

Corset

To see or wear a corset in your dream, indicates restraint and restrictions. You may be feeling limited. Alternatively, it may mean that you have a tendency to hold in your displeasure in order to please others.

Cosmetics

Please See Makeup.

Costume

To dream that you are wearing a costume, signifies that you are putting on a facade toward others. Your true self is not being revealed and you are not being completely honest with people around you.

Cottage

To see a cottage in your dream, represents comfort, peace and serenity. You prefer a life of simplicity. The cottage may represent an altered sense of reality and thus may be a means of escaping the responsibilities and problems that may be associated with your home. You need to approach life's difficulties one at a time.

Cotton

To dream that you are picking cotton, suggests that you are seeing little benefits from all your long hard work. It may also mean that aspects of yourself are in harmony.

To dream that you are wearing cotton, symbolizes simplicity.

Cotton Candy

To see or eat cotton candy in your dream, represents childhood pleasures or rewards. You are content with the way things are going in your life.

Couch

To see or dream that you are on a couch, represents rest, relaxation, laziness or boredom. It may also mean you need to clear you mind and thoughts. Consider also who is on the couch with you as the dream may also have sexual connotations.

Cougar

To see a cougar in your dream, symbolizes wild beauty, power, grace, and raw emotion. It often refers to feminine power and aggression. Alternatively, it also indicates lurking danger and death.

Coughing

To dream that you are coughing, represents your fear or dissatisfaction of the future. You need to put some distance between yourself and others. Alternatively, it indicates that you have made a negative choice in some important matter.

Counselor

To see a counselor or dream that you are one, suggests that you are seeking for some support and direction in your life. Pay important attention to what the counselor is saying and/or doing. Your dream is trying to convey a message that you need to think about and possibly act upon.

Counterfeit

To see counterfeit money in your dream, indicates that something is not what it appears to be. Perhaps you are feeling unworthy or someone is devaluing your talents or efforts. Alternatively, this dream symbol suggests that you are pretending to be something you are not.

Court

To dream that you are in court standing up for charges against you, signifies your struggle with issues of fear and guilt. A situation or circumstance in your life is giving your much distress and worry. You may feel that you are being judged in some way.

Cousins

To see your cousin in your dream, represents something or some aspect of your character that is somewhat familiar. Perhaps you need to spend more time in cultivating and developing some emerging ability or character. In particular, if you dream that your cousin is ignoring you indicates that you are not acknowledging some aspect of yourself that is represented by your cousin.

To dream that you or your sibling is in love with a cousin, represents your acceptance of each other and that you have acknowledge and embraced key qualities in one another.

Cow

To see a cow in your dream, signifies your obedience to authority without question. It symbolizes your passive and docile nature. Alternatively, it represents maternal instincts or the desire to be cared for. For some cultures, the cow represents divine qualities of fertility, nourishment and motherhood.

To see a cow with a skeleton face, suggests that you mother or motherly figure in your waking life is displaying a lack of emotions. She is being unresponsive to your needs.

To see a herd of cows, indicates your need to belong.

Coward

To dream that you or someone is a coward, indicates that you are afraid to see your true Self and to be who you are. You are hindering your own self-growth.

Cowboy

To see or dream that you are a cowboy, symbolizes masculinity, ruggedness, and toughness. You are in control of your animalistic and instinctual side.

Coworker

To see your coworkers in your dream, highlights aspects of your waking relationship with them, including difficulties/support. It signifies your ambition, struggles and competitive nature. If the coworkers in your dream are not your actual coworkers, then they may pertain to some psychological business that you need to work on.

To dream that you are training someone to take your place, suggests that you are moving on with respect to some task or inner development. You are leaving behind old attitudes and are looking toward the future.

Please see also Office.

Coyote

To see a coyote in your dream, denotes deception and weakness.

Crab

To see a crab in your dream, signifies you perseverance and tenacity. On an extreme note, you maybe be too clingy and dependant and hanging on to a hopeless endeavor. Crabs are also symbolic of your irritable personality, as in the pun, being "crabby".

Crackers

To see or eat a cracker in your dream, suggests that you tend to care for the needs of others besides your own. You spend your time looking of for other people and as a result, neglect your needs. The dream may also be a pun on "crack her". Perhaps you are trying to get someone to reveal certain information or secrets.

Cradle

To see a cradle in your dream, symbolizes a dependent relationship. You may feel the need to be protected and cared for. Your dream maybe telling you to regain some control and independence in your life. Alternatively, it represents a new project or fresh start.

Crane

To see a crane in your dream, represents happiness, maternal love, and your gestures of good will. You look out for those who are near and dear to you.

Crash

To dream that you are in a car crash, indicates that your beliefs, lifestyle, or goals are clashing with another's. It may also represent a shocking situation or painful experience. Alternatively, car crashes may forewarn of your dangerous or careless driving habits.

To dream that a plane crashes, signifies that you have set overly high and unrealistic goals for yourself and are in danger of having it come crashing down. Alternatively, your lack of confidence, self-defeating attitude and self-doubt toward the goals you have set for yourself is represented by the crashing airplane; you do not believe in your ability to attain those goals. Loss of power and uncertainty in achieving your goals are also signified.

***See The Meaning In Action: "_Plane Crash_"**

Crater

To see a crater in your dream, indicates that aspects of your unconscious are being slowly revealed to you. This dream symbol is also symbolic of past memories and experiences.

Crawling

To dream that you are crawling, indicates that you are approaching your goals with careful forethought and preparation. Alternatively, you may be lowering yourself and your standards. You may be doing less than your best.

To dream that you are crawling out of a wreck or ruins, represents your willpower.

To dream that someone is crawling towards you, signifies your need for power, revenge, superiority, or control.

Crayons

To see crayons in your dream, represents some childhood memories or a period of time where you were more carefree. It is also symbolic of creativity. You may need to think outside the lines into more unconventional thoughts and ways of doing things. Consider the symbolism of the color of the crayon.

Crazy

To dream that you are going crazy, suggests that you have lost sight of your goals. You may feel that you are no longer able to depend on someone. Alternatively, you may feel that your opinions, viewpoints or decisions are not being accepted or being ignored. You may feel like an outsider.

Cream

To see or eat cream in your dream, indicates that you appreciate the minor and sweet things in life. It is symbolic of nurturance and richness.

To see or apply face cream in your dream, represents a beautiful soul. It may also represent the character and personality you are portraying to others in your waking life.

Creatures

To see faceless creatures in your dream, indicates a situation you are refusing to see or confront, but are aware of it in some passive way. This dream also suggests that something in your life is bringing up feelings of fear and insecurities.

Credit Cards

To dream about credit cards, relates to your worth, value and/or credibility. Depending on your waking experiences, the credit cards may symbolize being in debt and your attitudes about money, work, and thrift.

To dream that you lose your credit cards, indicates your carelessness in some aspect of your waking life.

To dream that someone is stealing your credit cards, suggests that something or someone is robbing you of vital energy.

Creek

To see a creek in your dream, represents your own personal energy flow and steady emotional release.

To see a dried up creek, indicates that you are being cut off from your spiritual being and being out of touch with yourself. You may also feel physically or emotionally drained.

Cremains

To see cremains in your dream, symbolizes change. It also represents a return to your true Self and acceptance of who you are.

Cremation

To dream that someone is being cremated, represents purification and your strive for perfection.

Crescent

To see a crescent in your dream, represents the the emergence of your feminine character. It also indicates versatility and changes.

Crib

To see a crib in your dream, suggests that you are harvesting or "babying" a new idea, creation or project. Alternatively, it may refer to your nurturing, protective, and caring nature. A more literal interpretation of this symbol, suggests that you may be yearning for a baby or that you are expecting a baby.

Crickets

To see crickets in your dream, represents introspection. You are seeking guidance.

To hear crickets in your dream, suggests that you are letting minor things bother you.

Crime

To dream that you or someone commits a crime, represents feelings of guilt and shame. Your inner fears are hindering your growth and progress.

Cripple

*Please See Handicap.

Crocodile

To see a crocodile in your dream, forewarns of hidden danger. Someone near you is giving you bad advice and is trying to sway you into poor decisions. The crocodile may be an aspect of yourself and your aggressive and "snappy" attitude. Or maybe it reveals that you have displayed some false emotions and shedding "crocodile tears".

To dream that you are chased or bitten by a crocodile, denotes disappointments in love and in business.

**See The Meaning In Action: "Crocodile Chase"

Crop

To dream that you are tending to your crop, represents growth, self-love, and self-appreciation. In the end, your hard work is paying off.

Cross

To see a cross in your dream, signifies suffering, martyrdom, death, and/or sacrifice. Perhaps your dream is telling you that you have a cross to bear. Ask yourself what is causing you to suffer or what is causing you great difficulties.

Cross-Dressing

To dream that you or someone is cross-dressing, indicates that you need to express and acknowledge your masculine side if you are female or your feminine side if you are a man.

Crossroads

To dream that you are at a crossroad, signifies that you have come to a point in your life where you have several options to choose from which will take you various destinations. This dream suggests your need to make this important decision.

Crossword Puzzle

To see or do a crossword puzzle, suggests that you are being faced with a mental challenge. The dream may be a pun on "cross words" directed at your or aimed toward someone.

Crow

To see a crow in your dream, represents your annoying habits and the darker part of your character. The crow may serve as messengers from your unconscious.

Crowd

To dream that you are in or part of a crowd, signifies that you need to make some space for yourself. You need solitude to reflect on a situation at hand and recharge your energy. Consider also the familiar phrase of "going along with the crowd" which implies conformity and lack of individuality.

To see an unruly crowd in your dream, signifies that the worries and problems around you are pressing in on you. You will be be greatly distressed.

To see a happy, orderly crowd in your dream, denotes assured happiness, pleasant friends and opportunities for advancement.

Crown

To see a crown in your dream, symbolizes success and prominence.

Crucifix

To see a crucifix in your dream, is symbolic of new life, spiritual guidance, and liberation. The dream may serve as a connection with your inner Christ/love consciousness. Alternatively, it represents your difficulties and hardships. Do you feel you are being crucified for something occurring in your life?

Crucify

To dream that you are being crucified, indicates that you are punishing yourself.

Cruel

To dream that you or someone is being cruel, signifies the release of pent-up hostility and anger. You may need to acknowledge the shadow and negative aspects of your personality.

To dream that someone is being cruel to you, suggests that you need to develop your inner and outer strengths and become more emotionally strong.

Cruise

To dream that you are on a cruise, represents some emotional journey that you are going through. The dream may also be a pun on "cruising" through situations in your life with ease and little effort.

Crush

To dream that you are crushing something, denotes that you are under tremendous stress over a decision that you need to make.

To dream that you have a crush on somebody, is a literal reflection of your attraction and fascination for that person. To see your crush in your dream, represents your current infatuation with him or her. If you find yourself thinking about him during the day, then it is understandable that his image will appear in your dream during the night. If your dream that your crush rejects you, refers to not knowing how he or she really feels about you and whether he likes you or not.

If you dream that somebody has a crush on you, then it represent you own sense of worthiness and esteem.

To dream about a former crush, refers to that particular period in your life and what you were feeling. The former crush represents a point in time when you first had the crush on that person.

To dream that your crush rejects you or stood you up, represents your feelings of insecurities and anxieties. The idea of not knowing how your crush feels about you is driving you nuts. Assuming that he or she will reject you before you actually know, saves your from getting hurt. You are afraid to find out how he or she feels about you.

Crutches

To dream that you are on crutches, signifies your need to lean on others for help. Perhaps you are acting helpless in order to get out of some situation or obligation.

Cry

To dream that you are crying, signifies a release of negative emotions that is more likely caused by some waking situation rather than the events of the dream itself. Your dream is a way to regain some emotional balance and a way to safely let out your fears and frustrations. In our daily lives, we tend to ignore, deny, or repress our feelings. But in our dream state, our defense mechanisms are no longer on guard and thus allow for the release of such emotions.

To see someone else crying in your dream, may be a projection of your own feelings onto someone else. If you do not cry in your waking life, then seeing someone else cry may be a little easier to deal with then seeing yourself cry.

To wake up crying, suggest the grieving of your soul and that you need to change your ways and how you approach things.

To dream that no one hears or responds to your cries, represents your helplessness and difficulties and frustrations in trying to communicate with others. You feel that your words are falling on deaf ears. Perhaps your dream is telling you to be more vocal and work harder to get your point across.

Crystal

To see a crystal in your dream, signifies wholeness, purity, and unity. To dream that you are looking into a crystal, is indicative of how you are looking within yourself to find your true destiny.

Cub

To see a cub in your dream, represents innocence, playfulness and/or mischievousness. It is also symbolic of your children or siblings.

Cube

To see a cube in your dream, symbolizes material possessions and earthly things. It may also be a metaphor for "being square" or being too conservative.

Cuckoo

To see a cuckoo in your dream, represents timing and fate. You need to change your direction or alter your approach in how your pursue some situation. Alternatively, there may be someone in your life whose presence is unwelcome. The dream may also be a metaphor for someone who is behaving crazily.

Cucumber

To see or eat a cucumber in your dream, signifies recuperation and recovery. You need to regain your energy and health. Alternatively, it is symbolic of the phallus and have sexual connotations.

Cuddle

To dream that you are cuddling with someone, indicates your need for physical and/or emotional contact. Do not overlook the obvious meaning of this dream which suggests your heart's desire for that particular person. Also consider the symbolism of that person you are cuddling with and determine how you need to acknowledge, accept, and unify those qualities in yourself.

Cult

To dream that you are in a cult, suggests that you are in some destructive and/or manipulative relationship. You are being exploited. On a more positive note, you have the desire to strive for a better Self. It implies devotion and sense of community.

To see a cult in your dream, indicates that you are lacking any spiritual freedom.

To dream that you are a leader of a cult, signifies your authoritarian attitude. No one should question your motives or choices.

Cultivate

To dream that you are cultivating, indicates that you need to clear your mind of negative thoughts. Keeping an open mind will further allow you to grow as a person.

Cup

To see a cup in your dream, represents nurturance and the womb. The cup may also signify healing, rejuvenation, and healing. Alternatively, it indicates a transcendence into a realm of higher consciousness. Is the cup half-full or half-empty? Do you see life from an optimistic or pessimistic point of view.

To see a cup with a broken handle, indicates your feelings of inadequacy and anxieties of being unable to handle a particular situation.

To see a broken cup in your dream, denotes feelings of powerlessness, guilt and/or low self-esteem. Perhaps you feel unqualified or inadequate in dealing with a situation.

Cupboard

To dream that you are opening a cupboard, signifies that you are revealing some hidden truth or secret.

Cupid

To see cupid in your dream, represents a love relationship in your waking life. Its appearance in your dream may mean that you need to take a risk in love.

Curlers

To see curlers in your dream, suggests that you are thinking in circles. You may be going over the same problem/situation again and again without any conclusion.

Current

To see/notice an ocean or river current in your dream, represents the direction of your life and the decisions you have made along the way. It also represents the influences in your life and how they work in guiding you through your life's path. The dream may also be a metaphor for the current events or something that is going on in your life at the moment.

Curry

To see or taste curry in your dream, suggests that you are emotionally sensitive and easily irritable. Alternatively, it refers to your quick-wit, sharpness, and intellect. It may also mean that you feel like you are hot stuff.

Curse

To dream that you or someone is under a curse, suggests that you are getting caught up in your own guilt. You also need to proceed with caution in some situation or relationship.

To dream that you or someone is cursing, refers to your inner fears.

Curtains

To see or dream that you are shutting the curtains, signifies secrecy and a repression of thoughts. You are concealing a personal matter or an aspect of yourself. On the other hand, to dream that you are opening the curtains, indicates that you are ready to reveal something hidden.

Curtsy

To curtsy in your dream, suggests that you are acknowledging something that is greater than you and deserves your respect. You are submitting to a power larger than you.

Cut

To dream that you have a cut, suggests that you are being let down or being undermined. Alternatively, it refers to feminine sexuality and feminine attitudes toward sex. In particular, if the cuts are on your legs, then it symbolizes an imbalance. You are unable to stand up for yourself.

To dream that you are cutting yourself, indicates that you are experiencing some overwhelming turmoil or problems in your waking life. You are trying to disconnect yourself from the unbearable pain you are experiencing.

Cuticles

To notice your cuticles in our dream, suggests that you are being overly sensitive. You may be overreacting in some situation.

Cutting

To dream that you are cutting something, signifies a broken relationship or severed connection.

Cyclops

To see Cyclops in your dream, suggests that you may be narrow-minded and need to expand the scope of your vision. Alternatively, you may be too overly focused on one thing.

Cymbals

To dream that you are playing with cymbals, indicates that you are overreacting in some situation. You are making too much fuss over a small thing.

Cypress

To see a cypress tree in your dream, symbolizes death, the underworld, and the unconscious. It may also indicate a time of mourning and sadness.

D

Daffodil

To see daffodils in your dream, symbolizes renewal, inner growth, optimism, inspiration, and hope.

Dagger

To dream of being attacked by someone with a dagger, warns of physical injury from an enemy or a mugger. You may feel that you have been stabbed in the back by somebody.

To dream that you take a dagger from somebody's hand, means you will overcome hardships and misfortune.

Dahlias

To see dahlias in a dream, signifies good fortune in financial matters.

To see dahlias that are dying and wilting, signifies loss and sorrow.

Dairy

To dream that you are in a dairy, is a good omen. Much fortune will come your way and you will never be without the basic necessities in life.

Daisy

To see daisies in your dream, symbolizes freshness, beauty, innocence, simplicity, friendliness, and cleanliness.

To dream that someone gives you a bouquet of daisies, symbolizes sorrow and/or lost love.

To dream of walking in a field of daisies, represents good luck and prosperity. Someone will be there to offer you a helping hand and guidance for your problems.

Dalmatian

To see a Dalmatian in you dream, suggests that you tend to overlook your own feelings and tend to the needs of others. You are a people pleaser.

Dam

To see a dam in your dream, signifies repressed emotions or feelings that needs to be released. To dream of a bursting dam, denotes that you have lost control of your anger and are overwhelmed with emotions.

Damask Rose

To see a damask rosebush growing in the wild, foretells of a wedding in the family.

To dream that you receive a bouquet of damask rose, foretells that you will find a faithful and true lover.

For a woman, to dream that you receive a damask rose and places it in her hair, signifies that she will be deceived by someone who she thought was a good friend.

Damson

To see a damson tree full with fruit in your dream, signifies riches and that you will be well-rewarded.

To dream that you are picking the plums out of the damson tree and eating them, signifies that you will experience some loss and sorrow. A dark cloud will hover over you.

Dance

To dream that you are dancing, signifies freedom from constraints and harmony/balance with yourself. You are working in cooperation with yourself. It also represents frivolity, happiness, gracefulness, sensuality and sexual desires. Alternatively, it may signify intimacy and a union of the masculine and feminine aspects of yourself.

To dream that you are attending or going to a dance, indicates a celebration and your attempts to achieve happiness. Consider the phrase the "dance of life" which suggests creation, ecstasy, and going with what life has to offer you.

To see children dancing in your dream, signifies that you will have a comfortable home, and healthy, well-behaved children in the future.

To see ritualistic dancing in your dream, denotes your need to get in touch with the spirit within..

Dance Recital

To see a dance recital in your dream, signifies that you will be moving to another place to live.

To dream that you participate in a dance recital, signifies that you will be in conflict with your co-workers or classmates.

Dandelion

To see dandelions in your dream, foretells of pleasurable surroundings and joyous future for you and your lover.

To dream that you are eating dandelions, signifies that you need to take better care of your health or suffer ill consequences.

Dandruff

To dream that you have dandruff, indicates that you are misusing your energy. You may have been under a lot of stress and tension. You should rethink the way you are approaching any of your current problems. Alternatively, this dream may suggest a lack of self-esteem.

Danger

To dream that you are in danger and are wounded or killed, signifies substantial losses in business and discouraging prospects in love. You need to be more cautious in some aspect of your life.

To dream that you escape from danger, signifies that you will rise to a place of high position and honor in your business and social circle.

Darkness

To dream that darkness comes upon you, signifies failure in work you may attempt. Darkness is synonymous with ignorance, the unconscious, evil, death, and fear of the unknown. If the sun breaks through the darkness, then you will overcome your failures. If you feel safe in the dark, then it suggests that you like not knowing about certain things. As some might say, ignorance is bliss.

To dream that you cannot find someone in the darkness, signifies that you need to keep your temper in check. You have the tendency to let your emotions get out of control and lose your temper.

To dream that you are lost in the darkness, denotes feelings of desperation, depression, or insecurity.

To dream that you are groping around in the darkness, indicates that you have insufficient information to make a clear decision. Do your research and do not rush into making choices.

Darkroom

To dream that you are in a darkroom, suggests that you are waiting for something to happen or to see what might develop in a situation.

Dartboard

To see a dartboard in your dream, indicates that you are feeling hostility from someone. You need to express your anger and feelings more directly. Alternatively, the dartboard may symbolize a goal that you are aiming for. You need to try and take a shot at something new and overcome your fear of failure.

Darts

To dream that you are throwing darts in your dream, refers to some hurtful or harmful remarks that you or someone have said. Alternatively, it represents your goals and your "go-getter" attitude.

Date

To dream that you are on a date, suggests that you are getting to know some hidden aspects of yourself. You are acknowledging your hidden talents. Alternatively, it may reflect your anxieties about dating or finding acceptance.

Dates

To see plump ripe dates growing on a tree, signifies that the next few days will be happy occasions. Take this time to relax and find peace of mind.

To dream that you are eating dates, signifies distress. You are never happy with what you have. You are always concern with you wants and trying to acquiring these material things.

Daughter

To see your daughter in your dream, represents your waking relationship with your daughter and the qualities that she projects. If you do not have a daughter, then it symbolizes the feminine aspect within yourself.

Daughter-In-Law

To see your daughter-in-law in your dream, signifies that an unusual and unexpected incident will either give you much happiness or distress, depending on her demeanor in your dream.

Dawn

To see the dawn in your dream, signifies rejuvenation, enlightenment, and vitality. You may be emerging out of a new stage in life, possess a new understanding, or have a new start in life

Day

To dream of a sunny day, symbolizes clarity and/or pleasantness. You are seeing things clearly.

To dream of a gloomy or cloudy day, signifies loss.

Daybreak

To dream that the day breaks, signifies success in your projects and endeavors.

Dead

To see the dead in your dream, forewarns that you are being influenced by negative people and are hanging around the wrong crowd. You may suffer material loss. This dream may also be a way for you to resolve your feelings with those who have passed on.

If you dream of a person who has died a long time ago, then it suggests that a current situation or relationship in you life resembles the quality of that deceased person. The dream may depict how you need to let this situation or relationship die and end it.

To see and talk with your dead parents in your dreams, represents your fears of losing them or your way of coping with the loss. You may want that last opportunity to say your final good-byes to them.

To see your dead sibling, relative, or friend alive in your dream, indicates that you miss them and are trying to relive your old experiences you had with them. In trying to keep up with the pace of your daily waking life, you dreams may serve as your only outlet in coping and coming to terms with the loss of a loved one.

*Please see also Die.

Deaf

To dream that you are deaf, indicates that you are feeling secluded from the world, You may be closing yourself off from new experiences or shutting yourself out.

To dream that someone else is deaf, suggests that someone close to you is withdrawn.

Death

To dream about the death of a loved one, suggests that you are lacking a certain aspect or quality that the loved one embodies. Ask yourself what makes this person special or what do you like about him. It is that very quality that you are lacking in your own relationship or circumstances. Alternatively, it indicates that whatever that person represents has no part in your own life.

Debt

To dream that you are in debt, signifies struggle, worries and troubles in business and love.

Decapitation

To dream that you are decapitated, indicates that you are not thinking clearly are are refusing to see the truth. You need to confront the situation or the person despite the pain and discomfort you might feel in doing so. The dream also suggests that you have the tendency to act before you think.

*Please see also Behead.

Decay

To see something decay in your dream, signifies the degradation of a situation or circumstance. It may also represent the death of an old situation before the rebirth into a new stage.

December

To dream of the month of December, signifies increased wealth, but loss of friends.

Deceased

Please See Dead.

Deck

To dream that you are out on the deck, represents your connection with your Self and with nature. You need to be more aware of your surroundings and appreciate the environment.

Decorate

To dream that you are decorating an area, signifies a favorable turn in business or studies and increased social pleasures.

Deeds

To dream that you a signing a deed, foretells of a lawsuit in which you will most likely lose.

Deer

To see a deer in your dream, symbolizes grace, gentleness, and natural beauty. It has feminine qualities and may point to the feminine aspect within yourself. It also represents independence and virility. Consider the symbol to be a pun for someone who is "dear" to you.

If the deer is black, then it means that you are not acknowledging or are rejected the feminine qualities in you. You may not be in tune with your feminine side.

To dream that you kill a dear, suggests that you are trying to suppress those feminine qualities.

Defecate

To dream that you are defecating on someone, indicates your anger and hostility for that person.

To dream that you are being defecated on, represents feelings of guilt and unworthiness. You may be suffering from low self-esteem.

Please see also Bowel Movement or Feces.

Deformed

To dream that you or someone is deformed, represents undeveloped aspects of yourself that you may have ignored. You refusal to acknowledge these characteristics may be affecting your performance and creative flow.

Delight

To dream that you are experiencing delight, signifies a favorable and positive turn of events and much pleasantness.

Demons

To see demons in your dream, represents ignorance, negativity, distress or your shadow self. It also forewarns of overindulgence and letting lust give way to your better judgment. As a result, your physical and mental health may suffer.

To dream that you are possessed by demons, indicates ultimate helplessness.

Den

To dream that you are in the den, signifies work, industry, and efficiency.

Dentist

To dream that you are at the dentist, signifies periodic doubt over the sincerity and honor of some person. You may have some anxiety or fear of pain, but in the long run it will be for your own good.

To dream that the dentist working on somebody else's teeth, signifies that you will be shocked by scandal near you.

Deodorant

To see or put on deodorant in your dream, represents your inner strength and your ability to rid yourself of harmful and destructive behaviors.

Depression

To feel depressed in your dream, refers to your inability to make connections. You are unable to see the causes of your problems and consequences of your decisions.

Derrick

To see derricks in your dream, symbolizes obstacles standing in your road towards success.

Desert

To dream that you are walking through a desert, signifies loss and misfortune. You may be suffering from an attack on your reputation. Deserts are also symbolic of barrenness, loneliness and feelings of isolation and hopelessness.

Desk

To see or sit at your desk in your dream, suggests that you are evaluating and weighing your problems. It is indicative of self-exploration and discovery.

Despair

To dream that you are in despair, signifies that you will have many hardships and experience much cruelties in the working world.

To dream that others are in despair, denotes that some friend or relative will be in great distress and find themselves in a unhappy situation.

Dessert

To see a tasty dessert in your dream, represents indulgence, celebration, reward, or temptation. You are enjoying the good things in life.

Destruction

To dream about mass destruction, suggests that there is some chaos occurring in your life. Things may not be going the way you want it to. Perhaps the choices your are making are self-destructive.

Detective

To see a detective in your dream, signifies the thrills and dangers of an aspect of your waking life.

To dream that you are a detective, indicates that you are searching for your hidden abilities and talents. It also signifies that you are trying to solve a problem and seek the truth about an issue that is worrying you.

To dream that you are being followed by a detective, signifies guilt. Your character will be put under scrutiny and called into question.

Detergent

To see or use detergent in your dream, indicates that you need to resolve a major problem in your life. You may also need to clean up your image and attitude.

Determination

To dream that you have determination, represents your ambition and realization of your goals. It refers to your attitude and the restrictions that you or others impose onto you.

Detour

To see a detour in your dream, signifies that you have encountered an obstacle in some aspect of your life. You may not want to confront something directly and thus must try to find a way around it.

Devil

To see the devil in your dream, signifies negative aspects of yourself. It may also indicate feelings of guilt that you have been harboring. It is time to release these feelings. Alternatively, the devil may represent intelligence, cunningness, deception, and cleverness.

To dream that you fought off the devil, symbolizes that you will succeed in defeating your enemies.

To dream that the devil talks to you, signifies that you will find some temptations hard to resist even though you know it is not in your best interest.

To dream that you and the devils were in friendly terms, suggests that you may be seduced and tempted into doing something you do not want to do. You may be dealing with issues of morality.

Devotion

To dream that you are showing your devotion to your beliefs, serves as a reminder that nothing will be gained by deceit.

Dew

To dream that the dew is falling on your, signifies that you will be stricken with fever or some illness.

To see the dew sparkling in the grass, denotes honor and wealth.

Diadem

To see a diadem in your dream, signifies that some honor will soon be bestowed onto you.

Please Also See Crown.

Diamonds

To see diamonds in your dream, signifies the wholeness of the Self. You may be finding clarity in matters that have been clouding you. It may also point to your unchanging or unyielding nature. Alternatively, it represents vanity and conceit. You may be distancing yourself from others.

Diaper

To see or wear a diaper in your dream, symbolizes your childish or babyish attitudes/actions. You may be too dependent on others.

To dream that you are changing diapers, suggests a need to clean up you behavior and change your childish ways. Perhaps you need to change your attitude and approach regarding a new idea or project.

To see dirty diapers in your dream, indicates that you need to clean the mess you have created with your childishness.

Diarrhea

To dream that you have diarrhea, signifies that some part of your life is going out of control or that you can no longer contain your strong emotions. Alternatively, it may indicate a need for you to get something out of your system quickly. It may also indicate that you have not analyzed a situation long enough or that you do not want to deal with the problem at all.

Please see also Bowel Movement.

Diary

Please See Journal.

Dice

To see dice in your dream, signifies misfortune in the stock market and consequent misery and despair. They represent chance and fate.

To see your lover throwing dice, symbolizes his unworthiness.

Dictator

To see or dream that you are a dictator, suggests that you need to be more flexible and open-minded in our thinking and in your decision making. You are being too controlling.

Dictionary

To dream that you are using a dictionary, signifies that you rely too much on the opinions of others in the management of your own affairs.

Die

To dream that you die in your dream, symbolizes inner changes, transformation, self-discovery and positive development that is happening within you or in your life. Although such a dreams may bring about feelings of fear and anxiety, it is no cause for alarm and is often considered a positive symbol. Dreams of experiencing your own death usually means that big changes are ahead for you. You are moving on to new beginnings and leaving the past behind. These changes does not necessarily imply a negative turn of events. Metaphorically, dying can be seen as an end or a termination to your old ways and habits. So, dying does not always mean a physical death, but an ending of something.

On a negative note, to dream that you die may represent involvement in deeply painful relationships or unhealthy, destructive behaviors. You may feeling depressed or feel strangled by a situation or person in your waking life. Perhaps your mind is preoccupied with someone who is terminally ill or dying. Alternatively, you may be trying to get out of some obligation, responsibility or other situation.

To see someone dying in your dream, signifies that your feelings for that person are dead or that a significant change/loss is occurring in your relationship with that person. Alternatively, you may want to repress that aspect of yourself that is represented by the dying person.

Diet

To dream that you are on a diet, suggests that you are punishing yourself. You are feeling restrained from what you really want to do. Alternatively, it indicates self-control and self-discipline. You are giving up the things that are unhealthy in your life.

Difficulty

To dream that you are having difficulties, signifies temporary embarrassment and the threat of ill health.

To dream that you are having difficulties with your lover, denotes the contrary and that you will have a pleasant courtship.

Digging

To dream that you are digging, signifies that you are working too hard in trying to uncover the truth in a problem that is haunting you. You may also be preoccupied with trying to find out about yourself , your reputation, and your self-identity.

To dream that you dig a hole and find something shiny, signifies a favorable turn in your fortune.

To dream that you dig a hole and fill it with water, denotes that no matter how hard you try, your efforts will not make things go your way. You need to learn to compromise.

Dining Room

To dream that you are in a dining room, represents your quest for knowledge and understanding. You may be reaching an important decision in your life.

Dinner

To dream that you are eating dinner alone, indicates that you will need to do some serious thinking about your goals and direction in life. Alternatively, it may represent independence or lack of social skills.

To dream that you are eating dinner with others, signifies your acceptance or others, your interpersonal relationships, and how you behave in your social life. It is a time to reflect and share past experiences. It also suggests that you see everyone as an equal.

Dinosaur

To see a dinosaur in your dream, symbolizes an outdated attitude. You may need to discard your old ways of thinking and habits.

To dream that you are being chased by a dinosaur, indicates your fears of no longer being needed or useful. Alternatively, being chased by a dinosaur, may reflect old issues that are still coming back to haunt you.

Diploma

To see or receive a diploma in your dream, symbolizes completion and/or recognition for a job well done.

Directions

To dream that you are following directions, represents your need or ability to accept criticism. It also relates to your feelings about authority.

To dream that you are giving directions, refers to your goals and search for purpose. You are on a path toward self-realization.

Dirt

To see freshly stirred dirt in your dream, symbolizes thriftiness and frugalness. Dirt is also representative of situations where you have been less than honorable and may have acted in a devious manner.

To dream that someone throws dirt at you, denotes that enemies will try to attack your character and harm your reputation.

To dream that your clothes are soiled with dirt, signifies of a contagious disease that you have been stricken with.

Dirty

To dream that you or something is dirty, represents your anxieties and feelings toward sex. The dream stems from low self-esteem and feelings of being unworthy. You need to purify your mind, heart and body.

Disability

To dream that you have a disability, indicates that you are experiencing a lowered self-esteem. You have lost your power or direction in life. Perhaps you are not utilizing your full potential and skills. Consider the symbolism of the part of your body that is disabled.

Disappear

To dream that people or objects are disappearing right before your eyes, signifies your anxiety and insecurities over the notion that loved ones might disappear out of your life. You may feel that you cannot depend on someone and feel that you are alone and inadequate. You need to work on your self-image and self-esteem.

Alternatively, to dream that someone is disappearing suggests that you may not have given sufficient attention to those aspects/qualities of that person within your own self. Have you lost touch with some aspect of yourself?

Disappointment

To dream of disappointment, indicates real-life experiences of being continually disappointed. Such dreams often reflect repressed disappointments accumulated over a period of time. You dream serves as an emotional outlet which can provide ease of mind.

Disapproval

To dream of disapproval, indicates that you are rejecting or ignoring some aspect of yourself. It may also represent your own feelings of self-worth and being accepted.

Disaster

To dream that you are in a disaster, represents your fear of change. You are afraid of not knowing what is in store for you in the future.

Discovery

To dream of a discovery in your dream, signifies that you may be entering into a new phase of life or a new phase of personal development.

Please See Also Find.

Disease

To dream that you are inflicted with a disease, foretells that you will catch a slight cold or cough. Sometimes you dreams are able to spot an illness before you are aware of the symptoms.

To dream that you have an incurable disease, foretells that you will be single and loving it.

Disgrace

To dream that you have been disgraced, signifies that you have a low moral character and are lowering your reputation even more.

To dream that you are worried about the disgraceful conducts of others, symbolizes your unsatisfying hopes and pestering worries that continue to hover over your head.

affodil

To see daffodils in your dream, symbolizes renewal, inner growth, optimism, inspiration, and hope.

Dagger

To dream of being attacked by someone with a dagger, warns of physical injury from an enemy or a mugger. You may feel that you have been stabbed in the back by somebody.

To dream that you take a dagger from somebody's hand, means you will overcome hardships and misfortune.

Dahlias

To see dahlias in a dream, signifies good fortune in financial matters.

To see dahlias that are dying and wilting, signifies loss and sorrow.

Dairy

To dream that you are in a dairy, is a good omen. Much fortune will come your way and you will never be without the basic necessities in life.

Daisy

To see daisies in your dream, symbolizes freshness, beauty, innocence, simplicity, friendliness, and cleanliness.

To dream that someone gives you a bouquet of daisies, symbolizes sorrow and/or lost love.

To dream of walking in a field of daisies, represents good luck and prosperity. Someone will be there to offer you a helping hand and guidance for your problems.

Dalmatian

To see a Dalmatian in you dream, suggests that you tend to overlook your own feelings and tend to the needs of others. You are a people pleaser.

Dam

To see a dam in your dream, signifies repressed emotions or feelings that needs to be released. To dream of a bursting dam, denotes that you have lost control of your anger and are overwhelmed with emotions.

Damask Rose

To see a damask rosebush growing in the wild, foretells of a wedding in the family.

To dream that you receive a bouquet of damask rose, foretells that you will find a faithful and true lover.

For a woman, to dream that you receive a damask rose and places it in her hair, signifies that she will be deceived by someone who she thought was a good friend.

Damson

To see a damson tree full with fruit in your dream, signifies riches and that you will be well-rewarded.

To dream that you are picking the plums out of the damson tree and eating them, signifies that you will experience some loss and sorrow. A dark cloud will hover over you.

Dance

To dream that you are dancing, signifies freedom from constraints and harmony/balance with yourself. You are working in cooperation with yourself. It also represents frivolity, happiness, gracefulness, sensuality and sexual desires. Alternatively, it may signify intimacy and a union of the masculine and feminine aspects of yourself.

To dream that you are attending or going to a dance, indicates a celebration and your attempts to achieve happiness. Consider the phrase the "dance of life" which suggests creation, ecstasy, and going with what life has to offer you.

To see children dancing in your dream, signifies that you will have a comfortable home, and healthy, well-behaved children in the future.

To see ritualistic dancing in your dream, denotes your need to get in touch with the spirit within..

Dance Recital

To see a dance recital in your dream, signifies that you will be moving to another place to live.

To dream that you participate in a dance recital, signifies that you will be in conflict with your co-workers or classmates.

Dandelion

To see dandelions in your dream, foretells of pleasurable surroundings and joyous future for you and your lover.

To dream that you are eating dandelions, signifies that you need to take better care of your health or suffer ill consequences.

Dandruff

To dream that you have dandruff, indicates that you are misusing your energy. You may have been under a lot of stress and tension. You should rethink the way you are approaching any of your current problems. Alternatively, this dream may suggest a lack of self-esteem.

Danger

To dream that you are in danger and are wounded or killed, signifies substantial losses in business and discouraging prospects in love. You need to be more cautious in some aspect of your life.

To dream that you escape from danger, signifies that you will rise to a place of high position and honor in your business and social circle.

Darkness

To dream that darkness comes upon you, signifies failure in work you may attempt. Darkness is synonymous with ignorance, the unconscious, evil, death, and fear of the unknown. If the sun breaks through the darkness, then you will overcome your failures. If you feel safe in the dark, then it suggests that you like not knowing about certain things. As some might say, ignorance is bliss.

To dream that you cannot find someone in the darkness, signifies that you need to keep your temper in check. You have the tendency to let your emotions get out of control and lose your temper.

To dream that you are lost in the darkness, denotes feelings of desperation, depression, or insecurity.

To dream that you are groping around in the darkness, indicates that you have insufficient information to make a clear decision. Do your research and do not rush into making choices.

Darkroom

To dream that you are in a darkroom, suggests that you are waiting for something to happen or to see what might develop in a situation.

Dartboard

To see a dartboard in your dream, indicates that you are feeling hostility from someone. You need to express your anger and feelings more directly. Alternatively, the dartboard may symbolize a goal that you are aiming for. You need to try and take a shot at something new and overcome your fear of failure.

Darts

To dream that you are throwing darts in your dream, refers to some hurtful or harmful remarks that you or someone have said. Alternatively, it represents your goals and your "go-getter" attitude.

Date

To dream that you are on a date, suggests that you are getting to know some hidden aspects of yourself. You are acknowledging your hidden talents. Alternatively, it may reflect your anxieties about dating or finding acceptance.

Dates

To see plump ripe dates growing on a tree, signifies that the next few days will be happy occasions. Take this time to relax and find peace of mind.

To dream that you are eating dates, signifies distress. You are never happy with what you have. You are always concern with you wants and trying to acquiring these material things.

Daughter

To see your daughter in your dream, represents your waking relationship with your daughter and the qualities that she projects. If you do not have a daughter, then it symbolizes the feminine aspect within yourself.

Daughter-In-Law

To see your daughter-in-law in your dream, signifies that an unusual and unexpected incident will either give you much happiness or distress, depending on her demeanor in your dream.

Dawn

To see the dawn in your dream, signifies rejuvenation, enlightenment, and vitality. You may be emerging out of a new stage in life, possess a new understanding, or have a new start in life

Day

To dream of a sunny day, symbolizes clarity and/or pleasantness. You are seeing things clearly.

To dream of a gloomy or cloudy day, signifies loss.

Daybreak

To dream that the day breaks, signifies success in your projects and endeavors.

Dead

To see the dead in your dream, forewarns that you are being influenced by negative people and are hanging around the wrong crowd. You may suffer material loss. This dream may also be a way for you to resolve your feelings with those who have passed on.

If you dream of a person who has died a long time ago, then it suggests that a current situation or relationship in you life resembles the quality of that deceased person. The dream may depict how you need to let this situation or relationship die and end it.

To see and talk with your dead parents in your dreams, represents your fears of losing them or your way of coping with the loss. You may want that last opportunity to say your final good-byes to them.

To see your dead sibling, relative, or friend alive in your dream, indicates that you miss them and are trying to relive your old experiences you had with them. In trying to keep up with the pace of your daily waking life, you dreams may serve as your only outlet in coping and coming to terms with the loss of a loved one.

Please see also Die.

Deaf

To dream that you are deaf, indicates that you are feeling secluded from the world, You may be closing yourself off from new experiences or shutting yourself out.

To dream that someone else is deaf, suggests that someone close to you is withdrawn.

Death

To dream about the death of a loved one, suggests that you are lacking a certain aspect or quality that the loved one embodies. Ask yourself what makes this person special or what do you like about him. It is that very quality that you are lacking in your own relationship or circumstances. Alternatively, it indicates that whatever that person represents has no part in your own life.

Debt

To dream that you are in debt, signifies struggle, worries and troubles in business and love.

Decapitation

To dream that you are decapitated, indicates that you are not thinking clearly are are refusing to see the truth. You need to confront the situation or the person despite the pain and discomfort you might feel in doing so. The dream also suggests that you have the tendency to act before you think.

*Please see also Behead.

Decay

To see something decay in your dream, signifies the degradation of a situation or circumstance. It may also represent the death of an old situation before the rebirth into a new stage.

December

To dream of the month of December, signifies increased wealth, but loss of friends.

Deceased

*Please See Dead.

Deck

To dream that you are out on the deck, represents your connection with your Self and with nature. You need to be more aware of your surroundings and appreciate the environment.

Decorate

To dream that you are decorating an area, signifies a favorable turn in business or studies and increased social pleasures.

Deeds

To dream that you a signing a deed, foretells of a lawsuit in which you will most likely lose.

Deer

To see a deer in your dream, symbolizes grace, gentleness, and natural beauty. It has feminine qualities and may point to the feminine aspect within yourself. It also represents independence and virility. Consider the symbol to be a pun for someone who is "dear" to you.

If the deer is black, then it means that you are not acknowledging or are rejected the feminine qualities in you. You may not be in tune with your feminine side.

To dream that you kill a dear, suggests that you are trying to suppress those feminine qualities.

Defecate

To dream that you are defecating on someone, indicates your anger and hostility for that person.

To dream that you are being defecated on, represents feelings of guilt and unworthiness. You may be suffering from low self-esteem.

Please see also Bowel Movement or Feces.

Deformed

To dream that you or someone is deformed, represents undeveloped aspects of yourself that you may have ignored. You refusal to acknowledge these characteristics may be affecting your performance and creative flow.

Delight

To dream that you are experiencing delight, signifies a favorable and positive turn of events and much pleasantness.

Demons

To see demons in your dream, represents ignorance, negativity, distress or your shadow self. It also forewarns of overindulgence and letting lust give way to your better judgment. As a result, your physical and mental health may suffer.

To dream that you are possessed by demons, indicates ultimate helplessness.

Den

To dream that you are in the den, signifies work, industry, and efficiency.

Dentist

To dream that you are at the dentist, signifies periodic doubt over the sincerity and honor of some person. You may have some anxiety or fear of pain, but in the long run it will be for your own good.

To dream that the dentist working on somebody else's teeth, signifies that you will be shocked by scandal near you.

Deodorant

To see or put on deodorant in your dream, represents your inner strength and your ability to rid yourself of harmful and destructive behaviors.

Depression

To feel depressed in your dream, refers to your inability to make connections. You are unable to see the causes of your problems and consequences of your decisions.

Derrick

To see derricks in your dream, symbolizes obstacles standing in your road towards success.

Desert

To dream that you are walking through a desert, signifies loss and misfortune. You may be suffering from an attack on your reputation. Deserts are also symbolic of barrenness, loneliness and feelings of isolation and hopelessness.

Desk

To see or sit at your desk in your dream, suggests that you are evaluating and weighing your problems. It is indicative of self-exploration and discovery.

Despair

To dream that you are in despair, signifies that you will have many hardships and experience much cruelties in the working world.

To dream that others are in despair, denotes that some friend or relative will be in great distress and find themselves in a unhappy situation.

Dessert

To see a tasty dessert in your dream, represents indulgence, celebration, reward, or temptation. You are enjoying the good things in life.

Destruction

To dream about mass destruction, suggests that there is some chaos occurring in your life. Things may not be going the way you want it to. Perhaps the choices your are making are self-destructive.

Detective

To see a detective in your dream, signifies the thrills and dangers of an aspect of your waking life.

To dream that you are a detective, indicates that you are searching for your hidden abilities and talents. It also signifies that you are trying to solve a problem and seek the truth about an issue that is worrying you.

To dream that you are being followed by a detective, signifies guilt. Your character will be put under scrutiny and called into question.

Detergent

To see or use detergent in your dream, indicates that you need to resolve a major problem in your life. You may also need to clean up your image and attitude.

Determination

To dream that you have determination, represents your ambition and realization of your goals. It refers to your attitude and the restrictions that you or others impose onto you.

Detour

To see a detour in your dream, signifies that you have encountered an obstacle in some aspect of your life. You may not want to confront something directly and thus must try to find a way around it.

Devil

To see the devil in your dream, signifies negative aspects of yourself. It may also indicate feelings of guilt that you have been harboring. It is time to release these feelings. Alternatively, the devil may represent intelligence, cunningness, deception, and cleverness.

To dream that you fought off the devil, symbolizes that you will succeed in defeating your enemies.

To dream that the devil talks to you, signifies that you will find some temptations hard to resist even though you know it is not in your best interest.

To dream that you and the devils were in friendly terms, suggests that you may be seduced and tempted into doing something you do not want to do. You may be dealing with issues of morality.

Devotion

To dream that you are showing your devotion to your beliefs, serves as a reminder that nothing will be gained by deceit.

Dew

To dream that the dew is falling on your, signifies that you will be stricken with fever or some illness.

To see the dew sparkling in the grass, denotes honor and wealth.

Diadem

To see a diadem in your dream, signifies that some honor will soon be bestowed onto you.

Please Also See Crown.

Diamonds

To see diamonds in your dream, signifies the wholeness of the Self. You may be finding clarity in matters that have been clouding you. It may also point to your unchanging or unyielding nature. Alternatively, it represents vanity and conceit. You may be distancing yourself from others.

Diaper

To see or wear a diaper in your dream, symbolizes your childish or babyish attitudes/actions. You may be too dependent on others.

To dream that you are changing diapers, suggests a need to clean up you behavior and change your childish ways. Perhaps you need to change your attitude and approach regarding a new idea or project.

To see dirty diapers in your dream, indicates that you need to clean the mess you have created with your childishness.

Diarrhea

To dream that you have diarrhea, signifies that some part of your life is going out of control or that you can no longer contain your strong emotions. Alternatively, it may indicate a need for you to get something out of your system quickly. It may also indicate that you have not analyzed a situation long enough or that you do not want to deal with the problem at all.

Please see also Bowel Movement.

Diary

Please See Journal.

Dice

To see dice in your dream, signifies misfortune in the stock market and consequent misery and despair. They represent chance and fate.

To see your lover throwing dice, symbolizes his unworthiness.

Dictator

To see or dream that you are a dictator, suggests that you need to be more flexible and open-minded in our thinking and in your decision making. You are being too controlling.

Dictionary

To dream that you are using a dictionary, signifies that you rely too much on the opinions of others in the management of your own affairs.

Die

To dream that you die in your dream, symbolizes inner changes, transformation, self-discovery and positive development that is happening within you or in your life. Although such a dreams may bring about feelings of fear and anxiety, it is no cause for alarm and is often considered a positive symbol. Dreams of experiencing your own death usually means that big changes are ahead for you. You are moving on to new beginnings and leaving the past behind. These changes does not necessarily imply a negative turn of events. Metaphorically, dying can be seen as an end or a termination to your old ways and habits. So, dying does not always mean a physical death, but an ending of something.

On a negative note, to dream that you die may represent involvement in deeply painful relationships or unhealthy, destructive behaviors. You may feeling depressed or feel strangled by a situation or person in your waking life. Perhaps your mind is preoccupied with someone who is terminally ill or dying. Alternatively, you may be trying to get out of some obligation, responsibility or other situation.

To see someone dying in your dream, signifies that your feelings for that person are dead or that a significant change/loss is occurring in your relationship with that person. Alternatively, you may want to repress that aspect of yourself that is represented by the dying person.

Diet

To dream that you are on a diet, suggests that you are punishing yourself. You are feeling restrained from what you really want to do. Alternatively, it indicates self-control and self-discipline. You are giving up the things that are unhealthy in your life.

Difficulty

To dream that you are having difficulties, signifies temporary embarrassment and the threat of ill health.

To dream that you are having difficulties with your lover, denotes the contrary and that you will have a pleasant courtship.

Digging

To dream that you are digging, signifies that you are working too hard in trying to uncover the truth in a problem that is haunting you. You may also be preoccupied with trying to find out about yourself , your reputation, and your self-identity.

To dream that you dig a hole and find something shiny, signifies a favorable turn in your fortune.

To dream that you dig hole and fill it with water, denotes that no matter how hard you try, your efforts will not make things go your way. You need to learn to compromise.

Dining Room

To dream that you are in a dining room, represents your quest for knowledge and understanding. You may be reaching an important decision in your life.

Dinner

To dream that you are eating dinner alone, indicates that you will need to do some serious thinking about your goals and direction in life. Alternatively, it may represent independence or lack of social skills.

To dream that you are eating dinner with others, signifies your acceptance or others, your interpersonal relationships, and how you behave in your social life. It is a time to reflect and share past experiences. It also suggests that you see everyone as an equal.

Dinosaur

To see a dinosaur in your dream, symbolizes an outdated attitude. You may need to discard your old ways of thinking and habits.

To dream that you are being chased by a dinosaur, indicates your fears of no longer being needed or useful. Alternatively, being chased by a dinosaur, may reflect old issues that are still coming back to haunt you.

Diploma

To see or receive a diploma in your dream, symbolizes completion and/or recognition for a job well done.

Directions

To dream that you are following directions, represents your need or ability to accept criticism. It also relates to your feelings about authority.

To dream that you are giving directions, refers to your goals and search for purpose. You are on a path toward self-realization.

Dirt

To see freshly stirred dirt in your dream, symbolizes thriftiness and frugalness. Dirt is also representative of situations where you have been less than honorable and may have acted in a devious manner.

To dream that someone throws dirt at you, denotes that enemies will try to attack your character and harm your reputation.

To dream that your clothes are soiled with dirt, signifies of a contagious disease that you have been stricken with.

Dirty

To dream that you or something is dirty, represents your anxieties and feelings toward sex. The dream stems from low self-esteem and feelings of being unworthy. You need to purify your mind, heart and body.

Disability

To dream that you have a disability, indicates that you are experiencing a lowered self-esteem. You have lost your power or direction in life. Perhaps you are not utilizing your full potential and skills. Consider the symbolism of the part of your body that is disabled.

Disappear

To dream that people or objects are disappearing right before your eyes, signifies your anxiety and insecurities over the notion that loved ones might disappear out of your life. You may feel that you cannot depend on someone and feel that you are alone and inadequate. You need to work on your self-image and self-esteem.

Alternatively, to dream that someone is disappearing suggests that you may not have given sufficient attention to those aspects/qualities of that person within your own self. Have you lost touch with some aspect of yourself?

Disappointment

To dream of disappointment, indicates real-life experiences of being continually disappointed. Such dreams often reflect repressed disappointments accumulated over a period of time. You dream serves as an emotional outlet which can provide ease of mind.

Disapproval

To dream of disapproval, indicates that you are rejecting or ignoring some aspect of yourself. It may also represent your own feelings of self-worth and being accepted.

Disaster

To dream that you are in a disaster, represents your fear of change. You are afraid of not knowing what is in store for you in the future.

Discovery

To dream of a discovery in your dream, signifies that you may be entering into a new phase of life or a new phase of personal development.

*Please See Also Find.

Disease

To dream that you are inflicted with a disease, foretells that you will catch a slight cold or cough. Sometimes you dreams are able to spot an illness before you are aware of the symptoms.

To dream that you have an incurable disease, foretells that you will be single and loving it.

Disgrace

To dream that you have been disgraced, signifies that you have a low moral character and are lowering your reputation even more.

To dream that you are worried about the disgraceful conducts of others, symbolizes your unsatisfying hopes and pestering worries that continue to hover over your head.

Disguise

To dream that you are in a disguise. signifies that you are hiding from something or someone in your waking life. It is time to face reality and stop hiding behind a facade.

Dislike

To dream that you dislike someone or are disliked in your dream, represents an aspect of yourself that you do not like or are trying to suppress. Who are you inside and how you are acting on the outside are out of sync. You are not being true to yourself.

Disgust

To feel disgust in your dream, represents an unacknowledged or denied aspect of your own self. It also suggests that you fear confrontation and lack the means to defend and/or protect yourself.

Dishes

To see dishes in your dream, represents ideas, concepts, and attitudes. It may also be a fun for what you are "dishing" out to others. If the dishes are dirty and unwashed, then it signifies dissatisfaction and an unpromising outlook. You may have overlooked some problems in your life or you have not confronted your emotions.

To dream that you are washing dishes, suggests that you are moving on and planning for the next thing that comes your way.

To see shelves of polished dishes, suggests that you are doing your best and making the best out of a situation. You are trying to make a good impression.

To see broken dishes in your dream, signifies feelings of poverty, lack, and inadequacy. You may feel that you are not meeting the expectations of others.

Please See Also Plates.

Disinherited

To dream that you have been disinherited, forewarns that you should reevaluate your social and business standing. You may not be in such solid ground as you thought.

Diskette

To see a diskette in your dream, indicates that you are given some information which you should incorporate into some situation or aspect of your life. It may also refer to how ideas and advises are being passed on to others.

Dismemberment

To dream that you are dismembered, suggests that some situation or circumstance is falling apart in your waking life. You are feeling disempowered and experiencing some great and significant loss.

Disown

To dream that you have been disowned, signifies that you need to change your old habits and take charge of the situation.

Dispute

To dream that you are having disputes with your loved ones, signifies that a job transfer or relocation.

To dream that you are having disputes over trivial matters, signifies your unfairness in judging others.

Distress

To dream that you or others are in distress, suggest that things will turn out better than you expected. You will find that all your worries were for nothing and need to lighten up.

Ditch

To see a ditch in your dream, forewarns that there is something in your waking life that you need to avoid. Consider the symbol to also be pun and as en expression of your guilt for ditching school, work, appointment, etc.

To dream that you fall into a ditch, indicates that you may be headed into a pitfall.

Diving

To dream that you are diving into clear water, signifies an end to an embarrassing situation. Although you may experience some temporary setbacks, things will surely look up. Additionally, this dream may mean that you are trying to get to the bottom of a current situation and the root of your problems or feelings. It may also refer exploration of your unconscious.

To dream that you are diving into muddy water, signifies that you will suffer anxiety from the path of your affairs.

To see others diving in your dream, represents psychological and emotional balance.

To see animals diving in your dream, suggests that are exploring your instinctual and sexual urges which you have previously suppressed into your unconscious.

Divorce

To dream that you are getting a divorce, indicates that you need to differentiate between things in your life and prioritize them. Alternatively, it may mean that you have a fear of separation. Also you may be not be satisfied with your present relationship. Divorce dreams may reflect real-life events and the stress that it brings. You may be wondering if you have made a mistake in some situation or decision Divorce dreams suggest a transitional phase or a time to change your old habits.

Dizzy

To dream that you feel dizzy, symbolizes confusion. You are unable to make a decision or make up your mind about something. Concentrate of a focal point and learn to balance your choices.

DNA

To dream about DNA, suggests that you need to focus and carefully plot out everything in order to move ahead in life. Learn from the negativity that you have experienced. The dream may also represent the initials "D" and "A". Consider who or what in your life has these initials.

Docks

To dream that you are on the docks, suggests that you have successfully gotten through some tough times and emotions.

Doctor

To dream that you are seeing the doctor, denotes discouraging illness and strife amongst members of your family. It may signal your need for emotional and spiritual healing.

To dream of a doctor in a social atmosphere, foretells of good health and prosperity.

To dream that you marry a doctor, forewarns that you are being deceived by someone or a situation.

Dog

To see a dog in your dream, indicate a skill that you have ignored or forgotten, but needs to be activated. Alternatively, dogs may symbolize intuition, loyalty, generosity, protection, and fidelity. Your own values and intentions will enable you to go forward in the world and succeed. If the dog is vicious and/or growling, then it signifies some inner conflict within yourself. It may indicate betrayal and untrustworthiness. If the dog is dead or dying, then it indicates a loss of a good friend. Alternatively, it represents a deterioration of your instincts.

To dream that a dog bites your on the leg, suggests that you have lost your ability to balance aspects of your life. You may be hesitant in approaching a new situation or have no desire to move forward with your goals.

To see a happily barking dog in your dream, symbolizes pleasures and much social activity. If the dog is barking ferociously, then it represents your habit of making demands on people and controlling situations around you. It could also mean unfriendly companions.

To dream that you are buying a dog, indicates your tendency to buy your friends or buy compliments/favors. Alternatively, it suggest a need for you to find companionship.

To dream that you are dressing up your dog, signifies your attempts to cover up your own character flaws and habits.

Also consider the notions associated with the word dog, such as loyalty ("man's best friend") and to be "treated like a dog".

**See The Meaning In Action: "_The Bunny Dog_" & _Dogs In The Bathroom_"

Dog House

To see a dog house in your dream, may indicate that you are in big trouble. You are being punished for your actions.

Doll

To dream that a doll comes to life, signifies your desires to be someone else and escape from your present problems and responsibilities. Dolls may serve as a means to act out your wishes.

To see a doll in your dream, symbolizes childhood innocence and light-hearted fun.

To dream that you are playing with a doll, represents a lack of communication between you conscious and unconscious mind. You may also have an immature attitude towards the opposite sex.

Dollhouse

To see or play with a dollhouse in your dream, symbolizes your idealistic notions about family life. Alternatively, the dollhouse in your dream may serve as an indirect way to solve and work out waking problems with family members.

Dolphins

To see a dolphin in your dream, symbolizes spiritual guidance, your intellect, mental attributes and emotional trust. Utilize your mind to its capacity and you will move upward in life. Alternatively, it suggests that a line of communication has been established between the conscious and unconscious aspects of yourself. Dolphins represent your willingness and ability to explore and navigate through your emotions.

To dream that you are riding a dolphin, represents your optimism and social altruism.

Dome

To see a dome in your dream, signifies that you will never fully achieve your goals.

To dream that you are in the dome of a building, signifies some honor that will be bestowed upon you.

Dominoes

To dream that you are playing dominoes and win, foretells that you will be drawn into sinful pleasures, which will bring much distress to your family and relatives.

To dream that you are playing dominoes and lose, denotes that your indiscreetness with the opposite sex will bring much easiness to a friend who has much concern for your safety.

Donkey

To see a donkey in your dream, represents your stubbornness and unyielding personality. You are unwilling to cooperate with others. If the donkey is dead, then it denotes that your party hearty attitude will lead to unrestrained immorality.

To dream that you fall off or are thrown from a donkey, indicates disharmony in love which will lead to a separation.

To dream that you are kicked by a donkey, suggests that you are involved in illicit activities, which will bring your much anxiety and fear that you will be caught.

To dream that you are leading a donkey by a halter, signifies your leadership in every situation and your way of convincing people to see things your way.

Donuts

*Please see _Doughnuts_.

Door

To dream that you are entering through a door, signifies new opportunities that will be presented before you. You are entering into a new stage in your life and moving from one level of consciousness to another. In particular, a door that opens to the outside, signifies your need to be more accessible to others, whereas a door that opens into the inside, denotes your desire for inner exploration and self-discovery.

To see opened doors in your dream, symbolizes your receptiveness and willingness to accept new ideas/concepts. In particular, to see a light behind it suggests that you are moving toward greater enlightenment/spirituality.

To dream that the doors are locked, signifies opportunities that are denied and not available to you or that you have missed out on. In particular, if you are outside the locked door, then it suggests that you are having some anti-social tendencies. If you are inside the locked door, then it represents harsh lessons that need to be learned.

To dream that you are locking doors, suggests that you are closing yourself off from others. You are hesitant in letting others in and revealing your feelings. It is indicative of some fear and low self-worth.

To see revolving doors in your dream, suggests that you are literally moving in circles and going no where. You may feel that your opportunities and choices lead to a dead end.

Doorbell

To dream that you hear or ring a door bell, indicates that you are open to new experiences. The dream may also be calling attention to something that you have overlooked. Perhaps you do not yet realize that an opportunity is open to you.

Door Knocker

*Please see Knocker.

Dormitory

To dream that you are in a dormitory, represents the value you place on knowledge and education. You believe that you are always learning and not just in the classroom. If you are currently a college student who live in a dormitory, then this symbol may just be a reflection of your current surroundings and hold similar meaning as a house.

Doughnuts

To see a doughnut in your dream, represents the Self. It suggests that you may be feeling lost and still trying to find yourself and your purpose in life. Alternatively, it refers to growth, development and nurturance. You are not completely whole.

Doves

To see doves in your dream, symbolizes peace, tranquility, harmony, and innocence. In particular, to see white doves in your dream, symbolizes loyalty and friendships. It may also represent a message and blessing from the Holy Spirit. You have let go of your thoughts of hate and revenge.

To dream that doves are mating and building a nest, symbolizes a joyous home life filled with tranquility, pleasure and obedient children.

Down

To dream that you are moving down, suggests that you have made a wrong decision or headed toward the wrong direction in life. "Going down" may also sexual connotation and be a metaphor for oral sex.

Downtown

To dream that you are in downtown, represents your material concerns and possessions. It may indicate the hustle and bustle of your life.

Dowry

To dream that you fail to receive a dowry, signifies that you will have to work extremely hard in life and put up with the cutthroat business world or you may see yourself living in poverty.

Drafted

To dream that you have been drafted, indicates that the opinions and beliefs of others are being forced upon you. You are feeling pressure from those around you who want you to do something that you are not comfortable with.

Dragon

To see a dragon in your dream, signifies that you tend to let yourself get carried away by your passion. This kind of behavior may lead you into trouble. You need to exercise some self-control.

In the eastern cultures, dragons are seen as spiritual creatures symbolizing good luck and fortune.

To dream that you are a dragon and breathing fire and everyone, suggests that you are using your anger to get your own way.

Dragonfly

To see a dragonfly in your dream, symbolizes changes. It may also indicate that something in our life may not not appear as it seems.

To dream that you are eating a dragonfly, suggests that you are consumed by some sort of passion even at the risk of offending or hurting other's feelings.

Drain

To see a drain in your dream, signifies your need to release and channel your emotions. You should not kept you feeling inside. Alternatively, it may represent a wasted effort or loss. Consider the dream to also be a pun on something that may be draining you of your energy.

Drainer

To see a drainer in your dream, suggests that you are getting rid of your excessive emotions. Or on the other hand, it could imply that you are feeling emotionally drained.

Drama

To dream that you are writing a drama, denotes that you will suddenly find yourself submerged in debt and distress.

To see a drama in your dream, signifies that you will be reunited with old friends.

Drapes

To dream that you are closing the drapes, suggests that you are blocking out outside worries and problems. You are shielding yourself from the world.

Drawbridge

To see a drawbridge in your dream, represents protection. You may feel that some relationship or situation is too invasive. It may also mean that you are drawing the line and creating boundaries.

Drawers

To see drawers in your dream, signifies your inner and hidden state and being. So a disorderly drawer represents internal chaos and turmoil while an orderly drawer signifies order.

Drawing

To dream that you are drawing, may be an expression of your latent creative and artistic abilities.

Dreams

To dream that you are dreaming, signifies your emotional state. You are excessively worried and fearful about a situation or circumstance that you are going through.

Dress

To see or wear a dress in your dream, represents a feminine outlook or feminine perspective on a situation. You are freely expressing your femininity.

To dream that you are wearing a white dress, suggests that you want to appear pure and angelic toward others.

Dressing

To dream that you are having trouble getting dressed, signifies that some evil person will preoccupy your mind to the point where you are not able to enjoy your daily life and its pleasure.

To dream that you are dressed in white, foretells that you will have longevity and good health throughout your life.

Drill

To see a drill in your dream, indicates that you are headed toward a new direction in life. You are opening yourself up to new experiences and insights.

Drinking

To dream that you are drinking water, represents spiritual refreshment. You will find resolution by looking within yourself and your past.

To dream that you are drinking alcohol, denotes that you are seeking either pleasure or escape.

Dripping

To dream that something is dripping, suggests that you are slowly losing your spiritual will. You are experiencing something disturbing which is affecting your psyche and well-being.

Driver's License

To see your driver's license in your dream, suggests that you are facing identity crisis.

To lose your driver's license in your dream, indicates that you have lost your true identity. Perhaps you have lost the autonomy to move forward toward your goals.

Driveway

To see or drive up to a driveway in your dream, symbolizes an end to your journey. It also represents security and rest. Alternatively, it denotes your path toward achieving inner peace finding your spirituality.

Driving

To dream that you are driving a vehicle, signifies your life's journey and your path in life. The dream is telling of how you are moving and navigating through life. If you are driving and cannot see the road ahead of you, then it indicates that you do not know where you are headed in life and what you really want to do with yourself. You are lacking direction and goals. If you are driving on a curvy road, then it indicates that you are have difficulties in achieving your goals and the changes associated with it.

To dream that someone else is driving you, represents your dependence on the driver. You are not in control of your life and following the goals of others instead of your own. If you are driving from the passenger side of a car, then it suggests that you are trying to gain control of the path that your life is taking. You are beginning to make your own decisions.

To dream that you are driving a cab or bus, symbolizes menial labor with little opportunities for advancement.

To dream that you are driving a car in reverse, suggests that you are experiencing major setbacks in your goals. In particular, if you drive in reverse into a pool of water, then it means that you emotions are literally holding you back.

To dream that you are driving drunk, indicates that your life is out of control. Some relationship or somebody is dominating you.

To dream that you drive off a mountain road, suggests that the higher you climb in life, the harder it is to stay at the top. You feel that your advanced position is a precarious one. It takes hard work to remain at the top. You may also feel that you are not able to measure up to the expectations of others.

Dromedary

To see a dromedary in your dream, signifies unexpected gains and honor. You are a giving person and always there to lend a helping hand.

Drooling

To dream that you are drooling, suggests that you are feeling foolish or embarrassed by some situation. On the other hand, you may be taking things to seriously and need to let loose.

Drop

To dream that you are dropping things, indicates that you are letting go some project, relationship, person, or idea. Also analyze the significance of what is being dropped. Alternatively, it may represent your carelessness. Perhaps you are expressing some dismay or regret in how you let something slip through fingers.

Drowning

To dream that you are drowning, signifies that you are overwhelmed by emotions or repressed issues that is coming back to haunt you. You may be proceeding too quickly in trying to discover your unconscious thoughts and therefore must proceed more cautiously and slowly. If you drown to death, then is refers to an emotional rebirth. If your survive the drowning, then a waking relationship or situation will ultimately survive the turmoil.

To see someone drowning in your dream, suggests that you are becoming too deeply involved in something that is beyond your control. Alternatively, it represents a sense of loss in your own identity. You are unable to differentiate who you are anymore.

To dream that you rescue someone from drowning, indicates that you have successfully acknowledged certain emotions and characteristics that is symbolized by the drowning victim.

**See The Meaning In Action: "<u>Dogs In The Bathroom</u>"

Drugs

To dream that you are in possession of or taking drugs, signifies your need for a "quick fix". You may be turning to a potentially harmful alternative as an instant escape from your problems. Ask yourself why you need the drugs. What do you hope the drugs will achieve for you?

Drums

To dream that you are playing the drums, indicates that you progress through life by your own terms. You are strong willed and stick by the decisions you make.

Drunk

To dream that you are drunk, suggests that you are acting careless and insensible. You are losing control of your life and have lost a grip on reality.

Dryer

To dream that you are using a dryer, suggests that you need to start dealing with your emotions. The dream may also signify a dry idea that fails to bring any excitement and thrill.

Duck

To see ducks in your dream, either represents spiritual freedom (if flying) or it represents the unconscious (if swimming). Ducks are rather multi-talented animals that can walk, swim and fly and thus may represent your flexibility and in blending into various situations. Alternatively, the dream may also indicate that you are setting yourself up or being set up for the kill as associated by the phrase "sitting duck". Also, the duck may be a pun on "ducking" some issue or situation, instead of confronting it head-on.

To see a white duck in your dream, signifies falsehood and deceit.

Duel

To dream that you are in a duel, signifies inner conflicts in which you need to find a middle ground between the two extremes. You need to stop seeing things in black and white.

Dulcimer

To see a dulcimer in your dream, signifies carefree attitudes and a life where your desires will be happily realized.

Dumb

To dream that you are dumb, denotes your inability to persuade others to see your point of view.

Dump Truck

To see or drive a dump truck in your dream, suggests that you need to get rid of the burden that you have been carrying around with you. This dream symbol may be related to some major change.

Dummy

To see a dummy in your dream, indicates that a critical component is lacking in your relationship. You are feeling unchallenged and unfulfilled. The relationship is making you feel empty. The dream may also point to how you or someone has acted foolishly and stupidly in a situation.

Dungeon

To dream that you are in a dungeon, signifies that through some struggle and your wisdom, you will be able to overcome and surmount the obstacles in your life.

Dunghill

To see a dunghill in your dream, signifies that profits and fortune will come from the most unexpected of sources. For the single, you will also marry exceedingly well.

Dusk

To see the dusk of day in your dream, signifies defeated hopes and a dark, gloom outlook in your endeavors.

Dust

To see dust in your dream, suggest that aspects of yourself have been ignored or neglected.

To dream that you are covered in dust, signifies that the failure of others will adversely effect you.

To dream that you are dusting, symbolizes that you are clearing out all your past mistakes and starting fresh on a new slate.

Dwarf

To see a dwarf in your dream, suggests that you are well-grounded and connected to nature and the earth. Alternatively, a dwarf may mean an aspect of yourself that is not fully developed or has been repressed. You may be feeling inferior or insignificant.

Please See Also Troll.

Dye

To see the dyeing of cloths and garments in your dream, symbolizes either good or bad luck, depending on the color of the dye. (Find the color in this dictionary for further details.)

Dying

Please See Die.

Dynamite

To see dynamite in your dream, signifies a fast approaching and vast change in your life. You may be harboring aggression that is about to blow up.

E

Eagles

To see an eagle in your dream, symbolizes nobility, pride, fierceness, freedom, superiority, courage, and powerful intellectual ability. Eagles also indicate self-renewal. You will struggle fiercely and courageously to realize your highest ambitions and greatest desires.

To see an eagle chained down in your dream, represents a desperate situation where you are feeling restricted and confined. You are unable to express yourself and be who you really want to be. Consider also what the eagle is chained down to for additional clues as to what might be holding you back.

To see a nest of young eagles in your dream, signifies your advancement up to the top of the social ladder.

To dream that you killed an eagle, signifies your ruthlessness. You will let nothing stand in your way of ambitions and obtaining your goals, even if it means hurting those around you. If someone else kills an eagle, then it indicates that your fame, fortune and power will be ruthlessly taken from you.

To dream that you eat the flesh of an eagle, shows that your strong and powerful character will lead you to great wealth and influence.

Earphones

Please see Headphones.

Ears

To see ears in your dreams, suggests that you need to be more responsive or receptive to guidance and assistance from others. You may be relying too much on your own judgment and intuition. You need to listen more closely to what you are being told. Alternatively, it signifies your immaturity and lack of experience.

To dream that you are cleaning wax from your ears, suggests that you are not listening to those around you. There may be something that you are refusing to hear. Are you turning a deaf ear?

To dream of pain in your ear, indicates that you will be receive some bad or offensive news.

Earrings

To dream that you or someone is wearing earrings, suggests that you need to listen more carefully and pay attention.

To see broken earrings in your dreams, suggests that you are being talked about.

To dream that you are buying earrings, represents your desire for acceptance and affection.

Earth

To see the earth in your dream, signifies wholeness and global consciousness. It may also symbolize the sense of being "grounded" and your need to be realistic.

Earthquake

To dream of an earthquake, suggests that you are experiencing a major "shake-up" that is threatening your stability and foundation. The dream highlights you insecurity, fears and sense of helplessness. If you find cover from the quake, you will overcome these challenges. If you become trapped or injured during the quake, you will suffer loss of your business and assets.

Earwig

To see an earwig in your dream, signifies unpleasant news that will affect you and your business and family relations.

East

To dream that you are headed east, represents inner wisdom and spiritual enlightenment. You need to devote or dedicate yourself to your goals, family, career, etc. The direction east also symbolizes the sun. Since east is related to the direction right, it can suggest that you are headed in the right direction.

Easter

To dream about Easter, suggests that the worst of your problems are over. You will experience joy again after a period of darkness and sadness. You need to walk with your head held high and stop being ashamed. Alternatively, the dream symbolizes resurrection and spiritual rebirth.

Eating

To dream that you are eating alone, signifies loss, loneliness, and depression. You may feel rejected, excluded, and cut off from social/family ties. Eating may be a replacement for companionship and provide comfort for you. Alternatively, eating alone may reflect independent needs. Also consider the pun, "what's eating you up?" in reference to anxiety that you may be feeling.

To dream that you are eating with others, denotes prosperous undertakings, personal gain, and joyous spirits.

To dream that you are overeating or not eating enough, signifies your need and lack of spirituality and fulfillment in your waking life. Food can represent love, friendship, ambition, sex or pleasure in your life. Thus, food is seen as a metaphor to fulfill and gratify our hunger of love and desires.

To dream that someone clears away the food before you finish eating, foretells that you will have problems and issues from those beneath your or dependant upon you.

Ebony

To dream of ebony furniture or other articles of ebony, signifies distressing disputes, grievances and quarrels at home.

To dream of ebony nights, signifies despair and sadness.

Echo

To hear or make an echo in your dream, symbolizes your need to repeat yourself in order to be heard and for others to believe you. You should also pay attention to the power and impact of your own words. You are waiting and hoping for a reaction from those around you. It is also symbolic of the soul.

Eclipse

To dream of an eclipse of the sun, forewarns of enjoying life in excess. Too much partying and too much drinking will lead to major health problems. You will experience temporary failure in business.

To dream of an eclipse of the moon, signifies that some hidden aspect of yourself is coming to the surface.

Ecstasy

To dream of feeling ecstasy, signifies happiness an much joy with friends and family.

To dream of feeling ecstasy in the wake a disturbing dream, signifies much sorrow and disappointments. You may be on the mend from a broken heart.

Education

To dream you are are anxious to obtain an education, symbolizes your desire for knowledge will put you on a higher level than your associates. You will be distinguished amongst your peers.

*Please also see School.

Eel

To see an eel in your dream, indicates that you have issues with commitment. It also means that you have problems holding on to things.

Eggs

To see or eat eggs in your dream, symbolizes fertility, birth and your creative potential. It indicates that something new is about to happen.

To find a nest filled with eggs in your dream, signifies some financial gain; the more abundant and bigger the eggs, the more significant the gain.

To see cracked or broken eggs in your dream, denotes that you will suffer from many disappointments and misfortunes. It is indicative of a fragile state in your life and feelings of vulnerability. Alternatively, you may be breaking out of your shell and being comfortable with who you are.

To see bright colored eggs in your dream, symbolizes celebration of a happy event.

To dream of rotten eggs, signifies loss. You may have allowed some situation to take a turn for the worse.

To see fish eggs in your dream, represents an idea that has emerged from your unconscious.

Egypt

To dream of Egypt, indicates the roots and core of your own emotions and spirituality. It suggests of a time in life where things may have been simpler.

Elbows

To see your own elbows in your dream, indicates that you need to make a space for yourself. Your dream may express hesitance or fear in creating your own space for fear of being scrutinized.

To dream that your elbow is wounded, suggests your inability to function in some waking situation. It may also refer to some sexual anxiety. The right elbow relate to moral and ethical issues while the left elbow represents passiveness and your undeveloped characteristics.

Elderberries

To see elderberries in your dream, symbolizes domestic bliss and comfort.

Elderly

To see an elderly person in your dream, represents wisdom or spiritual power. Pay attention to the message or advise that they are conveying you. They help provide life answers and solutions to your problems and try to guide you toward the right direction.

Election

To dream that you are at an election, represents a choice that you need to make which may affect others.

Electric Guitar

To see or play an electric guitar in your dream, signifies the power and strength of your passion. You clearly express your feelings to others. Alternatively, it is symbolic of youth and rebellion.

Electricity

To dream of electricity, symbolizes vigor and life energy. You need to be revitalized.

To dream that the electricity is out, indicates your lack of insight and perspective on a situation.

Electrocution

To dream of an electrocution, signifies that the current course of your actions will lead to disaster, even death.

Elephant

To see an elephant in your dream, suggests that you either need to be more patient and understanding of others. The elephant is also a symbol of power, strength, and intellect. Alternatively, as a creature with an introverted nature, the elephant may thus be depicting your own personality.

To dream that you are riding an elephant, indicates that you are in control of your unconscious and aspects that you once were afraid of.

Elevator

To dream that you are ascending in an elevator, signifies that you will quickly rise to status and wealth. You may have risen to a higher level of consciousness and are looking at the world from an elevated viewpoint. Descending in an elevator, denotes that misfortunes will crush and discourage you. The up and down action of the elevator may represent the ups and downs of your life go emerging out of and submerging into your subconscious.

To dream that the elevator is out of order or that it is not letting you off, symbolizes that your emotions have gotten out of control.

Eleventh Hour

To dream of the eleventh hour, signifies that time is running out for you. This may be an approaching deadline for a project or a decision that needs to be made by you.

Elf

To see an elf in your dream, refers to some imbalance and disharmony in your life. The elf often serves as a guide of the soul. Alternatively, it suggests that you need to be more carefree, worry-free, and light-hearted.

Elk

To see an elk in your dream, symbolizes strength and endurance. It is an indication that you need to spend more time with friends and eat healthier.

Elopement

To dream of eloping is generally unfavorable and signifies disappointments in love.

To dream that your lover has eloped with someone else, symbolizes their unfaithfulness and infidelity.

For the married, to dream of an elopement signifies that you hold positions that you are unworthy of.

Eloquent

To dream that you are giving an eloquent speech, signifies pleasant news.

Email

To dream about email, indicates that you need to reach out to people who may not necessarily always physically be around. It could also very well mean that you have been spending too much time in front of the computer and this has carried over into your dreams.

Embankment

To dream that you are driving along an embankment, signifies the threat of trouble and unhappiness.

To dream that you are riding a horse along an embankment, denotes that you will fearlessly meet and overcome all obstacles in your road to wealth and happiness.

To dream that you are walking along an embankment, signifies your weary struggle for elevation and higher status.

Embarrassment

To dream that you are embarrassed, signifies hidden weaknesses, fears and lack of self-confidence. This dream also suggests of insecurities about your sexuality.

Embrace

To dream that you are embracing your lover, foretells of quarrels, disagreements, and accusations arising from infidelity.

To dream that you embrace a stranger, signifies of an unwelcome guest.

To dream that you are embracing relatives, signifies their sickness and unhappiness.

Embroidery

To dream that you are embroidering, symbolizes your ability to make the best of everything that comes your way.

Embryo

To dream of an embryo, symbolizes the emergence of a fresh idea. Also, your unconscious feelings may be surfacing. Alternatively, it may refer to your feelings of vulnerability and your need to be protected. However if you are pregnant, it is quite common to see the embryo in your dream.

Emerald

To see an emerald in your dream, represents strength. longevity, and durability. You may be entering the healing stages of some situation.

Emotionless

To dream that you are emotionless, suggests that you are closing yourself off from those around you. You may be neglecting your own feelings and should start paying more attention to them.

Emotions

Emotions expressed in dreams is a way for people to act out their feelings which they would not normally express if they were awake. This provides a "safe" outlet for these emotions instead of letting them be pent up.

Emperor

To see an emperor in your dream, represents completion and creativity.

Employment

To dream of losing your employment, denotes that you will have no fear of losing your job for you are a much desired help.

To dream that you are giving employment to others, signifies loss for yourself.

Empress

To see an empress in your dream, signifies that you will be honored highly, but your pride will make you very unpopular.

Emptiness

To dream of emptiness, signifies fruitless labor or that something is missing in your life. There is nothing to show for all the effort that you have dedicated to a project or development.

Enchantment

To dream that you are under the spell of enchantment, forewarns that you will be exposed to some evil in the form of pleasure if you are not careful.

To dream that your are trying to enchant others, foretells that you will fall into evil.

To resist enchantment, signifies that your good advise and counsel will be much sought after.

Enclosure

To dream that you are in an enclosure, indicates that you are in defensive mode. Some situation in your waking life has put you on guard and arouses the need to protect/defend yourself.

To dream that you are in an enclosure that is shrinking, indicates that you feel restrained and confined in some circumstance. It represents actual or perceived limitations. You need to start testing out your boundaries in order to grow.

To dream that you are in an enclosure made of glass, suggests that you are too critical about a person or situation.

Encyclopedia

To dream of seeing or searching through encyclopedias, symbolizes your pursuit for literary knowledge and the fine arts. Although these pursuits may not be financially beneficial, you are enriching you mind.

Enemy

To see your enemy in your dream, represents opposing ideas and contradictory attitudes. It also indicates something that you are in denial about or someone whom you are rejecting. Enemies may also represent the enemies within and your inner conflict with yourself.

To dream that you are dealing with the enemies, represents a resolution to some inner conflict or waking life problem.

Engagement

To dream that you are engaged to be married, represents sexual or relationship needs. You may be trying to resolve your feelings of loneliness.

To dream that you break an engagement, denotes a hasty and unwise decision in some important matter.

To dream of a business engagement, signifies concern and worries in an area of your work.

Engine

To see an engine in your dream, represents your heart and its power.

To dream that you engine is blown or disabled, indicates that you have been betrayed.

Engineer

To see an engineer in your dream, suggests that you are taking charge of your life. It also indicates that you are evaluating a situation and how various pieces fit together.

Entertainment

To dream of an entertainment filled with music and dancing, denotes health, prosperity, and pleasant tidings of the absent.

Entrails

To dream of human entrails (your own or another's), signifies horrible misery and despair and little hope for happiness.

To dream of the entrails of a wild animal or beast, denotes the defeat of your enemy.

To dream that you tear the entrails of another, signifies your own cruel intents to further your own interest and gain.

Please see also <u>Intestines.</u>

Envelope

To see envelopes in your dream, signifies anticipation or opportunity. To see unopened envelopes, indicates sorrow news and missed opportunities.

Envy

To dream that you are envious of others, signifies that you will make warm friends by your unselfish deference to the wishes of others.

To dream that you are being envied by others, denotes inconveniences from friends who are overanxious to please you.

Epaulet

To dream that you meet a person wearing epaulets, signifies unwise attachments that may result in scandal.

To dream that you are wearing epaulets, signifies temporary disfavor, but will eventually be acknowledged for your honors.

Epicure

To dream that you are an epicure, signifies that you will cultivate your taste to the finest and highest potential.

To dream that you are sitting at the table at epicure, signifies that you will enjoy some fine distinction, but will be surrounded by people of selfish means.

To dream that you are trying to satisfy an epicure, signifies that you will have a distinguished but tyrannical lover.

Epidemic

To dream of an epidemic, signifies worries of bothersome tasks.

Epilepsy

To dream that you have epilepsy, suggests that you are suppressing your feelings. You need to acknowledge and express these emotions.

Equator

To dream about the equator, indicates the search for Self. You are exploring aspect of yourself in order to become more whole.

Eraser

To see or use an eraser in your dream, suggests that you need to clear up some mistakes that you have made.

Erection

To dream that you have an erection, symbolizes your creative power and energy. You want to take action.

Ermine

To dream that you are wearing an ermine, signifies your quest for wealth and wants will lead to misery.

To see others wearing ermine, denotes that you will be associated with wealthy people who have a distinct taste for art and literature.

Errands

To dream that you are running errands, signifies harmony and mutual understanding in your domestic sphere.

To dream that you are sending someone on an errand, signifies that you will lose your lover through your indifference.

Eruption

To see an eruption in your dream, signifies a forceful and jolting outpour of repressed thoughts or urges. You may also be experiencing an upheaval in your life.

Escalator

To see an escalator in your dream, indicates movement between various levels of consciousness. If you are moving up in the escalator, then it suggests that you are addressing and confronting emotional issues. You are moving through your spiritual journey with great progress and ease. If you are going down the escalator, then it implies repression and descent back into your unconscious. It may be indication of a setback.

Escape

To dream that you escape from jail or some place of confinement, signifies your need to escape from a restrictive situation or attitude. On the other hand, it may mean that you are taking an escapist attitude and are refusing to face up to problems that are not going away.

To dream that you escape from injury, from an animal, or from any situation, signifies your good health and prosperity. You will experience a favorable turn of events.

Estate

To dream that you become an owner of an estate, signifies that your inheritance will be disappointing and not as you expected.

Eucalyptus

To see a eucalyptus in your dream, represents protection and the need to feel protected.

Europe

To dream of traveling to Europe, signifies a long journey which will give you some financial gain. Alternatively, it indicates original thought or old ways of thinking.

Evacuation

To dream of an evacuation, suggests that you are isolating yourself and holding back your emotions.

To dream that you are in a town that has been evacuated, indicates that you are feeling rejected by those around you. You are feeling unaccepted.

Eve

To see Eve in your dream, symbolizes your hesitance in accepting this biblical story as authentic and you will encounter opposition in your social and business circles.

To dream that you impersonate Eve, forewarns you to be careful when it comes to the persuasions of the opposites sex.

Evening

To dream that evening has arrived, denotes the end of a cycle, aging or death. It may also be symbolic of unrealized hopes.

Evening Gown

To see or wear an evening gown in your dream, represents enjoyment, social pleasures, grace and culture. Alternatively, it suggests that you are seeking or trying to attain some sense of happiness. Consider the color of the gown for additional significance.

Evergreen

To see evergreen in your dream, signifies wealth, happiness, immortality. and knowledge. Additionally, it may also mean that you will find hope in the midst of despair.

Eviction

To dream that you are being evicted, suggests that a present situation or relationship is making you feel helpless and powerless. You feel that you cannot fend for yourself and have a sense of not belonging. Alternatively, you believe that you are being unfairly treated.

Evil

To dream that someone or something is evil, denotes a repressed and/or forbidden aspect of yourself. This part of yourself may be seeking recognition and acknowledgment. Alternatively, evil may also be a reflection of your strong, negative emotions like hate, anger, etc.

Ex

To dream about your ex-boyfriend/girlfriend or ex-husband/wife or that you and your ex got back together again, suggests that something or someone in your current life that is bringing out similar feelings you felt during the relationship with your ex. The dream may be a way of alerting you to the same or similar behavior in a current relationship. What you learn from that previous relationship may need to be applied to the present one so that you do no repeat the same mistake. Alternatively, past lovers often highlight the positive experiences you had with that person.

In particular, to see your ex-husband/wife in your dream, indicates that you are finding yourself in a situation that you do not want to be in. It suggests that you are experiencing a similar relationship or situation which makes you feel unhappy and uncomfortable.

To see your mate's ex in your dream, suggests that you may be comparing yourself to the ex. The dream is trying to tell you not to make the same relationship mistakes that ended that relationship.

Alternatively, seeing your ex in your dream also signifies aspects of yourself that you have x'd out or neglected.

Ex-Boyfriend

To see an old ex-boyfriend from childhood in your dream, refers to a freer, less encumbered relationship. The dream servers to bring you back to a time where the responsibilities of adulthood (or marriage) didn't interfere with the spontaneity of romance. You need to recapture the excitement, freedom, and vitality of youth that is lacking in your present relationship.

To dream that your ex-boyfriend is giving you advice about your current relationship, suggests that you unconscious is telling you not to repeat the same mistakes that you had made with this ex-boyfriend.

To dream that you are being massaged by your ex-boyfriend, suggests that you need to let go of some of that defensiveness that you have been putting forth. You may have been putting up a wall or armor around you. You need to learn to trust people again.

To dream that you ex-boyfriend gives you a stuffed animal, suggests that you are seeking for reassuring and nurturing aspects of a relationship. This is not to imply that you want you ex-boyfriend back. Alternatively, the dream could represent some immature relationship which may (or may not) describe the relationship you had with your ex.

To dream that you see your ex-boyfriend dressed in a suit at a hospital, suggests that you have come to terms with that relationship and have completed the healing process.

Exam

To dream that you are taking an exam, signifies insecurities, fear of not meeting others' expectations, and fear of failure.

For an in depth analysis, click on Common Dreams: Exam.

Exchange

To dream of an exchange of any sorts, signifies a profitable gain and is seen as favorable.

Excrement

See Feces.

Execution

To see an execution in your dream, denotes that you will suffer some misfortune from the carelessness of others.

To dream that you miraculously escape your own execution, signifies that you will overcome your enemies and succeed in gaining wealth.

Exercise

To dream that you are exercising, signifies your worries about your health. You may be concerned about fitting into society's ideals of beauty. Alternatively, the dream may also indicate that you need to exercise your rights and power in some situation.

Exhausted

Please See Tired.

Exile

To dream that you are exiled, signifies that your journey will interfere with some engagement and pleasure.

See Also Banishment.

Exit

To see an exit in your dream, indicates that you are looking for a way out of a waking situation.

Exorcism

To dream that you or others are being exorcised, symbolizes your initiative to regain control and take steps toward the direction of your goals. Alternatively, you may not be taking responsibility for your actions and are looking for a scapegoat.

Experiment

To dream that you are working on an experiment, suggests that you need to be more daring and try something new and different. Take a chance.

Explosion

To see explosions in your dream, signifies a loss and displeasure in business. It may also mean that your repressed emotions and rage have come to the surface in a forceful and violent manner.

To dream that your face becomes blackened or mutilated by the explosion, signifies that will be confronted with unjust accusations and may suffer the consequences.

To dream that you are enveloped in flames or blown up into the air by an explosion, forewarns that unworthy friends will violate your rights and abuse your confidence.

To hear the sound of a loud explosion, but you did not see it, signifies that your troubles will soon be replaced with tranquility after you have overcome some small obstacle.

Extension Cord

To see an extension cord in your dream, suggests that you need to associate yourself with energetic people. Acknowledge those aspect of yourself which has been dormant.

Exterminator

To see or call an exterminator in your dream, indicates that you need to cut off ties from those who try to pull you down.

To dream that you are an exterminator, suggests that you need to confront your weakness and stand up to the challenges ahead.

Eyebrows

To notice eyebrows in your dream, represents expressions of amazement, disbelief, surprise, or doubt. It may also indicate concern or disapproval.

Eyeglasses

To dream that you are wearing eyeglasses and you do not normally wear them, suggests that you need a clearer view on a situation. There may have been a misunderstanding or a situation was misperceived and needs to be seen more clearly.

To see broken eyeglasses in your dream, indicates that your vision and perception is impaired. You are not seeing the facts correctly.

Eyelashes

To notice your eyelashes or dream that they are growing, indicates that you are trying to express yourself in some subtle or covert way. It also signifies good luck.

To dream that all your eyelashes fall off, suggests that you are having difficulties expressing yourself. It may also mean a loss in your feminine power. If only one eyelash falls off, then it also signifies good luck.

Eyes

To see your own eyes in your dream, represents enlightenment, knowledge, comprehension, understanding, and intellectual awareness. Unconscious thoughts may be coming onto the surface. The left eye is symbolic of the moon, while the right eye represents the sun. It may also be a pun on "I" or the self. If you dream that your eyes have turned inside your head and you can now see the inside of your head, then it symbolizes insight and something that you need to be aware of. This dream may be literally telling you that you need to look within yourself. Trust your intuition and instincts.

To dream that you have something in your eye, represents obstacles in your path. Alternatively, it may represent your critical view and how you tend to see faults in others.

To dream that you have one eye, indicates your refusal to accept another viewpoint. It suggests that you are one-sided in your ways of thinking.

To dream that you have a third eye, symbolizes inner vision and insight. You need to start looking within yourself.

To dream that your eyes are injured or closed, suggests your refusal to see the truth about something or the avoidance of intimacy. You may be expressing feelings of hurt, pain or sympathy.

To dream that you have crossed eyes, denotes that you are not seeing straight with regards to some situation. You may be getting your facts mixed up.

F

Fable

To dream of reading fables, represents your literary mind and romantic notions.

To dream that you are living a fable, symbolizes your need to face reality. It is better to face a situation head on then to retreat into a fantasy world.

Face

To see your own face in your dream, denotes the persona you choose to show to the world as oppose to the real you. It may refer to confrontations and your willingness to deal with problems and issues in your life.

To dream that you face is flawed or pimply, represents erupting emotions. You may have suffered an attack on your persona or your reputation.

Faceless

To see a faceless figure or person in your dream, indicates that you are still searching for your own identity and finding out who you are. Perhaps you are unsure of how to read people and their emotions. And therefore are expressing a desire to know and understand these people in a deeper level.

Facelift

To dream that you have a facelift, suggests that you are seeking a new self-identity and self-image. You may have experienced a surge in your confidence levels. Alternatively, it symbolizes vanity and you concerns about appearances rather than what is inside.

Factory

To dream that you are at a factory, represents repetitious thinking and old way of doing things. It is symbolic of predictability and unchanging habits.

Failure

To dream of failure, signifies your fears of inadequacy, low self-esteem and foretells that you are not applying yourself to the fullest potential. You are overwhelmed with anxiety and the pressure to excel.

To dream that your business is a failure, signifies bad management and that you need to be more aggressive and not let fear rule you.

Fainting

To dream that you are fainting, suggests your inability to confront some unconscious issue or feelings. You need to be more aware and acknowledge of those feelings.

To see a family member faint in your dream, signifies that you will hear some indiscreet activities from that person.

Fair

To dream that you are at the fair, suggests that you have overcame some minor obstacle and ready to move forward with renewed energy.

Fairy

To see a fairy in your dream, indicates that you are in search of some help or advise for a problem or decision, but may not want to directly admit you need help. In particular, if the fairy is evil, then it suggests that an aspect of yourself needs to be set free. The fairy is also symbolic of your soul and the feminine qualities and aspects of yourself.

Fairy Tale

To dream that you are a character in a fairy tale, suggests your need to be rescued or to be swept off your feet. It also indicates that you are exploring your limits and trying to awaken your fullest potential.

To dream that you are reading a fairy tale, indicates that you are a romantic at heart.

Faithless

To dream that you lover is faithless, has an opposite meaning that your lover is faithful and foretells of a happy marriage.

To dream that you friends are faithless, denotes that you are held in high regards and worthy esteem by them.

Fakir

To see a fakir in your dream, foretells of phenomenal changes in your life.

Falcon

To see a falcon in your dreams, foretells that your success will make you an object of jealousy.

To dream that you are hunting a falcon, forewarns that you are in danger of ruining your business reputation by being too aggressive and bringing harm to others.

Fall

To dream that you fall and are not frightened, signifies that you will overcome your adversities with ease.

To dream that you fall and are frightened, indicates a lack of control, insecurity, and/or lack of support in your waking life. You may be experiencing some major struggle and/or overwhelming problem. It may denote that you have failed to achieve a goal that you have set forth for yourself.

To dream that you are free-falling through water, indicates that you are feeling overwhelmed with emotions. You may feel that it is easier to give up then to try to stay afloat or prevent yourself from going under.

*For an in depth analysis, click on Common Dreams: Falling.

Fame

To dream that you have fame, denotes unrealized achievements and disappointed aspirations. It suggests your need to be admired by those around you.

To see famous people in your dream, signifies an increase to your prosperity and honor.

Famine

To dream of famine, signifies a negative turn in business and in health. This is generally a bad dream.

Famish

To dream that you are famished, foretells of a failure in some endeavor which you thought to be a promising success.

Family

To see your own family in high spirits in your dream, symbolizes harmony and happiness. To see them gloomy, foretells of disappointment and sadness.

Fan

To see a fan in your dream, refers to the changes in your life. It may also signifies your need to calm down after a highly charged emotional situation or state.

To dream that you are fanning yourself or that someone is fanning you, represents your lack of self-confidence.

Fangs

To see fangs in your dream, indicates that you have said some words that have been hurtful to others.

Farewell

To dream that you are saying farewell, foretells of unpleasant news from absent friends.

To dream that you are saying farewell to you lover, signifies your lover's indifference towards you.

Farm

To see or live on a farm in your dream, suggests that you need to develop aspect of yourself and utilize your potential. You are ready for growth.

Farmer

To see or dream that you are a farmer, points to your productivity. Are you utilizing your fullest potential? It may also suggest that you need to work harder in order to reap its benefits.

Farting

To dream that you are farting, suggests that you are being passive aggressive. You need to express your feelings in a more direct manner.

Fat

To dream that you are fat, signifies a fortunate change in your life or you may be overindulgent. A more literal interpretation of this dream is your fears of gaining weight. You have an skewed perception of your own image which may stem from low self-esteem.

To dream that others are fat, signifies prosperity.

Please see also Obese.

Father

To see your father in your dream, symbolizes authority and protection. It suggests that you need to be more self-reliant. Consider also your waking relationship with your father.

To dream that your father is dead, forewarns that you need to proceed with caution in conducting your business.

To dream that you are hitting your father. represents a desperate need for greater closeness with your father. You feel that he is not listening to you. In particular, if you are hitting your father with a rubber object, indicates that whatever you are doing or telling him has no significant effect on him. Things just literally bounces off him.

Father-In-Law

To see your father-in-law in your dream, signifies joyous occasions with friends and family.

Fatigue

To feel fatigue or see others fatigued in your dream, suggests that a relationship is worn out and near its ending point.

Faucet

To see a faucet in your dream, signifies how you control your emotions and which ones you allow to be expressed. It may also be indicative of sadness and depression.

To see a leaky faucet in your dream, represents sexual issues and problems.

Favor

To dream that you ask favors of anyone, signifies that you will enjoy abundance.

To dream that you grant favors, signifies a loss.

Fawn

To see a fawn in your dream, symbolizes true friends and faithfulness in love.

Fax Machine

To see or use a fax machine in your dream, indicates that you are receiving some message from your unconscious. This message will prove to be the real deal.

Fear

To dream that you feel fear, signifies that you achievements will not be as successful as you had anticipated. You are having anxieties in certain circumstances of your life.

Please see also Scared.

Feast

To see a feast in your dream, denotes your emotional needs or sexual appetite. Pleasant surprises may also be in your near future.

To see disorder at a feast, foretells of quarrels or unhappiness through the negligence or sickness of some person.

To arrive late to a feast, signifies of a bothersome event that will occupy your mind.

Feather

To dream of feathers floating in the air, signifies a life of ease, comfort, warmth and of financial gains. It may describe your lightheartedness and enjoyment for life. Alternatively, they may represent confusion, hastiness, and lost of dignity.

In particular, to see chicken feathers in your dream, signifies of minor annoyances. Eagle feathers represent the realization of your goals and aspirations. And to see peacock, ostrich, or any other ornamental feathers, denotes advancement up the social ladder. You will be met with much success in your future.

To dream that you are selling or buying feathers, symbolizes frugality and thriftiness.

February

To dream of the month of February, signifies ongoing ill health and gloom.

Feces

To see or come in contact with feces, signifies aspects of yourself that are dirty and negative and which you believe to be undesirable and repulsive. You need to acknowledge and express these feelings, even though it may be shameful. Release the negativity in your life. Alternatively, it may also refer to someone who is anal retentive.

To dream that you are unable to dispose of the feces, suggests that you are unwilling to let go of your emotions. You have a tendency to hold in and keep your feelings to yourself.

According to Freud, feces is related to possession, pride, shame, money/financial matters, or aggressive acts.

See The Meaning In Action: " Filthy Stalls"

Feeble

To dream that you are feeble, denotes unhealthy occupations and mental anxiety.

Feet

To see your own feet in your dream, symbolizes your foundation, stability and sense of understanding. It signifies your need to be more practical and sensible. Keep both feet on the ground. Alternatively, it represents mobility, independence and freedom. Perhaps you have taken a step in the right direction and are contemplating your goals or your next step. The sole of the foot may be a pun of being or feeling like the only support of some person/situation.

Consider also the pun of "putting your foot in your mouth".

To dream that you are washing your feet, indicates that others can easily take advantage of you.

In particular for the people of India, to dream of the feet may symbolize divine qualities since the feet are considered the holiest part of the body.

Fellatio

Please See Oral Sex.

Fence

To see a fence in your dream, signifies an obstacle or barrier that may be standing on your path. You may feel confined and restricted in expressing yourself. Are you feeling fenced in? Alternatively, it may symbolize a need for privacy. You may want to shut off the rest of the world.

To dream that you are climbing to the top of a fence, denotes success. If you climb over the fence, then it indicates that you will accomplish your desires via not so legitimate means.

To dream that you are building a fence, signifies a solid foundation for future wealth through your economical and industrious character.

To dream that you fall from a fence, denotes that you are in way over your head in regards to some project which you are incapable of dealing with.

To see animals jumping over a fence into an enclosure, foretells that you will receive assistance from an unexpected source. To see them jumping out, signifies loss in trade.

Ferns

To see ferns in your dream, symbolizes your future hopes and fears.

Ferret

To see a ferret in your dream, symbolizes distrust and suspicion of others. The dream may also be a pun on searching.

Ferry

To dream that you are riding on a ferry, indicates that you are going through some transitional phases in your life. It also means that you are setting your sights on a new goal.

To dream that you are waiting for a ferry, signifies unforeseen circumstances might hinder your desires and wishes.

Ferris Wheel

To see or ride on a Ferris wheel in your dream, suggests that you are going around in circles. You are headed no where. Alternatively, it is symbolic of wholeness and the circle of life. Life is full of ups and downs.

Fertilizer

To see or use fertilizer in your dream, refers to your growth. You need to continue to absorb knowledge and insights from your surroundings and experiences.

Festival

To dream that you are at festival, signifies indifference to the cold realities of life and you are acting to old before you time. You will never want, but will be largely dependent on others.

Fetus

To see a fetus in your dream, symbolizes a newly developing relationship or idea in your waking life. Something creative is happening. Alternatively, you may be expressing difficulties in some situation or relationship.

Fever

To dream that you have a fever, suggests that feelings of anger or hatred or threatening to come to your consciousness. You need to find a safe way to express these feelings.

Fiddle

To see a fiddle in your dream, signifies harmony in the home.

Field

To see green fields in your dream, symbolizes great abundance, freedom, and happiness. You may also be going through a period of personal growth. Alternatively, this dream may simply be an expression for your love of nature.`

To see freshly plowed fields in your dream, signifies growth, early rise to wealth and fortunate advancements to places of honor.

To see dead or barren fields, signifies lack, pessimism and your jaded prospects for the future.

Fiend

To see a fiend in your dream, signifies reckless living, loose morals and a blackened reputation.

Fife

To hear the sound of a fife, signifies that you will be unexpected call on to defend your honor.

To dream that you are playing a fife, signifies that your strong reputation will remain intact and withstand anything that is said about you.

Fig Leaf

To see a fig leaf in your dream, represents a loss of innocence or a fall from grace.

Fighting

To dream that you participate in a fight, indicates inner turmoil. Some aspect of yourself is in conflict with another aspect of yourself. Perhaps an unresolved or unacknowledged part is fighting for its right to be heard. It may also parallel a fight or struggle that you are going through in your waking life.

To see others fighting in your dream, suggests that you are unwilling to acknowledge your own problems and turmoil. You are not taking any responsibility or initiative in trying to resolve issues in your waking life.

To dream that you are fighting to the death, indicates that you are unwilling to acknowledge a waking conflict or your own inner turmoil. You are unwilling and refusing to change your old attitudes and habits.

Figs

To see figs in your dream, signifies a turn for the positive. To dream that you are eating figs, signifies a favorable turn in health. To see them growing, symbolizes profit and wealth. Figs are also often associated with sex and eroticism.

Figure

To see mysterious figures in your dream, signifies great mental distress.

Figurines

To see figurines in your dream, indicates that you are underestimating your own abilities and in yourself. You need to stop comparing yourself to others. Consider what the figurine depicts and how you are belittling that quality in yourself.

Filbert Nut

To see filbert nuts in your dream, signifies peace, harmony, and profitable business ventures.

To dream that you are eating filbert nuts, true and dependant friends.

File

To dream that you are filing away your bills or other important documents, signifies of unfavorable events which will be a source of much anxiety

File Cabinet

To see a file cabinet in your dream, suggests that you need to keep your facts and information straight. The file cabinet may also represent the memories or unnecessary details you keep stored in your mind and need to retrieve from time to time.

To dream that the drawers of the file cabinet are wide open, denotes your openness toward other viewpoints, opinions, suggestions, and criticism.

To dream that the file cabinet is locked, indicates that there is something that you do not want revealed to others. Alternatively, it may indicate that you are being close-minded.

Filer

To see a nail filer in your dream, suggests that you need to smooth out the rough edges of your personality or your relationship with others. You may be a little to harsh and abrasive toward others.

Film

To dream that you are watching a film, signifies that you are analyzing yourself and your own thoughts without being emotionally attached.

Find

To dream that you find something, suggests that you are coming into contact with some aspect of your psyche or unconscious. You are recognizing a part of yourself that was previously repressed or undeveloped. Alternatively, it represents change.

To dream that you find someone, indicates that you are identifying new facets of a relationship. You may be taking the relationship to a new level and/or direction.

Fingers

To see your fingers in you dream, symbolizes physical and mental dexterity. They indicate manipulation, action and non-verbal communication. If you dream that your fingers fall off, then it suggests that you are letting a situation dominate you or dictate how you behave. You may be literally losing your grip on life.

To dream that your fingers are injured or have been chopped off, denotes your anxieties about your ability to accomplish some demanding task or perform in some waking situation.

To dream of a finger pointing at you, signifies self-blame.

To dream about your little finger, represents mental power, intellect, memory, and the power of communication.

To dream of your forefinger, signifies authority, direction, judgment. Your dream may be trying to make a point.

To dream of your middle finger, denotes prudence, practicality, caution, responsibility, and hard work. Alternatively, the middle finger may symbolize the phallus.

To dream of your ring finger, represents success, popularity and creativity, It also has association with marriage, union, and commitments.

Fingernails

To dream that you fingernails break, suggests that you are trying to avoid some situation or trying to get out of a responsibility.

To dream that you are polishing your fingernails, represents glamour.

To dream that you are chewing your nails, indicates that a problem is too tough to handle. You are not sure how to go about resolving a situation in your waking life.

To dream that you fingernails are growing rapidly, refers to your desires to reach out to someone. You want to be able to extend a part of yourself to others.

To dream that a man has long red fingernails, suggests that he is very in touch with his sensitivity and emotions. It may also relate to issues of sexuality and sensuality.

Fire

Depending on the context of your dream, to see fire in your dream can symbolizes destruction, passion, desire, illumination, transformation, enlightenment, or anger. It may suggest that something old is passing and something new is entering your life. Your thoughts and views are changing. In particular, if the fire is under control or contained in one area, it is a metaphor of your own internal fire and inner transformation. It also represents your drive and motivation.

To dream of that you are being burned by fire, indicates that your temper is getting out of control. Some issue or situation is burning you up inside.

To dream that a house is on fire, indicates that you need to undergo some transformation. If you have recurring dreams of your family house on fire, then it suggests that you are still not ready for the change or that you are fighting against the change. Alternatively, it highlights passion and the love of those around you.

To dream that you put out a fire, signifies that you will overcome your obstacles in your life through much work and effort.

**See The Meaning In Action: "Line Of Fire" & "Smell Of Fire"

Fire Engine

To see a fire engine in your dream, suggests that you are tending to the needs of others and overlooking your own needs. You tend to worry and stress out in situations that are beyond your control. Stop trying to be in the middle of things and stop trying to fix things. Use more discretion.

Fighters

To see a fire fighter in your dream, represents your higher Self. You are experiencing a period of cleansing and purification.

Firebrand

To see a firebrand in your dream, signifies favorable fortune.

Fired

To dream that you are fired from your job. indicates that you are wanting to end some relationship or situation in your waking life. It also suggests that you are repressing what you really desire most.

Firecracker

To see a firecracker in your dream, represents your outbursts. Your anger is being misdirected.

Firefly

To see a firefly in your dream, represents bright ideas that are coming out of your unconscious.

Fireplace

To see a lit fireplace in your dream, symbolizes contentment, warmth, and comfort.

To dream of lighting or stirring a fireplace, suggests a burning a desire or your need to get to the heart of a matter/situation.

To see an unlit fireplace, is indicative of low energy, disinterest, or disheartenment.

Fireplace Damper

To see a fire damper in your dream, indicates the warmth of friends. You have a lot of love to offer. Alternatively, it may represent your pent up frustrations and anger. You are holding in your negative emotions. If the damper is broken, then it indicates a situation or relationship that has made you cold and bitter.

Fireworks

To see fireworks in your dream, symbolizes enthusiasm, creativity, and talent. It may also indicate that you are showing off and making a spectacle of yourself.

Fish

To see fish swimming in your dream, signifies insights from your unconscious mind. Thus to catch a fish, represents insights which have been brought to the surface. The fish is also an ancient symbol of Christianity and Christian beliefs. Consider also the common phrases "like a cold fish", "fish out of water" or something that is "fishy" about a situation. It may also imply a slippery or elusive situation.

To dream that you are eating fish, symbolizes your beliefs, spirituality, luck, energy and nourishment. It is food for the soul.

To dream of cooking fish, indicates that you are incorporating your new realizations with your spiritual feelings and knowledge.

To dream that you are cleaning fish, suggests that you are altering your emotional expression in a way that will be presentable to others. You are censoring yourself and not expressing how you completely feel.

Fish Market

To dream that you go to a fish market, signifies pleasure and joy.

To see decayed and rotting fish at the fish market, denotes distress that will come in the disguise of happiness.

Fisherman

To see a fisherman in your dream, signifies greater prosperity in the near future.

Fishhooks

To see fishhooks in your dream, refers to an idea or concept that you need to grasp. The dream may also indicate that you are getting hooked on something or being hooked in. You may be deceived into doing or believing something.

Fishing

To dream that you are fishing, indicates that you are confronting and bringing your repressed emotions to the surface. In particular, to dream that you are ice fishing, suggests that you are breaking through a hardened emotional barrier and confronting difficult feelings from your unconscious.

Consider the common phrase "fishing for compliments".

Fishing Rod

To see a fishing rod in your dream, represents your quest and exploration of your unconscious mind. You are ready to confront issues and emotions which you have suppressed.

Fishnet

To see a fishnet in your dream, indicates a fear of being found out or caught in the act.

Fishpond

To see a fishpond in your dream, represents unconscious material that is slowly revealing itself. Alternatively, it symbolizes feelings that you need to contain and keep in check.

Fist

To see a fist in your dream, symbolizes anger, power and aggression. It is also indicative of your readiness to fight and defend yourself.

Fits

To dream that you are having fits, signifies failing health and loss of employment.

To see others throwing fits, denotes unpleasantness and coldness amongst your social and/or business circle.

Fix

To dream that you are fixing something, indicates that you need to reevaluate and rethink a situation or relationship in your life.

Flag

To see your national flag in your dream, signifies peace and/or prosperity.

To see a flag of a foreign nation, denotes a breach of trust between friends.

Flame

To dream that you are fighting flames, signifies that you will need to invest your best efforts and energy in your road to success and wealth.

Please also see Fire.

Flamingo

To see a flamingo in your dream, represents you sense of community and cooperation. It also indicates new experiences or situations. Alternatively, you may be overly concerned with your physical appearance.

Flasher

To see a flasher in your dream, suggests that you are experiencing frustrations in your sex life. You are denying your sexual urges and needs.

Flashlight

To see a flashlight in your dream, suggests that you are questioning certain issues about yourself. You may be trying to shed light on your deeper thoughts and/or unconscious feelings. It symbolizes sudden awareness, insight, and the ability to find your way in a situation. Alternatively, the flashlight may imply sexual activities.

Flax

To see flax in your dream, signifies prosperity.

Fleas

To see fleas in your dream, signifies that you will be provoked into anger and manipulated into retaliation by someone close to you.

To dream that fleas bite you, signifies that vicious rumors by false friends will slander your character.

Fleet

To see a large, rapidly moving fleet in your dream, signifies a hasty change in the business market.

Flies

To see flies in your dream, symbolizes feelings of guilt or a breakdown of a plan. Flies may also forewarn of a contagious sickness or a surrounding of enemies.

To dream that you kill or exterminate the flies, signifies that you will regain your honor after you fell from grace and will be recapture the heart of your intended.

Flight

To dream of flight, signifies a sense of freedom where you had initially felt restricted and limited.

For an in depth analysis, click on Common Dreams: Flying.

Flirting

To dream that you are flirting or that someone is flirting with you, represents your need for intimacy and affection. You may be about to enter into a serious commitment or relationship in the near future.

Floating

To dream that you are floating, implies acceptance, letting go of your problems or worries and just going with the flow. You are experiencing new-found freedom. It also signifies that you will prove victorious in your obstacles that may presently seem overwhelming.

To dream that you are floating, but are afraid to move, suggests that you are questioning your own abilities. You are experiencing doubts in yourself.

Flock

To see a flock of birds in your dream, represents a lack of objectivity in your decision-making and thinking process.

Flogging

Please See Beating.

Flood

To see a raging flood with its muddy debris, represents emotional issues and tension. Your repressed emotions are overwhelming you. Consider where the flood for indications of where in your waking life may a situation be the source of stress and tension.

Floodlights

To see floodlights in your dreams, symbolizes your desire to open up so that everything is in the open and understood.

To see a floodlight burn out, symbolizes that you are being kept out in the dark about certain issues..

Floor

To see the floor in your dream, represents your support. It may also represent the division between the unconscious and conscious.

To see a polished, wooden floor in your dream, indicates that you are fully aware of your unconscious and keeping it suppressed.

To see a slanted floor in your dream, foretells that you are deviating too far from your original plans and goals.

Flour

To see flour in your dream, symbolizes a frugal but happy way of life. It also indicates hard work. This dream symbol may also be a pun on "flower".

Flower

To see colorful flowers in your dream, signifies kindness, compassion, gentleness, pleasure, beauty, and gain. It is also symbolic of perfection and spirituality. Your dream may be an expression of love, joy and happiness. Alternatively, flowers may denote a particular time or season. If the flowers are white, then it symbolizes sadness.

To see withered or dead flowers in your dream, denotes disappointments and gloomy situations. You may not be utilizing your full potential and talents.

To dream that you receive a bouquet of flowers, represents respect, approval, admiration, and rewards.

To see flowers blooming in barren soil, signifies that energy and cheerful nature will enable you to overcome your grievances.

Flute

To hear or play the flute in your dream, indicates harmony in your life. Everything is going well in your life.

Flying

To dream that you are flying, signifies a sense of freedom where you had initially felt restricted and limited.

To dream that you are flying with black wings, signifies bitter disappointments.

For an in depth analysis, click on Common Dreams: Flying.

Flying Fish

To see a flying fish in your dream, indicates that you are feeling emotionally free and uninhibited.

Flying Machine

To see a flying machine in your dream, foretells of steady satisfactory progress in your future endeavors.

Flying Saucer

Please See UFO.

Fly Paper

To see fly paper in your dream, signifies ill health and disrupted friendships.

Fly Trap

To see a fly trap in your dream, denotes a malicious plan set forth against you.

To see a fly trap full of flies, signifies of minor embarrassments.

Foal

To see a foal in your dream, signifies new undertakings and emergence of fresh energy.

Fog

To dream that you are going through a thick fog, signifies much confusion, troubles, scandal, and worries. You may not be seeing things the way they really are or you may have lost your sense of direction in life.

Folder

To see a folder in your dream, suggests that you need to sort out your feelings and re-organize issues in your waking life, especially if you've experienced some trauma or turmoil recently. Consider the contents of the folder for additional clues.

Followed

Please See Pursuit.

Food

To see food in your dream, represents physical and emotional nourishment and energies. The different types of food can symbolize a wide range of things. Generally, fruit is symbolic of sensuality. Frozen foods may imply your cold emotions and frigid ways. Eating certain foods refers to qualities that you need to incorporate within your own self.

To dream that you are hording or storing food, indicates a fear of deprivation. You do not trust what you already have.

To see or eat stale food in your dream, suggests that you are feeling sluggish and emotionally drained. You need to be invigorated and revitalized.

Please also see Eating.

Fool

Please see Minstrel.

Foot

To dream that you injured or hurt your foot, signifies a lack of progress, freedom, and independence. Alternatively, the dream may suggests that you have taken a step in the wrong direction. In particular, to dream that your foot gets cut by glass, then it indicates passivity. You are hesitant or reluctant in taking the first step toward a goal or decision.

Please See Also Feet.

Football

To dream that you are watching or playing football, signifies that you will have great satisfaction in your work and your goals will be achieved as you progress through your life.

To dream that you are on a football field, represents competition and showing off. There is a lack of cooperation in some area of your life.

Footprints

To see footprints in your dream, symbolize pride. and heritage. It may also suggest that you are following someone else's footsteps and hint toward your lack of originality and initiative. Alternatively, footprints indicate something or someone you have missed. Perhaps someone is never quite there for you.

Footstool

To see a footstool in your dream, suggests that in order to move up and advance in life, you need to learn to ask for help.

Forehead

To see a fine and smooth forehead in your dream, signifies your good judgment and fairness. It is also indicative of your intellectual capacities.

To see a wrinkled forehead, symbolizes worries and burdens. You may be deep in thought.

To dream that you feel the forehead of your child, denotes sincere praises.

Foreigner

To see a foreigner in your dream, represents an aspect of yourself that is unfamiliar or strange to you. You may be neglecting or ignoring some important feelings or talents.

Forest

To dream that you are in or walking through the forest, signifies a transitional phase. You may be following your instincts.

To dream that you are lost in a forest, signifies that you are searching through your unconscious for a better understanding of yourself.

Please see also Woods.

Forgetting

To dream that you keep forgetting, is your subconscious manifesting itself in your dream that you may have forgotten an appointment or date.

Fork In The Road

To see a fork in the road in your dream, represents an important decision that you need to make. It may indicate your choices or ambivalence about some situation. Alternatively, a fork symbolizes the union of opposites. Opposing views/aspects are coming together.

To see an oak tree at the fork in the road, signifies a decision that may be life-changing.

Fork

To see a fork in your dream, signifies an extension of your reach. You are setting forth in pursuing your goals. Alternatively, it may be a pun on "fork it over". Do you feel that you are being coerced or forced?

To dream of being stabbed with a fork, indicates that you are too picky with the ideas/suggestions presented to you.

To see someone eating with a fork, denotes that all his present worries will be cleared up through the help of a friend.

Forklift

To see or use a forklift in your dream, suggests that you need to rearrange some of your ideals in order to find a solution to a problem. It may also mean that you need t clear out your old emotions and/or memories.

Formaldehyde

To see or use formaldehyde in your dream, refers to something that you are holding to for too long. You need to let go of the past and quit dwelling on old emotions.

Fort

To dream that you are defending a fort, indicates that you are always having to be on guard and constantly defending yourself.

To dream that you attack and take a fort, signifies victory over your other.

Fortress

To see a fortress in your dream, symbolizes protection and healing. Alternatively, you may have put up a wall between you and others. You are shutting down emotionally.

Fortune Telling

To dream that you are having your fortune told, signifies fears and anxieties about the future. You have issues of control and the desire to know the unknown.

Fossils

To see fossils in your dream, symbolizes death. It is represents longevity and that which has last.

Found

To dream that you found something, suggests that you are coming into contact with some aspect of your psyche or unconscious. You are recognizing a part of yourself that was previously repressed or undeveloped. Alternatively, it represents change.

To dream that you found someone, indicates that you are identifying new facets of a relationship. You may be taking the relationship to a new level and/or direction. The dream may also be a metaphor for finding yourself.

Foundation

To see the foundation of a building, represents your belief system. You are well-prepared for any situation before you.

To dream that the foundation is shifting, suggests that you are changing your beliefs about something.

Fountain

To see a fountain in your dream, represents great joy, renewed pleasure and/or increased sensitivity. You may be entering into a new relationship.

To see a dry fountain in your dream, indicates that you are coming down from the "high" of a passionate relationship.

Fowl

To see a fowl in your dream, denotes temporary worry, illness, or disagreement with friends.

Fox

To see a fox lurking about in your dream, represents cleverness and resourcefulness. You need to use your insight and intellect to solve some problem. Perhaps you need to conceal your thoughts and/or remain silent. Alternatively, it indicates a period of isolation or loneliness. It is a good way for you to use this time to reflect.

Frame

To see a frame in your dream represents limitations and boundaries. You or someone else may be putting restrictions on you. Alternatively, it symbolizes vanity.

Framework

To see the framework of a house or other structures in your dream, signifies integrity and your basic, core characteristics. Houses in dreams represents your self and its framework is symbolic of your belief system and the traits and attributes that makes you stand up for yourself. In particular, a wooden framework signifies a warm and yielding quality, where as a steel framework represents a cold and unyielding quality.

Fraud

To dream that you are defrauding a person, signifies that you are of lowly character who indulges in degrading pleasures and will deceive and take advantage of others for your own gain.

To dream that a fraud has been committed against you, signifies that you feel cheated from what you rightly deserve.

Freckles

To dream that you have freckles on your face, signifies that displeasing incidents will be disguised as happiness and you are at risk of losing your lover.

Freeway

To dream that you are on a freeway, indicates that you are feeling liberated and free.

Freezer

To see a freezer in your dream, refers to you cold feelings. You are being too frigid. Alternatively, it suggests that you are preserving your ideas and energy so that you can access them later.

French

If you do no speak French and you hear French in your dream, signifies a sensual and romantic part of yourself. It is often referred to as the language of love. Perhaps you are unwilling to understand or not giving enough attention to some waking relationship.

To dream that you are speaking French, signifies an expression of love.

French Fries

To see or eat French Fries in your dream, suggests that you should not overlook the frivolous and seemingly minute things in life.

Friday

The days of the week have significant meaning to the individual person. To dream of your significant other on a Friday indicates that this is a meaningful day between you and your significant other. This may be the day you met, the day your broke up, or perhaps the day you two always went out. Whatever the significance, there is something personal between this particular day and which only you can correlate.

Fridge

*Please see Refrigerator.

Friend

To see your friends in your dream, signifies aspects of your personality that you have rejected, but are ready to integrate these rejected part of yourself. The relationships you have with those around you are important in learning about yourself. Additionally, this symbol foretells of happy tidings from them and the arrival of good news.

To see your childhood friend in your dream, signifies regression into your past where you had no responsibilities and things were much simpler and carefree. You may be wanting to escape the the pressures and stresses of adulthood. Consider the relationship you had with this friend and the lessons that were learned. Alternatively, the childhood friend may be suggesting that you have been acting in a childish manner and you need to start acting like an adult.

To dream that your best friend is dying, suggests that some aspect or quality that your best friend possess is dying within your own self.

Frightened

To dream that you are frightened at anything, signifies temporary and fleeting worries.

Fringe

To see fringe in your dream, suggests that you are feeling torn up inside. You are not sure how to express yourself. Alternatively, it indicates the beauty you find in others.

Frisbee

To see or play frisbee in your dream, represents an easy-going attitude and/or lack of competition. It also serves to remind your that situations and relationships in life or give and take.

Frog

To see a frog in your dream, represents a potential to change or to do the unexpected. The frog may be a prince in disguise. Alternatively, the frog may suggest uncleanness.

To see frogs leaping in your dream, may indicate your lack of commitment. You have the tendency to jump from one thing to another. Alternatively, it may suggest that you are taking major steps toward some goal.

To dream that you are catching a frog, signifies your carelessness concerning your health.

To hear the sounds of a frog in your dream, signifies that you visit with friends will not accomplish anything that you wanted it to.

Frosting

To see or taste frosting in your dream, represents the results of your creativity and/or hard work. You have renewed confidence and self-assurance. New opportunities are now opened to you.

Frozen

To dream that something is frozen, represents something that has been suppressed, rejected, or denied.

Fruit

To see fruit in your dream, signifies a period of growth, abundance and financial gain. Fruits generally represents lust and sexuality. In particular green fruit in your dream, denotes your hastiness and disappointed efforts. You need to work harder and longer in order to achieve your goals.

To see or eat rotting/bitter fruit, suggests your missed opportunities for growth and pleasure.

To dream that you buy or sell fruit, signifies much business but little profit in them.

See entries on specific fruits for more information.

Frustration

To dream that you feel frustrated, represents your difficulty in coping with a situation in your daily life. It may reflect your concerns that your life is not going in the direction you want.

Funeral

To dream of your own funeral, symbolizes an ending to a situation or aspect of yourself. You may be repressing some of your feelings or parts of yourself and the dream may be a signal for you to recognize and acknowledge those feelings. Instead of confronting a situation, you are dealing with it by burying it and trying to forget about it. If you are nearing death, a funeral dream may relate to your feelings/anxieties about your own death.

To dream that you are at somebody else's funeral, signifies that you are burying an old relationship and closing the lid on the past. You may be letting go some of the feelings (resentment, anger, hostility toward someone) that you've been clinging onto.

To dream that you are attending a funeral for a still-living parent, suggests that you need to separate yourself from your parent's restrictions and confines. The symbolic death may give you the courage you need to take the next step toward your independence and autonomy.

To dream that you are at the funeral of an unknown person, suggests that something in your life is supposed to put to rest or put aside so that you can make room for something new. You need to investigate further what aspect or component of your life you need to let go.

Please also see Burial.

Funhouse

To dream that you are in a funhouse, indicates that you have overcame your fears to the point where you can now chuckle at it.

Fungus

To see fungus in your dream, represents negative emotions that are expanding and growing in your unconscious. You need to find a productive way to express them before it grows out of control.

Furnace

To see a furnace in your dream, symbolizes power and energy.

Furniture

To see furniture in your dream, represents how you feel about yourself and your family. It refers to your relationships with others and how they fit into your life.

To dream that you are moving furniture, indicates that you are going out of your way to please others. Also, you may be changing your ways and trying to reevaluate your relationships/attitudes.

To see old or worn furniture in your dream, symbolizes outdated attitudes, former relationships, and/or old ways of thinking.

Please also refer to specific pieces of furniture.

Furs

To see furs in your dream, represents prosperity. You are shielded from poverty. The dream may also be symbolic of your animalistic and instinctual nature.

Future

To dream that you are in the future, signifies your hopes or your fears of how things will turn out depending on the scenario.

G

Gag

To dream that you are gagging, denotes that you are not able to express yourself in how you really feel about a situation. Alternatively, this dream may forewarn that you need to keep quiet before you put your foot in your mouth.

Galaxy

To see the galaxy in your dream, represents your creativity. It also means that you are looking at the broader picture and are more aware of your surroundings.

Gale

To dream of being caught in a gale, signifies business losses and your struggle against some problems.

Gallows

To see gallows in your dream, signifies frustration in your future plans.

To see yourself being led to the gallows, signifies unexplainable bad luck.

To see yourself standing on the gallows, signifies that you will suffer from the maliciousness of a false friend and will be betrayed by them.

Gambling

To dream that are gambling, suggests that you are participating in some risk-taking activity. You may also be relying on fate and not taking responsibility for you decisions.

If you are not a gambler and dream that you are gambling, denotes that you need to take a chance or let up on yourself.

Game

To dream that you are hunting, shooting at, or killing game, refers to the game of life. It also represents your ability to keep your animalistic nature in check and in control.

Games

To dream that you are playing games, signifies relaxation or competition. It may also represent the rules you play by.

Gang

To dream that you are a gang member, signifies your need to achieve and accomplish things through force and intimidation.

To dream that you are confronted or threatened by a gang, signifies circumstances or situations in your waking life which are overwhelming and you feel has ganged up on you.

Gangrene

To see someone affected with gangrene in your dream, foretells of grief, loss and possible death of someone near.

Gap

To see a gap in your dream, suggests that you need to bring two sides together. The dream may also indicate that there is something lacking in your idea or argument.

Garage

To dream that you are in a garage, signifies a period of inactivity and idleness in your life. You may feel that you have no direction or guidance toward achieving your goals.

To dream that you are pulling your car into the garage, represents security and stability brought about by your accomplishments and efforts.

To dream that you are opening the garage door, denotes that you have made a decision about a matter. You may have decided on the path you will take in reaching your opportunities and goals. On the other hand, if you are closing the garage door, then it suggests that you are putting off your goals for the sake of others around you.

Garbage

To dream that you are throwing away your garbage, suggests that you are kicking your old negative habits and throwing away your bad characteristics and unwanted traits.

To see piles of garbage in your dream, forewarns of scandal and that you need to change your old ways and bad habits.

To dream that you are disposing another's garbage, foretells that you will be inconvenienced to repair someone else's reputation.

Garden

To see a vegetable or fruit garden in your dream, indicates that your hard work and diligence will pay off in the end. It is also symbolic of stability and inner growth.

To see a flower garden in your dream, represents tranquility, comfort, love and domestic bliss. You need to be nurturing.

To see sparse, weed-infested garden, suggests that you have neglected your spiritual needs. You are not on top of things.

Gargoyle

To see a gargoyle in your dream, signifies hidden and embarrassing fears over secretive matters that you have not shared with anyone.

Garland

To see a garland in your dream, represents wholeness and completeness.

To dream that you are wearing a garland, suggests a bond.

Garlic

To dream that you are eating garlic, signifies your practicality and sensibility in matters of the heart; you look for security over love.

To see a garlic patch in your dream, foretells of your rise to wealth and prominence in your business.

Garret

To climb up to a garret in your dream, signifies your ease of bettering your life and increasing your finances.

Garter

To see or dream hat you are wearing a garter, represents seduction and titillation. You are looking to be more sexual adventurous.

Gas

To smell or see gas in your dream, indicates that your need to be reenergized.

To dream that you run out of gas, suggests that you are wearing yourself out. Take a time out.

Gas Station

To dream that you are at the gas station, indicates a need to reenergize and revitalize yourself. It may also suggest that to help and be an assistant to others.

Gasoline

To see gasoline in your dream, represents energy.

Gate

To see or pass through a gate in your dream, suggests that you are walking through a new phase of life. It also represents new opportunities and possibilities.

To see a closed gate in your dream, signifies your inability to overcome current difficulties. If you are unable to open the gate, then it indicates that your hard work will be seen as unsatisfactory. It may also mean that you are not ready or not prepared to move on to the next step.

Gauze

To dream that you are dressed in gauze, signifies uncertainty in wealth.

Gavel

To see a gavel in your dream, symbolizes justice. It may refer to a problem that you need to acknowledge and confront.

To dream that you are using a gavel, represents a resolution to a problem. Something has been decided.

Gay

Please See Homosexual.

Gazelle

To see a gazelle in your dream, symbolizes the soul. It suggests that you should not take life so seriously. Lighten up.

Gear

To dream that you are putting your car in gear, suggests that you are ready to move forward with a new project in your life. You are headed into a new direction.

Gecko

To see a gecko in your dream, represents an agreement or affirmation. The answer to a decision that you need to make is "yes".

Geese

To see geese in your dream, represents domesticity. You are well grounded.

Geisha

To see a geisha in your dream, represents beauty, charm, poise and grace.

To dream that you are a geisha, indicates that you are well-balanced in your personal, social, and professional life. You adjust well in various situations.

Gelatin

*Please See Jelly.

Gems

To see gems in your dream, foretells of a happy fate in love and business.

Genie

To see a genie in your dream, represents your creative and mind power.

Genitals

To dream of your genitals, represents your feelings toward sex/sexuality and your attitudes toward masculinity/femininity. It also relates to issues of commitment and pleasure.

*Please see also Penis and Vagina.

Geography

To dream that you are studying geography, foretells of much travels in your future.

Geranium

To see geranium in your dream, symbolizes long lasting beauty and enduring elegance.

German Shepherd

To see a German Shepherd in your dream, highlights your protective instincts and attentiveness to a situation. This is no time for your to be nervous and/or lose control.

To dream that you are training a German Shepherd, suggests that you are open to new ideas and/or easily influenced. You make be seeking some reassurance.

*Please see also Dog.

Germs

To have a dream about germs, represents small and irrational fears that you are feeling in your waking life. You may be lacking energy and motivation. Focus on your purpose and goals in life.

Geyser

To see a geyser in your dream, symbolizes an outburst of emotion. You need to acknowledge and express you pent up anger and feelings before they explode.

Ghost

In general, ghosts symbolizes aspects of yourself that you fear. This may involve a painful memory, guilt, or some repressed thoughts. You may be afraid of death and dying. Alternatively, ghosts are representative of something that is no longer obtainable or within reach. It indicates a feeling of disconnection from life and society. This dream may be a calling for you to move on and abandon your outdated modes of thinking and behavior.

To dream that you reach out to touch a ghost, but it disappears, indicates that you are taking steps to acknowledging some painful or repressed thoughts even though you are not ready to fully confront them.

To see the ghost of a living relative or friend in your dream, signifies that you are in danger of malice acts by that person.

To see the ghost of a dead friend/relative in your dream, suggests guilt and regrets concerning the past relationships with that particular person.

Ghoul

To see a ghoul in your dream, suggests that your habits and negative ways are hindering your growth. The dream may also represent a fresh beginning.

Giant

To see a giant in your dream, signifies of a great struggle between you and your opponents. This may prove to be a major and overwhelming obstacle for you to overcome. Alternatively, a giant may be symbolic of an issue or feeling that is dominating you.

To dream that you turn into a giant, indicates feelings of inferiority.

Gift

To dream that you are giving a gift, signifies your generosity towards others. Alternatively, you may be trying to express some feeling or have something awkward to say that has to be carefully packaged.

To dream that you receive a gift, denotes your tremendous luck in fortune and love. You are being rewarded for a job well done and are held in high esteem by those around you.

Gig

To dream of playing in a gig, signifies the threat of illness or your efforts to entertain unwelcome visitors.

Ginger

To see ginger in your dream, indicates security and comfort in your life. But you need to add some more excitement and variety to you life.

Ginseng

To see ginseng in your dream, represents virility and life.

Giraffe

To see a giraffe in your dream, suggests that you need to consider the overall picture. Take a broader view on your life and where it is headed.

To dream that you are riding a giraffe, represents your desire to stand up amongst the crowd. You want attention, but aren't getting it.

Girlfriend

To see your girlfriend in your dream, represents your waking relationship with her and how you feel about her.

Girdle

To dream that you are wearing a girdle, suggests that you are feeling restricted and limited in the expression of your ideas and feelings. Alternatively, you have the tendency to bear pain in order to please others.

Girls

To see a girl in your dream, represents your playful, innocent, and childlike nature. Perhaps you have been behaving prematurely.

To dream about a girl that you just met, represents your anxieties and thoughts of whether you had made a good impression on her and what she thought of you. If she told you that she disliked you in the dream, then it may be an excuse for you to dismiss her and not pursue a relationship that is beyond friendship.

For a man to dream that he is a girl, signifies that he aspires to be an actor and play female parts.

Glacier

To see a glacier in your dream, refers to your cold feelings. You are shutting down emotionally.

Gladiolas

To see gladiolas in your dream, symbolizes joy, happiness, and celebration.

Glass

To see glass in your dream, symbolizes passivity. To dream that you are drinking from a glass, is an omen of good luck.

To dream that you are looking through glass, represents your openness and non-defensiveness. Alternatively, you may be putting up an invisible emotional barrier around yourself.

To see broken glass in your dream, signifies a change in your life. You will find that a situation will come to an abrupt and untimely end.

To dream that you are eating glass, highlights your vulnerability, confusion and frailty. You may have difficulties in communicating your thoughts across and getting the right words out. Alternatively, it may symbolize your hurtful and cutting comments. Perhaps you have been hurt or disappointed by something that someone had said. Or you need to be careful in how you phrase and word things or run the risk of offending others.

Glass-Blower

To see a glass-blower in your dream, signifies that you are contemplating a change for the better in your business.

Glass House

To see a glass house in your dream, signifies that flattery is likely to hurt you.

To dream that you are living in a glass house, signifies the threatened loss of your reputation. Alternatively, it suggests that you are being watched.

Glass Slipper

To see or wear glass slippers in your dream, symbolizes truth and transformation.

Glasses

Please See Eyeglasses.

Gleaners

To see gleaners at their work in your dream, signifies a prosperity in business.

To dream that you are working with a gleaner, denotes that you will acquire some property after much disputes.

Glider

To see or ride a glider in your dream, represents your tendency to go with the flow of things instead of taking your own initiative and making changes in your life. It may also mean that things are a breeze for you.

Globe

To see a globe in your dream, denotes that you are in complete control of your life.

To see a spinning globe in your dream, signifies that your life is going out of control.

Gloomy

To be surrounded by gloomy things and situations in your dream, forewarns of rapidly approaching loss and unhappiness.

Gloves

To see or wear gloves in your dream, indicates how you handle things or how you may be getting a handle on something. Alternatively, it signifies your cautious demeanor and economical way in your dealings with others.

To dream that you are wearing work gloves, represents a hard job.

Glow

To see a glow in your dream, symbolizes enlightenment and that new light has been shed onto a situation. You have gained a fresh perspective and reached a welcomed understanding.

Glue

To see glue in your dream, indicates a fear of being trapped in some situation and not being able to get out of it. You may fear partnership or commitment and a general distrust of people around you.

To dream that you are gluing something together, suggests that you are piecing together aspects of yourself and acknowledging those previously rejected parts.

Gnome

To see a gnome in your dream, signifies the inner child and its fantasies.

Goat

To see goats in your dream, represents your lack of judgment and your gullibility. Also consider the associations with the goat as in "scapegoat" or "getting someone's goat".

To dream that a billy goat butts you, forewarns of enemies trying to get hold of your business plans.

Gag

To dream that you are gagging, denotes that you are not able to express yourself in how you really feel about a situation. Alternatively, this dream may forewarn that you need to keep quiet before you put your foot in your mouth.

Galaxy

To see the galaxy in your dream, represents your creativity. It also means that you are looking at the broader picture and are more aware of your surroundings.

Gale

To dream of being caught in a gale, signifies business losses and your struggle against some problems.

Gallows

To see gallows in your dream, signifies frustration in your future plans.

To see yourself being led to the gallows, signifies unexplainable bad luck.

To see yourself standing on the gallows, signifies that you will suffer from the maliciousness of a false friend and will be betrayed by them.

Gambling

To dream that are gambling, suggests that you are participating in some risk-taking activity. You may also be relying on fate and not taking responsibility for you decisions.

If you are not a gambler and dream that you are gambling, denotes that you need to take a chance or let up on yourself.

Game

To dream that you are hunting, shooting at, or killing game, refers to the game of life. It also represents your ability to keep your animalistic nature in check and in control.

Games

To dream that you are playing games, signifies relaxation or competition. It may also represent the rules you play by.

Gang

To dream that you are a gang member, signifies your need to achieve and accomplish things through force and intimidation.

To dream that you are confronted or threatened by a gang, signifies circumstances or situations in your waking life which are overwhelming and you feel has ganged up on you.

Gangrene

To see someone affected with gangrene in your dream, foretells of grief, loss and possible death of someone near.

Gap

To see a gap in your dream, suggests that you need to bring two sides together. The dream may also indicate that there is something lacking in your idea or argument.

Garage

To dream that you are in a garage, signifies a period of inactivity and idleness in your life. You may feel that you have no direction or guidance toward achieving your goals.

To dream that you are pulling your car into the garage, represents security and stability brought about by your accomplishments and efforts.

To dream that you are opening the garage door, denotes that you have made a decision about a matter. You may have decided on the path you will take in reaching your opportunities and goals. On the other hand, if you are closing the garage door, then it suggests that you are putting off your goals for the sake of others around you.

Garbage

To dream that you are throwing away your garbage, suggests that you are kicking your old negative habits and throwing away your bad characteristics and unwanted traits.

To see piles of garbage in your dream, forewarns of scandal and that you need to change your old ways and bad habits.

To dream that you are disposing another's garbage, foretells that you will be inconvenienced to repair someone else's reputation.

Garden

To see a vegetable or fruit garden in your dream, indicates that your hard work and diligence will pay off in the end. It is also symbolic of stability and inner growth.

To see a flower garden in your dream, represents tranquility, comfort, love and domestic bliss. You need to be nurturing.

To see sparse, weed-infested garden, suggests that you have neglected your spiritual needs. You are not on top of things.

Gargoyle

To see a gargoyle in your dream, signifies hidden and embarrassing fears over secretive matters that you have not shared with anyone.

Garland

To see a garland in your dream, represents wholeness and completeness.

To dream that you are wearing a garland, suggests a bond.

Garlic

To dream that you are eating garlic, signifies your practicality and sensibility in matters of the heart; you look for security over love.

To see a garlic patch in your dream, foretells of your rise to wealth and prominence in your business.

Garret

To climb up to a garret in your dream, signifies your ease of bettering your life and increasing your finances.

Garter

To see or dream hat you are wearing a garter, represents seduction and titillation. You are looking to be more sexual adventurous.

Gas

To smell or see gas in your dream, indicates that your need to be reenergized.

To dream that you run out of gas, suggests that you are wearing yourself out. Take a time out.

Gas Station

To dream that you are at the gas station, indicates a need to reenergize and revitalize yourself. It may also suggest that to help and be an assistant to others.

Gasoline

To see gasoline in your dream, represents energy.

Gate

To see or pass through a gate in your dream, suggests that you are walking through a new phase of life. It also represents new opportunities and possibilities.

To see a closed gate in your dream, signifies your inability to overcome current difficulties. If you are unable to open the gate, then it indicates that your hard work will be seen as unsatisfactory. It may also mean that you are not ready or not prepared to move on to the next step.

Gauze

To dream that you are dressed in gauze, signifies uncertainty in wealth.

Gavel

To see a gavel in your dream, symbolizes justice. It may refer to a problem that you need to acknowledge and confront.

To dream that you are using a gavel, represents a resolution to a problem. Something has been decided.

Gay

*Please See Homosexual.

Gazelle

To see a gazelle in your dream, symbolizes the soul. It suggests that you should not take life so seriously. Lighten up.

Gear

To dream that you are putting your car in gear, suggests that you are ready to move forward with a new project in your life. You are headed into a new direction.

Gecko

To see a gecko in your dream, represents an agreement or affirmation. The answer to a decision that you need to make is "yes".

Geese

To see geese in your dream, represents domesticity. You are well grounded.

Geisha

To see a geisha in your dream, represents beauty, charm, poise and grace.

To dream that you are a geisha, indicates that you are well-balanced in your personal, social, and professional life. You adjust well in various situations.

Gelatin

*Please See Jelly.

Gems

To see gems in your dream, foretells of a happy fate in love and business.

Genie

To see a genie in your dream, represents your creative and mind power.

Genitals

To dream of your genitals, represents your feelings toward sex/sexuality and your attitudes toward masculinity/femininity. It also relates to issues of commitment and pleasure.

*Please see also Penis and Vagina.

Geography

To dream that you are studying geography, foretells of much travels in your future.

Geranium

To see geranium in your dream, symbolizes long lasting beauty and enduring elegance.

German Shepherd

To see a German Shepherd in your dream, highlights your protective instincts and attentiveness to a situation. This is no time for your to be nervous and/or lose control.

To dream that you are training a German Shepherd, suggests that you are open to new ideas and/or easily influenced. You make be seeking some reassurance.

Please see also Dog.

Germs

To have a dream about germs, represents small and irrational fears that you are feeling in your waking life. You may be lacking energy and motivation. Focus on your purpose and goals in life.

Geyser

To see a geyser in your dream, symbolizes an outburst of emotion. You need to acknowledge and express you pent up anger and feelings before they explode.

Ghost

In general, ghosts symbolizes aspects of yourself that you fear. This may involve a painful memory, guilt, or some repressed thoughts. You may be afraid of death and dying. Alternatively, ghosts are representative of something that is no longer obtainable or within reach. It indicates a feeling of disconnection from life and society. This dream may be a calling for you to move on and abandon your outdated modes of thinking and behavior.

To dream that you reach out to touch a ghost, but it disappears, indicates that you are taking steps to acknowledging some painful or repressed thoughts even though you are not ready to fully confront them.

To see the ghost of a living relative or friend in your dream, signifies that you are in danger of malice acts by that person.

To see the ghost of a dead friend/relative in your dream, suggests guilt and regrets concerning the past relationships with that particular person.

Ghoul

To see a ghoul in your dream, suggests that your habits and negative ways are hindering your growth. The dream may also represent a fresh beginning.

Giant

To see a giant in your dream, signifies of a great struggle between you and your opponents. This may prove to be a major and overwhelming obstacle for you to overcome. Alternatively, a giant may be symbolic of an issue or feeling that is dominating you.

To dream that you turn into a giant, indicates feelings of inferiority.

Gift

To dream that you are giving a gift, signifies your generosity towards others. Alternatively, you may be trying to express some feeling or have something awkward to say that has to be carefully packaged.

To dream that you receive a gift, denotes your tremendous luck in fortune and love. You are being rewarded for a job well done and are held in high esteem by those around you.

Gig

To dream of playing in a gig, signifies the threat of illness or your efforts to entertain unwelcome visitors.

Ginger

To see ginger in your dream, indicates security and comfort in your life. But you need to add some more excitement and variety to you life.

Ginseng

To see ginseng in your dream, represents virility and life.

Giraffe

To see a giraffe in your dream, suggests that you need to consider the overall picture. Take a broader view on your life and where it is headed.

To dream that you are riding a giraffe, represents your desire to stand up amongst the crowd. You want attention, but aren't getting it.

Girlfriend

To see your girlfriend in your dream, represents your waking relationship with her and how you feel about her.

Girdle

To dream that you are wearing a girdle, suggests that you are feeling restricted and limited in the expression of your ideas and feelings. Alternatively, you have the tendency to bear pain in order to please others.

Girls

To see a girl in your dream, represents your playful, innocent, and childlike nature. Perhaps you have been behaving prematurely.

To dream about a girl that you just met, represents your anxieties and thoughts of whether you had made a good impression on her and what she thought of you. If she told you that she disliked you in the dream, then it may be an excuse for you to dismiss her and not pursue a relationship that is beyond friendship.

For a man to dream that he is a girl, signifies that he aspires to be an actor and play female parts.

Glacier

To see a glacier in your dream, refers to your cold feelings. You are shutting down emotionally.

Gladiolas

To see gladiolas in your dream, symbolizes joy, happiness, and celebration.

Glass

To see glass in your dream, symbolizes passivity. To dream that you are drinking from a glass, is an omen of good luck.

To dream that you are looking through glass, represents your openness and non-defensiveness. Alternatively, you may be putting up an invisible emotional barrier around yourself.

To see broken glass in your dream, signifies a change in your life. You will find that a situation will come to an abrupt and untimely end.

To dream that you are eating glass, highlights your vulnerability, confusion and frailty. You may have difficulties in communicating your thoughts across and getting the right words out. Alternatively, it may symbolize your hurtful and cutting comments. Perhaps you have been hurt or disappointed by something that someone had said. Or you need to be careful in how you phrase and word things or run the risk of offending others.

Glass-Blower

To see a glass-blower in your dream, signifies that you are contemplating a change for the better in your business.

Glass House

To see a glass house in your dream, signifies that flattery is likely to hurt you.

To dream that you are living in a glass house, signifies the threatened loss of your reputation. Alternatively, it suggests that you are being watched.

Glass Slipper

To see or wear glass slippers in your dream, symbolizes truth and transformation.

Glasses

Please See Eyeglasses.

Gleaners

To see gleaners at their work in your dream, signifies a prosperity in business.

To dream that you are working with a gleaner, denotes that you will acquire some property after much disputes.

Glider

To see or ride a glider in your dream, represents your tendency to go with the flow of things instead of taking your own initiative and making changes in your life. It may also mean that things are a breeze for you.

Globe

To see a globe in your dream, denotes that you are in complete control of your life.

To see a spinning globe in your dream, signifies that your life is going out of control.

Gloomy

To be surrounded by gloomy things and situations in your dream, forewarns of rapidly approaching loss and unhappiness.

Gloves

To see or wear gloves in your dream, indicates how you handle things or how you may be getting a handle on something. Alternatively, it signifies your cautious demeanor and economical way in your dealings with others.

To dream that you are wearing work gloves, represents a hard job.

Glow

To see a glow in your dream, symbolizes enlightenment and that new light has been shed onto a situation. You have gained a fresh perspective and reached a welcomed understanding.

Glue

To see glue in your dream, indicates a fear of being trapped in some situation and not being able to get out of it. You may fear partnership or commitment and a general distrust of people around you.

To dream that you are gluing something together, suggests that you are piecing together aspects of yourself and acknowledging those previously rejected parts.

Gnome

To see a gnome in your dream, signifies the inner child and its fantasies.

Goat

To see goats in your dream, represents your lack of judgment and your gullibility. Also consider the associations with the goat as in "scapegoat" or "getting someone's goat".

To dream that a billy goat butts you, forewarns of enemies trying to get hold of your business plans.

H

Hag

To see a hag in your dream, may represent the "Wise Old Woman" figure and thus refers to nurturance. Negatively, to see a hag in your dream, signifies the devouring mother.

Haggard

To see a haggard face in your dreams, suggests that you are growing tiresome or weary of a situation

To dream that your own face has grown haggard, forewarns that you may be stricken with an illness. You may be under a tremendous amount of stress.

Hail

To dream that you are caught in a hail storm, signifies mediocre returns in your projects.

To hear hail beating down on your roof, denotes that you will go through a period of difficult times.

Hair

To see hair in your dream, signifies sexual virility, seduction, sensuality, vanity, and health. It is indicative of your attitudes. If your hair is knotted or tangled, then it is symbolic of uncertainty and confusion in your life. You may be unable to think straight.

To dream that you are cutting your hair, suggests that you are experiencing a loss in strength. You may feel that someone is trying to censor you. Alternatively, you may be reshaping your thinking or ambitions and eliminating unwanted thoughts/habits.

To dream that you are combing, stroking or styling your hair, suggests that you are taking on and evaluating a new idea, concept, outlook, or way of thinking.

You may be putting your thoughts in order and getting your facts straight. A more literal interpretation suggests your concerns about your self-image and appearance.

To dream that you have long hair, indicates that you are thinking long and carefully before making some decision. You are concentrating on some plan or situation.

To dream that you are losing your hair, denotes that you are concerned with the notion that you are getting older and losing your sex appeal/virility. You are preoccupied with aging and your appearance. Losing you hair also signify a lack of strength and that you do not possess the power to succeed in an undertaking. You may be feeling weak and vulnerable.

To dream that someone is smelling your hair, indicates sexual curiosity and your need for some sensual stimulation. You have a lot to learn about a relationship. The way yours or someone else's hair smell may remind your of a particular person.

To dream that you are reaching for someone's hair, suggests that you are trying to connect with that person on a spiritual or intellectual level. It also refers to sympathy, protectiveness, and fraternal love.

To dream that the wind is blowing through your hair, signifies freedom to express uninhibited feelings. You are "letting your hair down".

To dream that your hair is white or turns white, indicates that something important has just been made aware to you. It is a symbol of wisdom and insight. The dream may also be a metaphor suggesting that you are feeling "light-headed".

Haircut

To dream that someone is giving you a haircut, suggests that you are experiencing a decreased sense of power. You may feel that you were criticized unfairly.

Hairdresser

To dream that you are a hairdresser, suggests that you are imposing your ideas and opinions on others. Perhaps you need to work on your self-image and improve on your image. Alternatively, it refers to your attitude toward your own sexuality.

*Please see also Salon.

Hairpiece

To dream that you are wearing a hairpiece, indicates some sort of deception. You may be giving off a false impression and passing the views of others as your own.

To dream that you lose your hairpiece, suggests that you are beginning to lose your mind or that you may be giving someone a piece of your mind. The dream may also be a pun on losing your "peace" of mind.

Half

To dream about half of something, indicates that something in your waking life is incomplete or unresolved. It may also indicate that you are only partially acknowledging your feelings. You or someone else is limiting or restricting you. Alternatively, the dream may suggest that you need to be open to compromise and meet halfway.

Hallways

To see a hallway in your dream, symbolizes the beginning of a path that you are taking in life or a journey into the unknown and self exploration. It represents spiritual, emotional, physical, or mental passages in your life. It is indicative of a transitional phase in your life.

Halloween

To dream of Halloween, signifies death and the underworld. Halloween also represents the temporary adoption of a new persona where you feel less inhibited and more comfortable to freely express yourself.

Hallucination

To have a hallucination in your dream, symbolizes an image from your unconscious. They can also represent repressed emotions and feelings that you do not want to confront. Your dream may be telling you to be more alert and to express yourself more clearly. Alternatively, it refers to self-deception. What are you trying to hide?

Halo

To dream that you have a halo. signifies that you are a perfectionist.

Halter

To dream that you are putting a halter on a horse, signifies that you are trying to persuade someone into mindset and your way of thinking.

Ham

To dream that you are eating ham, signifies festivities and togetherness.

To see hams in your dream, indicates that you are experiencing some emotional difficulties. The symbol may also be metaphor to suggest your desire for attention.

Hamburger

To see or eat a hamburger in your dream, suggests that you are lacking some emotional, intellectual, or physical component you need in order to feel whole again. You may be feeling unsatisfied with some situation or relationship. It is also symbolic of your experiences and how you need to learn from them. Look at the big picture.

Hammer

To see a hammer in your dream, signifies power, strength, virility, and masculine attitudes. It also symbolizes growth and construction.

To dream that you are using a hammer, signifies successful accomplishment in a task at hand. Alternatively, it suggests that you may be dealing with old demons and inner battles.

Hammock

To see a hammock in your dream, suggests that you need to devote more time to pleasure and leisurely activity.

To dream that you are lying in a hammock, indicates that you may be pushing people away.

To dream that you fall off a hammock, suggests that you are taking your valuable friends and loved ones for granted.

Hamper

To see a hamper in your dream, indicates that you need to find a more productive way to express your negative feelings.

Hamster

To see a hamster in your dream, represents underdeveloped emotions. You are distancing yourself from others so that you won't end up getting hurt. It may also indicate that issues of sexuality are trivial to you. You are able to separate sex and love.

Hand

To dream of your hands, represents your relationship to those around you and how you connect with the world. Hands serve as a form of communication. Perhaps you need to lend out a helping hand to someone. In particular, the left hand symbolizes your graciousness and feminine, receptive qualities. And the right hand symbolizes masculine, active attributes. It may also be a pun for some decision or something being "right".

To dream that you are holding hands with someone, represents your connection with that person. Your dream may also reflect anxieties about losing touch with him/her or that you are drifting apart.

To dream that you hands are injured, denotes an attack on your ego.

To dream that your hands are clasped or closed, signifies unity, completeness, acceptance or agreement. On a more negative note, it may suggest that you are close-minded, ungiving or unwilling to help.

To dream that you have unusually large hands, denotes much success in achieving your goals.

To dream that your hands are hairy or rough, implies your lack of gentleness in dealing with others. You may be too brash and abrasive.

To see blood on your hands, signifies that you are experiencing some sort of guilt.

To dream that you are washing your hands, represents a worrisome issue that you need to work through. Alternatively, it suggests that you are no longer taking responsibilities in some matter. You are letting go and getting things out of your system.

Handcuffs

To see a pair of handcuffs in your dream, signifies sickness and misfortune.

To dream that you are in handcuffs, suggests that something or someone is holding back your success. Opportunities are shut off to you. You are experiencing a loss of power and effectiveness.

To see others in handcuff in your dream, denotes that you will overcome your adversaries.

Handicap

To dream that you or someone is handicap, symbolizes your own weakness and neediness. You are confronted with many challenges and need to utilize your full potential. Consider which part of your body is handicap and its symbolism. Alternatively, it suggests that you are becoming too arrogant for your own good. You need to be more humble.

Handkerchiefs

To dream that you are waving good-bye with a handkerchief, signifies your social downfall. You will be disgraced in some way.

To dream that you lose you handkerchief, denotes a separation with your lover.

To dream that you handkerchief is soiled or torn, denotes that there is little likelihood of a reconciliation between you and your lover.

Handle

To see a handle in your dream, suggests that you are in control of the situation. The dream may a metaphor indicating that you have a handle on a situation or on life. If the handle is broken, then it may mean that you need to get a handle on who you are. Draw on your inner strength.

Handshake

To dream that you are shaking hands with someone, symbolizes either a new beginning or an ending to a situation. You have have reached an agreement or a decision to a problem. The dream may also mean that you are welcoming something new into your life. In particular, if you are shaking hands with someone famous or someone important, then it suggests that you are well regarded by others.

Handwriting

To dream that you are handwriting, represents your self-expression and creativity. Consider the symbolism of what you are handwriting and how it relates to your waking life.

Hang Gliding

To dream that you are hang gliding, symbolizes freedom in your personal life. It also represents trust and believing in destiny.

To dream that you crash a hang glider, represents a loss in faith.

Hanger

To see a hanger in your dream, suggests that you are getting the hang of some situation or some task. Or it may mean that you are just hanging in there. You need more motivation and encouragement.

Hanging

To watch a hanging in your dream, represents your feelings of insecurity. Consider also the image as a pun for something in your life which you have left hanging or unfinished.

To dream that you are hanging up clothes, suggests that you are clarifying your thoughts and elevating yourself to a new state of awareness.

Happy

To dream that you are happy, may be a compensatory dream and is often a dream of the contrary. You may be trying to compensate for the sadness or stress in your waking life.

Harbor

To see a harbor in your dream, signifies shelter from a stormy relationship or chaotic situation. You may be seeking refuge until you can recollect your thoughts and prepare for the challenges ahead.

Hardware Store

To dream that you are at the hardware store, indicates your need to make some self-improvements and adjust your attitudes.

Hare

To see a hare in your dream, signifies a transformation. It may also represent some personal attributes such as rashness and shallow cleverness.

Harem

To dream that your are part of a harem, signifies your repressed sexual energy and inhibitions. You need to be open to sexual experimentation.

To dream that you are held prisoner of a harem, suggests that you are seeking acceptance of your own sexuality.

To dream that you keep a harem, suggests that you are wasting your time and energy on frivolous pursuits. You need to rethink your goals and the direction you want to take in life.

Harmonica

To see or hear a harmonica in your dream, suggests that you need to let more joy and pleasure come into your life. It is also symbolic of a harmonious situation.

To dream that you are playing a harmonica, indicates that there is some emotions that you need to release and integrate into your daily life.

Harp

To see or play a harp in your dream, represents spiritual harmony. It is a healing symbol.

Harvesting

To dream that you are harvesting crops, denotes that you still have some way to go before fully developing your career and goals.

Hat

To see a hat in your dream, signifies that you are concealing something or covering up something. Alternatively, it may represent the role you play or the responsibilities you have in life.

To dream that you are wearing a top hat, denotes your aspirations for wealth. It is also symbolic of male elegance and formality.

Hate

To dream about hate, indicates repressed aggression and your fear of confrontations. On the other hand, you may forcing your views and opinions onto others. Consider the symbolism of other elements in the dream to find out what is it that you really hate.

Haunted

To dream that you are being haunted, indicates early unpleasant traumas and repressed feelings/memories. You are experiencing some fear or guilt about your past activities and thoughts.

Hawaii

To see or dream about Hawaii in your dream, symbolizes relaxation and leisure. You are trying to escape from your daily problems.

Hawk

To see a hawk in your dream, denotes suspicions are lurking around you and your activities. You need to proceed with caution.

Hay

To see hay in your dream, represents the necessity of hard work; nothing in life comes easy. You may also be feeling hopeless about a situation. Alternatively, hay indicates the need to nurture your maternal instincts, masculine energy, and/or your sexual urges. Consider also the symbol as a pun on "hey". Your dream may be trying to call your attention to something.

Head

To see a head in your dream, signifies wisdom, intellect, understanding and rationality. It may also represent your accomplishments, self-image, and perception of the world.

To dream that someone is trying to rip your head off, suggests that you are not see a situation or problem clearly. Perhaps you are refusing to see the truth. You have to confront the situation or the person despite the pain and discomfort you might feel in doing so.

Headache

To dream that you have a headache, suggests that you are heading in the wrong direction. You may be repressing your intellect and rational thinking. You need to utilize your mind and not let your emotions get out of control.

Headphones

To dream that you are wearing headphones, indicates that you are the only one getting the message. It also indicates that you are in tune with your intuition.

Headstone

To see a headstone in your dream, represents a forgotten or buried aspect of yourself which you need to acknowledge. Consider also the message on the headstone. It may indicate a statement about your life and its condition.

Healing

To dream of healing, represents your need for emotional and/or physical healing. You need to find the power to rectify and care for the matters in your life.

Hear

To dream that no one hears you, refers to a waking situation where you feel that no one is listening to you or paying attention to what you are saying. You feel you are being overlooked or overshadowed.

Hearing Aid

To see or wear a hearing aid in your dream, suggests that you are not paying enough attention to what someone is trying to tell you. You are not picking up on the cues.

Hearse

To see a hearse in your dream, indicates that you are moving into a new phase. You need to carry away and let go all of unfinished issues. Start taking action and making the necessary changes that will carry you into this new transitional level.

Heart

To see your heart in your dream, signifies truth, courage, love, and romance. It is representative of how you are currently dealing with your feelings and expressing your emotions. Also consider the saying "the heart of the matter" which implies that you may need to get down to the core of a situation before proceeding.

Heart Attack

To dream that you have a heart attack, refers to a lack of support and acceptance. Perhaps you also feel a loss of love.

Heartbeat

To hear a heartbeat in your dream, suggests that you are not confronting or recognizing your feelings. You need to approaching thing head-on. Alternatively, a heartbeat may symbolize life or fear. You are feeling threatened in some way.

Hearth

To see the hearth in your dream, signifies nurturance and family values.

Heat

To feel heat in your dream, indicates a feeling of shame or embarrassment. Alternatively, it represents purity and creative energy.

Heater

To see or use a heater in your dream, signifies warmth, nurturance, and comfort. It may also mean that you have opened up your feelings and allow yourself to love and be loved.

Heaven

To see heaven in your dream, signifies your desires to find perfect happiness. You may be trying to escape from the difficulties you are experiencing in your life. And your dream serves as a medium in which you can restore your faith, optimism, and hopes.

Heavy

To dream that something is too heavy, symbolizes your burdens, work load and responsibilities. You are carry too much on your shoulders and need to prioritize. Take a break and lighten up.

Hedge

To see hedges in your dream, symbolizes restrictions and obstacles that are inhibiting your progress.

To dream that you are trimming a hedge, denotes your acceptance of the restrictions you are facing and are now making the best out of a negative situation.

Hedgehog

To see a hedgehog in your dream, suggests that you are being overly sensitive. You tend to take everything too personally. Alternatively, it refers to losing your soul.

Heel

To see your heel in your dream, signifies oppression, lowliness, and vulnerability.

Height

To dream that you are at a great height, signifies that you have reached one of your highest goals or objectives.

To dream that you are afraid of heights, denotes that you are striving for goals that seem beyond your reach.

Helicopter

To see a helicopter in your dream, represents your ambition and achievements. You are in full pursuit of your goals.

To dream that you are in a helicopter, indicates that you are living beyond your means. You need to slow down and don't try to please everyone. Alternatively, you may be experiencing a higher level of consciousness, new-found freedom and greater awareness.

Hell

To dream of hell, denotes that you may be suffering from a seemingly inescapable situation. You may have placed your decision or course of action into someone else's hand. Alternatively, you may be possessing many inner fears and repressed guilty feelings. It is time to quit punishing yourself and take it easy for awhile.

Helmet

To see a helmet in your dream, signifies that you need to keep your thoughts and ideas closely guarded.

Help

To dream that you are helping someone, indicates your willingness to compromise your beliefs toward a greater accomplishment. It also represents your efforts to combine your talents or energies to achieve a mutual goal. In particular, if you are helping an enemy or someone you do not like, then it suggests that you need to come to an understanding or some sort of middle ground in order to move forward and on with your life.

To dream that you are calling or signaling for help, suggests that you are feeling lost, overwhelmed, and/or inadequate.

Helpless

To dream that you are or feel helpless, suggests that you are experiencing difficulties in confronting a situation or relationship. You feel that you are unable to take charge of yourself.

Hem

To dream that you are sewing a hem, represents your indecisiveness. Alternatively, it suggests that you are tying up the loose ends of a project.

Hemorrhage

To dream that you are hemorrhaging, suggests loss of vitality, loss of faith in yourself, and lack of self-confidence. Also consider where you are hemorrhaging from and analyze the symbolism of that body part.

Hen

To see a hen in your dream, symbolizes gossip and calamity. You have a tendency to brag about minor things. It may also suggest being "hen-pecked" or that you feel being picked on.

Herbs

To dream of herbs, indicates your need to take a new approach toward some situation or relationship. You need to look at things from a different perspective and live life with some zest.

Hercules

To see Hercules in your dream, suggests your individual struggle for freedom and immortality.

Herd

To see a herd in your dream, indicates that you are a follower. Learn to make your own decision and take initiative. The dream may also be a pun on "heard". Perhaps you heard something that was not meant for your ears. Consider also the specific animal in the herd.

Hermaphrodite

To see or dream that you are a hermaphrodite, represents the union of opposites.

Hermit

To dream that you are a hermit, represents your need to be alone or that you are feeling alone. You are withdrawing from daily life and distancing yourself from others. Find a way to get of out this rut.

Hero

To dream that you are a hero, signifies your inner strength and weaknesses. It may be representative of how you are bravely facing and challenging the secrets of your unconscious.

Heron

To see a heron in your dream, represents self-reliance, stability, and careful forethought. You will achieve much success through your efforts. Alternatively, it signifies your ability to explore and delve into your unconscious.

Herpes

To dream that you or someone has herpes, refers to your sexual anxiety and worries. Perhaps you have practiced unsafe sex and are expressing your regrets.

Hex

To dream that you are putting a hex on someone, represents your vengeful nature and vindictiveness.

To dream that someone is putting a hex on you, symbolizes angry and hurtful feelings. You are unable to cope in some painful situation.

Hexagram

To see a hexagram in your dream, symbolizes order and harmony in some aspect of your life.

Hiccup

To dream that you have hiccups, symbolizes minor interruptions and annoyances. You need to pace yourself and take your time in moving forward toward your goals.

Hickey

To dream that you have a hickey, represents a split between your rational thinking and your emotional thinking. You may be acting with your heart instead of thinking things out more clearly. Alternatively, you may be feeling emotionally or physically drained. You feel that you are giving too much of yourself in a relationship or situation.

Hiding

To dream that you are hiding, suggests that you are keeping some secret or withholding some information. You may not be facing up to a situation or not want to deal with an issue. However, you may be getting ready to reveal and confess before somebody finds out.

To dream that you are somebody else is hiding, indicates a need for security and protection. In particular, to dream that you are hiding from some authority figure (police, parents, teacher...), implies feelings of guilt.

Hieroglyphics

To see hieroglyphics in your dream, denotes that you will face many obstacles as you try to figure out your path in life.

High Heels

To dream that you are wearing high heels, represents femininity and glamour. You feel confident and self-assured. Alternatively, you may feel restricted and limited in your role as a female. You do not think that you can fully and freely express yourself.

High School

To dream about high school, refers to the bounds and friendships that you made while you were in high school. What spiritual lessons have you learned? The dream may also be telling you that you need to start preparing for the real world.

To dream that you have to repeat high school, suggests that you are doubting your accomplishments and the goals that you have already completed. You feel that you may not be measuring up to the expectation of others. The dream may occur because some recent situation may have awakened old anxieties and insecurities.

Please See Also School.

Highway

To see a highway in your dream, represents your sense of direction and your life's path. Consider the conditions of the highway which will reveal how much you feel in charge of your life. A smooth, straight highway signifies inner peace, while a winding, bumpy road reflects emotional distress/disharmony.

Hiking

To dream that you are hiking, represents progress and achievement. With perseverance and strong-will, you will make it far in life.

Hill

To dream that you are climbing a hill, signifies your struggles in achieving a goal. To dream that you are standing on top of a hill, signifies that you have succeeded in your endeavors or that you have now have the resources to complete a task at hand.

Hippie

To see a hippie in your dream, represents excess and freedom of expression.

To dream that you are a hippie, suggests that you want to be different. You are rejecting societal norms and conventional values.

Hippopotamus

To see a hippopotamus in your dream, symbolizes your hidden strengths. You have more influence and power than you realize.

Hips

To notice your hips in your dream, represents your mobility adaptability to some situation. It relates to getting things done. The dream may also be a pun on being hip.

Hit

To dream that you hit something or someone, is symbolic of unexpressed anger and aggression. You tend to keep your negative feelings inside instead of expressing them in a healthy way.

Hitchhiking

To dream that you are hitchhiking, suggests that that you have not earned or deserved to be where you are at . The dream may also be a metaphor that you are getting a free ride.

Hive

Please see Beehive.

Hives

To dream that you break out in hives, indicates that you are worried about some situation or decision. It also signifies nervousness and even fear.

Hockey

To dream that you are playing or watching hockey, symbolizes the achieving and protecting of your goals. It suggests that you may be be dealt with a lot of hard blows in your life.

Hoe

To see or use a hoe in your dream, suggests that you are breaking though the barriers and limits. You are ready for growth.

Hog

To see a hog in your dream, may be a pun on "hogging" everything instead of sharing.

Please Also See Pig.

Hole

To see a hole in the ground, denotes hidden aspects of your activities. On the other hand, it may mean that you are feeling hollow or empty inside. This dream may be an awakening for you in that you need to get out and expose your self to new interests and activities.

To dream that you fall into a hole, signifies a pitfall in a situation in your life or that you are stuck in a hole. Perhaps, you have dug yourself into a hole and can not get out of it.

Holidays

To dream of holidays, represent a need for a break or time for rest. You are expressing a wish to escape from your responsibilities. Depending on the activities related to the holiday, the dream may also indicate family issues, personal attitudes or some difficulty.

Hollow

To dream of something that is hollow, represents the womb and nurturance. It may also symbolize your hidden secrets. Alternatively, it may indicate that you are feeling empty, worthless, or insignificant in your waking life.

Holly

To see holly in your dream, represents holiday festivities and memories of friends and family.

Hologram

To see a hologram in your dream, suggests that you need to look at the whole picture instead of just pieces of it in order to get the whole story. Alternatively, the dream symbolizes your ideal self and your notions of perfection.

Home

To see your home in your dream, signifies security, basic needs, and values. You may feel at home at your new job or you finally feel settled and comfortable in a new environment.

In particular, to see your childhood home or a home that you no longer live in, suggests your own desires for building a family. It also reflects aspects of yourself that were prominent or developed during the time you lived in that home. You may experience some feelings or unfinished expression of emotions that are now being triggered by a waking situation.

To dream that you cannot find your way home, indicates that you have lost faith and belief in yourself. It may also signify a major transition in your life.

Homeless

To dream that you are homeless, indicates that you are feeling insecure. You are unsure of yourself and where you are headed.

Homosexual

To dream that you are homosexual (but you are not in your waking life), represents a union with aspects of yourself. It is symbolic of self-love, self-acceptance, and compassion. If, in your dream, you are not comfortable with homosexuality, then it suggests some fears/anxieties about your masculinity (if you are male) and femininity (if you are female). You may be experiencing some insecurity in your relations with the opposite sex.

To dream that the guy you like in real life is gay, represents your anxieties and fears that he won't like you back. If he was gay, then it would be easier to dismiss your feelings for him. And it would be easier for you to say that you have no chance with him.

On a side note, it is common for expectant fathers to have dreams of homosexual encounters.

If you are homosexual in your waking life, then the dream is simply a reflection of your own self.

Honey

To see honey in your dream, denotes that you need to be less meek and more honest in communicating with others. You need to assert yourself and make sure you are heard. On the other hand, to see honey in your dream represents sweetness, peace, and joy.

Honeycomb

To see a honeycomb in your dream, suggests that you are trying to hold on to the sweetness and pleasures that you are experiencing in your life. It is also symbolic of your desire for love and affection.

Hood

To see a hood in your dream, signifies that you are hiding and cowering from a person or situation. Consider also the saying, "having the hood pulled over your eyes".

Hoof

To see a hoof in your dream, represents balance, grace, and discipline. To dream that the hoof is broken, indicates you inability to balance various aspects of your life. You may also be lacking discipline.

Hookah

To see or smoke a hookah in your dream, represents ease and relaxation. Alternatively, it refers to the difficulties your are facing in your waking life. You may be bottling up your emotions.

Hooker

*Please See Prostitute.

Hooks

To see hooks in your dream, suggests that you will get caught for your mischievousness and deceit. It also indicates your quest for material gains or feelings of deprivation.

To dream that you are catching something with a hook, suggests that you need to acknowledge and incorporate some aspect or characteristic into your self-image. Alternatively, it may refer to your love or sexual relationship and issues of intimacy.

Hopscotch

To dream that you are playing hopscotch, represents your childish and/or immature behavior. Alternatively, it may indicate your tendency to jump from task to task or not being able to stay in one place.

Horizon

To see the horizon in your dream, symbolizes a new beginning or a somber conclusion. The horizon represents your goals and future plans. You are in a continual state of growth, rebirth, and regeneration.

Hornets

To see a hornet in your dream, symbolizes troubles and danger ahead for you. You may let your anger and temper get the best of you.

To dream that you are stung by a hornet, is an indication of revenge and vengeful attitudes. It may also represent some stinging remark.

Horn

To see or hear a horn in your dream, signifies your need to pay attention to your inner voices and intuition. Alternatively, you may be bragging and "blowing your own horn".

To see the horns of an animal in your dream, represents conflict and confrontation. You are at odds with someone. It may also indicate that you have been hardened.

Horse

To see a horse in your dream, represents a strong, physical energy. You need to tame the wild forces. The dream may imply that you have been horsing around. Or perhaps you need to be less arrogant and "get off your high horse".

To see a black or dark horse in your dream, signifies mystery, wildness, and the unknown. You may be taking a chance or gamble at some unknown area. It may even represents occult forces. If the horse is white, then it signifies purity, prosperity and good fortunes. To dream that you are being chased by a white horse, may be a pun on chaste. Perhaps you are having difficulties dealing with issues of intimacy and sexuality.

To see a dead horse in your dream, indicates that something in your life that initially offered you strength is now gone. This may refer to a relationship or situation.

To see a herd of wild horses in your dream, signifies a sense of freedom and lack of responsibilities/duties. Perhaps it may also indicated your uncontrolled emotions.

To dream that you are riding a horse, denotes that you will achieve success through underhanded means. You lack integrity. If you are riding a horse that is out of control, signifies that you are being carried away by your passions.

To see an armored or medieval horse in your dream, refers to your fierceness, aggression, power and/or rigidity. You may be seen as too confrontational. Alternatively, you may be trying to protect yourself from unconscious material or sexual desires that is emerging.

To dream that you are bathing a horse, represents a renewal of strength and vigor. You are experiencing a burst of energy in some aspect of your life.

Horserace

To dream that you are watching a horserace, represents the power and drive you need to move forward in life. You need to believe that you are capable of succeeding in all your endeavors. The dream also symbolizes your sexual energy or competitive nature.

Horseradish

To see or taste horseradish in your dream, suggests that you have made an overly strong statement. You may offend others without knowing it.

Horseshoe

To see a horseshoe in your dream signifies luck and success in your endeavors.

Hose

To see a hose in your dream, represents renewal, rejuvenation and cleansing. You need to heal those emotional wounds so that you can continue to grow as a person. Alternatively, it may be a metaphor for sex and sexual gratification.

Hospital

To see a hospital in your dream, symbolizes your need to heal or improve your physical or mental heath. You need to get back to the flow of everyday life.

Hospitality

To dream that you have hospitality, denotes your generosity and kindness toward others. You do things without expecting anything in return.

Hostage

To dream that you are a hostage, indicates that you are feeling victimized and powerlessness. You may also be feeling limited in your choices or physically immobilized. Perhaps this dream is paralleling some situation/difficulties in your daily life or relationship. Alternatively, it suggests that a part of yourself is not be fully expressed.

Hot

To dream that you are hot, signifies passion and emotion. You are lusting after someone. It may also reflect a situation that is potentially dangerous. The dream may also represent a person who is great looking. Perhaps you are feeling beautiful.

Hot Air Balloon

To see or dream that you are in a hot air balloon, suggests that it is time to overcome your depression. The dream may be a metaphor indicating that you are losing your ground or your foothold on some situation/problem. Alternatively, it represents the process of individuation and your quest to fulfill some spiritual needs. You feel the need to be elevated in someone's eyes.

Hot Dog

To see or eat a hot dog in your dream, is phallic symbol representing to masculinity, sexual energy, and vigor.

Hot Pepper

To see or eat hot pepper in your dream, symbolizes your hot temper. A debate or argument is becoming heated. Alternatively, it suggests that you need to add a little fire and spice into your relationship.

Hot Tub

To dream that you are in a hot tub, indicates that you are unveiling aspects of your unconscious. Alternatively, it refers to relaxation and recuperation. You are looking to escape from your daily problems. The dream may also be a metaphor suggests that you are in a lot of hot water or that you are in deep trouble.

Hotel

To see a hotel in your dream, signifies a new state of mind or a shift in personal identity. You need to move away from your old habits and old way of thinking.

Hour

To dream about the hour, refers to a passage of time. The dream may serve to remind you of an appointment, deadline, or anniversary. Consider the significance of a particular number or any superstitions that may be associated with a particular hour. For example, 12pm represents some confrontation or turning point.

To dream about happy hour, represents sensual enjoyment, stimulation, and relaxation. You are filled with inspirational power and enlightenment. Alternatively, it indicates avoidance in dealing with your problems and in facing your anxieties.

Hourglass

To see an hourglass in your dream, denotes that time is running out for you. This may be a deadline that you have to meet for school or work. Alternatively, it represents a situation that is being turned upside down.

House

To see a house in your dream, represents your own soul and self. Specific rooms in the house indicate a specific aspect of your psyche. In general, the attic represents your intellect, the basement represents the unconscious, etc. If the house is empty, then it indicates feelings of insecurity. If the house is shifting, then it suggests that you are going through some personal changes and changing your belief system.

To dream that you are cleaning your house, signifies your need to clear out your thoughts and getting rid of old ways. You are seeking self-improvement.

If you live with others in your waking life, but dream that you are living alone, suggests that you need to take new steps toward independence. You need to accept responsibilities and be more self-reliant.

To see an old, run-down house in your dream, represents your old beliefs, attitudes and how you used to think or feel. A situation in your current life may be bringing about those same old attitudes and feelings. Alternatively, the old house may symbolize your need to update you mode of thinking.

To see a new house in your dream, indicates that you are entering into a new phase or new area in your life.

To dream that your house is broken into, suggests that you are feeling violated. It may refer to a particular relationship or current situation in your life. Alternatively, it indicates that some unconscious material is attempting to make itself known. There are some aspects of yourself that you have denied.

To dream of a haunted house, signifies unfinished emotional business, related to your childhood family, dead relatives, or repressed memories and feelings.

To dream that a house disappeared, indicates that you are not feeling grounded. You feel uprooted by a particular circumstance or relationship in your life.

**See The Meaning In Action: "Haunted House"*

Howling

To dream that you are howling, represents wounded feelings and hidden fears.

To hear howling in your dream, refers to loneliness or solitude.

Hugging

To dream that you are hugging someone, symbolizes your loving and caring nature. You are holding someone or something close to your heart. Alternatively, it may indicate your need to be more affectionate.

Humid

To dream that it is humid, suggests that you may be lacking some understanding in a situation resulting in some anxiety for you.

Humidicrib

*Please See Incubator.

Hummingbird

To see hummingbirds in your dream, suggests that small ideas/concepts may possess much potential and power. Alternatively, it indicates your flighty thoughts and frivolous ideas. It may be a metaphor for your inability to commit to a relationship.

Hunger

To dream that you are hungry, signifies a feeling of unfulfilment in some area of your life. You may be starving for recognition, power, sex, wealth, or fame. You are longing to achieve something that you have desired for awhile. Or this dream may simply be that you are really feeling hungry and it is being manifested in your dream.

Hunting

To dream that you are hunting, denotes that you are seeking or pursuing to fulfill some inner desires, either emotional or physical. You may be in hunt for a solution or in pursuit of a sexual conquest.

To dream that you hunt and kill an animal, signifies that you are trying to repress or destroy an instinctive part of yourself.

To dream that you are being hunted, indicates that you are being overwhelmed by life's challenges.

To see someone else hunting an animal in your dream, suggests that you are trying to locate a hidden aspect of your own self. You be trying to indirectly approach a challenge or situation.

Hurdle

To see hurdles in your dream, symbolizes the barriers and obstacles that are in your way throughout your life. If you jump over the hurdles, then it indicates that you are goal-oriented and do not let anything get in your way of your success. If you knock over the hurdle, then it represents difficulties. You will need to work hard in achieving your goals.

Hurricane

To see a hurricane in your dream, indicates sudden and/or unexpected changes occurring in your life. You may be experiencing some destructive and powerful emotions.

To dream that you are swept up the hurricane, suggests that both your mental and emotional forces are building up inside and making themselves known. You may be literally consumed by your emotions.

Hurry

To dream that you are in a hurry, suggests that may be unprepared for a situation. There is a lack in your planning of things. Alternatively, you may be feeling out of place. This dream may also be a literal reflection of your daily life where you feel that you are always in a rush and that there is not enough time to do all the things you want to do. The dream may occur due to this type of stress.

Husband

To see your husband in your dream, signifies your relationship with your husband and the unconscious feelings you have towards him.

To dream that you have a husband (but you do not in your waking life), symbolizes some sort of partnership and/or commitment. Often, it is also representative of the qualities of your father in which you projected onto this figure or the masculine side of your own personality.

Hut

To see or live in a hut in your dream, represents the basic necessities and comforts. You need to simplify your life and get back to the bare basics. Accept what you already have and know that that is enough.

Hyacinth

To see hyacinth in your dream, symbolizes severe jealousy.

Hydrant

To see a hydrant in your dream, symbolizes renewal and rejuvenation. You are ready to make a fresh start.

To dream of a bursting fire hydrant, indicates an outburst of emotions. You need to acknowledge and express you pent up anger and feelings before they explode.

Hyena

To see a hyena in your dream, suggests that you are overwhelmed with responsibilities. You feel that someone is relying on you too much. Alternatively, a hyena may represent someone in your waking life with a sense of humor.

Hypnotize

To dream that you fail to be hypnotized, signifies that troubles hovering over you in which you and you alone can rise above.

Hysterectomy

To dream that you have a hysterectomy, indicates that you are going into new stage of growth in your life.

I

Ice

To see ice in your dream, suggests that you are lacking a flow of ideas and thoughts. You are not seeing in progress in your life. Alternatively, you may be feeling emotionally paralyzed or rigid. You need to let your feelings be known.

To dream that you are walking on ice, indicates that you are standing on shaky or instable ground. You are taking risks that you shouldn't be taking. Fear and caution are also implied.

To dream that you fall through ice, suggests that your emotions are threatening to come crashing through.

Ice Pick

To see an ice pick in your dream, symbolizes your cold feelings which have been suppressed.

Ice Cream

To see or eat ice cream in your dream, denotes pleasure and satisfaction with your life. It is also an indicative of good luck and success in love.

To dream that you are eating ice cream that is tasteless or sour, signifies sorrow, disillusionment, or betrayal.

To see ice cream melt in your dream, symbolizes failure to realize your hopes and desires.

Ice Skating

To dream that you or others are ice skating, suggests that you need to trust in yourself and your actions. The dream may also indicate that you need to proceed carefully into some situation or relationship.

Iceberg

To see an iceberg in your dream, suggests that you are not utilizing your fullest potential and strengths.

Icicles

To see icicles melting from trees in your dream, symbolizes hope and that your real estate and property problems will slow dissipate.

To see icicles forming in your dream, signifies problems that will soon manifest themselves.

Ideal

To dream that you meet the ideal person, signifies uninterrupted pleasure, love and devotion with a chosen mate.

To dream of having ideals, symbolizes utmost honesty in any legal matters you are involved in.

Identification

To see your I.D. in your dream, signifies your own self-confidence. To dream that you lose your I.D., denotes confusion about your own self-identity.

Idiot

To dream that you are an idiot or call somebody one, indicates that you are making a situation more difficult than it need by. Your train of thought is foggy and lack clarity.

Idle

To dream that you are idling, represents boredom and your lack of initiative to take action in what you really want to do.

To see idling people in your dream, signifies your tendency to not use your time and energy wisely in achieving your goals.

Idols

To dream that you are worshipping an idol, signifies little progress in attaining your goals. You are worshipping false values and ideas.

Ignition

To turn the ignition in your dream, suggests that you are set to move forward toward your goals. You are ready to grow.

Ignore

To dream that you are ignoring someone or being ignored, represents some aspect of yourself which you are not paying enough attention to. Alternatively, it may reflect your real waking experiences of being ignored by that person.

Iguana

To see an iguana in your dream, represents harshness, cold-heartedness, fierceness, and inhuman poise. It is an indication of both hostility and unstoppable determination. The iguana may remind you of someone or some situation in your waking life that you find frightening yet awe inspiring.

Illness

To dream of an illness in your dream, denotes despair, unpleasant changes, and an emotional breakdown. The illness may be symbolic of your inability to cope with a situation and you see that being ill is an easy way out. On a more direct note, this dream may signal you to pay close attention to your health especially to the areas of body revealed in the dream.

Please see also Sick.

Illumination

To see a strange illumination in your dream, foretells experience of distress, failure and trouble.

To see an illuminated face, signifies unfinished business that must be tended to immediately.

Imitation

To see imitations in your dream, forewarns that you should be cautious of trouble and loss to come.

To dream that someone is imitating your lover, forewarns of deception by that person.

Immobility

To dream that you are immobile, signifies feelings of being trapped or that you are rigid in your attitudes and decisions.

Please see also Paralyzed.

Immortal

To dream that you are immortal, represents longevity, continuity, or fearlessness. You feel that you are better than others. Alternatively, it signifies reluctance in starting over or in taking a new direction. You fear change.

Impale

To dream that you are being impaled, suggests a forceful, violent or passionate release of your repressed emotions. You have been symbolically set free from the physical limitations of your own psyche. You are more aggressive and direct about your pent up emotions. Consider which part of the body is being impaled and what that part of the body symbolizes.

Impeach

To dream that you or someone has been impeached, indicates your desire to challenge authority. You are not afraid in letting others know about your position, even though it is not a popular one.

Implements

To dream of implements, signifies unsatisfactory or underhanded means of accomplishing some work.

To see broken implements in your dream, denotes failure in business or serious illness of a friend or relative.

Impotence

To dream that you are impotent, signifies a fear of losing power. Maybe you are afraid that you won't measure up to a particular person or task in your life. A more direct interpretation suggest that you may be having problems with sex in your waking life.

Inauguration

To dream of inauguration, signifies a rise in your current state or position.

Incense

To dream that you are burning incense, indicates spiritual learning. It represents a high level of awareness.

Incest

If this dream relates to real-life experiences with incest, then you need to seek professional advice or counseling.

To dream of incestuous practices, signifies erotic desires. It may also be representative of the union between masculine and feminine aspects of yourself. You are in a phase in your life where you are not quite a child and not quite an adult, and thus this dream may be symbolic of the merging of the child and adult within yourself.

Incoherent

To dream that you are incoherent, symbolizes extreme nervousness and excitement.

Incubator

To see an incubator in your dream, suggests that you need some stability and calmness in your life. Alternatively, it is symbolic of fresh and new ideas, growth, and development of the Self.

To dream that you are in an incubator, indicates that you have been acting prematurely. It may also indicate that you are trying to escape from the burdens and responsibility of your waking life.

Independent

To dream that you are independent, signifies a rival who may do you wrong.

Indian

To see an Indian in your dream, represents the primitive and instinctual aspect of yourself. You need to be in more control of your waking-life situations and surroundings. You also need to be more self-reliant and exercise your personal power. Alternatively, this dream symbolizes honesty, dedication, and wisdom.

Indigo

To see indigo in your dream, signifies deceit of your friends for your own gain.

Indigestion

To dream of indigestion, symbolizes unhealthy and gloomy surroundings. Maybe you have made a decision or there is a situation that you are involved in that is not sitting well with you.

Infants

To see a newborn infant, symbolizes pleasant surprises.

To see a swimming infant, signifies a lucky escape from some entanglement.

Infection

To dream that you have an infection, represents minor problems and annoyances.

Infidelity

To dream of infidelity (either by you or someone else), forewarns of your actions with the opposite sex or you will suffer dire consequences. You are harboring guilt over a sexual relationship. Alternatively, you may feel unsatisfied with your current relationship and want to seek a more exotic sex life.

*Please see also Adultery.

Infertile

To dream that you are infertile, represents a lack of creativity. Something in your waking life is not working out in the way that you want. The dream may also reflect your own state of infertility and the struggles to have a baby.

Inheritance

To dream that you receive an inheritance, signifies success and ease of obtaining your desires. You have been given many opportunities in your life.

Injection

To dream that you are being injected for health reasons, suggests your need for healing behavior/ideas/attitudes. You need to develop yourself on a mental and spiritual level.

To dream that someone is forcibly injecting you, represents your negative attitudes about a particular situation/person. It also indicates the influence of peer pressure working against you. You are recognizing that someone is forcing their negative and unwelcome views/values on you.

*Please see also Syringe.

Injury

To dream that you are injured, suggests that you need to work on healing old wounds and hurts. You need to stop and slow down.

Ink

To see ink spilled over one's clothing, symbolizes bitterness, spite and envy.

To see ink on your fingers, signifies jealous and rage toward someone.

To see bottles of ink in your dream, suggests that a solution to your problem will soon become apparent.

In-Law

To see your in-law in your dream, represents a working relationship which can take many different turns. The dream may also be a pun on being more careful and playing by the rules.

Inn

To see a welcoming, well-furnished inn in your dream, signifies prosperity and pleasures.

To see a run-down inn, denotes unhappy journeys and poor success.

Insanity

To dream that you or someone is insane, represents your retreat from reality. You have difficulties in telling what is right and wrong.

Inscription

To see an inscription in your dream, foretells of bad and unpleasant news.

To dream that you are writing an inscription, signifies loss of a valuable friend.

To dream that you are reading an inscription on a tomb, signifies distress and sickness.

Insect

To see insects in your dream, signifies minor obstacles that you must overcome. There are small problems and annoyances that need to be dealt with. Something or someone may be "bugging" or "pestering" you. Alternatively, insects are also said to be symbolic of precision, alertness, and sensitivity. You may need to organize your thoughts and sort out your values. Sometimes they are seen as divine messengers.

Insurance

To dream that you are buying insurance, refers to a lack of trust. You are afraid of losing something that means a lot to you. Alternatively, it represents your need for security.

Intercom

To see or use an intercom in your dream, suggests that you are always readily available to those who need your help. It also symbolizes your acute awareness to your surroundings and to those around you.

To hear a voice over an intercom, represents messages from your unconscious. Your unconscious is trying to make you aware of a solution to a problem.

Intercourse

*Please See Sex.

Intermarriage

To dream that you intermarry, signifies quarrels and manifestations of trouble and loss.

Internet

To dream of the internet, signifies your need to communicate with a larger network of people.

Interrupt

To dream that you are being interrupted, suggests that things in your waking life are not going as smoothly as you would like. You may feel that you are continually being sidetracked or that you are unable to get your point across.

Intersection

To dream that you are at an intersection, represents a decision or choice that you need to make.

Interstate

*Please See Highway.

Interview

To dream that you are at an interview, denotes your anxiety over being judged by others.

Intestines

To see intestines in your dream, signifies evil, disaster, and extreme misfortune.

Intoxicated

To dream that you are intoxicated, foretells of illicit pleasures and desires.

*Please See also Drunk.

Intruder

To see an intruder in your dream, represents your feelings of guilt. Consider also what unfamiliar feelings or thoughts may be breaking into your peace of mind. Alternatively, an intruder symbolizes self-indulgent behavior or unwanted sexual attention.

Invasion

To dream of an invasion, represents your need to be more assertive. Stand up for yourself and let your voice be known.

Inventor

To see an inventor in your dream, signifies unique and honorable achievement.

To dream that you are an inventor, symbolizes your aspirations for fortune and success.

Investigator

Please See Detective.

Invisible

To dream that you are invisible, signifies feelings of not being noticed or recognized for what is important to you. Alternatively, you may be trying to withdraw from the realities of life.

Invitation

To see or respond to an invitation in your dream, suggests that you need to join or incorporate certain characteristics into yourself

Iris

To see an iris in your dream, symbolizes wisdom, faith, and valor.

Iron

To see iron in your dream, symbolizes harshness and ruthlessness. On a positive note, it may signify strength and willpower.

To see red, hot iron in your dream, denotes failure resulting from displaced energy.

To see old, rusty iron in your dream, signifies poverty and disappointment.

Ironing

To dream that you are ironing, signifies domestic comfort and orderliness. You may be trying to "iron the wrinkles" out of your life.

To dream that you burn your hands while ironing, signifies loss of tranquility, illness, or jealousy.

Island

To see an island or dream that you are on an in your dream, signifies ease, relaxation and comfort.

To dream that you are in stranded on a island, signifies that you are in a rut and do not quite know what to do with your life. On the other hand, you may be seeking some solitude. Perhaps you are running away from a situation instead of trying to confront it.

Itch

To dream that you have an itch, refers to sexual urges. Alternatively, you may have been anticipating to do something for a long time.

Please see also Scratch.

Ivory

To see ivory in your dream, symbolizes purity, strength, and endurance.

Ivy

To see ivy in your dream, signifies mounting joy, excellent health and increased fortune. Your close ties and relationships with those around you will bring your much security and comfort.

To see withered ivy in your dream, denotes broken engagements and sadness.

J

Jab

To dream that you are jabbing someone, suggests that you need to take more initiative and stop doubting your own abilities.

Jack

To see or use a jack in your dream, suggests that you are looking to balance your life. The dream may also symbolize a person named "Jack" in your life.

Jackal

To see a jackal in your dream, refers to manipulation. You have a tendency to feed off of others.

Jackdaw

To see a jackdaw in your dream, signifies ill health, disputes, and quarrels.

Jacket

To see or wear a jacket in your dream, represents the image that you want to present and project to the outside world. Alternatively, it symbolizes your protective and defensive persona. You tend to distant your feelings and as a result, you may be isolating yourself. Consider also the color, appearance, and type of jacket for additional significance.

Jackhammer

To see a jackhammer in your dream, suggests that you need to make some drastic changes in your life. Break away from your old outdated attitudes and habits.

Jacuzzi

To dream that you are in a jacuzzi, suggests that you need to cleanse your emotions and rid yourself of all the negativity you are experiencing in your sex life.

Jade

To see jade in your dream, indicates healing powers, immortality, and truth. Additionally, it also represents growth, shaping and development of your personality.

Jaguar

To see a jaguar in your dream, represents speed, agility, and power.

Jail

To dream that your lover is in jail, signifies that this lover is deceitful and untrustworthy.

To dream that you are in jail, signifies your feelings of confinement and suffocation.

To dream that others are in jail, signifies your unsettled feeling to grant privileges to an unworthy person.

To dream that children are in jail, signifies negligence and worry.

Jailer

To see a jailer in your dream, forewarns of low morality, treachery, and/or loss.

Jam

To dream that you are eating jam, signifies pleasant surprises and new discoveries. Consider also the pun, "caught in a jam" which mean that you may find yourself in a little problem.

To dream that you are making jam, foretells of a happy home life.

To dream that you are spreading jam, indicates that you may be spreading yourself too thin. You have too many responsibilities and commitments and need to learn to say no.

Janitor

To see an idle janitor in your dream, signifies many problems and setbacks in your business endeavors.

To see a busy janitor, foretells of pleasant news.

January

To dream of the month of January, signifies loss of love and companionship.

Jar

To see an empty jar in your dream, signifies impoverishment and distress.

To see a full jar in your dream, symbolizes success and victory.

To see a broken jar in your dream, denotes illness and heartbreak.

Jasmine

To see jasmine in your dream, signifies love and protection. It is also an indication of short-lived pleasures.

Jasper

To see jasper in your dream, signifies longevity and healing.

To dream that a jasper stone is placed in your mouth, signifies that the truth will soon be revealed to you.

Jaundice

To dream that you have jaundice, denotes you will have great good fortune after a period of temporary loss and embarrassment.

To dream that others have jaundice, signifies bothersome people and unpleasant companions.

Javelin

To dream that you are stabbed by a javelin, signifies a threat to your safety and freedom.

Jaw

To dream that you are in the jaws of an animal, signifies misunderstandings and hasty judgments, which may threaten your happiness.

To see your own jaw in your dream, represents your stubbornness, determination and forcefulness. You may need to have more willpower and fortitude in some situation. To dream that your jaws are tight, indicates unexpressed angers and other powerful feelings which you are holding back.

To dream that you break or dislocated your jaw, suggests that you are compromising your own beliefs and principles.

Jawbreaker

To see or eat a jawbreaker in your dream, indicates that a situation may look tempting and inviting but it is really difficult to handle and control.

Jaybird

To see a jaybird in your dream, signifies pleasant, but unproductive labor.

To see a dead jaybird in your dream, signifies domestic quarreling.

Jealousy

To dream that you are jealous of another person, signifies that such feelings may be carried over from your waking life This dream may reveal you unconscious feelings of jealousy toward that particular person. Alternatively, it represents your vulnerability and your fear of intimacy. You need to work on self-love and acknowledging your self-worth.

Jelly

To see or eat jelly in your dream, represents some suspicion or insight into a situation you are wondering about. The dream may be a metaphor for something that is finally taking shape. You have come to some understanding. Alternatively, it indicates that you are preserving or maintaining a sweet relationship.

Jellyfish

To see a jellyfish in your dream, represents painful memories that is emerging from your unconscious. There may be hidden hostility or aggression in some aspect of your waking relationship or situation. Alternatively, it may indicate feelings of inadequacy and a lack of self-esteem. Perhaps there is some situation in which you are unable to assert yourself.

Jester

To see a jester in your dream, symbolizes that petty things and silly pastimes will cause you to ignore important matters.

Jesus

To see Jesus in your dream, foretells that your greatest desires and goals will be realized. This dream serves to console and strengthen you in your times of adversity, hardship and struggle. You will rise above any situation and circumstance and become victorious.

To dream that Jesus speaks to you or that you are praying with Him, signifies that you will be blessed with true peace of mind, joy and contentment.

Jet Ski

To see or dream that you are on a jet ski, represents a journey of self-discovery. You are confronting and exploring aspects of your unconscious in full force. Alternatively, the dream relates to some sexual adventure or relationship.

Jets

To see a jet flying overhead in your dream, signifies of bad news from distant friends or misfortune in business.

Jewelry

To see jewelry in your dream, signifies your own sense of self worth and personal value. It is also symbolic of knowledge, identity, or whatever qualities you hold precious in your life. They highlight the importance of spirituality and psychological riches. A particular piece of jewelry that you own, may symbolize aspects of a waking relationship.

To dream that you receive jewelries as gifts, indicates that you need to acknowledge and incorporate those corresponding qualities within your own self.

To see broken jewelry in your dream, signifies disappointment in achieving your goals and attaining your highest desires.

Jewelry Box

To see a jewelry box in your dream, represents your own sense of self-worth, self-value, and potential. You need to unleash your stored potential and quit keeping them hidden.

Jewels

To see or wear jewels in your dream, signifies a value within yourself or others in which your admire and cherish. It also symbolizes pleasure, riches, ambition and spiritual protection.

To find jewels in your dream, signifies rapid advancement.

Jigsaw Puzzle

To see a jigsaw puzzle in your dream, represents a mental challenge or a problem in your waking life that you need to solve. If there are pieces missing in the puzzle, then it suggests that you do not have all the facts in order to make a good and sound decision.

Job

To dream that you are looking for a job, suggests that you are unfulfilled and feeling frustrated in your current phase of your life.

To dream about your current job, represents your satisfaction and contentment in the way things are going in your life. It may also mean that there is something or some task that must be done at once.

Jockey

To see a jockey in your dream, foretells of a gift from an unexpected source.

To dream that a jockey is thrown from his house, signifies your assistance will be called on by strangers.

Jogging

To dream that you are jogging, suggests that you are proceeding through life in a steady pace. You are not really taking any action toward changes.

Joint

To feel or notice your joints in your dream, represent flexibility. It also refers to a give and take situation and the need to work together as a team.

To dream that you are having joint problems, suggests that things are not coming together the way you want it to. You are experiencing difficulties in your progress.

Joke

To dream that you are telling a joke, denotes that you are not being taken seriously and as a result you are feeling frustrated. On the other hand, you may not be taking an issue seriously.

To hear a joke in your dream, signifies that you are doing something that is either pointless or ridiculous. It may also mean a release from tension that had been bothering you.

Joshua Tree

To see a Joshua Tree in your dream, symbolizes spirituality, purity and natural achievement. It also represents strength and courage.

Journal

To see or read a journal in your dream, suggests that you are trying to change or rewrite the past to suit your own needs. Consider what is written in the journal and how it is similar or dissimilar to actual events in your waking life. Alternatively, it symbolizes memories and history.

To dream that someone is reading your journal, indicates that you are keeping secrets. You have difficulties telling others how you really feel.

Journey

To dream that you are going on a journey, signifies profits, self-discovery or progress. The scenery you see in your journey is telling of your feelings and circumstances you may be currently experiencing.

To dream that your friends go on a journey, signifies delightful and welcomed change and harmony.

Joy

To dream that you are joyful, denotes harmony amongst friends and loved ones.

Jubilee

To dream of a jubilee, signifies pleasurable endeavors and even matrimony.

Judge

To see a judge in your dream, denotes feelings of guilt or fear of being caught. Your dream may be helping and guiding you in making your own judgments. On a more direct note, your dream may indicate that disputes will be resolved through legal proceedings.

Jug

To see filled jugs in your dream, signifies reunion of friends.

To see empty jugs in your dream, foretells of estrangement by friends due to your conduct.

To see broken jugs in your dream, signifies sickness and failures in employment.

Juggling

To dream that you are juggling, indicates that you are trying to do much at one time.

Juice

To drink juice in your dream, represents the gift of life and vitality.

Jukebox

To see a jukebox in your dream, represents your second best. You are not trying your hardest. Consider the type of music that it is playing and how that relates to your morale, beliefs, and mood.

July

To dream of the month of July, foretells of gloomy outlooks followed by unexpected pleasure and good fortune.

Jumping

To dream that you are jumping, indicates that you need to take a risk and go for it. You will find progress toward your goals

To dream that you fail to jump, indicates that you are afraid of the uncertain. You do not like change.

Jump Rope

To dream that you are jumping rope, signifies that your thrilling and sensational escapades will shock your friends.

To dream that you are jumping rope with children, signifies that you are selfish and arrogant.

June

To dream of the month of June, signifies unusual gains in all your endeavors.

Jungle

To dream that you are in a jungle, signifies aspects of yourself and your personality that may have been inhibited

Juniper

To see a juniper tree in your dream, signifies happiness and wealth out of disappointments, sorrow and depressed conditions.

Junk

To see junk in your dream, symbolizes your need to get rid of and discard old ways of thinking and old habits.

Junkyard

To dream that you in in a junkyard, represents fear, frustration, and anger which you have kept inside. It may also signify your discarded attitudes, old habits, and former beliefs.

Jupiter

To see Jupiter in your dream, symbolizes success, optimism. generosity, and extravagance.

Jury

To see a jury in your dream, suggests that you are placed under scrutiny by others. You feel that others are judging you and your actions.

To dream that you are part of a jury, indicates that tend to past judgment on others.

Justice

To dream that you demand justice, signifies that you are threatened with embarrassment from false statements and accusations.

To dream that others demand justice from you, signifies your conduct and reputation are being questioned.

K

Kaleidoscope

To see a kaleidoscope in your dream, signifies diversity and fragments or various aspects that is coming together. It also foretells that you will have difficulties in choosing a career path.

Kangaroo

To see a kangaroo in your dreams, refers to maternal and paternal protection. You may be expressing your nurturing and mothering nature. Alternatively, a kangaroo may symbolize aggression.

To dream that a kangaroo attacks you, foretells that false accusations will damage and jeopardize your reputation.

Karaoke

To dream that you are taking part in karaoke, suggests that you are acting too overly confident in your abilities or in your accomplishments. Alternatively, you may not be utilizing your talents to its fullest potential.

Karate

To dream that you know karate, suggests that you need to direct your energy and concentrate them toward your goals.

Katydids

To see katydids in your dream, forewarns that you are in danger of losing your love due to your laid-back attitude.

To hear katydids in your dream, signifies your over-reliance on others.

Keg

To see a keg in your dream, symbolizes your struggle against adversity. If the keg is full, continue with the methods you are using to win the struggle and if the keg is empty, change your methods.

To see a keg that is cracked or broken, signifies family quarrels or family separation.

To see a loose band around the keg, foretells of a break up or divorce if you do no not act to change your circumstance.

Kelp

To see kelp in your dream, symbolizes emotional difficulties that you go through and get caught up in at some point in your life.

Kettle

To see a kettle of boiling water in your dreams, signifies great and laborious work ahead, but your struggles will soon be over.

To see a light-colored kettle in your dream, signifies freedom, while a dark-colored kettle, denotes disappointment in love and heartbreak.

For a woman to dream of boiling clothes in a kettle, signifies an end to her problems and the beginning of a better life.

Key

To see a key in your dream, symbolizes opportunities, access, control, secrets, or responsibilities. You may be locking away your own inner feelings and emotions.

To dream that you lose your keys, signifies your fear of losing your position or status in life. You may have lost control of yourself. It may also foretells of unexpected changes and unpleasant adventures. If you give your key away, then it suggests that you have given up control of some situation or responsibility.

To dream that you find keys, signifies that you have found a solution to a problem.

To see broken keys in your dream, signifies many quarrels and possibly a break-up.

To hear the sounds of keys rattling, indicates that you have the right attitude toward life. You are heading in the right direction and asking all the right questions in the process. It is also a sign of decisive action.

Keyhole

To dream that you are peeping through a keyhole, forewarns that you will be in danger of hurting a good friend by revealing a secret.

To dream that you catch others peeping through a keyhole, forewarns that you should be cautious of jealous friends who try to blemish your reputation.

To dream that you cannot find the keyhole in the dark, signifies that you have unconsciously hurt a friend's feeling.

Khakis

To wear khakis in your dream, suggests that there is something that you are not seeing clearly on. Or that something may not be what it seems.

Kid

To see a kid (baby goat) in your dream, forewarns that your unscrupulous ways will bring about grief to a loved one.

To see a kid in a meadow, denotes that too much of your time is spent on pleasure and your business or educational pursuits will eventually suffer.

*Please See Also Children.

Kidnapper

To dream that you are being kidnapped, denotes feelings of being trapped and restricted. Someone or some situation may be diverting your concentration and your attention away from your goals.

To dream that someone has been kidnapped, indicates that you are not letting aspects and characteristics of that person be expressed within you. You are trying to contain and/or suppress those qualities of the kidnapped person.

To dream that you are a kidnapper, signifies that you are holding on to something that you need to let go. You may be forcing your views and opinions on others.

**See The Meaning In Action: "Kidnapped By Aliens"

Kidneys

To see your own kidneys in your dream, signifies an impending illness or a broken marriage.

To dream that you are eating kidney stew, a secret love affair will be revealed to you.

Killing

To dream that you kill someone, indicates that heavy stress may cause you to lose your temper and self-control. Consider the person you have killed and ask yourself if you feel any rage towards him or her in your waking life. You may very well be expressing some anger or hatred toward this person. Alternatively, you may be trying to kill or put an end to an aspect of yourself that is represented by the person killed. Identify the characteristics of this person and ask yourself how you do not want to be like him or her.

To dream that you have been killed, suggests that your actions are disconnected from your emotions. Alternatively, it refers to drastic changes that are happening in your life.

This dream may also represent a part of you or your life that you wish would leave you alone and stop creating a nuisance. Killing may represent the killing off of old parts of yourself and old habits.

*Please see also Murder.

Killer

To see a killer in your dream, suggests that an essential aspect of your emotions have been cut off. You feel that you are losing your identity and your individuality. Alternatively, this dream may represent purification and the healing process. You are standing up for yourself and putting a dramatic end to something.

King

To see a king in your dream, signifies much success and prestige to be headed your way. It is symbolic of power and control.

To dream that you are the king, suggests that you will rise above your problems and adversities. Alternatively, it is an expression of your masculine power.

Kiss

To dream of a kiss, denotes love, affection, tranquility, harmony, and contentment. To see others kissing in your dream, suggests that you are too involved in their personal lives and relationship. You need to give them some space. If the dream ends just about you are about to kiss someone, indicates that you are unsure of how he or she really feels about you. You are looking for some sort of relationship with this person but you are not sure about how to go about achieving it. If you are heterosexual and you dream that you are kissing someone of the same sex, then it represents self-acceptance. You are acknowledging the feminine or masculine side.

To dream that you are kissing someone's hand, signifies respect.

To dream that you are kissing someone else's boyfriend or girlfriend, indicates your wish to be in a relationship and to experience the energy of love. You may be sexually acting out and desire to awaken your passion. Alternatively, it indicates a lack of integrity on your part.

If you are kissing a close friend, then it represents your respect and adoration for your friend. You are seeking some intimate closeness that is lacking in some waking relationship. It may or may not signify a romantic interest for him or her.

To dream of kissing an enemy, signifies betrayal, hostility, or reconciliation with an angry friend. Consider also the saying "this kiss of death". If you are kissed by a stranger, then your dream is one of self-discovery. You need to get more acquainted with some aspect of yourself.

Kitchen

To see a kitchen in your dream, signifies your need for spiritual nourishment. It also forewarns that you will be met with some depressing news.

Kite

To dream that you are flying a kite, suggests that you have high ambitions and goals, but still remain well-grounded. Persistence will pay off in the end no matter how difficult your current task may be. Alternatively, it is symbolic of your spiritual or childlike awareness.

Kitten

To see a white kitten in your dream, signifies deceit and trouble.

To see non-white or soiled kittens, indicates trouble ahead for you.

Knapsack

To see or carry a knapsack in your dream, represents your hopes, desires, and secrets. It also signifies the emotional baggage and responsibilities that you are carrying and weighing you down.

Knee

To dream of your knees, symbolizes a level of support your may be receiving. It also indicates that you are feeling very emotional. Feelings of inadequacy and issues of power/control also come into play. You may have more than you can handle.

Knife

To dream that you are carrying a knife, signifies anger, aggression and/or separation. There may be something in your life that you need to cut out and get rid of.

To see a dull knife in your dream, denotes that your hard work is accompanied by little or no gain.

To dream that you are wounded by a knife, suggests that you or someone is affected by hurtful remarks or malicious gossip.

To see an electric knife in your dream, indicates your power to get down to the truth of a situation quickly.

See The Meaning In Action: "Boiling A Rabbit"

Knife Grinder

To see a knife grinder in your dream, signifies a loss of freedom.

Knight

To see a knight in your dream, signifies protection and security. The knight can be seen as a savior or someone who sweeps you off your feet, as in the "knight in shining armor".

Knitting

To dream that you are knitting, signifies a quiet, peaceful and loving home life. It may also refer to someone in your life (past or present) who you associate with knitting. Alternatively, it symbolizes your creativity, accomplishments or your need to take time out from your regular routine.

Knob

To see knobs in your dream, signifies turning issues or conditions around you. You need to get a handle on these things.

Knocker

To see or use a knocker in your dream, symbolizes opportunities and welcomed expectations. You may be seeking for assistance and spiritual guidance. On a negative note, to see a knocker in your dream signifies repressed thoughts. death, and dreaded expectations.

Consider also a knocker as a sexual innuendo referring to a woman's breasts.

Knocking

To hear knocking in your dreams, suggests that your unconscious is trying to attract your attention to some aspect of yourself or to some waking situation. A new opportunity may be presented to you.

Knots

To see knots in your dream, signifies much worry over trifling affairs. You may be trying to find a resolution to a situation. It also denotes constraints and restrictions in your thoughts, feelings and actions.

To dream that you are tying a knot, symbolizes your independent and unyielding nature. You have everything under control. It may also mean a union of two people or a commitment to a relationship as indicated by the coming phrase "tying the knot".

Knuckles

To see knuckles in your dream, represent hard work and diligence.

Koala

To see a koala in your dream, represents your link the physical world, the unconscious, and the spiritual realm. The koala also symbolizes security, nurturance, protection, and/or feminine qualities. You may be expressing a desire to regress back into infantile dependence and escape from your daily responsibilities/problems.

Krishna

To see Krishna in your dream, symbolizes divine love and spiritual knowledge.

Kumquats

To see kumquats in your dream, symbolizes luck and prosperity.

L

Label

To dream that you are putting labels on items, denotes that your need for organization and order. It may also indicate that you are too quick to label something and pigeon hole it.

To see or read labels in your dream, signifies that you have unknowingly let an enemy see the inside of your private affairs, as a result of your carelessness and neglect.

Labor

To dream that you are laboring, foretells of favorable outlook in any new undertaking.

To see men laboring in your dream, signifies fruitful enterprise and vitality in your health.

Laboratory

To dream that you are in a laboratory, signifies that you are experimenting with your inner feelings, beliefs, and fears and testing yourself. Alternatively, you may be going through some sort of transformation.

Labyrinth

To see a labyrinth in your dream, signifies that you will be involved with my complicated situations where your domestic sphere will be quite intolerable.

To dream that you are in a labyrinth of green vines and timber, signifies an unexpected turn of happiness where despair and loss was anticipated.

To dream that you are in a labyrinth of night or darkness, denotes bitter trouble and sickness.

Lace

To see lace in your dream, represents your sensuality and the realization of your heart's desires. It may also indicate that you are being overly practical in some area of your life.

Ladder

To dream that you are climbing up a ladder, suggests that you have reached a new level of achievement and higher awareness. It is indicative of prosperity, hard work and efforts. You may also be looking things from a different perspective. Alternatively, it may indicate meditation and prayer. You are setting forth on a spiritual path. Consider also the phrase of "climbing the social ladder" in which you have achieved status, power, or an important goal.

To dream that you are climbing down a ladder, suggests that you are escaping from your spiritual responsibilities. It is an indication of much disappointments.

To dream that someone is holding a ladder for you, signifies that you will find success and rise to prominence with the support of others.

To dream that you fall from a ladder, denotes the hardships, risks or failures you are faced with in your endeavors.

To see a broken ladder in your dream, indicates consistent failures in your undertakings. You may feel handicapped in pursuit of your goals.

To dream that you escape by means of a ladder, signifies that you will be successful after much struggle and obstacles.

**See The Meaning In Action: "Stuck At The Top"*

Ladle

To see a ladle in your dream, signifies that children will be a great source of your joy and pride.

To see a broken ladle, denotes grief and sorrow in love.

Ladybug

To see a lady in your dream, is symbolic of good luck. It also signifies happiness at work.

Lagoon

To see a lagoon in your dream, denotes that there is a misunderstanding and doubt in your words.

Lake

To see a lake in your dream, signifies your emotional state of mind. If the lake is clear and calm, then it symbolize your inner peace. If the lake is disturbed, then you may be going through some emotional turmoil.

Lamb

To see a lamb in your dream, denotes that you will have many companions. Consider also the metaphor "as gentle as a lamb". Lambs are representative of all that is pure and innocent.

To dream that you are holding a lamb in your arms, signifies that you will rise to a position of wealth through hard work and ethical means.

Lame

To dream that someone is lame, signifies failure in realizing your hopes and desires and much disappointments. As yourself who or what is holding you back.

Lament

To dream that you lament a loss, is a bad omen signaling distress, illness, and struggle. Only after overcoming such adversity will you enjoy pleasure and personal gains.

Lamp

To see a lamp in your dream, symbolizes guidance, hope, inspiration, enlightenment and reassurance.

To see a broken lamp in your dream, suggests that you are shutting out those who are trying to help you. It is also symbolic of misfortune and the approach of bad luck.

To see a lamp explode in your dream, suggests that you will make enemies with whom used to be your friends.

To see a dimly-lit or unlit lamp in your dream, signifies that you are being overwhelmed by emotional issues. You have lost your ability to find your own way.

Lamppost

To see a lamppost in your dream, denotes that someone who you least expect will prove to be a great friend in your time of need.

Lampshade

To see a lamp shade in your dream, indicates a need for protection form some intense energy or power. You may be trying to hide or be less noticeable.

Lanai

To see or dream that you are in a lanai, indicates that you are open-mined and easy-going. You are receptive to new ideas. As a Hawaiian island, it may symbolize your need to escape and get away from your daily responsibilities. Give yourself a vacation.

Lance

To see a lance in your dream, represents initiative and have set you sight on a direct goal or path. You have taken a stance.

To dream that you are wounded by a lance, denotes that you have made a poor judgment and is facing the consequences.

To dream that you break a lance, signifies that you will succeed in overcoming what was a seemingly impossible task.

Land

To see land in your dream, represents nurturance and you need to be grounded. You are seeking for a strong foundation and some sort of stability.

To see rocky or barren land, denotes failure in your undertakings.

Landing

To see the landing of an aircraft in your dream, signifies completion of a journey or some task. There may have been some issues in which you felt out of control in trying to handle but are now being grounded.

Landau

To dream that you are riding in a landau, signifies that you will meet a fun, light-hearted person who will bring you much pleasure.

To see an overturned landau in your dream, signifies that your pleasure will come to an abrupt end.

Landlord

To see your landlord in your dream, represents the part of yourself that is always in control. It refers to your rational and responsible side. Perhaps you need to show more restraint and control of the other aspects of your psyche.

Landscape

To dream of various landscapes in your dream, represents where you are in your life or in your relationships. How do you see yourself with respect to the rest of the world and those around you? According to Freud, the landscape symbolizes the human body.

To dream of ever changing landscapes, indicates psychological transitions or emotional progress. It represents the various stages in your life. Alternatively, it may be offering you various viewpoints in looking at the same idea or situation. Consider the symbolism of key elements in the landscape.

Landslide

To see a landslide in your dream, represents emotions that you have been holding back for a long time. You are at the risk of emotional overload. Your emotions are erupting in an unexpected or violent way. The dream may also symbolize the stresses in your life and the responsibilities that rest on your shoulders.

Language

To dream that you are studying a language, denotes that you are having difficulties expressing your thoughts.

To hear foul language in your dream, signifies that you will soon find yourself in an embarrassing situation.

Lantern

To see or buy a lantern in your dream, denotes unexpected wealth and fortunate dealings.

To dream that you are carrying a lantern, signifies that you generosity and kindness will attract many friends.

To dream that a lantern goes out, foretells that you will fail to rise to prestige.

To dream that you blow out a lantern, signifies that you will miss an opportunity of getting married.

Lap

To notice your lap in your dream, implies opportunities and/or problems. It may also indicate loneliness and loss.

To dream that you are sitting someone's lap, signifies that you will find stability and security after some difficult situations.

To dream that you are holding someone on your lap, denotes that you will be open to unfavorable criticism.

Lapis

To see a lapis in your dream, suggests that no one is perfect. You need to accept yourself with all your imperfections and look within your own self.

Laptop

To see or use laptop in your dream, suggests that you need to be able to reach out and communicate with others in any circumstance.

Lard

To see lard in your dream, denotes that you will have much gratification over your rise in fortune.

To dream that your hands are in melted lard, signifies disappointments and failure to achieve prominence within your social circles.

Large

Please See Big.

Lark

To see larks flying in your dream, symbolizes high aspirations. If they fall during flight, then it indicates that you will be overcome with despair in the midst of your pleasure and joy.

To hear larks singing in your dream, foretells of success in business. You will find happiness in a change of environment.

To see a wounded or dead lark in your dream, denotes sadness and gloom.

To dream that you kill a lark, signifies a loss of innocence as a result of giving in to your urges and desires.

Larva

To see a larva in your dream, symbolizes a rebirth. You are undergoing some inner changes and transformation.

Las Vegas

To dream that you are in Las Vegas, refers to excess and overindulgence. You need to show some restraint in some area of your life. Alternatively, it suggests that your good judgment is being clouded by all the emotional turmoil and chaos.

Laser

To see a laser in your dream, symbolizes clarity and truth. You are seeing and understanding things much more clearly. Alternatively, it suggests that you need to focus your attention and concentrate on one task at a time.

Lasso

To dream that you are skillfully swinging a lasso, denotes contentment in love and happiness in your family affairs.

To dream that you signifies that you will be embarrassed.

To dream that you lasso an animal, signifies that you will succeed in gaining the heart of your true love.

Latch

To see a latch in your dream, signifies that you will receive an unwelcome appeal for aid.

To see a broken latch in your dream, signifies that you and a good friend will be in a major disagreement.

Late

To dream that you are late, denotes your fear of change and your ambivalence about seizing an opportunity. You may feel unready, unworthy, or unsupported in your current circumstances. Additionally, you may be overwhelmed or conflicted with decisions about your future.

Latin

To dream that you are studying Latin, signifies that you will rise to a position of prominence and distinction.

Laudanum

To dream that you are taking laudanum, signifies weak-will and that you are easily persuaded and influenced by others.

To see your lover taking laudanum, denotes unhappiness and loss of a friend.

To dream that you prevent others from taking laudanum, denotes that you will create a lot of joy and pleasure for others.

Laughing

To dream that you are laughing, suggests that you need to lighten up and let go of your problems. Don't put so much pressure on yourself. Laughing is also a sign of joyous release and pleasure.

To hear the cheerful laughter of children, denotes splendid joy and vital health.

To hear evil, demonic laughing in your dream, represents feelings of humiliation and/or helplessness.

Laundry

To dream that you are doing your laundry, suggests that you are cleaning up your act or change your image. You are concerned about how you appear to others.

To dream that you are having someone else do your laundry, denotes gossip.

To dream that you are sorting the laundry, indicates that you are trying to understand your own feelings and sorting your attitudes.

To see a laundry chute in your dream, suggests that you are not allowing others dictate how your should look or act. Your mind is your own. Alternatively, it signifies your exploration of your unconscious and/or negative emotions.

Laurel

To see laurel in your dream, signifies forthcoming success and prestige. Love will also enter your life.

To dream that you put a wreath of laurel on your lover's head, denotes that your lover will be an honest and faithful partner.

Lava

To see lava in your dream, signifies an expression of anger which you have kept inside for awhile.

**See The Meaning In Action: "_Lava_"*

Lavender

To see lavender in you dream, indicates mysticism and spirituality.

Lawsuits

To dream that you are entangled in a lawsuit, forewarns that you rivals are publicly defaming your character.

To dream that you are studying law, denotes that you will make a rapid rise in your chosen career path.

Lawn

To see a green lawn, represents hope, pleasure, and well-being. You are in control and making steady and smooth progress.

To see a dead or brown lawn in your dream, signifies dissatisfaction with some aspect of your home life. You may also be too concerned about what other people think.

Lawn Mower

To see a lawn mower in your dream, suggests that you need to channel those negative thinking into positive energy. You need to keep your temper and attitude under control.

Lawyer

To see or dream that you are a lawyer, suggests that help is available to you if you ask. You need to put aside your pride and look upon others for their assistance.

Laxative

To see or take a laxative in your dream, suggests that you need to let go of the emotional hurt and fears that you are still harboring inside. It is time to cleanse your body and spirits.

Lazy

To dream that you are feeling lazy, signifies that you will make a terrible error in a business deal resulting in bitter disappointments.

To dream that you lover is lazy, signifies that you will have many rocky and insecure love relationships.

Lead

To see lead in your dream, indicates that there is a problem or issue that is burdening you. Perhaps a relationship or guilt is weighing you down.

To see a lead mine in your dream, denotes deceit.

Leader

To dream that you are a leader, represents you ability to assert your ideas and/or offer guidance to others. The dream may also be telling you that you are being too passive and need to take a more active role in a situation. Take more control over your life and behavior.

Leak

To see a leak in your dream, signifies great loss and distress for you. You are wasting your energy on fruitless endeavors. Alternatively, the dream may indicate some repressed feelings emerging from your unconscious.

Leaping

To dream that you are leaping over an object, signifies that you will eventually achieve your desires and goals after some efforts and struggle.

Learn

To dream that you are learning something, signifies your interest and never-ending quest in acquiring knowledge.

To dream that you are in places of learning, foretells that you will rise to distinction.

Leash

To dream that you are holding a leash, indicates a need for more control in your life.

To dream that you are wearing a leash, suggests that you need to show more restraint with regards to your sexual urges and desires.

Leather

To see or wear leather in your dream, represents toughness and ruggedness. It also refers to your instinctual and animalistic nature.

Leaves

To see leaves in your dream, signifies new found happiness and an improvement in various aspects of your life. It is symbolic of growth and openness.

To see brown or withered leaves in your dream, signifies fallen hopes, despair, and loss.

Lecture

To dream that you are giving a lecture, suggests that you are becoming somewhat of a bore. You may need to improve your communications skills. Alternatively, your dream may serve as a continuation of your intellectual thinking carried over from your waking hours.

Ledge

To dream that you are standing on a ledge, indicates that you are feeling tense, anxious and/or excited. Consider what direction you are looking? Up? Down? Straight Ahead? The direction to which you are looking relates to your viewpoint, whether it be an optimistic one, pessimistic one or realistic one. On a more positive note, this dream may signify a sense of freedom and liberation.

To dream that someone is standing on a ledge, denotes a sign of desperation and a cry for help.

Ledger

To dream that you are keeping a ledger, denotes that you will find yourself in a complicated situation that you will be left to combat on your own. If the accounts are the ledger are in good standing, then it denotes that you situation will improve in the end. If the accounts on the ledger are worthless, then it signifies that you will suffer some losses in your situation.

To dream that you misplaced your ledger, signifies that your plans will not go accordingly as a result of your neglect.

To dream that there are errors in your ledger, denotes that you will be involved in some minor disputes and experience small losses.

Leeches

To see or be bitten by leeches in your dream, refers to something in your life that is draining the energy and vigor out of you. The dream may refer to people, habits, or negative emotions that are sucking you out of your vitality. Alternatively, if your body is covered in leeches, then you are feeling disgusted by your own body or repulsed by something you have done.

Leek

To see a leek in your dream, symbolizes victory and protection.

Leeward

To dream that you are sailing leeward, denotes pleasant journeys.

Left

To dream of the direction left, symbolizes the unconscious and your repressed thoughts/emotions. It is an indication of passivity.

Legislature

To dream that you are a member of a legislature, denotes that you are boastful of your possessions and find that you have no real economic and social advancement.

Legs

To see your legs in your dream, indicate that you have regained confidence to stand up and take control again. It also implies progress and your ability to navigate through life. If your legs are weak, then you may be feeling emotionally vulnerable.

To see someone else's legs in your dream, represents your admiration for that person. You need to adopt some of the ways that this person does things.

To dream that you legs are wounded or crippled, signifies a lack of balance, autonomy, or independence in your life. You may be unable or unwilling to stand up for yourself. Perhaps you are lacking courage and refuse to make a stand.

To dream that one of your leg is shorter than the other, suggests that there is some imbalance in some aspect of your life. You are placing more emphasis and weight on one thing, while ignoring other important aspects that need attention as well.

To dream that you have three or more legs, denotes that you are undertaking too many projects than you can handle. Unfortunately, you will find these projects to be unfruitful and a waste of time.

**See The Meaning In Action: "Wounded Leg"*

Legumes

To see legumes in your dream, symbolizes small annoyances and minor problems.

Lei

To dream that someone is giving you a lie, signifies a welcoming, acceptance, and acknowledgement. The dream may also be a pun on "getting laid".

*Please also see Garland.

Lemonade

To dream that you are drinking lemonade, signifies that you will go to great lengths in pleasing others even at your own expense.

Lemons

To see a lemon in your dream, indicates something that is inferior in quality.

To eat or suck on a lemon in your dream, refers to your need for cleansing or healing.

To dream that you are squeezing a lemon, suggest your need to be more economical.

Lending

To dream that you are lending money, denotes financial difficulties and piling debts.

To dream that you refuse to lend out anything, signifies that you look out for your own interest

To dream that others lend you things, denotes close friendship ties and bright prospects for financial gain.

Lens

To see lens in your dream, symbolize the need for you to take a closer and better look at things. You need to concentrate and focus on a situation that has long been neglected.

Lentil

To see lentils in your dream, signifies that you surroundings are emotionally straining and unhealthful.

Leopard

To see a leopard in the wild in your dream, signifies that through persistent efforts, you will eventually overcome your difficulties. If the leopard is in a cage, then it suggests that you will overcome any obstacles.

To dream that you kill a leopard, suggests that you will definitely succeed in your projects.

To dream that a leopard is attacking you, signifies that you are overly confident in your success for the future and not realizing the difficulties and struggles that you need to endure.

To see the skin of a leopard in your dream, signifies that you have befriended a dishonest person who means you harm.

Leprechaun

To see a leprechaun in your dream, suggests that you will reap the benefits and rewards of your hard work through perseverance and dedication. Alternatively, you may be trying to take the quick and easy path to success.

To dream that you are a leprechaun, refers to the mischievous aspect of your personality.

Leprosy

To dream that you have leprosy, suggests that you are not utilizing your full potential. You are wasting away your talents and abilities.

Lesbian

To dream that you are a lesbian (but you are not in your waking life), signifies a union with aspects of yourself. It is symbolic of self-love, self-acceptance, and passion. You are comfortable with your sexuality and femininity. If, in your dream you abhor the notion of lesbianism, then it represents your fears and rejection of parts of your own sexuality.

If you are a lesbian in your waking life, then the dream is simply a reflection of your own self.

Letter

To dream that you receive a letter, signifies a new opportunity or challenge. Alternatively, the letter represents a message from your unconscious mind. The contents of the letter may offer you some guidance in a current situation. Consider also how the letter may be a pun on "let her".

Letters

To see letters of the alphabet in your dream, symbolizes any object, animal, place associated with or resembling that particular letter. For example, the letter "T" may refer to a type intersection in a road. Alternatively, you may still be trying to understand some concept or emotion that is still in the primitive stages.

Lettuce

To see lettuce growing in your dream, signifies that you will finally have a moment of pure bliss and pleasure.

To dream that you are eating lettuce, signifies that jealousy will cause a major rift between you and your lover or friends.

To dream that you are planting lettuce, forewarns that you will be the cause of your own illness and premature death.

To dream that you are buying a head of lettuce, signifies that you will experience a downfall that will be your own doing.

Levitation

To dream that you are levitating, signifies that you are holding on to far-fetched ideas and need to grasp on to more realistic notions. Alternatively, you may be cut off from feeling grounded and safe. It represents a feeling of being disconnected with those around you and feeling helpless.

Liar

To dream that someone is calling you a liar, denotes that you will be irked by some deceitful person.

To dream that you are lying, suggests that you are trying to deceive yourself into believing in something that goes against your natural instincts or long held values. Ask yourself what are you hiding from yourself or from others.

To dream that someone is a liar, indicates your growing distrust for that person. You may have lost your faith in that individual. Alternatively, it suggests that you are no longer as confident.

To dream that you lover is a liar, forewarns that your disagreeable disposition will turn valued friendships away.

Library

To dream that you are in a library, signifies the search for knowledge and the hunger for ideas. You may be trying to seek out new meanings in life or you need to study and evaluate your situation before taking action.

To see a library in your dream, symbolizes the knowledge you have accumulated over the years.

Lice

To see lice in your dream, signifies frustrations, distress and feelings of guilt. You may also be feeling emotionally or physically unclean. Alternatively, the lice my represent a person, situation, or relationship that you want to distance yourself from. You may be feeling used or taken advantage of.

License Plate

To see a license plate in your dream represents liberty and freedom to run your own life.

Lick

To dream that you are licking something, signifies your tendency to be cautious before proceeding on to new situations or adventures. Alternatively, it may also represent satisfaction in some minor matters.

To dream that you are licked by an animal, denotes that you will be called upon for advice.

Lie

*Please see <u>Liar</u>.

Life Jacket

To dream that you are wearing a life jacket, symbolizes security and reinforcement. You are in need of some support.

To dream that you are not wearing a life jacket, indicates that you want to approach your emotions and problems head on, despite the notion that it may be painful or uncomfortable.

Lifeguard

To see or dream that you are a lifeguard, suggests that you are keeping your emotions well guarded. You may be seeking guidance and support while you carefully explore aspects of your unconscious.

Lift

To dream that you are being lifted, represents that you are rising above unpleasant conditions or issues.

Light

To see light in your dream, denotes a clear mind, plain understanding, and insight. Light has been shed on a once cloudy situation or problem. You have found the truth to a situation or an answer to a problem.

To see a bright light in your dream, indicates that you need to move toward a higher level of awareness and feeling. Bright light dreams are sometimes common for those who are near death.

Light Bulb

To see a light bulb in your dream, suggests that you are ready to accept and/or face reality. It refers to your consciousness. The dream also symbolizes spiritual enlightenment, hope, new ideas and visions. You are approaching a situation in a new direction.

Lighthouse

To see a lighthouse in your dream, signifies that you are seeking guidance during your times of hardships and turmoil..

Lightning

To see lightning in your dream, signifies sudden awareness, insight, and purification. Alternatively, lightning may imply a shocking turn of events. It suggests the many forces governing your life may be beyond your control.

To dream that you are struck by lightning, symbolizes irreversible changes occurring in your life. It is a transformation of sorts.

Lilac

To see lilac in your dream, indicates disappointments and rejection. Also you should not always rely on what you see or hear.

Lily

To see lilies in your dream, symbolizes tranquility, spirituality, peace, and bliss.

Lime

To see a lime in your dream, signifies that you will experience a temporary period of hard times but you will arise from it with greater and richer prosperity than before.

Limousine

To see a limousine in your dream, indicates that you have an exaggerated sense of self-worth and self-importance. You may also feel the need to show off and impress others. In addition to the above, if the limousine is black, then it suggests that your are unwilling to make changes or yield to others. Alternatively, it may symbolize prestige, wealth, and power.

Limping

To dream that you are limping, refers to a lack of balance in some relationship in your life. You feel that the relationship is one-sided. Perhaps you feel that you are giving more than you are getting back or vice-versa.

Line

To see a line in your dream, symbolizes duality. It also relates to movement or non-movement. A line also represents limits and boundaries. And thus to dream that you are crossing a line, suggest that you are overstepping your boundaries or that you are moving beyond any limits.

To see a line of people or objects, indicates that you need to be more aware of some situation or relationship.

To dream that you are standing in line, indicates your need for patience. You should be prepared to wait for something and not have it right away.

Lingerie

To dream that you are wearing lingerie, represents your sexual identity, body image and your self-esteem. You may finally be recognizing and acknowledging an aspect of yourself that was not previously expressed.

To dream that you are buying or shopping for lingerie, indicates that you are compensating for your inner feelings of emptiness. You may be trying to fulfill some sexual/emotional need. Alternatively, you may be seeking to change your image and attitude. You may feel one way on the inside but behave another way on the outside.

*Please see also <u>Underwear</u>.

Lions

To see a lion in your dream, symbolizes great strength, aggression and power. You will overcome your emotions and/or difficulties. As king of the jungle, the lion also represents royalty, leadership, pride and dominion. You have much influence over others. You may also need to exercise restraint in your own personal and social life.

To dream that you are attacked by a lion, indicates that you have many obstacles to overcome. You must resist the force that is driving you to self-destruction.

Liposuction

To dream that you have liposuction, represents your preoccupation with your physical shape and appearance. Alternatively, it suggests that you are taking drastic measures to rid yourself of all the responsibilities and things that are weighing you down. The dream may also refer to your anxiety about actual liposuction that you are having.

Lips

To see lips in your dream, signifies sensuality, sex, love, and romance. They are also seen as a means of communication as in the familiar phrase "read my lips".

Lipstick

To buy, see, or wear lipstick in your dream, suggests that you are not entirely truthful about something.

List

To dream that you are making a list, suggests that you are worried about a problem or situation in your waking life.

Listen

To dream that you are listening to something, indicates that you need to pay more close attention to what you are being told and what you are seeing. Perhaps your dream is telling you to be more receptive towards the guidance/criticism of others.

Litter

To see or dream that you litter, suggests that you need to prioritize and organize your ideas and aspects of your life. Your ideas may be lost in the clutter.

Little

*Please See Small.

Liver

To see yours or someone else's liver in your dream, suggests the possibility of a physical disorder. The dream forewarns that you need to reduce your alcohol consumption. Alternatively, it indicates that someone in your life who may not be looking out for your best interest at heart. You may be feeling belittled or angry.

Living Room

To dream that you are in the living room, represents the image that you portray to others and the way which you go about your life. It is representative of your basic beliefs about yourself and who you are.

Lizard

To see a lizard in your dream, signifies your primal instincts and reactions toward sex, food, etc. and your anxieties toward these feelings. The lizard can also be representative of a person who you view as cold-blooded, fearful, or thick-skinned. On a more positive note, the lizard also symbolizes emerging creativity, renewal, and revitalization. It may also suggest that you are well-grounded.

**See The Meaning In Action: "I'm A Lizard"

Llama

To see a llama in your dream, represents deep trust, strength and endurance. It may also mean that you are worrying too much and carrying too many problems.

Loan

To dream that you need a loan, signifies your worry over money matters. Alternatively, you may be too self-reliant and your dream is telling you that it is okay to ask for help and lean on the support from friends and family.

Lobby

To dream that you are in a lobby, indicates that you are trying to make something known.

Lobster

To see a lobster in your dream, represents strength and persistence. You will hold your own ground and overcome minor difficulties and problems.

To dream that you are eating lobster, indicates that you will regain your confidence.

Lock

To see a lock in your dream, signifies your inability to get what you want or being kept out. Perhaps an aspect of yourself is locked up inside and needs to be expressed.

To dream that a lock is accidentally shut around your wrist, suggests that you are debating on whether to be more open about your feelings or keep them to yourself. You feel that you are taking a major risk in letting your feelings known.

Locked

To dream that you are locked out, suggests that you are feeling alienated or unaccepted. You have difficulties getting in touch with your feelings. Consider what and where you are being locked out of.

Locker

To see or use a locker in your dream, signifies aspects of yourself which you have kept hidden inside. Consider what items and belongings are in the locker. In particular, to dream of a school locker, denotes hidden feelings, knowledge, and attitudes that you need to learn and/or acknowledge.

To dream that you cannot open a locker or that your forgot the combination, suggests that you are unsure of where you stand in a particular situation. You feel that you are on shaky ground. If you cannot find your locker, then it also symbolizes your insecurities about your role or position in a situation.

Locker Room

To dream that you are in a locker room, suggests that you need time to cool off and calm down. It also indicates that you are involved in some tough competition or overcoming an obstacle in your life. Perhaps you are trying to pursue a love interest.

Locusts

To see locusts in your dream, signifies a lack of psychological nourishment. You may feel that your are lacking in creativity or that your creativity is being destroyed. Alternatively, it may represent cycles and transformation.

Logs

To see logs in your dream, represents unconscious ideas and a significant and meaning aspect of yourself. Alternatively, it signifies a transformation. You are headed toward a new direction in your life.

To dream that you are sitting on a log, indicates personal satisfaction and joy in you life.

To see a log floating in water, represents new opportunities. You may be overlooking something important.

Lollipop

To see or lick a lollipop in your dream, indicates surprises, new experiences and adventures. It also represents indulgence, sensuality and the pleasant aspects of life. Alternatively, the lollipop may be a pun for "sucker" and thus suggests that you need to proceed with caution in some relationship or situation.

Loneliness

Please see Alone.

Long

To dream of anything long, refers to the penis and/or issues of power and prowess. It may reflect comparison or evaluation issues, how you and others may perceive you. Metaphorically, it may indicate that a situation or relationship has gone on too long.

Loon

To see a loon in your dream, suggests that you have the ability to dig deep and bring up unconscious wisdom. You are looking within yourself for answers. It is time for self-exploration, self-reflection and introspection. You need to get tot he bottom of some situation. The dream may also be a metaphor for someone who is "loony" or crazy.

Lose

To dream that you lose something may mean that you really have misplaced something that you had not realized yet. It may also be a signal for you to clean out and reorganize your life. You have become overwhelmed and distracted with the hustle and bustle of day-to-day life.

On a symbolic note, losing things in your dream may signify lost opportunities, past relationships or forgotten aspects of yourself. Your personal associations to the thing you lose will clue you into the emotional meaning and interpretation of your dream.

Lost

To dream that you are lost, suggests that you have lost your direction in life or that you have lost sight of your goals. You may be feeling worried and insecure about the path you are taking in life. Alternatively, you may be trying to adjust and get accustomed to a new situation in which the rules and conditions are ever changing.

To dream that someone else is lost, represents unresolved issues or feelings regarding the person that is lost. Consider also what aspect of that person you may have lost within your own self. Perhaps you need to recapture and re-acknowledge those aspects.

Lotion

*Please See Cream.

Lottery

To dream of playing the lottery, suggests that you are relying too much on fate instead of taking responsibility for your own actions/decisions. You need to reconsider some issue/situation before committing to it.

To dream that you win the lottery, represents your inner desires to live without having to worry about financial and material troubles.

Lotus

To see a lotus in your dream, represents growth, purity, beauty and expansion of the soul.

Louse

Please See Lice.

Love

To dream of love of being in love, suggests intense feelings carried over from a waking relationship. It implies happiness and contentment with what you have and where you are in life. On the other hand, you may not be getting enough love in your daily life. We naturally long for the sense to belong and to be accepted.

To see a couple in love or expressing love to each other, indicates much success ahead for you.

To dream that your friend is in love with you, may be one of wish fulfillment. Perhaps you have developed have developed feelings for your best friend and are wondering how he or she feels. You are so preoccupied with these thoughts that it is evitable that it find its way into your dreaming mind. On the other hand, the dream may also suggests that you have accepted certain qualities of your best best friend and incorporated into your own character.

To dream that you are making love in public or in different places, relates to some overt sexual issue or need. Your dream may be telling you that you need to express yourself more openly. Alternatively, it represents your perceptions about your own sexuality in the context of politic and social norms. You may be questioning your feelings about sex, marriage, love, and gender roles.

Lover

To see a lover in your dream, symbolizes acceptance, self-worth, and acknowledgement of your true inner value. It may also indicate integration of masculine and feminine traits into yourself. You are feeling complete or whole.

To dream of an old or former lover, signifies unfinished/unresolved issues related to that specific relationship. Your current relationship may be awakening some of those same issues.

Loveseat

Please see Couch.

LSD

To dream that you take LSD, represents an awakening and expanded consciousness. You are looking at things from a new perspective.

Luggage

To see luggage in your dream, signifies the many desires, worries, and needs that you carry with you and weighing you down. You need to reduce you desires and problems and alleviate the pressure you are putting on yourself.

Lumber

To see lumber in your dream, indicates your need for a fresh start and to reorganize your life. You may need to start over and rebuild.

Lunatic

To see a lunatic in your dream, represents an acknowledged aspect of yourself. You may feel that your opinions and suggestions don't matter or are being ignored. You feel like an outsider. Alternatively, you may feel that you have lost a person, situation, or relationship which you frequently depended on.

Lungs

To see lungs in your dream, symbolize insight, creativity, and inspiration. Alternatively, lungs may indicate a stressful situation and refer to a relationship/situation in which you feel suffocated.

Lust

To dream of lust, suggests that you are lacking or feeling unfulfilled in some aspect of your life. Alternatively, you need to exercise some self-control.

Lute

To see or play the lute in your dream, symbolizes pureness and faith.

Lynching

To see a lynching in your dream, represents feelings of self-guilt.

Lynx

To see a lynx in your dream, symbolizes secrecy. There is more to be known and more to be learned. You need to expose and examine those secrets and learn from them.

Lyre

To see al lyre in your dream, represents joy and harmony. The symbol may also be a pun on "liar".

M

Macadamize

To see or travel on a macadamized road in your dream , denotes a pleasant journey that will prove beneficial and profitable.

Macaroni

To dream that you are eating macaroni, denotes small losses. To see macaroni in large quantities, signifies that need for you to be frugal, economize, and save money.

Mace

To see or use mace in your dream, represents your quest for objectivity over subjectivity. You do not let your emotions rule your actions.

Machinery

To see machinery in your dream, suggests that you are going about your way without much thought. You are making decisions without thinking it through. You need to get out of your boring pattern. Alternatively, it indicates that your self-image or a relationship may be in need of repair.

Mad Dog

To see a mad dog in your dream, denotes that you and your friends will be the verbally assaulted by your lowly rivals..

To dream that you kill a mad dog, signifies that you will overcome the adverse opinions of others and rise to prosperity.

Madness

To dream that you are diagnosed with madness or that you are mad, forewarns of trouble, loss, and overwhelming grief. You may have been behaving in an inappropriate way in your waking life.

To see others suffering from madness, signifies a gloomy end to hopeful prospects.

Madonna

To see the Madonna in your dream, symbolizes the mystical mother and the giver of life and beauty. It also signifies blessings.

Mafia

To dream that you are a member of a mafia, suggests that you are allowing others to manipulate you. Or you are using your power against others.

To dream that you come in contact with the mafia, indicates that you are experiencing some inner conflict and turmoil.

Magazine

To read a magazine in your dream, indicates that you are opened to various new ideas. Consider also the theme and name of the magazine and its symbolism.

Maggot

To see maggots in your dream, represents your anxieties about death. It may also be indicative of some issue or problem that you have been rejecting and it is now "eating away" at you . You need to confront it for it is destroying your sense of harmony and balance.

In particular, to dream that you are stepping on maggots, indicates guilt and impurity. You are trying to repress your immoral thoughts or behavior . On a positive note, it may symbolize your resilience, persistence, and your ability to bounce back from adversity.

Magic

To dream that you are performing magic, signifies many pleasant surprises. It may also represent a creative mind and that events will turn out the way you had hoped for.

To see others performing magic in your dream, denotes profitable endeavors.

To dream of black magic, represents that you have obtained your wishes and wants through underhanded tricks. It also symbolizes evil and treachery.

Magic Carpet

To dream that you are riding a magic carpet, indicates that you are overcoming your obstacles and physical limitations.

Magician

To see or dream that you are a magician, signifies that an issue or a task at hand may be trickier than you had anticipated. You may be disillusioned. The dream may also mean that you are trying to fool yourself or someone into believing something that you know is not true.

Magistrate

To see a magistrate in your dream, signifies that you will be involved in a lawsuit or experience loss in business.

Magnet

To see a magnet in your dream, symbolizes negative forces that are drawing you towards a path of dishonor and ruin. It may also signify personal empowerment.

Magnifying Glass

To look through a magnifying glass in your dream, signifies failure to accomplish your work in a satisfactory manner.

Magnolia

To see magnolias in your dream, symbolizes beauty, grace and elegance.

Magnolia Tree

To see a magnolia tree in your dream, indicates your need for attention and to be noticed. You are being overly confident in your abilities. Alternatively, it represents your need to feel protected and safe from life's problems.

Magpie

To see a magpie in your dream, signifies dissatisfaction and disagreements and that you need to be careful of what you say and do.

To see a dead magpie in your dream, symbolizes that malicious rumors will lead to the downfall of another.

Maid

To see or have a maid in your dream, suggests that you are depending too much on others for their help. You need to be more independent and look after your own self.

To dream that you are a maid, indicates that you need to clear up the clutter in your life. You may also need to nurture yourself and cleanse your emotions.

Mail

To dream that receive mail, indicates that you need to communicate or re-establish contact with someone from your present/past. It may also represent messages from your unconscious or intuition. The mail may also be a pun on a "male" in your life.

If you receive mail from someone you don't know, then it suggests that some hidden aspect of yourself is trying to tell you something.

Mailbox

To see a mail box in your dream, represents important information that you are about to receive. Pay particular attention to your dream and what message it is trying to convey to you from your unconscious. If the mailbox is full, then it indicates that you have not digested or accepted these messages.

Mailman

To see a mailman in your dream, symbolizes your communications with others. You need to get the word out about something.

To dream that you are a mailman, suggests that a message is being channeled to you from your unconscious. Pay close attention to the message of this dream.

Makeup

To dream that you are applying make-up, signifies that you are trying to cover up or conceal a hidden aspect of yourself. Alternatively, it may signify that you are putting on your best face forward. You are trying to enhance your self-image and increase your sense of self-confidence.

To dream that you are wearing too much make-up, indicates that you are putting more emphasis on beauty and outside appearances rather than what is inside.

Making Out

To dream that you are making out with someone you don't like in that way, suggests that you need to acknowledge and incorporate aspects and characteristics of this person into your own character. Consider specific traits that this person possess.

To dream that you are making our with a friend, suggests that you have an unconscious desire to pursue the relationship but fear that it will jeopardize the friendship.

Malice

To dream that you have malice toward others, signifies that others will look down on you because of your ill temper. You need to control your temper.

To dream that others have malice towards you, denotes a false friend who is working on harming you.

Mall

To dream that you are at the mall, represents your attempts in making a favorable impression on someone. The mall is also symbolic of materialism and the need to keep up with the trends, fads, and/or the latest technology.

Mallet

To see a mallet in your dream, signifies chaos in the home. You will be treated unkindly and insensitively by friends even though you are in ill health.

Malpractice

To dream that you are sued for malpractice, signifies a need to change your ways and attitude.

Malt

To see malted drinks in your dream, signifies that you will be wrapped up in an intriguing but dangerous affair.

Man

To see a man in your dream, denotes the masculine aspect of yourself - the side that is assertive, rational, aggressive, and/or competitive. If the man is known to you, then the dream may reflect you feelings and concerns you have about him.

If you are a woman and dream that you are in the arms of a man, suggests that you are accepting and welcoming your stronger assertive personality . It may also highlight your desires to be in a relationship and your image of the ideal man.

To see an old man in your dream, represents wisdom or forgiveness.

Manager

To dream that you are a manager, indicates that you need to be more organized and efficient.

Mandala

To see a mandala in your dream, signifies that positive changes are occurring in your waking life. It also symbolizes wholeness, unity, healing, spirituality, and harmony.

Mango

To see or eat a mango in your dream, symbolizes fertility, sexual desires, and lust. Alternatively, the mango may also be a pun to mean "man go" in reference to a relationship in which you should let go and move on.

Manicure

To dream that you are getting a manicure, represents glamour and beauty. You are seeking attention for the work you have done. You may also be expressing something beautiful and positive through your work.

Mannequin

To see a mannequin in your dream, represents an extension of your own self that you are projecting. You may feel that you are not playing an active enough role in some situation. Consider how the mannequin is dressed for clues as to what you may wish to act out, but have not done so.

Manners

To see well-mannered persons, signifies a pleasant and favorable turn in what you thought was a bleak situation.

To see bad-mannered persons, denotes that conflict and disagreements with an associate or a teammate will lead to failure to carry out the task at hand.

Man Of War

To see a man of war in your dream, signifies long journeys and separation from friends.

To see a man of war sailing upon rough seas in your dream, denotes that foreign forces may affect you daily life.

Mansion

To see a mansion in your dream, symbolizes your greatest potential and growth. You may feel that your current situation or relationship is in a rut.

Manslaughter

To dream of manslaughter, signifies fear and scandal.

Mantilla

To see a mantilla in your dream, signifies that an unwise deal will bring your name shame and disfavor.

Manure

To see manure in your dream, suggests that you are learning from past experiences. You are drawing from those experiences and putting it to use in your current situation.

Manuscript

To dream that you are writing a manuscript, signifies fears in not accomplishing your greatest desires.

To dream that your manuscript is rejected by a publisher, denotes that you will experience temporary hopelessness. Once you overcome this period, your hopes will eventually be realized.

To dream that a manuscript is on fire, signifies that your own hard work will result in profit and a rise in the social ladder.

Map

To dream that you see or study a map, signifies that you are being guided and led in a direction that will fulfill your needs and goals. It also denotes a new change in your business which will be followed by temporary disappointments and then stable profits.

Maple

To see a maple in your dream, symbolizes humility, warmth, and openness. It also indicates positive gains, happiness and fullness of life.

To see a falling maple tree, indicates family disharmony and broken ties.

To see a maple leaf in your dream, represents each of the five senses and what it has to offer. It also denotes a helping or protective hand.

Marble

To dream that you are polishing marble, represents your enduring efforts and perseverance.

March

To dream of the month of march, signifies disappointing returns in business and your honor and trust will be called into question.

Marching

To dream that you are marching to the beat of music, signifies teamwork. It also denotes your aspirations in becoming a soldier or a public office holder.

To see people marching in your dream, denotes your desires in wanting to associate with people in public positions.

Mardi Gras

To dream of Mardi Gras, indicates your need to release your inhibitions and let yourself go.

Mare

To see a mare or several mares in your dream, represents your intuition.

To see a white mare in your dream, symbolizes spirit and creativity.

Marigold

To see marigolds in your dream, denotes health and longevity.

Marijuana

To see, smell or use marijuana in your dream, suggests that you are experiencing an expanded sense of awareness and consciousness. You need to take advantage and draw insight from this new consciousness. The dream may also mean that you need to look on your inner strength for stimulation instead of relying on outside forces.

Mariner

To dream that you are a mariner, signifies a long and pleasant journey to foreign country.

Marijuana

To dream that you are using marijuana, signifies illicit activity or ill health.

Market

To dream that you are in a market, represents some emotional of physical need that you are currently lacking in your life. You may be in need of nurturance and some fulfillment. Consider the specific items that you are shopping for. Alternatively, the market signifies frugality.

To see an barren market in your dream, signifies depression and gloominess. There is a void in your life.

Marmalade

To dream that you are eating marmalade, signifies illness for you.

To dream that you are making marmalade, denotes an unhappy domestic life.

Marmot

To see a marmot in your dream, signifies that a person of your opposite sex is serving as a lure to your downfall.

Marriage

To see a marriage in your dream, signifies commitment, harmony or transition. You will undergo an important developmental transitional phase. It may also represent the unification of formerly separate or opposite aspects of yourself. In particular, it may represent the union of masculine or feminine aspects of yourself.

To dream of a proposal of marriage, suggests that some situation will take a turn for the worse.

To dream that you are getting married to your ex, suggests that you have accepted aspects of that relationship and learned from those past mistakes. Alternatively, it means that a current relationship shares some commonality with your previous relationship with your ex. However, you will not make those same mistakes.

*Please see also Wedding.

Mars

To see Mars in your dream, signifies that cruel friends will make you feel miserable and depressed over life.

Marsh

To dream that you are walking through marshy areas, suggests instability in your emotional realm.

*Please see also Swamp.

Marshmallows

To see or eat marshmallows in your dream, represents timidity and lack of self-confidence. You need to learn to be more assertive and stand up for yourself.

To dream that you are roasting marshmallows, indicates growth and motivation.

Martyr

To dream that you are a martyr, suggests that you are tending to the needs of others and neglecting your own needs. The dream is also indicates of a lack of self-love and not being able to forgive yourself.

Mascara

To dream that you are wearing mascara. suggests that you need to open your eyes and be more attentive to a situation or relationship.

To dream that your mascara is smeared, indicates that your reputation is being called into question by rumors.

Mask

To dream that you are wearing a mask, signifies temporary trouble as a result of some misunderstanding and misinterpretation of your actions and conduct. Alternatively, you may be pretending to be someone you are not or are hiding your true feelings.

To see others wearing a mask in your dream, denotes that you will battle against deceit, falsehood, and jealousy.

To see others unmask in your dream, symbolizes failure in gaining the admiration and/or respect of someone sought for.

Mason

To dream that you are a mason, signifies a rise in your current circumstances and a more satisfying social surrounding.

Masquerade

To dream that you are at a masquerade ball, signifies that your indulgence in sinful and foolish pleasures will lead to the neglect of your business and domestic duties.

Massacre

To witness a massacre in your dream, suggests that you are a follower. You follow the ideals of others without question and hesitation.

Massage

To dream that you are getting a massage, suggests that you are lacking sensual or sexual stimulation in your waking life. You may also need to take better care of your body. It also represents nurturance and comfort. Alternatively, it suggests that you need to let go and stop being so defensive.

Mast

To see the masts of ships in your dream, signifies long and pleasant journeys and new companionships.

To see the masts of wrecked ships in your dream, denotes sudden changes in your situation.

Mastectomy

To dream that you have a mastectomy, indicates your lack of sensitivity. You are feeling disconnected from those around you. From a positive perspective, this dream signifies your independence and autonomy. If you have been diagnosed with breast cancer, then this dream represents fear and worry.

Master

To dream that you are a master, signifies that you will hold high positions and gain much wealth.

To dream that you have a master, denotes your feelings of inadequacy and that you need a strong-willed leader to guide you.

Masturbation

To dream that you are masturbating, represents your unacknowledged and unexpressed sexual needs/desires. It may also indicate you need to take care of yourself in sensual or emotional ways which are not necessarily sexual. You may need to put forth a little more effort toward some relationship.

To see others masturbating in your dreams, denotes your anxieties and concerns about your inhibitions. It may also be a reflection that something in your waking life is not as satisfying as it might be. Keep in mind that this dream may not necessarily represent sexual inhibitions or satisfaction, but may be analogous to some situation or relationship.

Mat

To see mats in your dream, signifies the approach of sorrow and disappointments.

Matador

To see or dream that you are a matador, suggests that you need to challenge yourself and prepare for the obstacles ahead. Work on your bravery.

Matches

To see or strike a match in your dream, suggests that there is something that you need to ignite and rekindle in your life.

Mathematics

To dream about mathematics, indicates that you are evaluating a situation in your waking life where you need to be more rational in your thinking. Try not to act on your emotions

To dream that you are unable to solve a mathematical problem or equation, parallels a waking problem where you may be confused about. The dream may offer a hint toward a new approach to the waking problem.

Mattress

To see a mattress in your dream, signifies that you will have new responsibilities and duties that will need your attention for a short time.

To dream that you are sleeping on a new mattress, symbolizes happiness in your present stage of life.

Mausoleum

To see a mausoleum in your dream, signifies illness, trouble, and possibly death of some close friend.

To dream that you are in a mausoleum, denotes illness and health problems ahead for you.

May

To dream of the month of May, signifies prosperity and times of pleasure.

Mayonnaise

To see or eat mayonnaise in your dream, represents disappointment in your waking life. It also indicates the occurrence of insults and disrespect in some situation or relationship.

Maypole Dance

To see or participate in a maypole dance, indicates that you are celebrating an end to your old ways and welcoming in a new beginning. Alternatively, it signifies male sexuality and fertility.

Maze

To dream that you are in a maze, denotes that you need to deal with the task on hand at a more direct level. You are making the situation harder than it really is. Alternatively, the maze may symbolize your life and its twists and turns.

Meadow

To see a meadow in your dream, represents openness and security. You are taking time out to appreciate your accomplishments.

Meadowlark

To see meadowlark in your dream, indicates your cheerful disposition and outlook on life. You make the best out of every situation.

Meals

To see meals in your dream, signifies that you dwell too much on trivial matters and it will divert your attention from more important engagements and matters.

Measles

To dream that you have measles, signifies much worry and anxiety in your life that will interfere with your job or schooling.

To see others with measles in your dream, denotes that the troubling situation and condition of others will give you much worry.

Measurement

To see or dream about your measurements, indicates that you are setting standards for yourself or what you think others expect of you. You need to stop comparing yourself to others.

Meat

To see raw meat in your dream, signifies that there will be many obstacles and discouragement in achieving your goals. Alternatively, it may reflect your untamed, animalistic nature and raw emotions.

To see cooked meat in you dream, denotes that you will see others obtain the object for which you have been striving for.

To dream that you are eating meat, signifies that you are getting to the heart of the matter.

To see rotten meat in your dream, suggests a degradation of your physical and psychological being. The dream may be a metaphor for some health problems.

Mechanic

To see a mechanic in your dream, suggests that you need to work on healing your past hurts and trauma.

Mercury

To see Mercury in your dream, symbolizes alertness, awareness, reason, and versatility. You are exhibiting efficiency in your work.

Medal

To see medals in your dream, signifies that you will attain some honor through hard work.

To lose a medal in your dream, denotes misfortune through the unfaithfulness of others.

Media

Please See Press.

Medicine

To dream that you are giving medicine to others, signifies that you will conspire to harm someone who trust you.

To dream that you are taking medicine, represents a period of emotional and/or spiritual healing. It also indicates that the troubles you are experiencing are only temporary and will prove to be for the best in the long run,

Medicine Man

To see a traditional medicine man in your dream, signifies that you have the support of good friends to help you in your quest for success.

Medieval

To dream of Medieval times, represents old habits/attitudes and old ways of thinking. It is important to analyze the activities that occur in the dreams so that you will find out what aspect of yourself or your life that needs updating.

Meditate

To dream that you are meditating, represents self-acceptance and enlightenment. It also suggests that you need to be less judgmental on others and don't be so hard on yourself.

Medium

To dream that you are a medium, indicates that you are getting in touch with your intuitive side and being more sensitive to your instincts and how your perceive things. It also suggests increased knowledge of your unconscious.

Medusa

To see Medusa in your dream, signifies cunningness.

Meeting

To dream that you are in a meeting, suggests that you need to redirect your energies toward a more productive endeavor. Alternatively, you are learning to accept various aspects of yourself and integrating these various parts.

To dream that you are late or miss a meeting, signifies anxieties that you are not measuring when it comes to your professional life and toward achieving your goals. You may feel unprepared in some situation or challenge in your waking life.

Megaphone

To dream that you are using a megaphone, indicates that you need to be more vocal and expressive about your feelings. Speak up and express yourself. Perhaps you feel that you are overlooked and feel that your voice is not being heard.

Melancholy

To dream that you are feeling melancholy, signifies disappointment in an event that was assumed to be a success.

To see others melancholy in your dream, signifies unpleasant interruptions in your affairs that need to be tended to immediately.

Melon

To see melons in your dream, symbolizes ill health and misfortune in business deals.

To dream that you are eating melons, signifies that hastiness will lead to much anxiety in the end.

To see melons growing on vines, signifies that your current problems will lead to fortune for you in the end.

Melting

To see melting ice or snow, signifies that you are letting go or releasing negative or cold emotions that you have been feeling. You are warming up to a situation.

Memorandum

To dream that you are making a memoranda, denotes unfruitful business with little or no gain, but much worry and distress.

To see others making memorandum in your dream, signifies that you will be called upon to aid a person in need.

Memorial

To see a memorial in your dream, denotes that you will need to show kindness and compassion towards your relatives who will be experiencing some trouble and/or illness.

Memory

To dream about a memory, suggests that your are ready to rid yourself of your old ways and undergo some sort of transformation and new outlook in life. Recalling a memory in your dream may also be less of a shock then if you had recalled the memory in your waken state. It indicates that you may have learned something from your past.

Men

If you are a woman and dream that you are in a room full of men, highlights the masculine aspect of yourself and forces you to acknowledge your authorities and aggressive side. Consider also how the men are dressed as this will provide a clue as to what area in your life you need to assert more power.

*Please Also See Man.

Menagerie

To dream that you are at a menagerie, signifies varying degrees of problems

Mendicant

To see mendicants in your dream, signifies interruptions in your plans.

Mending

To dream that you are mending a garment, symbolizes your attempts in fixing a problem. It also foretells of success and gains to your fortune.

Menopause

To dream about menopause, suggests that you are smothering the people around you. You need to be less codependent.

Menorah

To see a Menorah in your dream, represents the seven days of the week. It is also symbolic of the sun, the moon, and the five main planets. Alternatively, it symbolizes beauty, strength, and wisdom. This dream imagery may also be a reflection of your religious faith.

Menstruation

To dream of menstruation, indicates that you are releasing your pent-up tension and worry. It signals an end to your difficult times and the beginning of relaxation. Alternatively, you may be denying your feminine side.

For women in particular, dreaming of their menstrual cycle when it is not time yet, may indicate your anxiety about your cycle or may sometimes signal an early or unexpected period.

**See The Meaning In Action: "Menstruation"

Mental Institution

To dream that you are in a mental institution, indicates a need for rest and reset your mind. You need to not be afraid to ask for help/assistance when you need it.

To dream that you are outside a mental institution, suggests that you are feeling ostracized or shunned. You may be close to a mental breakdown. Or you are feeling left out, excluded, and ignored.

Mercury

To see mercury in your dream, represents quick movement. You need to speak up first and think it through later. Trust your intuition.

Mermaid

To see a mermaid in your dream, signifies the female aspect of yourself that is mysterious and secretive. It may also show a fear of sex. In particular, for a man to dream of a mermaid, it indicates that he is having fears of being drowned by the feminine aspect of his psyche. For a woman, it suggests doubts over her femininity.

Merry

To dream that you are merry or in merry company, signifies a time of pleasant engagements and profitable affairs.

Merry-Go-Round

To dream that you are on a merry-go-round, indicates a fear of reliving your childhood. You may feel that you are going nowhere or in a state of stagnation. Or you may be expressing some anxiety about your transition into adulthood. Alternatively, it suggests that you are in the beginning stages of romantic love.

To see a merry-go-round in your dream, represents childish joy.

Meshes

To dream that you are entangled in the meshes of a net, denotes that your rivals will succeed in getting the best of you during your times of promising hope and prosperity.

To dream that you are able to untangle yourself from the meshes, signifies that you will narrowly escape slander.

Message

To dream that you are sending a message, forewarns that you will be put into an unpleasant situation.

To dream that you are receiving a message, signifies changes in your affairs.

*Please see also Letter.

Metal

To see metal in your dream, signifies strength and character. It may also symbolize the inhumane side of society.

Metamorphosis

To see a metamorphosis take place in your dream, denotes sudden and rapid changes in your personal life. If the metamorphosis is a smooth one, then it indicates necessary changes for you to adapt to a new situation. However, if the metamorphosis is a complicated and unpleasant one, then it suggests that you are ill prepared for the changes in your life.

Meteor

To see a meteor in your dream, suggests that you will experience success in a project. You are trying to realize your greatest desires.

To see a meteor shower in your dream, signifies romantic thoughts and idealistic notions

Mice

To see mice in your dream, symbolizes domestic problems, business loss, deceit, and insincere friends. It represents minor problems in which you are spending too much time dwelling on.

To dream that you kill a mouse, signifies that you will overcome your rivals.

To dream that a mouse jumps on you or into your clothing, foretells of scandal in which you will largely figure in.

To dream that you or someone is eating mice, indicates that there is something that has been nagging your conscience and you need to get off your chest.

Microphone

To see a microphone in your dream, suggests that you need to make be more assertive. You need to voice your opinions more strongly and make your views known. The microphone may also be a pun on someone in your life who is named "Mike"

Microscope

To see a microscope in your dream, suggests that you need to take a closer look at some situation. Something that may seemingly be insignificant may actually be a hindrance.

Microwave

To see a microwave in your dream, represents your quick thinking and quick-action. You need to consider new and better way of doing things.

Midget

To see a midget in your dream, suggests that you are feeling small and insignificant. Do you feel helpless in some situation or have a deflated sense of self-worth?

Midwife

To see a midwife in your dream, denotes illness that is almost life-threatening.

Mildew

To see mildew in your dream, symbolizes neglected feelings and emotions that you are unwilling to confront. It is time to bring those feelings to the surface and work through them.

Military

To see the military in your dream, signifies rigid authority and emotional repression. Disciplinary action may be brought upon you.

If you have served with the military, then this dream may represent our actual life experiences and memories.

Milk

To see milk in your dream, symbolizes maternal instincts and motherly love. It also denotes human kindness, wholesomeness, and compassion for new acquaintances.

To dream that you are drinking milk, signifies domestic bliss and inner nourishment. It may also imply your need to strengthen your ties and relationships with others.

To spill milk in your dream, symbolizes a loss of faith, opportunity, and trust. It may indicate that your friends will cause you much temporary disappointment and unhappiness..

To dream of milk that is sour or impure, denotes small problems that will torment you and give you much distress.

To dream of hot milk, signifies that you will undergo a struggle before accomplishing your rise to fortune.

To dream that you are bathing in milk, denotes a stable circle of reliable and pleasant friends.

To dream that you are choking on milk, indicates that you are being overprotected. You may be feeling smothered in some relationship.

Milking

To dream that you are milking a cow, signifies that great opportunities are being put before you but out of your reach. Through perseverance, you will win out in the end.

Mill

To see a mill in your dream, symbolizes frugality and fortunate endeavors.

Miller

To see a miller in your dream, foretells of growing hopes in your current situation.

Mime

To see or dream that you are a mime, suggests that you are having difficulties verbally communicating your thoughts and feelings across. Others around you may not understand your erratic behavior. You are trying to make light of how you really feel.

Mine

To dream that you are in a mine, signifies that you are getting to depth or core of an issue or condition. It also forewarns that will fail in your endeavors.

To dream that you own a mine, signifies future riches.

Minefield

To dream that you are in a minefield, indicates that you are facing much difficulties in your waking life. You are worried about how to resolve your problems. Don't be afraid to reach out for advice and for help.

Mineral

To see minerals in your dream, signifies that your current bleak outlook look look more promising in the future.

Mineral Water

To dream that you are drinking mineral water, denotes that you will have a solid foundation of fortune to satisfy you taste for the finer things in life.

Mining

To see mining in your dream, signifies that your rivals is seeking your downfall by stirring up your past mistakes.

Minister

To see or dream that you are a minister, suggest that you need to be more compassionate and understanding in some situation or relationship. Alternatively, it indicates that you have overstep your boundaries and into another's rights.

Mink

To see a mink in your dream, symbolizes value. It may also represent your understanding of your unconscious and its motivation.

Minotaur

To see a minotaur in your dream, denotes a union between your intelligence and powerful instincts. A situation in your waking life may be larger than you can handle. You are feeling overwhelmed.

Minstrel

To see a minstrel in your dream, indicates the start of some new journey or life path.

Minuet

To see a minuet in your dream, pleasant surroundings and joyous friendships.

To dream that you are dancing in a minuet, foretells of domestic bliss and prosperity.

Minx

To see a minx in your dream, signifies that you will have to overcome sneaky rivals.

To dream that you kill a minx, denotes that you will achieve your desires.

To see minx furs in your dream, symbolizes security and that you will have an extremely jealous lover.

Miracle

To see a miracle in your dream, suggests that you are goal-oriented and plan for the future. You have a lot of confidence in our accomplishments.

Mirage

To see a mirage in your dream, signifies your disillusionment. What you think is true about others may turn out to be the contrary.

Mire

To dream that you are going through a mire, signifies a minor interruption in your plans.

Mirror

To see your own reflection in the mirror, suggests that you are pondering thoughts about your inner self. The reflection in the mirror is how you perceive yourself or how you want others to see you. You may be contemplating on strengthening and changing aspects of your character.

To dream that you are looking through a two-way mirror, indicates that you are coming face to face with some inner or worldly issue. What you see is related to your persona and unconscious. Seeing images through the mirror may be a safe way for you to consider and/or confront material from your unconscious. Mirrors symbolize the imagination and a link between the conscious and unconscious.

To dream that you are being watched through a two-way mirror, suggests that you feel you are being scrutinized and criticized. Alternatively, you may be blocking or unwilling to acknowledge your unconscious emotions.

To break a mirror in your dream, suggests that you are breaking an old image of yourself. You may be putting an end to an old habit. Breaking a mirror is also an old symbol for seven years of bad luck.

To see a cracked or broken mirror in your dream. represents a poor or distorted self-image. Alternatively, it suggests that you have put an end to your old habits and ways.

To see a fogged mirror in your dream, signifies a hazy concept of who you are and questions about your self-identity. You are confused in your goals in life an you may have a lack of clarity in a purpose.

Miscarriage

To dream that you have a miscarriage, suggests that some idea or plan did not follow through or has gone awry. The dream may also serve as a warning against your continued course of action. You should alter your path or may risk losing something of significance and value to you. Alternatively, the dream may indicate that you have been wronged in some way.

For expectant mothers, dreams of miscarriages are common in the second trimester of pregnancy.

Miser

To see or dream that you are a miser, indicates a low sense of self-worth. You may be limiting yourself and not recognizing your full potential and the resources that are available to you.

Misshapen

*Please See Deformed.

Missile

To dream that you are attacked by a missile, represents feelings of helplessness and forces beyond your control. Alternatively, missile may indicate insecurities about sex.

Missing

To dream that you are missing something, denotes a sense of being out of control and being disorganized.

Mist

To dream that you are caught in a mist, signifies confusion and unhappiness in your home life and uncertain fortune. You need to see things more clearly.

To see others caught in a mist, signifies that you will gain from the misfortune of others.

Mistake

To dream that you make a mistake, indicates that you are doubting yourself in the choices and decisions you have made.

Mistletoe

To see mistletoe in your dream, symbolizes joyous occasions and much happiness. It also indicates that you are feeling attracted toward someone around you.

Mistress

To dream that you (or your mate) have a mistress, suggests your unconscious desire to end your current relationship and are finding ways to sabotage it. Alternatively, you feel neglected in the relationship. Perhaps you feel that you are not measuring up to the expectations of others, in particular to your mate.

To dream that you are a mistress, indicates your desires for the finer things in life.

To see a mistress in your dream, suggests that you or someone is being lured or tempted into some negative activity.

Mittens

To see or dream that you are wearing mittens, suggests that you are handling things in a childish manner.

Mixing

To dream that you are mixing something, signifies a blending of opposite ends of your personality. The result is acceptance of an attitude that is more flexible.

Moat

To see a moat in your dream, suggests that you have put up an emotional wall around you. You are shutting others out and trying to block out the hurt.

Mob

To see a mob in your dream, represents chaos and disorganization. Your are experiencing a conflict in ideas and interest. It is time to be more assertive and take control of your life.

Mocassins

To see or wear mocassins in your dream, signifies your respect for nature and its beings. It also suggests that you walking peacefully or treading lightly on some situation.

Mocking

To dream that someone is mocking you or making fun on you, indicates that you are suffering from low self-esteem.

Mockingbird

To see or hear a mockingbird in your dream, represents cockiness, cleverness, or independence. You may be taking credit for the work of others. You also have the tendency to get what you want.

Models

To see or dream that you are a model, represents an image that you are trying to portray. You are trying to be something that you are not.

Modest

To dream that you are being modest, indicates that you need to be less arrogant and/or assertive in your real-life situations. You need to show more humility and be more even-tempered. Alternatively, it suggests that you have some minor concerns about a situation.

Moisturizer

To use or apply moisturizer in your dream, represents the persona you are portraying to others. It also symbolic of a renewal. You have a fresh outlook in life.

Molasses

To see molasses in your dream, signifies that you will receive much pleasure and fortunate surprises through the hospitality of others.

To dream that you are eating molasses, denotes disappointments in love.

To dream that molasses gets on your clothing, signifies business losses and disagreeable offers of marriage.

Mold

To see mold in your dream, indicates that something in your life has been ignored or is no longer of any use. It may also represent transformation and new growth.

To see a broken mold in your dream, suggests that you need to break away from your old habits and explore new things. You may be rigid and lacking creativity.

Moles

To see a mole in your dream, represents destruction and unforeseen danger. You are secretly plotting against others or someone else is working against you. Someone around you may have their own hidden agendas. Alternatively, a mole is symbolic of your unconscious drives and things that are not on the surface. You need to go deeper and uncover what is going on.

To dream that you have a mole on your face or body, suggests that something is interfering with your personal esteem or that you are unable to obtain the esteem of others.

Monastery

To dream that you are at a monastery, indicates that you need to learn and explore more about yourself. It is a time for self-reflection and self-exploration.

Money

To see or win money in your dream, symbolizes that success and prosperity is within your reach. Money may represent confidence, self-worth, success, or values. You have much belief in yourself. Alternatively, dreaming about money, refers to your attitudes about love and matters of the heart. It is frequently a symbol for sexuality and power. In particular, finding money indicates your quest for love or for power.

To dream that you lose money, signifies temporary unhappiness in the home and a few setbacks in your affairs. You may be feeling weak, vulnerable, and out of control in your waking life. Additionally, you may be lacking ambition, power and self-esteem.

To dream about giving money away, is analogous to giving love. You are looking for love. To see others giving money away, suggests that you are feeling ignored or neglected. Someone is not paying enough attention and showing enough affection toward you.

To dream that you have no money, denotes that you have a fear of losing your place in the world or that you feel that you lack the abilities needed to achieve some desired goal. You may be overlooked or neglected by others.

To dream that you steal money, forewarns that you are in danger and need to be cautious. On a positive note, it may mean that you are finally going after or reaching out towards attributes that you associate with things of value.

Monk

To see a monk in your dream, signifies devotion, faith, and spiritual enlightenment.

To dream that you are a monk, symbolizes the introspective aspect of yourself. You need to emotionally withdraw yourself from a situation and regain some control, structure, and order.

Monkey

To see a monkey in your dream, symbolizes deceit people are working to advance their own interest. Monkeys also symbolize a playful and mischievous side of your own personality or an immature attitude.

To see a monkey hanging or swinging from a tree, denotes that you be troubled by young ones.

To dream that you are feeding a monkey, denotes that you betrayed by someone whom you thought cared about your interests.

Monster

To dream that you are followed by a monster, signifies that grief and misfortune are in your immediate future. Monsters represent parts of yourself that you find brutish and ugly. You may possess some fears or some repressed emotions.

To dream that you kill a monster, signifies that you will successfully deal with your rivals and advance to a higher and better position.

**See The Meaning In Action: "_Monsters On Bikes_"

Monument

To see a monument in your dream, signifies your legacy and how you want to be remembered. It also symbolizes your self-worth and the qualities you value in yourself.

Moon

To see the moon in your your dream, represents something hidden, mystery and the feminine aspect of your self. In particular, a full moon signifies completion, whereas a new moon symbolizes new beginnings.

To dream that the moon in odd in any way, signifies infidelity of your lover and disappointments in business.

To see the eclipse of the moon in your dream, signifies that your feminine side is being overshadowed. It also foretells of illness of someone near you.

To see the crescent moon in your dream, indicates cyclic changes, renewal, and movement. You are progressing smoothly toward your life path.

Moose

To see a moose in your dream, represents long life and longevity. It may refer to the elders around you. Alternatively, a moose may also indicate that you can be both powerful and gentle.

Mop

To dream that you are mopping, suggests that you are letting go of something. You need to release your emotions and express it in a productive way.

To see a mop in your dream, symbolizes domesticity. It may also represent the work needed to maintain and keep a household together.

Morgue

To dream that you are in a morgue and looking for someone, foretells shocking and dreadful news of the death of a relative or close friend.

To dream that there are many corpses in the morgue, denotes much grief and trouble for you.

Morning

To dream that it is morning, denotes that fortune and pleasure are within near reach. It may also denotes new beginnings, renewal, an awakening or starting over.

To dream that the morning is cloudy, signifies that an important situation will burden you for a while.

Morocco

To see morocco in your dream, signifies that you will receive assistance from people whom you least expect it from.

Morph

To dream that you or someone is morphing into another person, suggests that you need to incorporate aspects of this other person into your own character. You are in need of some change. Alternatively, you need to learn to see things from someone else's perspective and expand your awareness.

Mortgage

To dream that you hold a mortgage, represents how you utilize your energies and put it to worthy pursuits.

Morose

To dream that you are morose, denotes that you pessimistic about the world around you and find that it is going terribly wrong.

To see others morose in your dream, signifies unpleasant situations and disagreeable companions.

Mortify

To dream that you feel mortified over your conduct, signifies that will find yourself in an embarrassing situation before those whom you wish to appear most honorable.

Mortuary

To see or dream that you are in a mortuary, suggests that you are hindering your own self-growth by not utilizing your abilities and talents. Alternatively, it represents aspects of yourself that you need to discard and rid yourself of.

Mosaic

To see a mosaic in your dream, represents the various aspects and components that make up life as a whole. You need to consider things from a wider perspective. Things may look insignificant and meaningless, but you need to stand back and consider the overall picture.

Moses

To see Moses in your dream, signifies personal gains and self gratification .

Mosquito

To see mosquitoes in your dream, suggests that some situation or somebody has been draining you of your energy and resources. Alternatively, it signifies that you will try in vain to resist attacks from others.

To dream that you are killing mosquitoes, denotes that you will eventually overcome your obstacles and enjoy happiness and fortune.

Moss

To see moss growing in your dream, indicates an extremely slow progress in some project or relationship. You need to be more patient.

Motel

To see or live in a motel in your dream, represents your potential to achieve your goals. You are going through a transitional phase.

Moth

To see a moth in your dream, indicates that unseen irritations and damage will not surface until it is too late. It is important to pay attention to minor details and not overlook things or others. Alternatively, the moth may symbolize your weaknesses and character flaws.

Mother

To see your mother in your dream, represents the nurturing aspect of your own character. Mothers offer shelter, comfort, life, guidance and protection. Some people may have problems freeing themselves from their mothers and are thus seeking their own individuality and development.

To dream that you are having a conversation with your mother, denotes a matter that has preoccupied your mind and you are not sure how to deal with it in your waking life. It indicates unresolved problems that still need to be worked out with your mother.

To hear your mother call you in our dream, signifies that you have been negligent in your duties and responsibilities. You are pursuing down the wrong path.

To hear your mother cry in your dream, denotes some illness or affliction.

Mother-In-Law

To see your mother-in-law in your dream, foretells that after much bitter disagreements. things will be resolved in a pleasant and amicable manner.

To dream that you are in a dispute with your mother-in-law, signifies that you will be greatly annoyed by callous and unfeeling people around you.

Motor Home

To dream that you live in a motor home, suggests that you need to move on with regards to some aspect of your life. You may be dwelling too much on a situation and it is time to move forward. Alternatively, you may be expressing your desire to be more independent and self-sufficient.

Motorcycle

To see or ride a motorcycle in your dream, symbolizes your desire for freedom and need for adventure. You may be trying to escape from some situation or some other responsibility in your waking life. A motorcycle is also symbolic of raw sexuality.

To dream that you are speeding on a motorcycle, indicates that you are moving too fast.

Mountain Lion

To see a mountain lion in your dream, represents lurking danger, aggression and raw emotions. You need to keep your attitude and emotions in check. Alternatively, mountain lions symbolize pride and grace.

Mountains

To see mountains in your dream, signifies many major obstacles and challenges that you have to overcome. If you are on top of the mountain, then it signifies that you have achieved and realized your goals. Alternatively, mountains denotes a higher realm of consciousness, knowledge, and spiritual truth.

To dream that you are climbing a mountain, signifies your determination and ambition.

To dream that you fall off a mountain, suggests that you are in a hurry to succeed without thoroughly thinking about your path to success. It also means that you have a tendency to give up or escape from demanding situations.

Mourning

To dream that you are in mourning, refers to your inability to let go of the past. You need clear those old experiences and make way for the new.

To dream that you are wearing mourning, symbolizes grief, bad luck, and unhappiness.

To see others wearing mourning in your dream, signifies disturbing influences and misunderstanding amongst your friends that may result in loss, disappointments, or possible separation.

Mouse

To see a mouse in your dream, indicates fear, meekness, and a lack of assertiveness. You possess feelings of inadequacy and not measuring up. Alternatively, it may symbolize minor irritations and annoyances.

Please Also See Mice.

Mouse Trap

To see a mouse trap in your dream, denotes that you need to be cautious of shady people around you who have designs against you.

To dream that you are setting a mouse trap, signifies that you will outwit your opponents.

To see a mouse caught in the trap, signifies that you will fall into the hands of your rivals.

Mouth

To see a mouth in your dream, signifies your need to express yourself or talk about an issue that's bothering you. On the other hand, perhaps you have said too much and you need to keep your mouth shut.

Mouthwash

To see or use mouthwash in your dream, indicates that you need to literally wash your mouth as a result of something you said. Perhaps you need to think first before saying something you might regret.

Movement

To see normal movement in your dream, represents your ability to cope with various situations. You are able to adapt to the changing environments that you find yourself in.

To see quick, smooth movement, represents self-acceptance and/or your quick wit. You are able to easily express your feelings.

To see slow, difficult movement, indicates a fear of failure. Something is holding you back and preventing you to take chances.

Movie

To dream that you are watching a movie, suggests that you are watching life pass you by. Perhaps you are living vicariously through the actions of others.

Consider also how the movie parallels to situations in your waking life. Observe how the characters relate to you and how they may represent an aspect of yourself.

To dream that you are playing a role in the movie, foretells that something from your unconscious is about to emerge or be revealed. It may also represent memories of images or scenes from your past. Alternatively, the dream may be pointing you toward a new role that you might be undertaking. Your unconscious is psychologically preparing you for this new role.

Movie Theater

To dream that you are in a movie theater, indicates that you are attempting to protect yourself from your emotions and/or actions. Viewing them on a movie screen projects them onto another person and thus makes those feelings/actions distant . You may be protecting yourself from experiencing them.

Moving

To dream that you are moving away, signifies your desire or need for change. It may also mean an end to a situation or relationship and your are moving on. Alternatively, it indicates your determination and issues regarding dependence/independence.

Mud

To see mud in your dream, suggests that you are involved in a messy and sticky situation. It also suggests that some internal cleansing is needed.

To dream that you are walking in mud, suggests that you are feeling weighed down by a situation, problem, or relationship.

To dream that mud has gotten on your clothing, signifies that your reputation is being attacked and called into question. Consider the term "mud-slinging" to refer to some politicians.

Muff

To dream that you are wearing a muff, signifies a solid foundation of fortune.

Muffins

To dream that you are baking muffins, denotes that you are a hard worker and will reap the fruits of your labor.

To dream that you are eating muffins, signifies your taste for exquisite and expensive things in life.

Mulberries

To see mulberries in your dream, signifies that illness will be a major setback for you in achieving your goals. Either your own illness will hinder your path or you will be called on to tend to the sickness of others.

To dream that you are eating mulberries, denotes bitter disappointments.

Mule

To see a mule in your dream, represents stubbornness. You may be overbearing at time.

To dream that you are riding a mule, denotes that you are undertaking responsibilities that will give you a lot of anxiety.

To dream that you are kicked by a mule, foretells disappointments in love and marriage.

To see a dead mule in your dream, signifies broken promises and a decline in social status. It is also an indication of your long sufferings.

Mutilate

To dream that someone or something is mutilated, indicates that your integrity is put into question.

Mummy

To see a mummy in your dream, denotes you feeling of being trapped in a situation. You may also feel that you are not being heard.

Mumps

To dream that you have the mumps, suggests that you are unable to communicate your point across. Your voice is not being heard. Alternatively, it indicates pent up frustration and anger.

Murder

To dream that you have committed a murder, indicates that you are putting an end to an old habit and your former ways of thinking. This could also mean an end to an addiction. Alternatively, you may have some repressed aggression or rage at yourself or at others.

To dream that you witness a murder, indicates deep-seated anger towards somebody. Consider how the victim represents aspects of yourself that you want to destroy or eliminate.

To dream that you are murdered, suggests that some important and significant relationship has been severed and you are trying to disconnect yourself from your emotions. It also represents your unused talents.

Note also that dreams of murder occur frequently during periods of depression.

Please also see Killing   See the Meaning In Action: "Premonition of Murder"

Muscle

To see muscles in your dream, symbolizes power and strength. You need to develop these qualities and become a more stronger and confident person.

Museum

To see a museum in your dream, indicates that your non-traditional path to success will make you unique and stand out from the rest. Alternatively, the museum may represent a history of yourself and your past. There are many things you can learn from your past and your family's past. Consider what you have gained from these experiences and apply them to your current circumstances.

To dream that you are in a museum, gives you the opportunity for you to review and reflect on the things you value in life.

Mushroom

To see mushrooms in your dream, signifies unhealthy pleasures and unwise haste in amassing wealth, for it may disappear in lawsuits and vain pleasures.

To dream that you are eating mushrooms, denotes that you will be humiliated and disgraced by love. You will have many uphill battles and challenging situations and relationships.

Music

To hear harmonious and soothing music in your dream, is a good omen of prosperity, pleasure and the expression of your emotions in a positive way. Music serves to heal the soul.

To hear discordant music in your dream, signifies unhappiness and troubles in the home.

Musical Instruments

To see musical instruments in your dream, symbolizes the expectation of fun and pleasures.

To see broken musical instruments in your dream, denotes that pleasures will be interrupted by mean spirited friends.

Musk

To smell musk in your dream, denotes that you will find joy in situations that you least expect it.

Mussels

To see mussels in your dream, signifies minor gains in fortune, but you will be filled with much joy and domestic bliss.

Mustache

To dream that you have a mustache when you don't actually have one, signifies that you are hiding an aspect of yourself. You are putting on a disguise or showing a different aspect of your personality.

To dream that you shave off your mustache, denotes that you are revealing your true self. You no longer have to hide under some disguise or some shield. Alternatively, you will try to attempt to reinstate yourself to a position of honor and status and abandon your associations will illicit pleasures and evil companions.

If you are a woman and dream that you have a mustache, indicates that you are expressing your power through your words and your verbal expression.

Mustard

To see mustard growing in your dream, signifies success and wealth.

To dream that you are eating mustard seeds, denotes that you will bitterly regret some hasty action that you are now suffering for.

Mute

To dream that you are mute, indicates that you are afraid to say something for fear of being criticized or judged. There may also be a situation in your waking life that has left you speechless.

Myrrh

To see myrrh in your dream, signifies wise and satisfying investments and pleasant surprises.

Myrtle

To see a myrtle in your dream, symbolizes happiness, peace, and properity,

N

Nails

To see yourself hammering nails in your dream, signifies your tenacity and ability to drive a hard bargain. Consider also the pun, "getting nailed" which may mean getting caught at something or a sexual innuendo. Another popular phrase "hitting the nail on the head" suggests that you have fully resolved a situation.

To see nails in your dream, symbolizes long and hard work for little compensation and pay.

To see bent, broken and rusty nails in your dream, indicates illness or failure in business.

To dream that you hurt yourself with a nail, denotes that you should be careful of what you say.

Please see also Fingernails.

Naked

To dream that you are naked, denotes the fear of being found out and exposed about your activities and misjudgment.

To dream that you suddenly discover your nudity and are trying to cover up, signifies your vulnerability to a situation.

To see a naked person in your dream and you are disgusted by it, signifies some anxiety about discovering the naked truth about that person or situation. It may also foretell of an illicit love affairs, loss of prestige and scandalous activities. On the other hand, if you do not have any problem with another's nudity, then it implies that you see through people and accept them for who and what they are.

For an in depth analysis, click on Common Dreams: Naked.

Name

To dream that you forget your name or someone else's name, suggests that you be feeling overwhelmed and burdened. It may also indicate that you have forgotten your true self or your family roots.

To hear your name being called, indicates that you are in touch and in tune with your spirituality. It also makes you aware of your own uniqueness and highlights your individuality.

To see a familiar name written in your dream, symbolizes the way you feel about that person. Your intuition about them may turn out to be true.

Nap

To dream that you are taking a nap, suggests that you need to take a little time off to relax and take it easy. Give yourself a break.

Napkin

To see a napkin in your dream, signifies neatness and cleanliness. You may be preparing yourself to hear some goodness.

To see soiled napkins being placed on the dining table, symbolizes a major marital or relationship problem.

Narcissus

To see a narcissus in your dream, represents vanity. This dream symbol may be a metaphor for someone in your life who is narcissistic. Alternatively, it symbolizes divine love.

Narcotics

Please see Drugs.

Narrow

To dream about narrow spaces, suggests that great struggles await you on your journey. You may feel restricted and confined. Alternatively, it is symbolic of female sexuality.

Native American

To see a Native American in your dream, represents the instinctual and untamed aspect of your character. You desire more freedom from cultural and society restraints.

Nativity

To see the nativity in your dream, indicates that you have made a startling discovery about yourself and your capabilities. It also points to the importance of spiritual enlightenment and inner strength as opposed to material richness.

Nature

To dream of nature, denotes freedom, tranquility, restoration, and renewal. It may represent that your internal instincts are experienced and expressed.

Nausea

To dream that you have nausea, signifies that you are suffering from a sickening situation or condition in which you are trying to rid yourself of.

Navel

To see your navel in your dream, represents your being and self. The dream may indicate that you need to find your center and middle ground. In particular for males, dreams of their navel signify the bonding to their mother.

Navy

To dream that you are in the Navy, symbolizes your need for organization, discipline and structure in your life.

To dream that you are rescued by a Navy person, foretells of assistance from an authoritative source.

Nazi

To see a Nazi in your dream, represents a form of evil and merciless force that cannot be reasoned with. You may feel that others are putting you down.

Nearsighted

To dream that you are nearsighted, signifies that your efforts and energies are too focused on short term goals and not on preparing for the long term of the future. This dream may also denote an embarrassing failure or unexpected and unwelcome visitors.

Neck

To see your neck in your dream, signifies the relationship between the mind/mental and the body/physical. It represents willpower, self-restriction and your need to control your feelings and keep them in check. Consider the familiar phrase, "don't stick your neck out" which serves as a warning against a situation.

To dream that your neck is injured, indicates a separation between your heart and mind.

To dream of a thick neck, signifies that you are becoming very quarrelsome and quick-tempered.

Necklace

To see or wear a necklace in your dream, represents unsatisfied desires. It also highlights your intellect and your desire to have more influence and power over others.

To see a broken necklace in your dream, indicates that your rational thinking is in accordance with your emotional thinking. You need to act on your gut instinct about some situation or relationship.

To dream that you lost a necklace, signifies sadness and grief.

Necktie

To dream of a loose-fitting necktie around your neck, signifies that you have unfinished business to tend to.

To dream of a tight-fitting necktie, denotes that you feel trapped in a situation or condition.

Necromancer

To dream of a necromancer, signifies the threat of evil by a strange acquaintance.

*See also Hypnotist

Need

To dream that you are in need, signifies the danger of losing your fortunes through gambling and speculation.

To dream that others are in need, denotes that your actions and misfortune will affect others.

Needle

To use a needle in your dream, indicates that you need to mend some relationship or situation that has gotten out of hand or driven to the extreme. A needle is also symbolic of some emotional or physical pain.

To dream that someone is using a needle, suggests that you need to incorporate and join together various aspects of your consciousness.

To look for a needle in your dream, symbolizes useless worries over small, trivial matters.

To dream that you are threading a needle, represents unfinished issues that you need to tend to and perhaps even repair.

Negligee

To see or wear a negligee in your dream, indicates your suggestiveness. Perhaps you feel that people can see right through to who you are and your intents. The symbol may also be a pun on your negligence of some situation.

Neighbor

To dream of having a good neighbor, signifies enjoyment and tranquility at home.

To dream of having an angry neighbor, signifies quarrels, dissensions and possibly relocation from your home.

Neighborhood

To dream about your neighborhood, represents a sense of community and the need to be more active. You are expressing a need to develop new friends and new ties. Consider your waking feelings toward your neighbors.

Nephew

To dream of your nephew in a pleasing disposition, foretells that you will soon find yourself in a pleasant and congenial surrounding.

To dream of your nephew in an unpleasant disposition, signifies illness or loss of business.

Neptune

To see Neptune in your dream, represents inspiration, imagination, and devotion. You may need to show some more compassion and understanding.

Nerd

To see or dream that you are a nerd, indicates feelings of inferiority and/or ineffectiveness. You feel that you have been overlooked.

Nervous

To dream that you are nervous about something, indicates that you are experiencing self-doubt and feelings of insecurity.

Nervous Breakdown

To dream that you or someone has a nervous breakdown, suggests that you have lost a frame of reference in a relationship or situation. You are seeking more clarity and insight. The dream also indicates that you are having difficulties trusting your own judgment and decisions.

Nest

To see a bird's nest in your dream, signifies comfort, safety, and protection. The dream may also symbolize new opportunities.

To see a nest filled with broken or bad eggs, symbolizes disappointments and failure.

Net

To see a net in your dream, signifies that you find yourself caught in a complicated life situation.

Nettles

To dream that you walk among nettles without being stung, signifies prosperity for you you.

To dream that you walk among nettles and get sting, signifies discontentment and unhappiness for you and others around you.

For a young woman to dream that she is passing through nettles, foretells that she will have many marriage proposals by different men.

New

To see a new house in your dream, indicates that you are taking on a new identify and developing new strengths. You are trying to be more emotionally mature about things.

To see new shoes in your dream, suggests that you are overconfident in your success. Alternatively you may be on a life path that is unfamiliar to you.

To dream that you are at a new school, signifies that you are feeling out of place in some situation.

Generally speaking, to dream about new things and new places corresponds to what is new in your waking life. You may be trying to learn and analyze what you already know from past experiences.

Newborn

*Please See Baby.

News

To hear good news in your dream, signifies that you will be fortunate in your endeavors and will have many harmonious companions. The contrary is true if you dream of hearing bad news.

Newspaper

To see newspapers in your dream, signifies that new light and insight will be shed on a problem that has been on your mind. You are seeking knowledge and answers to a problem. Alternatively, to see newspapers in your dream, implies that you need to be more vocal and express yourself. In other words, you need to make headlines.

To dream that you try but fail to read a newspaper, signifies your failure in some uncertain enterprise or that your reputation is in jeopardy.

Newspaper Reporter

To dream that you are a newspaper reporter, foretells of many travels in your future, attached with some honor and gain.

New Year

To dream of the New Year, signifies prosperity and hope.

Nickname

To hear a nickname in your dream, represents your feelings and memories of the person who is referred to by that nickname. If the nickname is not familiar, then it may be a pun on something or a metaphor.

To dream that someone is calling you by a nickname, suggests that you are trying to change they way you and others see you.

Niece

To see your niece in your dream, signifies unexpected trials and useless worries of the future.

Night

To have a dream that takes place at night, represents some major setbacks and obstacles in achieving your goals. There are some issues in your life that you are facing that are not too clear. You should put the issues aside so you can clear your head before coming back to it.

Please also see Darkness

Nightclub

To dream that you are in a fun-filled nightclub, signifies a happening social life is in your future.

To dream that you are in a depressing and dimly-lit nightclub, signifies an a financial crisis or and end to a lover affair.

Nightgown

To dream that you are in your nightgown, suggests that you are acknowledging and expression aspects of yourself that you were previously uncomfortable about.

Nightmare

To dream that you are having a nightmare, denotes failure in business, disappointments, or decline in health. You may have been indulgent in things and need to cut back on such activities. Allow the mind and body to rest and heal.

Nightingale

To see silent nightingales in your dream, signifies minor misunderstandings among your friends.

To hear the songs of the nightingale, denotes a pleasant and healthy surrounding.

Ninepins

To dream that you play ninepins, signifies that you are foolishly wasting your energy and letting opportunities slip away. It may also forewarn to select your companions carefully.

Nipples

To see nipples in your dream, relate to infantile needs and a regression into dependency.

To dream that you are squeezing pus out of your nipples, refers to your negative feelings about relationships. You are feeling sexually inadequate.

Please see also Breasts.

Nobility

To dream that you are associated with nobility, signifies that you prefer show, pleasure and status as opposed to the cultivation of the mind.

Noise

To hear a strange noise in your dream, signifies the unexpected and the unknown. You may be expressing some fear or confusion concerning a particular situation in your waking life. The noise in your dream may serve as a way to attract your attention to that issue. Alternatively, noise may represent a breakthrough in your personal struggles. Perhaps you have burst through a barrier of resistance which had been holding you back for a long time.

Noodles

To see noodles in your dream, signifies an abnormal appetite and desire.

Noose

To see a noose hanging from a tree, denotes fear and anxiety.

To see a noose around someone else's neck, signifies repressed anger and rage at a that person or towards a particular condition.

North

To dream of the direction north, symbolizes reality. It also indicates that you are making progress and moving forward in life.

North Pole

To dream that you are at the north pole, signifies completion and an ending to some journey, situation, or relationship. You have successfully completed your transformation.

Northern Lights

To see the northern lights in your dream, represents renewed energy, vitality, and youth. A situation or relationship is finally made clear to you. Alternatively, it indicates that you know what you need to do, but may be too lazy or too afraid to jump into action.

Nose

To see your own nose in your dream, signifies a conscious effort to achieve whatever endeavor you chose to undertake. The nose represents energy, intuition, and wisdom. Alternatively, the nose symbolizes curiosity. You dream may suggest your need to learn more about a situation at hand.

To dream that hair is growing on your nose, signifies extraordinary undertakings that need to be carried through a strong will and character.

To dream that a bug or insect is coming out of your nose, indicates that you are being nosy to the point where it is "bugging" and bothering others. You need to learn to when to get out of people's business and respect their privacy.

Notary

To see a notary in your dream, foretells of unsatisfied desires and probable lawsuits.

Notebook

To see a notebook in your dream, denotes that you are trying to stay on top of things and keep detailed records.

November

To dream of the month of November, signifies of an indifferent success in all affairs.

Nude

Please See Naked.

Nuclear Bomb

To dream of a nuclear bomb, suggests feelings of helplessness, being threatened and loss of control. You may be experiencing great hostility and rage to the point of being destructive. Alternatively, you may be expressing a desire to wipe out some aspect of yourself. It may also be an indication that something crucial and precious to you has ended and important changes are about to occur.

Numbness

To dream that you feel numbness, indicates that you are letting fear take over. You are afraid of taking any risk and failing.

Numbers

To see numbers in your dream, signifies unsettled conditions in business resulting in uneasiness and dissatisfaction.

For a specific number, please see Dream Themes: Numbers.

Nuns

To see nuns in your dream, signifies purity, chastity and obedience. It also indicates that you need to live up to the vows and promises you have made. It also foretells that material fortune and gain will interfere with your spirituality. Consider also the pun of being "none" or "nothing".

For a woman to dream that she is a nun, signifies her unhappiness of her current situation and environment.

To see a dead nun in your dream, denotes poverty and despair over the unfaithfulness of loved ones.

Nuptial

To dream of your nuptials, foretells of an engagement that will lead to much joy and harmony.

Please also see Marriage.

Nurse

To dream that you are a nurse, suggests that you need to show more compassion in a situation.

To see a nurse in your dream, denotes that you need to be taken care of and a time of healing, either mentally, physically or spiritually.

Nursing

To see someone nursing or dream that you are nursing, suggests that you are nurturing a hidden aspect of yourself.

Please see also <u>Breast Feeding.</u>

Nuts

To see nuts in your dream, signifies craziness or confusion. It may also refer to someone who is "nuts" or someone who is driving you crazy. You may be approaching a waking situation all wrong and need to look at it from a different perspective. Also consider nuts as a pun on "testicles" and thus allude to some sexual innuendo.

To dream that you are eating nuts, signifies prosperity and attainment of your desires. You may also be trying to get to the core of a matter or situation.

Nymph

To see nymphs in your dream, denotes that passionate desires will be joyously realized.

O

Oak Tree

To see an oak tree in your dream, symbolizes longevity, stability, strength, tolerance, wisdom, and prosperity.

To see an oak tree with acorns, signifies a promotion or increase in the social ladder.

Oar

To see or use an oar in your dream, signifies control over your emotions. You are seeking guidance.

To dream that you are paddling with one oar, signifies your need for help or assistance.

Oasis

To dream that you are searching for an oasis, symbolizes inner fears, insecurities, and overwhelming conditions.

To dream that you are resting at an oasis, signifies success in business and financial matters. You may also be in need of a vacation.

Oath

To dream that you are taking an oath in your dream, signifies strife and disharmony in your present situation.

To dream that you refuse to take an oath, denotes an immediate change for the better.

Oatmeal

To dream that you are eating oatmeal, suggests that you are well-grounded.

To dream that you are cooking and serving oatmeal, signifies that you have control over the destiny of someone close to you.

Oats

To dream that oats are being fed to a horse, denotes luxury and ease entering your life.

To dream that oats are being refused by the animal, signifies a poorly-made decision regarding your finances or living conditions.

To see decayed oats. denotes poverty or great sorrow coming your way.

Obedience

To dream that you are obedient, symbolizes that you are a good worker who will go far in your occupation.

To dream that others are obedient towards you, signifies good fortune and success in your business.

Obelisk

To see an obelisk in your dream, signifies your cold, stern nature and the need to warm up to others and soften your nature.

To see an obelisk in your dream may also have phallic implications.

Obsidian

To see obsidian in your dream, suggests that you are well-grounded or that you need to be more grounded.

Obese

To dream that you are obese, denotes lack of self-esteem and overindulgence. It may signify your hopelessness and helplessness to express and assert power and authority. This dream may also mean that you are trying to insulate yourself from your surroundings. You want to protect yourself from any involvement in a situation.

Please see also Fat.

Obituary

To see or read an obituary in your dream, represents the end to your old attitudes and outdated beliefs.

Obligation

To dream that someone is obligated to you, means that you will succeed to soaring heights in your personal life and business undertakings.

To dream that you are obligated to someone, signifies thoughtlessness.

Obscene

To see something obscene in your dream, refers to aspects of yourself that you have rejected or refuse to acknowledge.

Observatory

To see an observatory in your dream, signifies your high goals and aspirations.

Occultist

To dream that you are influenced by an occultist, signifies your generosity towards the ones less fortunate and the strive to elevate their socially and economically.

Ocean

To see an ocean in your dream, represents the state of your emotions and feelings. It is indicative of some spiritual refreshment, tranquility and renewal.

To dream that you are traveling across the ocean, signifies new found freedom and independence. You are showing great courage.

*Please See Also Water.

Octagon

To see an octagon in your dream, indicates a spiritual reawakening.

October

To dream of the month of October, signifies gratifying success in your endeavors.

Octopus

To see an octopus in your dream, signifies that you are entangled in some difficult matter or situation. Or it may mean that you are overly possessive and too clingy in a relationship.

Odor

To smell an odor in your dream, indicates a memory or past experience. Your dream be trying to convey your personal feeling and associations with that odor.

Offense

To dream of being offended, signifies of error in your conduct which has caused you to stand up for yourself.

To dream that you are giving offense, foretells of struggles and obstacles toward your goals.

Offering

To dream that you are bringing or making an offering, signifies hypocrisy.

Office

To dream of your work office, indicates that you cannot seem to leave your work at the office. You may be overworked or have too much on your mind. Alternatively, it symbolizes your status, accomplishments and your place in the world.

To dream that you hold public office, symbolizes that your aspirations may lead you to a dangerous path, but your courage will be rewarded with success.

Offspring

To see your offspring in your dream, symbolizes cheerfulness and joyous moments.

Ogre

To see an ogre in your dream, signifies self-criticism and discipline.

Oil

To see oil in your dream, suggests a need to have thing run more smoothly. You may need to show more love and compassion in your life.

To see baby oil in your dream, indicates that you need to soothe the child within you. You need to release that child in you once in a while.

To see crude oil in your dream, signifies great wealth and riches. Alternatively, you need too socialize more.

Oil Spill

To see an oil spill in your dream, suggests that you are in emotional turmoil. You are experiencing problems and distress in your personal relationships.

Ointment

To see ointment in your dream, signifies a healing process. It also implies the forming of new friendships that will prove beneficial and enjoyable.

Old

To see something old in your dream, suggests that there is something in your life that you need to replace or get rid of.

Olives

To see or eat olives, symbolizes contentment and faithful friends. It also refers to immortality.

To see an olive branch, signifies reconciliation, peace, and hope. You may also find a resolution to your conflicts and have a burden lifted off you.

Omelet

To see an omelet in your dream, signifies betrayal, deceit and flattery that will be used against you.

One-Eyed

To dream that you have one eye, indicates your refusal to accept another viewpoint. It suggests that you are one-sided in your ways of thinking.

Onions

To see onions in your dream, signifies that you will be a target of jealousy, spite, and envy as a result of your success. It may also mean that there are deep layers you need to get through and discover regarding an issue or situation at hand.

To dream that you eat an onion, symbolizes that you will overcome all oppositions.

To see cooked onions, denotes minor gains in business.

To dream that you are cutting onions, signifies your defeat by your rivals.

Onyx

To see onyx in your dream, represents spiritual and mental balance. It also symbolizes peace of mind.

Opal

To see an opal in your dream, refers to your libido and sexual desire. The dream indicates that you need to be more passionate in your love life

Opening

To see an opening in your dream, signifies a new influence or new-found inspiration entering your life.

To dream that you are opening something, suggests that you are unleashing your potential. It may also mean new opportunities.

Opera

To watch an opera in your dream, represents your quest for the grander things in life. You may be acting a little overly dramatic in some situations.

Operation

To dream that you are in operation, suggests that you need to get something out of your system. Perhaps you need to let go of something or change your habits. You need to cut something out of your life.

To dream that you are operating on someone, denotes that you are facing and dealing with some deep issues or repressed thoughts.

*Please see also Surgery.

Opium

To dream of opium, foretells that strangers will obstruct your chances of improving your fortunes, by sly and seductive means.

Opossum

*Please see Possum.

Opponent

To dream that you have an opponent, signifies an aspect of yourself in which you are in conflict with.

Oral Sex

To dream that you are giving or receiving oral sex, signifies your willingness to give or receive pleasure/joy. It is symbolic of your creative energy and reaffirms that you are headed in the right direction in life. The dream may also be a pun on talking about sex. You may need to communicate with your mate about your sexual needs and desires. Perhaps you are acting out your sexual wishes.

To dream that you are performing oral sex on yourself, represents your need for self-gratification.

Oranges

To see orange trees in your dream, signifies health and prosperity.

To dream that you are eating oranges, denotes negative vibes, dissatisfaction in your business circles, illness in the family, or separation/loss of a lover.

Orangutan

To see an orangutan in your dream, signifies unfaithfulness in a lover or that some person is manipulating for their own advancement.

Orca

To see an orca in your dream, signifies distrust and suspicious motives.

Orchard

To dream of passing through a blossoming orchard, signifies a happy home life, longevity, faithfulness, and loyalty.

To see a storm-swept or barren orchard, signifies unwelcome guests or duties or lost opportunities.

Orchestra

To dream that you are in an orchestra, represents inner integration and harmony. It also indicates resolution.

To hear the music of an orchestra, denotes that your knowledge of humanity will prove you to be a much-liked person.

Orchids

To see orchids in your dream, symbolizes gentleness, romance. beauty and sensuality. It may suggest that you need to give some special attention or care to a situation or may represent a special occasion.

Organ

To hear the grand anthems of an organ in your dream, symbolizes long lasting friendships and well-grounded fortune.

To see an organ in a church, denotes sad separation of families.

To dream that you are playing an organ, signifies that fortune will fall on your and social distinction will be given to you.

Organist

To see an organist in your dream, signifies that the hasty actions of a friend will create much inconvenience for you.

Orgasm

To dream that you are having an orgasm, represents an exciting end to something. What is complete for you? Alternatively, it may mean that you are not getting enough sex. You need to relieve some of your sexual tensions.

Orgy

To see an orgy in your dream, signifies repressed desires of your own sexuality and passion. It may also mean that there is some sort of confusion in where you distribute your energies. You may be going in to many direction and as a result, is spread too thin.

Orient

To dream that you are in the orient, signifies spiritual awakening.

Ornament

To see or hang an ornament in your dream, refers to the things in your life and the things you do to make you feel good about yourself. It is also symbolic of a spiritual gift.

Oriole

To see an oriole in your dream, represents the sun, light and happiness. It may denote the season of summer.

Orphan

To see an orphan in your dream, signifies fears of abandonment and feelings of loneliness and rejection..

To dream that you are condoling with orphans, symbolizes that the unhappiness of others will touch your sympathies and cause you to sacrifice much personal enjoyment.

Ostrich

To see an ostrich in your dream, suggests that you are not facing reality and living in a world of your own. You may be in denial or unwilling to accept a situation. Alternatively, the ostrich can symbolize truth and justice.

**See The Meaning In Action: "Alligator In Ostrich Suit"*

Otter

To see otters in your dream, symbolizes happiness and good fortune. You will find ideal enjoyment or unusual tenderness with your loved one.

Ottoman

To dream that you are relaxing upon an ottoman and discussing the topic of love, signifies that envious rival will seek to defame you in the eyes of your lover.

Ouija Board

To see an Ouija board in your dream, indicates that some relationship or situation will fall apart. It may also mean that nothing is going to go according to planned.

To dream that the Oiuja board fails to function, symbolizes complications caused by substituting pleasure for work or what needs to be done.

Outer Space

To dream of outer space, represents your creativity. It may also indicate that something or someone has just came out of nowhere.

Oval

To see an oval in your dream, represents the vagina, womb and female qualities. It also symbolizes your aura and your spiritual energy.

Oven

To see a red hot oven in your dream, symbolizes you will be loved by friends and family for your devotion and unselfish nature. Alternatively, it symbolizes the womb. You may be in anticipation or fear of having children. Consider the phrase " a bun in the oven".

To dream that your oven is broken, signifies many vexations from children.

Overcoat

To dream of an overcoat, signifies others indifferences towards you.

To dream that you borrow an overcoat, denotes that the mistakes of strangers will effect you and cause you misfortune.

Overall

To dream that you are wearing overalls, represents your sloppy attitudes and incoherent thoughts.

Owl

To see an owl in your dream, symbolizes wisdom, insight and virtue. The owl is also synonymous with death and darkness.

To hear the hoot of an owl, denotes disappointments and forewarns that death creeps closely in the wake of joy and health.

To see a dead owl, signifies a narrow escape from desperate illness and death. Death in this sense may also represent a symbolic death, as in an important transition in life.

Ox

To see an ox in your dream, represents the balance of masculine power and strength with feminine mystique. Consider also the familiar metaphor, "as stubborn as an ox".

Oxygen

To dream of oxygen, symbolizes life, your inner spirit, and creative energy.

To dream that you do not have enough oxygen, suggests that you are feeling suffocated or smothered by a situation in your life.

Oysters

To dream that you are eating oysters, indicates sexual urges and gratification. signifies that you will lose all your senses and morality in the pursuit of low pleasures and indulgences.

To see oysters in your dream, symbolizes beauty, humility, wealth, wisdom, and a laid-back atmosphere. It may also indicate that tend to shut others out.

To see oyster shells in your dream, signifies that you will be frustrated in your attempt to secure the fortune of another

P

Pacifier

To see a pacifier in your dream, represents emotional nurturance. You may be expressing a desire to escape from your daily responsibilities and demands.

To dream that you are sucking on a pacifier, implies that you are trying to "suck up to" someone in your waking life.

Pacify

To dream that you are trying to pacify someone or a situation, signifies that you will be will admired and respected for you kindness.

Package

To see a package in your dream, represents hidden creative energy, skills., and/or feelings. If you receive a package, it indicates that you are acknowledging certain feelings or acquiring new resources. If you are giving or sending a package, then it suggests that you are projecting your feelings onto another and not dealing with them.

Packing

To dream that you are packing, signifies big changes ahead for you. You are putting past issues and/or relationships to rest and behind you. Alternatively, it represents the burdens that you carry.

To dream that you are packing, unpacking and packing and unpacking again, represents chaos in your life. You are having trouble juggling various components of your life. You are carrying around too many burdens but have trouble letting go some of these burdens. Consider what unfinished business you have to tend to. Try to resolve these issues so they can finally be put to rest.

Paddle

Please See Oar.

Paddleboat

Please See Rowboat.

Page

To see a page in your dream, signifies that you are on the rebound from a broken relationship. As a result, you will enter into a hasty relationship will someone ill-suited for you.

To see a blank page in your dream, suggests that you are not doing anything with your life. You are stagnant and feel that you are going nowhere.

To dream that you are a page, denotes that you will find yourself in foolish amusements and fruitless pleasure.

Pageant

To watch or dream that you are in a beauty pageant, refers to your own insecurities about your appearances. You are constantly comparing yourself to others and how you measure up to them. You may also be subscribing to society's standards of beauty.

Pager

To see a pager in your dream, suggests that someone is trying hard to communicate their thoughts to you. They are trying to get through to you one way or another. On the other hand, you may feel that someone is pushing their beliefs onto you.

Pagoda

To see a pagoda in your dream, foretells of a short journey.

Pail

To see or carry a pail in your dream, indicates an improvement in your current situation. If the pail is filled pail, then it signifies abundance, love and wealth. If the pail is empty, then it signifies that you will overcome some loss or conflict. The dream may also be a pun on pale.

Pain

To dream that you are in pain, signifies that you are being too hard on yourself with regards to a situation that was out of your control. It may also be a true reflection of real pain that exists somewhere in your body. Dreams can reveal and warn about health problems.

To dream that you are inflicting pain to yourself, indicates that you are experiencing some overwhelming turmoil or problems in your waking life. You are trying to disconnect yourself from your reality by concentrating on the pain that you inflicted to yourself.

Paintbrush

To see or use a paintbrush in your dream, symbolizes harmony, creativity and artistic talents.

Painting

To dream that you are painting your house, signifies that you will find much success in a new project and that you will be promoted to a coveted position. You may be expressing your creativity. Alternatively, it may also mean your are covering up something. Consider the color of the paint to determine any additional significance. For example, red colored paint may imply painting the town red and releasing your pent up excitement.

To dream that paint has gotten on your clothes, signifies that you are too easily offended by criticism about you.

To see a painting in your dream, represents your need for self-expression. The painting is symbolic of your intuition and inner realizations.

Pajamas

To see or wear pajamas in your dream, suggests that you need to relax and get some rest. In particular, if you dream that you are wearing pajamas in public, then it means that you are unaware of some important that may be right in front of you. You may be just drifting through life without fully paying attention to what is going on around you.

Palace

To see a palace in your dream, symbolizes prominence and wealth. You are ready to utilize your full potential.

To dream that you are the owner of a palace, signifies that success is right within your reach.

Pall

To see a pall in your dream, forewarns of approaching bad news.

To dream that you raise the pall from a corpse, signifies bereavement and grief.

Pallbearer

To see a pallbearer in your dream, denotes that you have to keep your temper in check for someone is trying to push your buttons.

To see a pallbearer carrying a coffin in your dream, signifies change, whether it be a change in jobs or a change in social status.

Pallet

To dream that you are making a pallet on the floor, signifies separation of lovers.

To dream that you are sleeping on a pallet, signifies of sleeping on a pallet shows that you have a rival who is very jealous of your success.

Palm

To notice your palm in your dream, suggests that you hold all the knowledge you need in you own hands. You need to reach and utilize your full potential.

Palm Reading

To dream that you are having your palms reads, represents your life goals and ambition. The dream shows how you want to live your life and where you want to be headed.

Palm Tree

To see palm trees in your dream, denotes tranquility, high aspirations, victory, and hopes.

Pan

To see a pan in your dream, symbolizes your attitudes and stance on a particular situation. It may also represent criticism and anger. If the pan is made of glass, then it represents being conscious and aware about a particular situation.

To see a frying pan in your dream, represents completeness in love. Alternatively, it suggests that you need to start accepting the consequences of your actions. You may have found yourself in an inescapable situation.

Pancake

To make or eat pancakes in your dream, represents gratification and pleasure in your current situation. It may also mean that take pleasure and comfort in your work.

Panda

To see a panda in your dream, suggests that you are having difficulties coming to a compromise in a waking situation. You need to find a middle ground so that all parties involved will be satisfied. Alternatively, it is symbolic of your own childlike qualities or something that is cuddly.

Pandora's Box

To dream of a Pandora's box, indicates hope. You will soon experience a turn for the better. Alternatively, it symbolizes your curiosity, your unconscious thoughts and your need to express them.

Panic

To dream that you are in a panic, indicates a lack of control and power in your life. You may be feeling helpless in some situation or unable to make a clear decision.

Pansy

To see a pansy in your dream, represents thoughts and nobility of the mind. Alternatively, it suggests that you are being too gullible.

Panther

To see a panther in your dream, signifies lurking danger and enemies working to do you harm. It represents darkness, death, and rebirth. On a more positive note, panthers signify power, beauty and/or grace.

Panties

To see or wear panties in your dream, represents your feminine attitudes and feelings. It reflects a female point of view.

To dream that you are taking off your panties, signifies your ideas of sexuality. It may also indicate your need to get to the bottom of things. You may want to find a way out of a situation.

Pants

To see or wear pants in your dream, suggests that you are questioning your role in some situation. Consider the material and color of the pants for additional interpretation.

To dream that you are wearing velvet pants, signifies your sensual side.

Paper

To see a blank white paper in your dream, signifies your desire to make a fresh start in your life. It may represent you desire to express yourself through writing or art. You need to work on being more communicative.

To see a stack of papers in your dream, denotes overwhelming responsibilities and stress that you are having to cope with.

Paper Clip

To see or use a paper clip in your dream, suggests that you feel that you need to hold a relationship together. Perhaps you need to organize certain aspects of your life.

Papyrus

To see a papyrus in your dream, indicates that you are looking back into the past. You can learn a lot from your previous interactions.

Parachute

To dream that you are in a parachute, signifies that you have protection and security during a time in which many risks and turmoil surround you. Alternatively, it may also imply that it is time to bail out of a situation or abandon an old idea/habit.

To dream that you have difficulties with a parachute, denotes that you will be let down by someone you relied on and trusted.

Parade

To dream that you are watching a parade, indicates that you are being sidetracked or distracted from achieving your goals. For fear of failure, you may stop yourself from even pursuing your goals and desires. Alternatively, the parade symbolizes cycles, passage of time, or a special event in your life. Consider also the symbolism of whatever figures/animals/floats are in the parade. They may reflect a need for you to possess or control those attributes.

Paradise

To dream that you are in paradise, symbolizes your desire to achieve spiritual perfection. You may be trying to retreat from the stresses of the real world.

Parakeets

To see a parakeet in your dream, indicates that you lack initiative and new idea. You need to be more unconventional and spontaneous. The dream also relates to dependency and immaturity.

Paralyzed

To dream that you are paralyzed, may reflect the current state of your body while you are dreaming. During the REM state of sleep you really are immobile and paralyzed. However symbolically, dreaming that you are paralyzed may mean you are feeling helpless or pinned down in some aspect or circumstances of your waking life. You may feel unable to deal with a situation or that you can't do or change anything. Alternatively, you may feel emotionally paralyzed. You may have difficulties in expressing yourself.

Please see also Immobility. See The Meaning In Action: "Smell Of Fire" and "Paralyzed"

Paranoia

To dream that you are paranoid, indicates your hesitance in moving forward in some situation or relationship. You are not ready for that major step in your life and are overcome with fear and suspicion.

Parasite

To see a parasite in your dream, suggests loss of vitality and feeling physically drained. You are becoming too dependent on others. It is also an indication that you are taking without giving back.

Parents

To see your parents in your dream, symbolizes both power, shelter, and love. You may be expressing your concerns and worries about your own parents. Alternatively, it represents the merging of the female and male aspects of your character.

*See Father and Mother.

Paris

To dream that you are in Paris, symbolizes your need for romance and passion. It also suggests that you are a person of distinction. You own personal experiences and knowledge of Paris will supercede the suggested interpretation here.

Park

To dream that you are at a park, represents a temporary escape from reality. It indicates renewal, meditation, and spirituality. It is also an indication of a readjustment period after a serious personal conflict or an ending of a passionate affair.

To dream that you are lost in a park, indicates your struggles with your career, relationship, or other problem. You may feel alienated by society.

To dream that you parked your car in a non-parking zone,

Parking Lot

To dream that you are in parking lot, suggests that you need to slow down and take some time to relax from your daily activities.

To dream that you cannot find a parking space, indicates your inability to find your place in life. You may still be on your quest to find your talent or niche where you belong. Alternatively, it may reflect your busy life and the lack of time you have.

Parking Meter

To see a parking meter in your dream, indicates that your leisurely and carefree days are soon coming to an end. You need to decide on a goal and what you want to do with your life before your time runs out. Alternatively, a parking meter suggests that you need to adjust your attitude or run the risk of offending others.

Parking Ticket

To dream that you are getting a parking ticket, suggests that you are experiencing a lost sense of not knowing what you want to do with your life. You feel that you are being judged and criticized for the path you want to take. The dream may also be analogous to your lack of accomplishments or to the setbacks in your life.

Parrots

To see a parrot in your dream, represents gossip. A message is being conveyed to you. It may also mean that you or someone is being repetitive or even mocking you. Alternatively, the parrot can denote a person in your waking life who is eccentric or obnoxious.

Parsley

To see parsley in your dream, represents success. You achievements will be recognized.

Partner

To see a partner in your dream, suggests that you need to seek the help of others in order to accomplish mutual goals.

Partridge

To see a partridge in your dream, signifies independence and highlights your leadership abilities. Alternatively, it represents deception and temptation.

Party

To dream that you are at a party, suggests that you need to get out more and enjoy yourself. If the party is bad, then it indicates that you are unsure of your social skills.

Passageway

To discover secret passageways in your dream, parallels to something new and/or exciting that is occurring in your waking life. It may refer to new opportunities, a new relationship, or a new attitude toward life. If you wake up before fully exploring these passageways, then it suggests that you may not know how to go about taking advantage of these opportunities or how to move forward with a relationship. Perhaps the newness and uncertainty of this discovery also makes you a little more cautious. This is a positive dream.

Passenger

To dream that you are a passenger, suggests that you are not in control of your life and are letting others decide for you. To see other passengers signifies, that you are spending too much energy pleasing others. You may feel that others are leeching on you.

Passport

To see a passport in your dream, signifies your identity and your ability to traverse various situations. You may going through a period of finding yourself and discovering who you are.

To dream that you lose your passport, indicates that are are trying to find yourself and get a sense of who you are. Alternatively, you may feel that opportunities are being close off to you.

Pastel

To dream of pastel colors, indicates that you are not completely recognizing and dealing with some part of your emotions. It also implies ambiguity in your life.

Pastry

To see or eat a pastry in your dream, refers to indulgence, sensual pleasure and satisfaction. You are enjoying life and reaping its rewards.

Path

To walk through a quiet, open path, signifies clarity of thought and peace of mind. It may also symbolize your progress.

To see a blocked or windy path, denotes that you need to give serious attention to the direction you are heading in your personal and/or business life. You also need to take time out to consider and rethink the consequences before acting on your choices.

Patient

To dream that you are a patient, suggests that you are going through a healing process. Alternatively, this dream may be a pun for you to be more patient.

Patio

To dream that you are in the patio, suggests your openness toward a particular situation.

To dream that the doors to the patio are opened, represents your receptive state of mind. If they are closed, then it indicates that you are not being opened to a situation. Patio doors also represent the merging of your mental and spiritual state.

Pauper

To dream that you are a pauper, suggests that you are not utilizing your inner talents and full potential. You are not acknowledging your own self-worth.

Pavement

To see or walk on pavement in your dream, suggests that you have a clear understanding and grasp of a situation. You are standing on solid ground. The dream may also indicate that you have paved and laid out the path toward your life goals.

Paying

To dream that you are paying for something, indicates the price you pay for your decisions and actions.

Paw

To see an animal paw in your dream, suggests that you need to trust your intuition and animal instincts. The dream may also be a pun on your "Pa" or father.

Peace

To dream of peace and tranquility, indicates an end or a resolution to an emotional issue or inner conflict. It may signal and end of a cycle and the pause before the beginning of a new endeavor. It also suggest that you have reached a new level of stability and calmness. Alternatively, the maddening quietness may refer to the calm before the storm.

Peach

To see a peach in your dream, represents pleasure and joy, You take pleasure in the minor, trivial things in life. The dream may also imply that something in your life is just "peachy" and going well. Alternatively, a peach may be indicative of lust and sensuality. Consider how it my be a metaphor for your sweetheart or loved one.

Peacock

To see a peacock in your dream, represents spring, birth, and new growth. It is a good omen, signaling prestige, much success and contentment with your career. It may also be telling of your confidence and even arrogance over your success.

Peak

To dream that you are at the peak of a mountain, symbolizes your success and achievements. You will go far in your life. The dream may also be a pun on "peek". Perhaps you saw something that you should not have or you are curious about something.

Peanut Butter

To see or eat peanut butter in your dream, suggests that you are having difficulties communicating your thoughts and ideas. It may also mean a misunderstanding; your words are coming out all wrong.

Peanuts

To see peanuts in your dream, symbolize the need to get to the truth or core of something. You may also need to start pushing yourself and utilizing your full potential, Consider the peanuts in your dream to be a pun for money and what little you have of it. It may represent your financial difficulties.

Pear

To see a pear in your dream, symbolizes the womb, fertility and thus may refer to some female in your life. It is also often associated with the Virgin Mary. The dream may also be a pun on a "pair" of something.

To see a pear tree in your dream, represents new opportunities.

Pearl

To see pearls in your dream, signifies wisdom in your new ventures or ideas. It also symbolizes the human soul.

Peas

To see peas in your dream, symbolizes some minor problems and annoyances that are continually bothering you.

Pebbles

To see pebble in your dream, represents minor difficulties and annoyances in your life.

To dream that you are throwing pebbles, suggests that you are feeling hurt be the little things that may seem insignificant. It is symbolic of criticism and gossip.

Pedestal

To dream that you are on a pedestal, indicates that you are an object of admiration. Alternatively, it may suggest that you ego is becoming over-inflated. You are showing off.

To see a pedestal in your dream, refers to something or someone that you look up to.

Peel

To dream that you are peeling something, represents the shedding away of old ways, habits and conditions. It may also mean that you are finally getting rid of and discarding unneeded exterior pretenses.

Pelican

To see a pelican in your dream, represents nurturance and caring for others.

Pelvis

To see your pelvis in your dream, represents sexual issues and you sense of masculinity and femininity. You may be dealing with issues of creativity and self-expression.

Pen

To see a pen in your dream, signifies self-expression and communication. Consider also the phrase of how the the pen is mightier than the sword.

Pencil

To see a pencil in your dream, indicates that you are making a temporary impact in a situation. It may also suggest that a relationship may not last long.

To dream that you are sharpening a pencil, suggests that you need to be more flexible in your way of thinking. Listen to what others have to say; don't be so quick to reject their views and opinions.

Pendant

To see a pendant in your dream, represents your relationships and the desire for unconditional love. You are feeling connected so someone. The dream may also indicates that you are feeling emotionally touched by some situation or by someone.

Pendulum

To see the back and forth swinging of a pendulum, suggests that you are experiencing some difficulties/confusion in making an important choice in your life. You may be afraid of change. People around you are anxiously awaiting your decision.

Penguin

To see a penguin in your dream, signifies that your problems are not as serious as you may think. It serves as a reminder for you to keep you cool and remain level-headed. Alternatively, a penguin seen in your dream suggests that you are being weighed down by your emotions or by a negative situation. You need to find some balance and inner harmony.

Penis

To see a penis in your dream, signifies sexual energy, power and fertility. To see an exceptionally large penis, suggests doubts and anxieties about your sexual drive and libido.

Penny

To see pennies in your dream, indicates your fear of poverty or some financial loss. It is also often connected with your talents, energies, and perseverance. Do not underestimate your ability. If the penny is shiny, then it signifies luck.

To find pennies in your dream, it suggests that you are discovering your hidden talents and ready to unleash your potential.

Pentagram

To see a pentagram in your dream, represents the connection of your spirit to the earth, air, fire, and water. These elements contribute to various aspect of your well-being. It signifies protection.

To see an inverted pentagram, signifies conflict, negativity and aggression. It is often associated with Satanism and evil. Are you feeling guilty about something? Alternatively, it represents the physical world. It points to the notion that you may be on the materialistic side.

Penthouse

To dream that you are in a penthouse, represents the creative and spiritual aspect of yourself. You are looking a life from a new perspective abd accessing your highest potential.

Peony

To see a peony in your dream, represents your well thought-out plans and ideas. You need to draw wisdom from your past experiences. Alternatively, it represents shyness or bashfulness. You are being overly cautious in your pursuits.

People

To see people you know in your dream, signifies qualities and feelings of those people that you desire for yourself.

To see people you don't know in your dream, denotes hidden aspects of yourself that you need to confront.

To see people from your past in your dream, refers to your shadow and other unacknowledged aspects of yourself. It can represent a waking situation that is bringing out similar feelings as your past relationships.

Pepper

To see pepper in your dream, indicates that you need to put a little more spice and variety in your life. Alternatively, there may be something that is bothering or irritating you and your dream may be trying to point to the source.

Percolator

To see or hear a percolator in your dream, suggests that you need to take things a little slower. You need to think things through before taking any action.

Perfume

To dream that you are spraying or wearing perfume, suggests that you are seeking for more pleasure in your life. It is symbolic of your sexuality, sensuality, and indulgence.

Period

*Please See Menstruation.

Perm

To dream that that you are getting a perm, signifies a change in your outlook and way of thinking. You need to start to look at things from another point of view.

Perpetual Motion

To dream of perpetual motion, indicates that you are experiencing general anxiety and nervousness over a situation. You may desire a change from the repetitive and/or predictable behavior from your job, relationship or daily life.

Perspire

Please see Sweat.

Petals

To see petals in your dream, indicates a broken relationship or a rift in a friendship. It also represents regret and guilt.

Pet Store

To see or dream that you are at a pet store, represents the responsibilities that you bear. Consider also the symbolism of the pet that you see or purchase and how you may need to incorporate certain qualities of the animals into your own self.

Pets

To see your or someone else's pet in your dream, represents civilized instincts. You are keeping your temper in line. Alternatively, it indicates a need for love and acceptance. You are lacking attention from others and are feeling neglected. The pet may also be a pun for "petting" as in some sexual behavior.

To see a pet that has been dead for awhile, suggests that something that you had thought was left in the past is coming back to haunt you. Similarly to seeing your childhood home, a past pet serves the same function as trying to bring you back into that particular time period. A situation in your current life may parallel a situation in your past and the dream is providing a means of resolving it.

Petticoat

To dream that you are wearing a petticoat, represents your reluctance in revealing something about yourself. Others may see you as modest or conservative.

Pewter

To see items made of pewter in your dream, suggests that you are holding on to the past. Your ways of thinking may be outdated.

Phantom

To see a phantom in your dream, represents guilt, fear, and/or repressed memories. Your dream is serving as a medium for you to face your fears and thus it is important to pay attention to what message the phantom is trying to convey.

Please see also Ghost.

Pharaoh

To see or dream that you are a pharaoh, indicates that you are acknowledging the authority within yourself. It may also signify your connection with your spirituality and the divine.

Pharmacy

To dream that you are in pharmacy, suggests that you need to correct your thinking and readjust your attitude. You should look within yourself for the solution to a problem instead of relying on outside help.

Pheasant

To see a pheasant in your dream, symbolizes motherhood and nurturance.

Philanthropist

To dream that you are a philanthropist, represents your generosity and giving nature. The dream may also mean that you are ready to share an important part of yourself.

Phobia

To dream that you have a phobia, suggests that you need to confront your fears. Do not let your fears control your life. Consider the specific phobia for additional clues in interpreting your dreams. For example, if you dream that have a phobia of heights, then it may mean that you your position at the top is a precarious one. You are afraid that you may fall from grace.

Phoenix

To see a phoenix in your dream, symbolizes immortality and renewal. It may also mean that your past continues to haunt you.

Phone

Please see Telephone.

Phone Number

To see a phone number in your dream, suggests that you need to make contact with someone and reach out for help.

To dream that you cannot remember or find a phone number, suggests that you need to start being more independent and responsible.

Photo Album

To dream that you are looking through a photo album, suggests that you are unwilling to let go of your memories and the past. You are idealizing about the past.

Photograph

To see a photograph in your dream, indicates that there is a relationship that needs your attention. It may also be telling of a false image and that something is not what it seems to be. Alternatively, it suggests that you are clinging on to the past or to some false hope.

Please see also Picture. See The Meaning In Action: "Black Wedding"

Photographer

To dream that you are a photographer, represents your need to hold on to an image from a point in your life.

Physician

Please see Doctor.

Piano

To dream that you are playing a piano, indicates your quest for harmony in your life. Consider where the piano is placed as a clue as to what aspect of you life needs accordance.

To dream that you hear the sound of a piano, suggests harmony in your life. You are pleased with the way you life is going.

To dream that the piano needs to be tuned, indicates some aspect of your life is in discord. You need to pay more attention to some situation. You may also need to repair or devote some more time toward a relationship, family duties, project, or other situation.

Pickaxe

To see or use a pickaxe in your dream, represents a level of sexual aggression or sexual tension. You need to loosen up

Pickle

To see a pickle in your dream, signifies some anxiety, fear or realization that you will be in trouble.

Alternatively, a pickle may be seen as a symbol for the penis. Sexual messages from the unconscious are usually disguised in symbols.

Pick-up Truck

To see a pick-up truck in your dream, represents hard work. It also suggests the need to return to the basics.

Picnic

To dream that you are at a picnic, signifies a joyful and tranquil domestic life.

To see a picnic basket in your dream, indicates an opportunity to learn and share your ideas and opinions.

Picture

To see a picture in your dream, symbolizes a mental imprint that remains persistent in your mind. There may be permanence in your actions. Also consider the pun on "picture this" or "seeing the big picture" in a situation.

To dream that you are hanging a picture, represents acceptance or acknowledgement of the image that is depicted in the picture. You have come to an understanding or compromise regarding a situation.

To dream that you are taking a picture, suggests that you need to get a good understanding and gain more information on some issue. You need to focus more attention to some situation or relationship. Perhaps you feel that you need to recapture some past moments in a relationship.

To see a black and white picture in your dream, indicates that you need to consider opposing views/values. Alternatively, it may denote you need to add more color and pizazz to you life.

To see a blurry picture in your dream, suggests that your memory of the depicted event, incident, or people, is fading. Perhaps you need to let go of the past and stop holding on to what was and concentrate on what is. On the other hand, you are attempting to disguise a situation and refusing to see it as it really is. You need to learn acceptance.

Pie

To see a pie in your dream, symbolizes that there will be some reward for your hard work. It also indicates that perhaps you are reaching beyond your abilities. Alternatively, it may be a metaphor for getting your fair share, as in your "piece of the pie".

Pier

To see or dream that you are on a pier, represents self-reflection and an introspect into your unconscious. You are ready to explore and grow as an individual. The dream signal emotional and spiritual growth.

Piercing

To dream that you are getting your tongue or lip pieced, suggests that you have said some stinging and hurtful words and are regretting it.

To dream that someone is getting their eyebrow pierced, may be a metaphor for their "piercing eyes". The dream could draw attention to something disturbing that was seen or that they saw something they shouldn't have.

Less symbolically, dreams of getting pierced, may just be your waking desire or anxiety on getting pierced.

Pig

To see a pig in your dream, symbolizes dirtiness, greediness, stubbornness or selfishness. The pig may also represent opulence and overindulgence.

Pigeon

To see a pigeon in your dream, suggests that you are taking the blame for the actions of others. Pigeons also represent gossip or news. You may be expressing a desire to return home.

Pilgrim

To see a pilgrim in your dream, indicates a spiritual journey. You are striving toward greater understanding and awareness of who you are and the world you live in.

Pill

To see a pill in your dream, signifies a restoration of your inner harmony. It is a period of healing and an end to those negative ideas in your mind.

Pillow

To see a pillow in your dream, represents comfort. relaxation, ease, and/or luxury. It may indicates laziness or on the other hand, a need to take it easy on yourself.

To dream that you are lying on a pillow, suggests that you are in need of some mental support.

Pilot

To dream that you are a pilot, indicates that you are in complete control of your destination in life. You are confident and self-assured in your decisions and accomplishments.

Pimples

To dream that you have pimples, relates to issues about your self-esteem and self-image. You are feeling awkward or out of place in some situation or relationship.

To dream that you are popping your pimples, indicates that negative emotions about need to be expressed and acknowledge. Those emotions that you are holding back are on the verge of erupting.

Pin

To dream that you are pricked by a pin, signifies a sticky situation or irritating relationship. It may refer to a situation that is falling apart or that is unstable. You may be feeling anxious or feeling the need to hold together a particular relationship. Consider the pun of someone who may be a "prick".

Alternatively, to see pins in your dream may denote a feeling of being trapped or immobilized, as exemplified by the phrase "being pinned down".

Pin Cushion

To see or use a pin cushion in your dream, signifies stinging remarks or hurtful comments. You are feeling used and manipulated. Alternatively, you may be trying to harm others with your sharp words and negative attitude.

Pinball

To see a pinball machine or dream that you are playing pinball, suggests that with patience, control, and precision, you will succeed in your goals. Something that may look risky or challenging at first can be tackled if you break it down.

Pine Tree

To see a pine tree in your dream, symbolizes immortality, life, and/or fertility.

Pineapple

To see a pineapple in your dream, represents self-confidence, ambition and success. You are self-assured in what you do. Alternatively, it indicates sexual problems and issues of losing control.

Pinky Finger

To notice your pinky finger in your dream, represents mental power, intellect, memory, and the power of communication.

Pioneer

To dream that you are a pioneer, suggests that you are exploring aspects of your unconscious. You are looking for a new way to express yourself and expand your thinking.

Pipe

To see a pipe in your dream, indicates that you are open and receptive to new ideas. It may also represent your connection to those around you.

To dream that you are smoking a pipe in your dream, denotes knowledge or contemplation.

Piranha

To see piranhas in your dream, suggests that something is eating away at your unconscious. You need to release some of those pent up feelings and confront those issues that are causing much internal conflict.

Pirate

To see a pirate in your dream, signifies that some person or situation is adding chaos to your emotional life. You may feel that someone has violated your integrity or creativity. Alternatively, the pirate may symbolize freedom and one who defies authority. You may have desires to explore new adventures and take riskier ventures.

Pistol

To dream that you are aiming a pistol, denotes that you are trying to target a specific goal. However, if the overtones of the dream is that of fear, anger and aggression, then the pistol signifies power by which you need to defend yourself against the fear and anger.

*Please see also Gun.

Pit

To dream that you are in a pit, signifies feelings of hopelessness about some situation or circumstance. Also consider the familiar phrase of "being in the pits".

Pitcher

To see a pitcher in your dream, symbolizes the outpouring of ideas, knowledge, or emotions. You may be spilling your guts out to others and sharing aspects of yourself which you have previously kept to yourself.

Pixie

To see a pixie in your dream, indicates your childish ways. It may also represent unrecognized energy and your hidden potential. Alternatively, you may need to seek some outside advice.

Pizza

To see or eat pizza in your dream, represents abundance, choices, and variety. It may also indicate that you are lacking or feeling deprived of something.

Place Mat

To see or put a place mat on a table, suggests that you are welcoming a new person into your life. You may be entering into a new relationship, either on a friendship level or romantic level.

Placenta

To see a placenta in your dream, suggests that there is something in your life that is no longer needed. You need to let go of some of the unnecessary burden.

Plague

To dream of a plague, indicates that you are facing a very broad problem, such as an intimate relationship or career situation.

Plaid

To dream that you are wearing plaid, suggests that your conservative views are in conflict with your liberal and wild side.

Plains

To see the plains in your dream, represents wholesomeness. and something that is homegrown. Alternatively, it signifies that you have a clear and smooth path ahead. The dream may also be a metaphor for someone who is plain.

Planet

To see a planet in your dream, signifies creativity, exploration, and new adventures.

Plants

To see plants in your dream, indicates fertility, spiritual development, growth or the potential for growth. Alternatively, the appearance of plants in your dreams reflects your caring and loving nature.

In particular, to see indoor plants in your dream, suggests that your growth is being hindered or slowed in some way. You are experiencing a lack of independence. Alternatively, the dream signify your desire to be closer to nature.

If you are estranged from your children, then the plants can be seen as a representative for your your children.

Plastic

To see plastic objects in your dream, suggests that you are being fake and artificial. You are not being genuine and true to yourself.

Plastic Surgery

To dream that you are having plastic surgery, suggests that you are rebuilding your self-esteem and trying to improve your self-image. The dream may also occur if you are considering plastic surgery or scheduled to go in for plastic surgery.

Plates

To see a plate in your dream, indicates your social advantages and a hunger for life.

To see an empty plate in your dream, indicates that there is an emotional void in your waking life. You may be feeling left out. Alternatively, it suggests that you need to rethink your priorities.

Please See Also Dishes.

Plateau

To dream that you are on a plateau, suggests that you are in a rut or that you are taking a breather from life's fast pace. There is little excitement in your life. Alternatively, the plateau symbolizes a high state of consciousness.

Platinum

To see platinum in your dream, symbolizes success, prosperity and wealth. Your achievements and accomplishments are attributed to your determination and drive. Do not ever believe that your goals are unattainable. Alternatively, it indicates a coldness or toughness to your exterior persona.

Platter

To see a platter in your dream, indicates that you are feeling lazy or envious. Perhaps you are wanting everything handed to you "on a silver platter".

Platypus

To see a platypus in your dream, suggests your tendency to wallow and dwell on your emotions. It may also suggest that your repressed thoughts and unconscious material are slowly coming to the surface and making their presence known. Alternatively, it is indicative of shyness and reservation, especially in social situations.

Play

To dream that you are playing, suggests your tendency to go against the norm and break the rules of convention. You have unrestricted creativity. Alternatively, it may be an indication that you are all work and no play.

To dream that you are watching a play, represents the parts you play in your life and the various acts and personas you put on.

Playground

To dream that you are on a playground, indicates your desires to escape from your daily responsibilities. Consider also objects in the playground as expressing or your need to express some aspect of yourself. Perhaps you need to be more carefree or have some fun getting to know some of your talents and abilities that you have long ignored or disregarded.

Playpen

To see a playpen in your dream, suggests that you need to make time for leisure and pleasure.

Pliers

To see a pair of pliers in your dream, suggests that you need to draw out all the details of a situation before you make a decision about it. Alternatively, you may need to rid yourself of something from your life. and pull it out of the way.

Plough

To see a plough in your dream, represents growth, expansion and the cultivation of new ideas and projects.

Plum

To see or eat a plum in your dream. symbolizes youth and vitality. The plum may also represent you self-image and the way you are feeling about your body. You may be feeling a little "plump".

To see a plum tree dream in your dream, represents youth, vitality, and innocence. The dream also indicates that you will overcome your difficulties.

Plumbing

To see plumbing in your dream, symbolizes the flow of emotions. If the plumbing is clogged up, then it signifies repressed or pent up emotions needed to be released and expressed.

Plunge

To dream that something is plunging in your chest or someone else's chest, suggests that some truths are being hidden and/or ignored. You are refusing to acknowledge and confront the truth.

Pluto

To see Pluto in your dream, symbolizes death and destruction. It may also indicate a rebirth or transformation.

Pocket

To see a pocket in your dream, represents hidden talents and undeveloped abilities. You have not utilized your strengths to the fullest potential.

Pocketknife

To see a pocketknife in your dream, suggests a good friend is hiding his or his true feelings.

Poetry

To see or read poetry in your dream, signifies inspiration and idealistic notions. It also suggests that you need to improve the lines of communications with someone.

Poison

To see poison in your dream, denotes that you need to get rid of something in your life that is causing you much sickness, distress, or negativity.

To dream that you consume poison, implies that you are introducing something into yourself that is harmful to your well-being. This may be feelings of bitterness, jealousy or other bad feelings that is consuming you.

Poison Ivy

To see poison ivy in your dream, suggests that you are having vengeful or devious thoughts. It is indicative of resentment, jealousy, and revenge. Alternatively, it may represent a situation or condition that you should avoid.

Poker

To dream that you are playing poker, suggests that a situation in your waking life requires strategy and careful planning. You need to think things out before carrying out your actions. The dream may also be a pun on "poke her". Are you trying to get a girl's attention?

Pole

To see a pole in your dream, represents security and stability. You always have something or someone you can lean on.

Police

To see the police in your dream, indicates some failure to perform or to honor obligations and commitments. The police also symbolize structure, rules, and control. A more direct interpretation of seeing the police in your dream forewarns that you should avoid reckless behavior.

To dream that you are arrested by the police, suggests that you feel sexually or emotionally restrained because of guilt.

To dream that you are a police officer, represents your own sense of morality and conscience. The dream may serve to guide you down a straight path. If you have recurring dreams that you are a police officer, then it may mean that your past actions have left you feeling guilty. Consider your behavior/actions as the cop.

To dream that you are having difficulties contacting the police, suggests that you have yet to acknowledge your own authoritativeness in a situation. You need to take control and be in command of the direction of your life.

To dream that you are pulled over by the police, suggests that you need to slow down and take things down a notch.

To see or dream that you are a police officer chasing a felon, indicates that your naughty and more devious side is in conflict with your moral standards.

Politician

To dream that you are a politician, indicates that you are being deceptive and manipulative. You are trying to persuade others to support your views and ideas.

To see a politician in your dream, suggests that you need to choose and take a side. The dream parallels a decision that you need to make in your waking life.

Pollen

To see or inhale pollen in your dream, represents annoyances. You may be feeling irritable. Alternatively, it signifies the sharing and spreading of new ideas.

Pollution

To dream of pollution, indicates that you need to clean your words and thoughts.

Polo

To dream that you are playing polo, denotes a life of wealth and prestige. It also refers to a patriarchy and how we may be living in a male-dominated world.

Poltergeist

To see or hear a poltergeist in your dream, signifies a lack of control in your life. You may be experiencing some disruptions that are hindering your goals.

Polyester

To dream that something is made of polyester, suggests that you are just getting by and are satisfied with mediocrity.

Pomegranate

To see pomegranates in your dream, signifies fertility, good health, life and longevity. The allure and invitation of sex is also indicated. Alternatively, it represents bloo

Pond

To see a pond in your dream, represents tranquility and desire for more quiet time to yourself. It is a time to reflect on your situation and what is going on in your life. Alternatively, it suggests that you keep your feelings contained and in check. You are experiencing and emotional calm in your life.

Pony

To see a pony in your dream, signifies the playful aspects of your life. It is representative of your unexplored, underdeveloped, or undisciplined power.

Pool

To see a pool of water in your dream, denotes that you will find much happiness and pleasure in love and marriage. Your social life will keep you busy.

To dream that you are playing or shooting pool, represents your competitive nature. You need to learn to win or lose gracefully. Alternatively, it may mean that you need to concentrate harder on a problem in your waking life.

Pool Table

To see a pool table in your dream, suggests that you need to practice more cooperation. Perhaps you need to "pool" your efforts together.

Poor

To dream that you are poor, symbolizes neglect of your sexual nature. You may be taking on too many responsibilities and working too hard that you are not taking the time to cater to your sexual self.

Popcorn

To see popcorn in your dream, suggests that you are full of ideas. It may also indicate that certain truths/facts are being made aware to you.

Pope

To see a pope in your dream, represents your spiritual guidance, beliefs, and spiritual self. The dream serves to be an inspiration. Alternatively, it may indicate your own self-righteousness, narrow-mindedness, and holier-than-thou attitudes.

Poplar

To see a poplar in your dream, symbolizes life and vitality.

Porcupine

To see a porcupine in your dream, suggests that you need to look out for yourself and protect yourself from emotional or psychological harm. Trust and honesty are important qualities. Alternatively, it indicates that there is a situation which you need to approach with openness. Someone in your waking life may not be revealing their vulnerability.

Porch

To dream of a porch, represents your personality, your social self, your facade and how you portray yourself to others. Consider the condition and size of the porch. In particular to dream of an enclosed porch, suggests of your tendency to distance yourself from others and your desires for privacy. To dream of an opened porch, signifies your outgoing nature and welcoming attitude.

Pornography

To dream that you are watching pornography, indicates your issues with intimacy, power, control, and effectiveness. You may be having concerns about your won sexual performance. Alternatively, you may be afraid in exposing some aspect of yourself.

To dream that you in a porno film, suggests your desire to be more sexually adventurous. It also implies lust and wish-fulfillment.

Porpoise

Please see Dolphins.

Port

Please See Harbor.

Possessed

To dream that you are possessed, represents your state of helplessness and not being in control of things.

Possum

To see a possum in your dream, indicates that something may not be what it appears to be. You need to dig deeper and look for the hidden meaning of some situation or circumstance.

Postcard

To see or read a postcard in your dream, represents your desire to be more open.

Postman

Please See Mailman.

Post Office

To dream that you are in a post office, signifies an important message from your unconscious or inner wisdom. It may relate to your need to reach out and communicate with others. You may be trying to maintain your beliefs or reestablish contact with someone from your past.

Pot

To see a pot in your dream, represents your attitudes and may reveal hidden anger or frustration. Consider also how it may be a reference to marijuana and/or drug use.

To dream that the pot is boiling or bubbling over, suggests that you are filled with enthusiasm, excitement and/or ideas. Alternatively, it may indicate that you have more than you can handle. You may be overwhelmed with emotions.

Potato

To see potatoes in your dream, symbolizes laziness and/or stupidity.

To see or eat mashed potatoes in your dream, suggests that you are experiencing concerns over financial matters.

Potato Chips

To see or eat potato chips in your dream, symbolizes your overindulgent behavior.

Potholes

To see potholes in your dream, represents difficulties and setbacks in achieving your goals. You may need to make some changes in how you approach your goals. The dream may also indicate that things are not going smoothly for you in some aspect or situation in your waking life.

Potion

To see a potion in your dream, indicates misfortune and negative consequences. You should not try to purposely alter the normal rhythm of things.

Power

To dream that you have power, indicates your growing confidence, high self-esteem and increasing skills. Alternatively, your dream of power may try to compensate for a waking situation in which you were powerless.

To dream that you do not have any power or feel powerless, refers to a waking situation in which you felt unable to do anything.

Power Lines

To see or become entangled in power lines, represents your struggle for power and empowerment. You are experiencing an obstacle toward your career goals or in your relationship.

Prawn

Please See Shrimp.

Praying

To dream that you are praying, signifies a need to turn over some matter to a higher force and let it go. You need to learn to relinquish and let go of your worries. It may also be an indication that you need to pray more.

Praying Mantis

To see a praying mantis in your dream, suggests that you are in a destructive relationship. It may also indicate that you are preying on others.

See The Meaning In Action: "Devil In Disguise?"

Preacher

To see a preacher in your dream, represents a harsh personal lesson that you need to learn. You may be harboring feelings of guilt and self-punishment. You need to quit being so hard on yourself.

Precipice

Please See Cliff.

Pregnant

To dream that you are pregnant, symbolizes an aspect of yourself or some aspect of your personal life that is growing and developing. You may not be ready to talk about it or act on it. This may also represent the birth of a new idea, direction, project or goal.

To dream that you are pregnant with the baby dying inside of you suggests that a project you had put a lot of effort into is falling apart and slowly deteriorating. Nothing works out the way you want it to.

If you are pregnant and having this dream, then it represents your anxieties about the pregnancy. In the first trimester, your dreams usually consists of tiny creatures, fuzzy animals, flowers, fruit and water. In the second trimester, your dreams will reflect your anxiety about being a good mother and concerns about possible complications with the birth. Dreams of giving birth to a non-human baby are also common during this period of the pregnancy. Finally, in the third trimester, you will tend to dream about your own mother.

For a man to dream that he got a girl pregnant, forewarns that his indiscriminate sexual activities may come back to haunt him.

*Please see also Birth or Belly. See The Meaning In Action: "Pregnant Mother"

Pregnancy Test

To dream that you are taking a pregnancy test, may be a metaphor for a new phase you are entering in your life (a new job, relationship, etc.) You may feel that you are being put to the test as to whether you are prepared or ready for these changes. Alternatively, this dream may be literal in meaning and address your anxieties/fears of getting pregnant.

Presents

*Please see Gift.

President

To see the president of your country in your dream, symbolizes authority, power and control. It may also represent your own personal views and opinions of the presidents and his actions.

Press

To see the press in your dream, suggests that there is a messages that you need to convey and get across to others. You need to pay more attention to the outside world and not be so self-absorbed.

To dream that the press is chasing you, indicates your lack of privacy. You may feel that someone or some situation is invading into your space.

Pretzel

To see a pretzel in your dream, symbolizes devotion, spiritual beliefs and life's sweet rewards. You are embracing life and extending yourself to help others. Alternatively, it may indicate that you are preoccupied with some complex issue and are not sure how to handle it.

Prickerbush

To see a prickerbush in your dream, indicates that you are experiencing problems and difficulties in some waking relationship. You may need to put up your defenses and stand up for yourself. Alternatively, it may refer to someone in your life who is a "prick".

Pride

To dream that you have pride, denotes that you will have to stand up and fight against attacks to your integrity. You will be challenged.

To dream that others are displaying pride, signifies that you will soon be invited to be part of a project or accepted into a group.

Priest

To see a priest in your dream, signifies spiritual needs, regulation, religious belief and guidance. It also symbolizes chastity and abstinence. You may view sexuality as immoral.

To see a dictatorial or condemning priest in your dream, signifies unyielding authority and over-protectiveness.

Primrose

To see primrose in your dream, symbolizes purity, youth, and vitality.

Prince

To dream that you are a prince, suggests your need to feel important and needed. You may be admiring yourself and you accomplishments.

To see a prince in your dream, signifies honor and recognition will be bestowed upon you. Alternatively, it indicates your wishes for romance and meeting that Prince Charming.

Princess

To dream that you are a princess, indicates that you are recognizing your full potential. You still need to grow more and develop your full character. Alternatively, you may be too demanding and perhaps acting like a spoiled brat.

For a male, to see a princess in your dream, represents his sister or an important female figure in your life. It also suggests your desires for the ideal woman.

Printer

To see a printer in your dream, suggests that you are trying to express a thought or idea in a way that others can understand.

To dream that the printer is not functioning, indicates your difficulties and frustrations in communicating your thoughts across.

Prism

To see a prism in your dream, represents your connection to your spirituality and your colorful personality within. Perhaps you need to be more in tune with your spiritual side.

Prison

To dream that you are in prison, signifies that you are being censored and not allowed to express yourself.

To dream that someone else is in prison, signifies an aspect of yourself that you are unable to express freely.

To dream that you or someone is released from prison, denotes that you need to make major changes to your waking life. Eventually, you will overcome your misfortune.

Please also see Jail.

Prisoner

Please See Convict.

Privacy

To dream that you have no privacy, suggests that you are feeling exposed and unprotected. What are you trying to hide? Alternatively, it indicates that you are repressing your emotions and not allowing them to be fully expressed. You are worried that others will see the real you and criticize you.

Prize

To dream that you receive a prize, denotes that you have achieved some outstanding accomplishment or had made significant progress in personal endeavors. You feel pleased and proud of yourself.

Procession

To see a procession in your dream, suggests that you are ready to stand up for your beliefs.

Professor

To see a professor in your dream, symbolizes higher learning and wisdom. You will have prominence in some field.

Prom

To dream that you are at a prom, represents cycles and the passage of time. This dream signals an end to something and the beginning of something else. This dream may also signify your anticipation of your own upcoming prom in real life.

Proposal

To dream that you are being proposed to, indicates that you are merging a previously unknown aspect of yourself More directly, the dream suggests you are thinking about marriage or some serious long-term commitment/project/situation. Your reaction to the proposal indicates your true feelings about marriage or commitment.

Prostitute

To dream that you are a prostitute, indicates your desires for more sexual freedom/expression and sexual power. You want to be less inhibited and possibly explore other areas of sexuality. Your waking principle are too rigid. On a negative side, you may be harboring feelings of guilt and negative attitudes toward relationships. You are having difficulties integrating love and sexuality.

To dream that you are with a prostitute, suggests that you are feeling sexually deprived/needy. Alternatively, you may be feeling that sexual relationships were more simple and straightforward.

Protection

To dream that you are being protected or need protection, indicates that you are feeling helpless in some situation. Life's difficulties has made you dependable on others. You need to start taking charge of the situation.

To dream that you are protecting someone, suggests that you are putting up an emotional wall or barrier between you and others around you. Consider who or what you are protecting for clues as to what aspect of your own self you are afraid of letting out and letting others know.

Prune

To dream that you are pruning, represents growth. You need to get rid and cut away at your old habits and former ways. Get rid of what you no longer need.

Prunes

To see prunes in your dream, symbolizes an emotional or creative blockage. It may also represent aging as implied by the metaphor "as wrinkled as a prune".

Psychic

To dream that you see a psychic, represents your desires to know the unknown, your fate and hopes. You may be experiencing anxieties about the future and in achieving your goals. Additionally, you may feel a lack of control in the path that you life is taking.

To dream that you are psychic, indicates the sensitive side of your personality.

Psychokinesis

To dream that you have psychokinesis, indicates your tendency to manipulate your surroundings. You are being over controlling.

Pubic Hair

To see pubic hair in your dream, suggests that you are coyly making your sexual feelings known.

Puddle

To see a puddle in your dream, represents feelings that have been downplayed and overlooked. Although these feelings may be minor, it is still worth addressing before it threatens to explode unexpectedly.

Pulling

To dream that you are pulling something, indicates your struggles with getting things accomplished. It may represent your responsibilities, relationships, or situations which you should unload and/or let go. Consider what or who you are pulling.

Puke

Please See Vomiting.

Pumpkin

To see a pumpkin in your dream, implies openness and your receptiveness to new ideas and experiences. A pumpkin is also symbolic of the female sexuality. Alternatively, it may relate to the popular fairy tale of Cinderella where a carriage turns back into a pumpkin. In this regard, it may represent some situation in which time is running out.

Punch

To dream that you are punching someone or something, represents hidden anger and aggression. It may also be a symbol of power and your ability to draw strength from within yourself.

To dream that you are unable to throw a punch, indicates that you are feeling helpless. You may have self-esteem and confidence issues.

To dream that you are drinking punch, represents vitality and renewal.

Punishment

To dream that you are punished, signifies guilt or shame about your actions. You need to learn to forgive yourself. Are you punishing yourself?

To dream that you are punishing others, signifies hidden resentment towards that person. Alternatively, they may represent aspects of your own personality that you fear.

Puppet

To see a puppet in your dream, suggests that you are allowing others to control you. You are easily swayed by others and feel that you can not stand up for yourself.

Puppeteer

To dream that you are a puppeteer, suggests that you are trying to control or manipulate somebody.

Puppy

To see a puppy in your dream, symbolizes your playfulness and carefree nature. It also represents a blossoming friendship or that your friendships will grow stronger.

To see a litter of newborn puppies in your dream, is indicative of the amount of time that an idea has been developing or will take to develop. Look to the number of puppies to give you that approximate amount of time.

To dream that you are taking care of some puppies, indicates that you are a trustworthy and loyal friend especially in difficult times.

Purse

To dream that you are carrying a purse, signifies secrets which are being closely held and guarded.

To dream that you lost your purse, denotes loss of power and control of possessions. It also suggests that you may have lost touch with your real identity.

Pursuit

To dream that someone or something is in pursuit of you, indicates that you are refusing to acknowledge a certain viewpoint or idea.

To dream that you are in pursuit of someone or something, suggests that you are being denied of your power and influence. You need to re-evaluate your strengths and concentrate your efforts in something more worthwhile.

*Please also see Common Dreams: Chase

Pus

To see pus in your dream, suggests that something needs to be expressed. You may be harboring some prejudices, attitudes, or some other negative emotion that attempting to be released. You need to acknowledge these feelings and deal with them. Also consider the symbolism of where on the body the pus is located.

Push

To dream that you are pushing something, symbolizes energy, effort, encouragement and a new drive to succeed in life. Consider also how you are someone in your life may be a "pushover".

To dream that you are pushed or being pushed, signifies that you are being pressure or feel coerced into doing something. Alternatively, it implies your need for perfection. You may be finding that you do not have enough time to complete a task.

Pushpins

To see or use pushpins in your dream, indicates that you need to open your eyes and look at what is in front on you. You may be overlooking something that is in plain view.

Putty

To dream that you are handling putty, signifies that your risk taking approach to things will cause you to lose your fortune.

Puzzle

To see a jigsaw puzzle in your dream, represents a mental challenge or a problem in your waking life that you need to solve. If there are pieces missing in the puzzle, then it suggests that you do not have all the facts in order to make a good and sound decision.

To see or do a crossword puzzle, suggests that you are being faced with a mental challenge. The dream may be a pun on "cross words" directed at your or aimed toward someone.

Pyramid

To see pyramids in your dream, signifies that many new and major changes will be occurring in a short amount of time. It is a symbol of longevity, stability, and a firm foundation.

To dream that you are climbing a pyramid, denotes that you will wander aimlessly for awhile before finding the gratification of your desires.

Python

To see a python in your dream, represents danger, sin, and overt sexuality. Alternatively, it may symbolize your determination.

To see a python suffocate and kill its prey, suggests that you are feeling emotionally stressed and anxious.

Q

Quack Doctor

To see a quack doctor in your dreams, forewarns that you should check your doctor's credentials to insure that you are getting qualified and quality care during an illness. It is also a warning to be cautious of people who claim to be what they are not.

Quack Medicine

To dream of taking quack medicines, signifies that you are taking the wrong course of action with regards to your problems and affairs.

Quadrille

For a woman to dream that she is dancing in a quadrille, foretells happiness and a coming marriage.

For a man to dream that he is dancing in a quadrille, foretells that he will enjoy popularity with the honeys and business success may soon follow.

Quadruplets

To see quadruplets in your dream, represents wholeness. You are close to becoming who you really want to be. There will be calmness and peace after a period of much chaos and problems.

Quagmire

To see yourself bogged down in a quagmire, signifies your inability to meet obligations and that you are stuck in a daily non-exciting routine.

To see others bogged down in a quagmire, denotes that you will be effected by the failures of others.

Quail

To see a live quail in your dream, symbolizes good fortune.

To see a dead quail in your dream, symbolizes bad luck, especially in gambling.

To shoot a quail in your dream, foretells of an argument with your best friend.

To eat quail in your dream. forewarns of danger over extravagant spending.

Quake

Please see Earthquake.

Quaker

To see a Quaker in your dream, signifies that you will make many faithful new friends and have much success in business based on good business ethics.

To dream that you are a Quaker, symbolizes your fairness and honorable manner toward an enemy.

Quarantine

To dream that you are placed in quarantine, symbolizes your helplessness by a false friend who is spreading malicious gossip. It may also signify your need to distance yourself from others or a situation.

To dream that you are seeing a sick friend in quarantine, signifies that a friend desperately needs your help but is afraid to ask.

Quarrel

To dream that you are quarreling with a certain person, signifies that there is some hidden hard feelings and conflict toward that person and you are having difficulties talking about. This dream functions to help open that line of communication with that person in your waking life.

To overhear quarreling in your dream, denotes unsatisfactory business dealings.

Quarry

To see a quarry in your dream, denotes that hard work will lead to an advancement in your present job. Alternatively, you may have dug yourself into an emotional hole.

To dream of an idle quarry, signifies disappointment and failure and possibly death.

Quartet

To dream that you are in a quartet, signifies that you will have an enjoyable life filled with many companions. You may also be seeking out a companions and partnerships to work together in a harmonious way.

To see a quarter that you cannot join, signifies your attempt to do a job that is beyond your capacity.

Quartz

To see quartz in your dream, suggests rigidity and an unyielding personality. Alternatively, quartz can symbolize the union of masculine and feminine energies. Some situation is finally becoming clear.

Quay

To see many ships docked at the quay, signifies fulfillment of your wishes.

To see many ships being unloaded while you stand on the quay, foretells that you will take a long ocean voyage.

Queen

To see a queen in your dream, symbolizes intuition and personal growth. The queen is also a symbol for your mother.

For a woman to dream that she is a queen, indicates your desire for increased status and power. Alternatively, it may indicate that you need to listen to others.

Question

To question something in your dream, signifies your suspicions toward a love one.

To ask a question in your dream, foretells that you will strive to attain the truth.

To be questioned in a dream, denotes that you will be unfairly dealt with.

Queue

*Please see Line.

Quicksand

To dream that you are sinking in quicksand, signifies that your assumption that you are on solid ground will prove misleading and you will slowly find yourself in an expected situation.

To dream that you are rescued from quicksand by a lover, signifies a worthy and faithful lover.

Quills

To see quills in your dream, denotes success, social status, sophistication and prestige.

For a woman to dream that she is putting a quill on her hat, signifies that she will attempt many conquests, with her success depending on her charm.

Quilts

To see a quilt in your dream, signifies harmony, protection, warmth, and pleasant and comfortable circumstances.

To see a soiled quilt in your dream, signifies carelessness in dress and manner.

Quinine

To dream of quinine, foretells that you have great happiness but your prospect for wealth may be meager.

To dream that you are taking quinine, foretells an improvement in health and energy.

Quinsy

To dream that you afflicted with quinsy, denotes discouraging employments.

To see others being afflicted with quinsy, signifies your anxiety towards sickness.

Quintuplets

To see quintuplets in your dream, represents the five senses: sight, smell, taste, hearing, and touch. It may also symbolize the essential and fundamental human being. Alternatively, it represents the connection between the female and the male.

Quoits

To play at quoits in your dream, foretells low engagement and loss of employment.

R

Rabbits

To see a rabbit in your dream, foretells of luck, magic and of a favorable turn of events and a positive outlook in your future endeavors. Alternatively, rabbits symbolize your sexual activity.

To see a white rabbit in your dream, symbolizes faithfulness of a lover.

To see many rabbits hopping about the meadows, signifies fertility and that children will bring you much joy.

**See The Meaning In Action: "_The Bunny Dog_", "_Black Rabbit_", "_Boiling A Rabbit_" & "_Turned Into A Bunny_"

Rabies

To dream that an animal with rabies bites you, indicates that you are harboring extreme inner feelings of anger and unexpressed hostility. Your anger might erupt in violence if not expressed in a controlled manner.

Raccoon

To see a raccoon in your dream, signifies deceit, thievery, and of false friends secretly conspiring against you.

Race

To dream that you are in a race, signifies that others are envious of your achievements and want it for themselves. If you win the race, then it denotes that you will overcome your competitors. Alternatively, this dream may also be an indication for you to slow down or take a different coarse in life. Often this dream can reveal your competitive nature and how you tend to measure yourself against others.

Race Car

To see a race car in your dream, symbolizes your hard driving and headstrong attitudes. It may also reflect your competitive nature and the need to win. Alternatively, the symbol may be a pun for your issues with race and ethnicity.

To dream that you are driving a race car, represents your fast paced lifestyle. You may be jeopardizing your health with your reckless behavior.

To see race tracks in your dream, represents life in the fast lane for you. The tracks may be a metaphor for your quest to get ahead in life. Alternatively, you may feel that you are going in circles. Or that you have a set path of thinking and doing things and are unwilling to deviate from it.

Racism

To see racism in your dream, indicates that you may be too judgmental and discriminatory in some situation of your waking life. Perhaps you have falsely pre-judged someone because of the way he or she appeared.

To dream that you are racist, indicates your unwillingness and refusal to be pushed aside. You refuse to be dismissed.

If you believe in racism, then the dream is a reflection of your waking ideals and beliefs.

Rack

To see an empty rack in your dream, signifies your preoccupation with a problem that has given you much anxiety.

To see a rack of clothes in your dream, signifies your indecisiveness and the lingering uncertainty and doubt over the faithfulness of your lover.

Racket

To hear a racket be made in your dream, signifies disappointments after being let down in some anticipated pleasure.

Radio

To dream that you are listening to the radio, symbolizes your awareness and intuition toward a particular situation. What you hear through the radio also represents messages from your unconscious. It is possible that it is some for of ESP or telepathic communication.

To dream that a radio is turned off, indicates that you have the ability to help or assist in some situation, but you are refusing to do so.

Radish

To see a garden of radishes in your dream, signifies prosperous business and kind friends.

To dream that you are eating a radish, denotes that your feelings will be slightly hurt as a result of the thoughtlessness of someone near you.

To dream that you are planting radishes, foretells that your heart's desires will be happily realized.

Raffle

To dream that you are raffling an item, signifies risky speculation and investment ventures.

To dream that you are attending a church raffle, foretells of bitter disappointments in your future.

Raft

To see a raft in your dream, indicates that you have not built a firm foundation for yourself. There is still much work ahead.

To dream that you are floating on a raft, suggests that you are drifting through life, not knowing where you are headed. You are confused about your purpose and direction in life.

To dream that you are white water rafting, signifies that after going through some turbulent times, your sadness and pain will slowly disappear.

Rage

To dream that you are in rage, is symbolic of your bad temper and negative outbursts. Work on empowering your inner strengths.

Rags

To see old, tattered rags in your dream, signifies that you are cleaning up old problems and issues.

To dream that you are wearing rags, signifies anxieties and concerns over your self-image.

Railing

To dream that you are holding on to a railing, signifies that you are desperately holding out for a chance to obtain the object of you affection.

Railroad

To see a railroad in your dream, signifies that you have laid out a set track toward achieving your goals.

To see an obstruction on the railroad, denotes the path toward your goals will not be an easy one. It may also indicate that you have lost track of your goals,

To dream that you are walking alongside the railroad tracks, signifies much happiness from your skillful completion of your tasks.

Rain

To dream that you get wet from the rain, signifies that you will soon be cleansed from your troubles and problems. Rain also symbolizes fertility and renewal.

To see and hear rain falling, symbolizes forgiveness and grace.

To dream that you are watching the rain from a window, indicates that spiritual ideas and insights are being brought to you awareness. It may also symbolize fortune and love.

To hear the tapping of the rain on the roof, denotes spiritual ideas and blessings coming to mind. It may also suggests that you will receive much joy from your home life.

Rainbow

To see a rainbow in your dream, signifies much hope, success and good fortune in the form of money, prestige, or fame. The rainbow is a bridge between your earthly, grounded self and the higher, spiritual self.

For lovers to see a rainbow, symbolizes overwhelming happiness from their union.

Raincoat

To dream that you are wearing a raincoat, suggests that you are shielding yourself from your emotions. You are not able to face the nastiness. It also refers to your pessimistic outlook.

Raisins

To dream that you are eating raisins, signifies that negative forces and discouraging comments will seek to diminish your hopes when they are about to be realized.

Rake

To dream that you are using a rake, signifies that work will never be accomplished unless you do it yourself.

To see others raking, denotes that you will be happy on the well-being and livelihood of others.

To see a broken rake in your dream, signifies that some illness or accident will interrupt your plans, resulting in its failure.

Ram

To see a ram in your dream, signifies aggression, energy, and impulsiveness. You may be pursuing a decision that should be approached with more tact and consideration. It may also symbolize strong and powerful friends who will use their influence and best efforts for your good.

To dream that a ram is pursing you, signifies the threat of misfortune.

Ramp

To dream that you are going up a ramp, signifies your struggles in achieving a goal. It is symbolic of your determination and ambition. If you fail to go up a ramp, then it suggests that you are not able to overcome your difficulties. There are still obstacles standing on your way.

To dream that you are going down a ramp, refers to some instability in your life.

Ranch

To dream that you are at a ranch, suggests that you need to take stock of your life and what you hope to achieve and gain. The dream may also refer to your own livelihood and concerns about money.

Ransom

To dream that somebody is demanding ransom from you, signifies that you have been deceived.

Rape

To dream that you have been raped, suggests a sadistic expression of sexual desire. You may be expressing an unconscious desire to be violated, conquered, or forced into forbidden territory. Some women have a desire to be sexually overpowered, but not hurt. It also indicates vengeful feelings toward the opposite sex. Alternatively, it suggests that you are feeling violated in some way. Something or someone is jeopardizing your self-esteem and emotional well-being. You feel that someone or something is being forced upon you. Dreams of rape are also common for those who were actually raped in their waking life.

To see a rape being committed in your dream, denotes sexual dysfunction or uncertainty.

Rapids

To dream that you are carried away by the rapids, suggests that you are experiencing some intense feelings.

Rash

To dream that you have a rash, indicates repressed anger, frustrations and annoyances. You may be holding in your anger and frustrations and not revealing your negative feelings to others.

Raspberry

To see raspberries in your dream, signifies dangerous but interesting affairs.

To dream that you are eating raspberries, denotes distress over some malicious gossip that is being spread about you.

Rats

To see rats in your dream, signifies feelings of doubts, guilt and/or envy. You are having unworthy thoughts that you are keeping to yourself but are eating you up inside. Alternatively, it denotes repulsion. The dream may also be a pun on someone who is a rat.

To see a black rat, represents deceit and covert activities.

To see a white rat in your dream, denotes that in your time of distress, you will receive assistance from an unexpected source.

To dream that a rat is biting your feet, symbolizes the rat race that you are experiencing in your waking life.

Rattle

To see a baby playing with a rattle in your dream, signifies tranquility and contentment in the home.

To dream that you give a baby a rattle, signifies unfortunate investments.

Rattlesnake

To see a rattlesnake in your dream, represents the passage of time.

*Please see Snake.

Raven

To see a raven in your dream, symbolizes betrayal, disharmony, misfortune, and death.

Razor

To see a razor in your dream, suggests that there is a situation or problem that you need to smooth out.

Reading

To dream that you are reading, signifies that you need to obtain more information or knowledge before making a decision. You should review your thoughts, think things through and consider other options.

To dream that you or someone is reading incoherently, signifies worries and disappointments.

Reapers

To see reapers working hard in your dream, denotes prosperity and pleasure.

To see an idle reaper in your dream, a discouraging event will interrupt your prosperous times.

Rebirth

To dream that you are born again, indicates that you need to deal with issues that you have been avoiding. You may have been given a second chance to regain what was previously thought to be lost. Alternatively, you are starting or entering a new stage in your life. You are looking toward the future without dwelling on the past.

Receipt

To see a receipt in your dream, indicates that you are accepting or acknowledging some aspect of yourself. It is a reflection of your openness and genuineness. What is the receipt for? Alternatively, it suggests guaranteed success and better times ahead.

Reception

To dream that you are attending a reception, signifies many pleasant engagements and social gatherings.

Recipe

To dream of a recipe, symbolizes your creativity, talents and enjoyment of life. You need to take advantage of life's pleasures. Consider what is the recipe for. Desserts suggest that your need to indulge in life and devote some time to leisure. A recipe for preparing meat generally represents your desires for physical/emotional satisfaction.

Reconcilement

To dream about a reconcilement, represents a person in your waking life that you need to reconnect with. You need to rid yourself of some burden that has been weighing you down.

Record

To see or listen to a record in your dream, suggests that you need to consider both sides of a situation. You need to be more in tune with your instincts. Alternatively, it represents a need for enjoyment and sensual pleasure.

Rectangle

To see a rectangle in your dream, represents permanence, materialism and stability. Because of its four corners and four sides, it is also symbolic of the number 4.

Redhead

To dream that you are a redhead, suggests that you need more spontaneity and vitality in your life. Make some dramatic changes.

Reeds

To see reeds in your dream, symbolizes your flexibility in various situations.

Reef

To see a reef in your dream, suggests that you are blocking out unconscious material from emerging onto the surface.

Referee

To see a referee in your dream, signifies an inner battle between your own ideals and values and between the ideals and values of others.

Reflection

To see your reflection in your dream, represents your true self; it is time to look within. The reflection may highlight both your flaws and positive attributes. Learn from your flaws and how to improve on them and at the same time appreciate your good qualities. Alternatively, your reflection could also indicate how you want others to perceive you.

Refrigerator

To see or open a refrigerator in your dream, represents your chilling personality and/or cold emotions. The dream may also be telling you need to put some goal, plan, or situation on hold. Alternatively, it signifies that you have found and accomplished what you have been unconsciously seeking.

Refugee

To dream that you are a refugee, signifies your feeling of not belonging anywhere. You feel socially rejected or emotionally isolated. Alternatively, you may be trying to escape a situation or issue instead of confronting it.

Register

To dream that you register at a hotel under an alias, signifies that you will undertake some guilty enterprise that will give you much distress. You will lose your peace of mind.

To dream that someone else is registering into a hotel using your name, signifies that you will leave some work that others will have to finish for you.

Rehabilitation

To dream that you are in a rehabilitation center, indicates that you are ready for a fresh new start. You are rebuilding a new self-image.

Rehearsal

To dream that you are attending a rehearsal, suggests that you are getting ready for life or enter into the real world.

Reindeer

To see a reindeer in your dream, signifies your loyalty toward your friends who may be going through a tough time.

Rejection

To dream that you are rejecting something, indicates that there are feelings or situations that you want to be rid of. Alternatively, you may be refusing to accept a situation that is being imposed and forced upon you.

To dream that you are being rejected, signifies a lack of self-worth and alienation of others.

Relationships

To dream about your waking relationships, indicates wish-fulfillment. In your dream state, you may be able to confront issues that you would normally ignore or are afraid of bringing up. Compare your dream relationship with your waking relationship.

To dream about a relationship with a stranger, represents the different sides of your personality.

Relatives

To see your relatives in your dream, signifies family issues or feelings. They represent some aspect of your own self.

Relief

To dream about relief, suggests that you are trying to reduce the affect of the dream message and images. You may be having a disturbing dream and your conscious is seeking to alleviate the impact. You need to take some time out. Evaluate your decisions and judgment carefully.

Religion

To dream that you are deeply religious, foretells of a negative turn to your business affairs and a disruption to your life.

To dream that you are over religious, signifies that your goody goody character will repulsed your lover or mate.

Remodeling

To dream that you are remodeling, indicates that you are reevaluating your values and making changes to your belief system.

Remote Control

To see a remote control in your dream, symbolizes that your buttons are being pushed by someone, a relationship or situation that is too controlling

Renovate

To dream that you are renovating, signifies that old ideas or habits are being replaced by new ways of looking at the world and interacting with others. It is also an indication that you have triumph over much adversity.

Rent

To dream that you are paying rent, signifies satisfactory finances.

To dream that you cannot pay rent, is a bad omen by which you will see much failure in trade.

To dream that you are renting a house, denotes new and profitable dealings.

Repair

To dream that you are repairing something, signifies that you are going through a period of recovery from an upsetting situation. The item that you are repairing is indicative of the area in your life that you are working on.

Reprieve

To dream that you are granted a reprieve, signifies that you will overcome some difficulty that has given you much anxiety.

Reptile

To dream that you are attacked by a reptile, forewarns of a serious problem ahead for you. A friend will betray and slander you.

To dream that you are handling a reptile without harm to yourself, signifies that you are letting the ill humor and bitterness of your friends bring you down. You will eventually succeed in regaining their pleasant relations.

To dream that you are bitten by a reptile, signifies that you will lose your lover to a rival.

To dream that a dead reptile comes to life, symbolizes that your old problems that you thought were resolved and settled will resurface again.

Rescue

To dream that you are being rescued or rescue others, represents an aspect of yourself that has been neglected or ignored. You are trying to find a way to express this neglected part of yourself.

In particular, to dream that you rescue someone from drowning, indicates that you have successfully acknowledged certain emotions and characteristics that is symbolized by the drowning victim.

Reservoir

To see a filled reservoir in your dream, symbolizes stored up or repressed emotions. To see an empty reservoir in your dream, denotes that you have expended all your energy and emotions on others.

Resign

To dream that you resign from any position, signifies of unfortunate endeavors and make some foolish choices.

Resort

To dream that you are on a resort, represents your need for some relaxation and escape from the pressures of everyday life. You need to re-energize yourself. The dream may also be a pun a "last resort". Don't be afraid to turn to someone for help.

Restaurant

To dream that you are in a restaurant, suggests that you are feeling overwhelmed by decisions/choices that you need to make in your life. Alternatively, it indicates that you are seeking for emotional nourishment outside of your social support system.

Résumé

To see a résumé in your dream, suggests that you are evaluating your own abilities and performance in some situation. Depending on how you feel about the résumé, it may indicate whether or not you feel you have what it takes for the task at hand.

Restrained

To dream that you are restrained, indicates that you are holding yourself back and not fully expressing yourself. The dream may also be a reflection of the actual state of your body, known as REM paralysis.

Please See Paralyzed.

Resurrection

To dream that you or others are resurrected from the dead, suggests that you will eventually overcome your current obstacles and achieve your goals. It signals an awakening of your spirituality and renewed energy.

Resuscitate

To dream that you are being resuscitated, signifies that you will have heavy losses.

To dream that you resuscitate another, denotes that new friendships will be formed giving you much pleasure.

Retarded

To dream that you are retarded, indicates that you are having feelings of self-doubt. You are afraid of being left out or left behind.

To see a retarded person in your dream, suggests that someone around you is feeling ignored or overlooked. Perhaps you have failed to listen to what they have to say and as a result are alienating them.

Reunion

To dream that you are attending a reunion, suggests that there are feelings from the past which you need to acknowledge and recognize. Alternatively, it indicates that you have incorporated the various aspects/qualities of the people in your dream reunion.

Revelation

To dream that you are having a bright and pleasant revelation, signifies a positive outlook in business and/or love.

To dream that you are having a gloomy revelation, signifies you will be met with a lot of discouraging obstacles.

Revenge

To dream that you are taking revenge, symbolizes your weak character and bitter heart, which will lead to loss of friends and cause your more problems.

To dream that others take revenge on you, denotes that you are surrounded my enemies and have reason to be fearful.

Reverend

To see a reverend in your dream, indicates that you are looking for respect and guidance. The dream may also mean that you need to be more selfless and reach out to others in their time of need.

Revolt

To see a revolt in your dream, indicates peer pressure is working on you and that you may not want to go along with the crowd.

Revolver

To see a revolver in your dream, symbolizes the lingering of danger.

To see your lover with a revolver in your dream, signifies a disagreement with some friend and a possible break-up with your lover.

Please also see Pistol or Gun.

Revolving Door

Please see Door.

Rheumatism

To dream that you have rheumatism, signifies that an unexpected interruption will delay the achievement of your goals and plans.

To dream that others have rheumatism, symbolizes disappointment.

Rhinestones

To see rhinestones in your dream, signifies short-lived pleasures.

Rhinoceros

To see a rhinoceros in your dream, suggests that you need to forge ahead toward your goals and do not take "no" for an answer. Do not let any obstacles sidetrack you from your destination. You need to be more aggressive.

Rhubarb

To see rhubarb growing in your dream, signifies that you are freeing yourself out of an unwanted situation or relationship. It also suggests that pleasant times will be lingering around for awhile.

To dream that you are cooking rhubarb, signifies an argument which will result in a loss of a friend.

To dream that you are eating rhubarb, denotes disappointment in your present job.

Rib

To see ribs in your dream, symbolizes poverty and misery.

Ribbon

To see floating ribbons floating in your dream, signifies pleasant companions.

For a single person to dream that you are decorating yourself with ribbons, foretells that you may enter into a marriage based on frivolity. This may be a mistake.

To see others decorated with ribbons in your dream, denotes that you will encounter a rivalry and have much obstacles in securing a husband or a commitment to a stable relationship.

Rice

To see grains of rice in your dream, symbolizes success, prosperity, luck, fertility and warm friendships.

To dream that you are eating rice, denotes happiness and tranquility in the home.

To dream that you are cooking rice, signifies that new responsibilities will bring you much joy.

To see rice mixed with dirt in your dream, signifies illness and separation from friends.

Riches

To dream that you are rich, suggests that you will succeed in life with perseverance and strive.

Please also see Wealth.

Riddles

To dream that you are trying to solve a riddle, signifies that your patience will be tested in some endeavor you have chosen to undertake. You can also expect that this task will tie up some of your finances.

Ride

To dream that you are riding an animal or vehicle, symbolizes the path and direction of your life. Alternatively, it may indicate that you are going along with another's plans and ideas.

In particular, to dream that you are riding a bicycle, motorcycle, or horse symbolizes the rhythm of some sexual act.

Right

To dream of the right, represents conscious reality, deliberate action and rational thoughts. It may also be a pun on the rightness of an idea, decision, or plan. You are doing the right thing.

Ring

To see a ring on your finger in your dream, signifies your commitment to a relationship or a successful new endeavor. It also indicates your loyalty to your ideals, responsibilities, and beliefs.

To see a broken ring in your dream, signifies an attack on your loyalty. It is indicative of disappointments and separation.

To dream that you lose a ring or someone has stolen your ring, suggests that you will lose something or someone near and dear to you.

To dream that you receive a ring, denotes that your suspicions and worries over you lover will end. You will come to realize that he is true to his heart and will devote himself to your interest.

Ringmaster

To see or dream that you are a ringmaster, suggests that you are taking control of your hectic life. You are attempting to find order in your life.

Ringworms

To dream that you have ringworms, forewarns that you will catch a slight illness.

Riot

To see or participate in a riot in your dream, represents a loss of your individuality. You are involved in a situation that is destructive to your being. It is time to stand up for yourself.

Rising

To dream that you are rising high into the air, signifies that you will find unexpected wealth and pleasures.

To dream that you are rising to a high position, signifies that determination and knowledge will bring you desired wealth.

Rival

To dream that you have a rival, signifies that you are too hesitant in asserting you rights and standing up for yourself. Consequently, you will lose the favor of some distinguished people.

To dream that you have been outwitted by a rival, signifies that you have neglected your duties and business affairs for the pursuit of leisure and ease. Your neglect of these matters will prove detrimental.

To dream that you outwitted a rival, denotes that you will find a loveable companion. You will also be advancing to higher a higher position.

River

To see a clear, calm-flowing river in your dream, signifies that you are allowing your life to float away and it is time that you take a more decisive hand in directing your life. A river also symbolizes joyful pleasures, peace and prosperity.

To see a raging river, signifies that your life is feeling out of control.

To see a muddy and/or raging river, signifies tumultuous times and jealousy in your life.

To dream that a river is comprised of flowing red chili, refers to the raw emotion, intense passion or anger that is flowing through you and yearning to be expressed.

Roaches

To see roaches in your dream, represents an undesirable aspect of yourself in which you need to confront. Alternatively, it may be a pun for smoking marijuana. On a positive note, roaches may also be symbolic of tenacity and longevity.

Please also see Cockroach. See the meaning in action: "Crawling Cockroaches"

Road

To see a road in your dream, indicates your sense of direction and pursuit of your goals. To see a winding, curvy, or bumpy road in your dream, suggests that you will experience many obstacles and setbacks in achieving your goals. You may be met with unexpected difficulties. If the road is dark, then it reflects the darker or more frightening choices which you have made or are making.

To see a smooth road bordered by green trees and flowers, denotes a steady progress and steady climb up the social ladder. If the road is straight and narrow, then it means that your path to success is going according as planned.

To see an unknown road in your dream, signifies that you new project will cause more grief than it is worth and a waste of time.

To dream that a threatening creature is on a road, parallels a hostile situation/person you are encountering in your waking life. It is an obstacle that you need to overcome, no matter how intimidating the situation or person may appear.

*Please see also Street.

Road Signs

To see road signs in your dream, represent advice and messages that your unconscious is trying to convey. Consider what the road sign is saying and how you need to apply its message to an aspect of your daily life.

*Please See Stop Sign or U-Turn.

Roadblock

To see a roadblock in your dream, signifies obstacles in your business or personal life. You may be more persistent and diligent in trying to overcome the obstacles that come your way.

Roadrunner

To see a roadrunner in your dream, represents mental agility. You tend to run toward one idea after another. You also have the ability to stop at a moment's notice and consider your next plan of action.

Roast

To see or eat roast in your dream, signifies melancholy in the home, betrayal, and/or secrets.

Robbery

To dream that you have been robbed, denotes that you are experiencing an identity crisis or you are suffering some sort of loss in your life. Alternatively, you may feel that someone has stolen your success or has taken credit for something you did.

Robe

To see or wear a robe in your dream, signifies personal issues that you need to confront. The dream may also refer to your secret desire to let loose.

Robin

To see a robin in your dream, represents new beginnings and time for growth. It may also be a pun on someone whose name is Robin.

Robot

To see a robot in your dream, indicates that you are going about life in a mechanical and rigid way. You have lost the ability to express your feelings. Alternatively, a robot may symbolize the way you view your working life.

Rocket

To see a rocket shooting up into the air in your dream, signifies faithfulness in marriage or the winning over the heart of your crush. Your plans or ideas may also be taking off and you are quickly achieving success.

To see a rocket descending from the air in your dream, denotes unhappy unions.

Rocking Chair

To see an occupied rocking chair in your dream, signifies friendly surroundings and jovial pleasures.

To see a vacant rocking chair in your dream, foretells of grief and estrangement.

Rocks

To see rocks in your dream, signifies permanence and stability as expressed in the familiar phrase "as solid as a rock". It may also indicate that you are making a commitment to a relationship. Or you may be contemplating some changes in your life that will lay the groundwork for a more solid foundation. On the other hand rocks may also symbolize stubbornness, disharmony and unhappiness.

To dream that you are climbing a steep rock, signifies struggles, obstacles, and disappointments.

Please also see Stones.

Rodeo

To dream that you are at the rodeo, suggests that you need to take control of your animalistic forces and primal urges.

Rogue

To dream that you are rogue, foretells that your friends will worry about you over a poor decision that you have made and gone through with.

To dream that your lover is rogue, signifies that you will be greatly distressed over the neglect and inconsideration of a friend.

Roller Blades

To dream that you are on roller blades, suggests that you are moving rapidly through life with tremendous ease and determination. You are experiencing a sense of liberation and freedom.

Roller Coaster

To dream that you are riding a roller coaster, signifies that you are experiencing erratic behavior brought on by yourself or a situation. You are experiencing frequent ups and downs in your waking life.

Rolling Pin

To see or use a rolling pin in your dream, represents your creative ability. You are feeling productive and being optimistic.

To dream that you are using a rolling pin as a weapon, indicates that you are being being too hasty and on the verge of losing your temper.

Roof

To see a roof in your dream, symbolizes a barrier between two states of consciousness. It represents a protection of your consciousness, mentality, and beliefs. It is an overview of how you see yourself and who you think you are.

To dream that you are on a roof, symbolizes boundless success. If you fall off the roof, suggests that you do not have a firm grip and solid foundation on your advanced position.

To dream that the roof is leaking, represents distractions, annoyances, and unwanted influences in your life. It may also indicate that new information will dawn on you. Alternatively, it may suggest that something is finally getting through to you. Perhaps someone is imposing and intruding their thoughts and opinions on you.

To dream that the roof is falling in, indicates that you high ideals are crashing down on you. Perhaps you are unable to live up to your own high expectations.

Rooks

To see rooks in your dream, signifies that your modest friends are not meeting your needs in your pursuit for pleasure, vitality and joy.

To see a dead rook in your dream, forewarns of a serious illness or death in your family.

Room

To dream that you are in a room, represents a particular aspect of yourself or a particular relationship. Dreams about various rooms often relate to hidden areas of the conscious mind and different aspects of your personality.

To dream that you find or discover new rooms, suggests that you are developing new strengths and taking on new roles. You may be growing emotionally.

To see an appealing or comfortable room in your dream, signifies opulence and satisfaction in life.

To see a dark, eerie or confining room, denotes that that you feel trapped or repressed in a situation.

*Please see also Bathroom. or Kitchen,.

Rooster

To see a rooster in your dream, indicates that you or someone is being a show-off. It is an indication of cockiness and arrogance. You have little or no regards for others.

To hear a rooster in your dream, symbolizes bragging and self-glorification.

To see roosters fighting in your dream, signifies rivalry and quarreling.

Roots

To see roots of the trees or plants in your dream, symbolizes the depths and core of your unconscious mind and soul. It represents your values and belief system. Alternatively, it denotes your family ties and bonds. You may be searching into your past

Ropes

To see ropes in your dream, represents some connection or a way to tie/hold things together.

To dream that you are walking on a rope, denotes that you will engage in a doubtful investment but it will prove to be successful.

To dream that you are climbing up a rope, indicates your determination to succeed and overcome adversity. It may also represent your climb to the top. If you are climbing down a rope, then it indicates that you are experiencing disappointments and decline in some business affair.

To dream that you are tied up in ropes, signifies that you will let your heart guide you contrary to your better judgment.

Rosary

To see or hold a rosary in your dream, symbolizes comfort, solace, or satisfaction. It is also connected to the act of giving and asking.

Rosebush

To see a rosebush in your dream, foretells of a period of prosperity.

To see a dead rosebush in your dream, denotes misfortune and illness to strike you or your relatives.

Rosemary

To see rosemary in your dream, symbolizes sadness and remembrance. You are reflecting on something in your dream.

Roses

To see roses blooming in your dream, signifies faithfulness in love and the arrival of a much joyous occasion. Roses also symbolize love, passion, femininity, and romance, particularly if they are red roses. If you see a white rose, then it symbolizes virginity, pureness, and secrecy. It you see a yellow rose, then it refers to infidelity or jealousy.

To see withered roses in your dream, signifies death or the parting or absence of loved ones.

To smell roses in your dream, denotes unimaginable happiness and pleasure.

Rosette

To dream that you or others are wearing rosettes, signifies a waste of time on frivolous pursuits which will bring you much disappointments in the end.

Rotten

To dream that something is rotten, suggests that you are wasting away your potential. You have failed to make use of the opportunities that have come your way.

Rouge

To dream that you are wearing or putting on rouge, signifies that you will obtain your desires through deceitful ways.

To see others with rouge on their face, denotes that you are being cleverly manipulated to further the gains of a deceitful person.

To dream that rouge is coming off of your face, signifies that you will be humiliated before your rival and lose your lover at the same time.

Rowboat

To dream that you are in a rowboat, symbolizes hard work and perseverance. You are coping with your own problems and emotions in your own way and at your own pace. Consider the condition of the water.

Rowing

To dream that you are rowing, indicates a hard and difficult journey or path. It may be telling you that you are doing things the hard way. Alternatively, it may represent your spiritual progress and emotional journey.

Rubber

To see rubber in your dream, represents your adaptability and versatility to various situations.

To dream that you are hitting someone with a rubber object, indicates that things literally bounce off of them. They are less effected by what is going around them.

Rubber Band

To see or use a rubber band in your dream, suggests that you need to be more accommodating to others. You may need to expand your attitude, imagination and way of thinking.

To dream that a rubber band snaps, indicates that you have outstretched yourself into too many responsibilities.

Ruby

To see a ruby in your dream, symbolizes passion, vitality and sexual desire.

To see ruby slippers in your dream, represents your path to spiritual enlightenment. You need to venture onto a journey in order to find who you are as a person.

Rudder

To see a rudder in your dream, foretells of new friendships through your journeys to foreign lands.

To see a broken rudder in your dream, forewarns of illness and disappointments.

Rug

To see a rug in your dream, suggests that you are trying to shield yourself from some harsh reality. There may also be something that you are trying to hide. Consider the design and condition of the rug. If it is old and worn, then it suggests that you feel that you are being taken advantage of or stepped on by others.

Ruins

To see ruins in your dream, forewarns of break-ups with lovers, ill turn in business, destruction to crops and/or property, and failing health.

To see ancient ruins in your dream, signifies the absence of a friend. You will experience a note of sadness in your travels.

To see your property in ruins after a fire, signifies that some unforeseen good fortune will arise even though you may see no hope and feel like giving up.

Ruler

To see a ruler in your dream, indicates your concerns of not measuring up to the standards of others. It may also mean that you need to be careful in making a decision or judgment.

Rum

To drink rum in your dream, signifies that you will have wealth but will lack class and moral refinement. You wallow in pleasure and overindulgence.

Runaway

To dream that you are a runaway, indicates that you are dealing with issues of belonging and acceptance.

Running

To dream that you are running away from someone, indicates an issue that you are trying to avoid. You are not taking or accepting responsibility for your actions. In particular, if you are running from an attacker or any danger, then it suggests that you are not facing and confronting your fears.

To dream that you are trying to run but cannot make your feet move as fast as you want them to, signifies lack of self-esteem and self-confidence. It may also reflect your actual state of REM paralysis while in the dream state.

To dream that you are running alone, signifies that you will advance to a higher position and surpass your friends in the race for wealth. Alternatively, you may be running from some situation or from temptation.

To dream that you are running with others, signifies festive and prosperous times.

Rust

To see rust forming on iron or tin, signifies neglect or old age. It is also indicative of depressing surroundings, characterized by a decline in fortune and false friends.

RV

To see an RV in your dream, suggests that you are feeling empowered. You need to enjoy life to the fullest.

Rye

To see rye or fields of rye in your dream, symbolizes prosperity in your future.

To see or eat rye bread in your dream, foretells of a cheerful and tranquil home.

S

Sabotage

To dream that you have been sabotaged, represents waking conflicts. An overwhelming anxiety is threatening the boundary between your unconscious and your ego. You need to get rid of your old attitudes and former ways of thinking.

Sacrifice

To dream that you are being sacrificed, signifies your tendency to punish yourself. You may also feel that others do not appreciate your talents and efforts. Alternatively, you may need to eliminate certain conditions to make time and space for more productive and rewarding experiences.

Sad

To dream that you are sad, suggests that you need to learn from your disappointments and make yourself happy. Try not to dwell on the negative.

Saddle

To see a saddle in your dream, suggests that you need to freely pursue your goals. Do not let anyone hold you back from achieving goals.

To dream that you are sitting on a saddle, signifies that you will rise to a position of prominence and power.

Safari

To dream that you are on a safari, represents freedom from societal norms and rules. You are trying to break free from the confines of civilization.

Safe

To see a safe in your dream, signifies that you are hiding your sense of self worth and self value. It may also symbolize security or a keeping of a secret.

To see an empty safe, signifies loss or lack.

Safety Pin

To see a safety pin in your dream, indicates that a situation is on the verge of falling apart causing much anxiety or fear. You feel that the livelihood of the relationship depends on you.

Saffron

To see saffron growing in your dream, signifies a deceitful lover or false friend.

To dream that you are using saffron in food, denotes a peaceful resolution to your problems and quarrels.

Sage

To see sage in your dream, signifies frugality and practicality.

To dream that you use sage in food, signifies that your extravagant lifestyle will leave you penniless in the end.

Sailboat

To see a sailboat in your dream, represents success.

Sailing

To dream that you are sailing on peaceful waters, suggests that you are living life with ease. You will achieve success without major barriers.

Sailor

To see a sailor in your dream, signifies your desires for adventure and exploration. You may be ready to venture into deeper waters, particularly in personal relationships.

For a woman to dream that you are attracted to a sailor, signifies that your lover's jealousy will doom the relationship.

Saint

To see a saint in your dream, indicates that a special message is being given to you from the spiritual realm.

Salad

To see or eat a salad in your dream, suggests that you need to express your feelings and take in the positive influences in your life in order to create personal growth. Alternatively, it indicates that you are longing for nature and good heath.

Salamander

To see a salamander in your dream, represents your ability to survive through shame, misfortune, and/or embarrassment.

Salami

To see salami in your dream, suggests that you are having issues related to your self-image. It may also be indicative of sexual or relationship problems.

Sale

To dream that something is on sale, represents opportunities that are readily available to you.

Salesperson

To see or dream that you are a salesperson, suggests that there is something you need to include in your life.

Saliva

To see saliva in your dream, symbolizes sexual/sensual appetites or some creative energy.

To dream that you are spitting out your saliva, implies that you are having some anxieties about losing control, either physically or emotionally.

To see the saliva of an animal in your dream, denotes intense feelings of anger and rage.

Salmon

To see a salmon in your dream, represents determination. You are able to overcome adversity and achieve success. Alternatively, it suggests that you are comfortable with expressing your emotions and dealing with them.

Salon

To dream that you are at the salon, indicates your consciousness of your appearance and beauty. You may be trying too hard to impress others. It may also suggests deception and cover-up of some situation. Alternatively, it may denote a new outlook toward life.

Salt

To see salt in your dream, represents added flavor and a new found flare in the experience of life. You may be experiencing and elevated sense of individual worthiness and increased zest and vigor in your life. Your efforts are paying off. Alternatively, salt also symbolizes dependability, truth, dedication and longevity.

To dream that you are salting meat, signifies piling debt and as a result you will be constantly harassed by bill collectors.

Saltpeter

To see saltpeter in your dream, signifies that you will experience a tremendous grief over an extended period of time.

Salve

To dream that salve is being applied on you, denotes that you will overcome your struggles.

To dream that you are applying salve on someone else, signifies that you are a reliable and dependable person who will be there for a friend in need.

Samples

To see a variety of product samples in your dream, signifies that opportunities will come knocking on your door time and time again.

Samurai

To see or dream that you are a samurai, symbolizes honor and duty. You need to work on your issues with commitment.

Sand

To see sand in your dream, signifies a shift in perspective or a change in your attitude. Consider also the familiar phrase, "the sands of time" in which it may be suggesting that you are wasting your time or letting time pass you by.

To see wet sand in your dream, indicates that you are lacking a sense of balance in your life.

Sand Dunes

To see a sand dune in your dream, signifies your desires to be sheltered from the bitterness of reality.

Sandals

To see or wear sandals in your dream, signifies comfort and ease. You have an open understanding of others. The dream may also indicate that you need to tread lightly around certain people or risk offending them.

Sandbox

To see or play in a sandbox in your dream, suggests that you are taking a situation too seriously. You need to lighten up and enjoy the experience.

Sandpaper

To see sandpaper in your dream, suggests that you need to smooth over some rough spots in your situation or relationship. Alternatively, it may indicate that you may be a little too abrasive or harsh in your words or attitude.

Sandwich

To see a sandwich in your dream, suggests that a lot of pressure and stress is being put on you. It also reflects your ability to do two things at once. However, sometimes a sandwich is just a sandwich.

To see or eat a fish sandwich in your dream, indicates conflict between your spiritual beliefs and what is practical.

Santa Claus

To see Santa Claus in your dream, indicates that you need to be more giving, accepting, and/or forgiving. You need to acknowledge and tend to some aspect of yourself.

To dream that you or someone is dressed as Santa Claus, suggests that you need to treat others as you would like to be treated. Put yourself in someone else's shoe and determine how they might feel.

Sap

To see sap in your dream, signifies physical health and vigor. It may also represent someone who is excessively gullible or sentimental.

Sapphires

To see sapphires in your dream, represents protection, heaven, and divinity. It also represents an unlocking and understanding of your unconscious. This stone may refer to a person who is born in September.

Satan

To see Satan in your dream, denotes that there is some wrongdoing or evil workings in your life or environment.

Please see also Devil.

Satellite Dish

To see a satellite dish in your dream, represents global awareness and your understanding about worldly issues.

Saturn

To see Saturn in your dream, represents discipline, constraints, and a conservative attitude. It is also indicative of the lessons of life.

Satyr

To see a Satyr or dream that you are a Satyr, suggests that you are seeking sexual freedom. You need to integrate your mind and your body.

Sauce

To see or taste some sort of sauce in your dream, represents your sense of wisdom and intellect. Consider the color and flavor of the sauce for additional significance.

The dream may also be a pun on being "saucy". You may need to be more bold and direct with your feelings or opinions even though it may not seem to be an appropriate time.

Sauna

To dream of a sauna, suggests that you need to be more open and receptive to others opinions and ideas. You may also need to rid yourself of the negativities in your life. Alternatively, it may relate to eroticism and your sexual desires.

Sausage

To see or eat sausage in your dream, symbolizes material values. It also represents the phallus and thus refers to sexual feelings or tension.

Savanna

To see or dream that you are in a savanna, suggests that you need to learn to adjust the various situations and circumstances in your life. Appreciate the different experiences in your life even though they are not what you may be accustomed to.

Saw

To see or use a saw in your dream, indicates that you need to quit doing something. The dream may also be a pun on something you saw or are seeing.

To see an electric saw in your dream, signifies your ability to get down to the core of the problem. You know how to get to the point quickly.

Sawdust

To see sawdust in your dream, suggests that you need to clear up emotional wound that was recently opened.

Saxophone

To see or play a saxophone in your dream, indicates that there is something you need to express from deep within your soul. Perhaps you have made a deep connection with someone.

Scales

To see scales in your dream, signifies a decision that you need to make. Alternatively, the scales may suggest your need to take a balanced view of a situation and not get so emotional. Don't be so black and white and consider the gray in the situation.

Scallop

To see a scallop shell in your dream, signifies female sexuality.

Scar

To see a scar in your dream, symbolizes struggles and/or painful memories and bad feelings which may have never entirely healed and still continue to linger in your mind. It suggests that your past still has some influence or effect on your life. Alternatively, a scar may represent deep-seeded insecurities which may be holding you back from accomplishing your goals.

Scarab

To see a scarab in your dream, symbolizes your ability to survive, adapt, and change. It also represents immortality. You may be experiencing anxieties about death and aging.

Scarecrow

To see a scarecrow in your dream, indicates depression. You are going through some crisis in your life.

Scared

To dream that you are scared, indicates that you are experiencing self-doubt and feelings of incompetence. You may be feeling a lack of control. Anger often masquerades as fear, so also consider issues about which you are angry about in your waking life.

Scarf

To see a scarf in your dream, symbolizes self-restrictions. You may be too controlling of your emotions instead of expressing them. Or you may feel that your voice is being muffled.

To dream that you are wearing a scarf, suggests that you are separating your mind from your body. You may be relying too much on how you think, rather than how you feel or vice versa. Alternatively, you need to tell yourself that it is mind over matter.

Scent

*Please see Smell.

Scepter

To see a scepter in your dream, represents individual power and how one person can make a difference.

School

To dream that you are in school, signifies feelings of inadequacy and childhood insecurities that have never been resolved. It may relate to anxieties about performance and abilities. You may also be going through a "spiritual learning" experience. If you are still in school and dream about school, then it will naturally serve as a backdrop to your dream world. Alternatively, a dream that takes place in school may be a metaphor for the lessons that you are learning from your waking life.

*Please see also Teacher.

School Bus

To see a school bus in your dream, suggests that you are about to venture on a life journey needed for your own personal growth.

To dream that you drive a school bus, indicates that you like to take charge of others and watch out for their best interest.

Scientist

To dream that you are a scientist, signifies experimentation, invention, and to a certain degree, eccentricity.

Scissors

To dream that you are using scissors, denotes decisiveness and control in your waking life. Alternatively, it may suggests that you need to get rid of something in your life. It also represents your ability to cut things or people out of your life.

**See The Meaning In Action: "_Scissors In The Forest_"

Scooter

To see or ride a scooter in your dream, suggests that you are enjoying your position of power.

Scorpion

To see a scorpion in your dream, represents a situation in your waking life which may have been painful or hurtful. It is also indicative of destructive feelings, "stinging" remarks, bitter words and/or negative thoughts being expressed by or aimed against you. Your dream forewarns of a self-destructive and self-defeating path. The scorpion is also a symbol of death and rebirth. You need to get rid of the old and make room for something new. Alternatively, the scorpion may also represent a person who is born under the astrological sign for Scorpio.

To see scorpions floating in water, suggests that you need to let go of some pain and learn to accept the situation. You may be going through the three-step process of denial, acceptance, and finally moving on.

Scratch

To dream that you are scratching yourself, symbolizes a minor irritation or frustration. Perhaps something that began as minor may have the potential to become worse. Or that somebody may have hit a sore spot in you.

To see a scratch in your dream, suggests that you are feeling anxiety about having to start over or begin something "from scratch".

Scream

To dream that you are screaming, symbolizes anger and fear. It is an expression of your powerful emotions which you have kept pent up inside.

If you try to scream, but no sound comes out, then is suggests that you need to immediately confront some situation. Perhaps you are unable to pinpoint your fears or feelings.

Screw

To see a screw in your dream, represents your feelings of being taken advantaged or that you are messing things up. It may also mean that you have overlooked the little details that keeps and holds everything together. Alternatively, it may be a metaphor for having sex.

Screwdriver

To see a screwdriver in your dream, indicates the need to hold some situation or relationship together. Consider also if there someone in your life who is "all screwed up" or whom you would like to "put the screws on"?

Sculptor

To dream that you are a sculptor, suggests that you are able to create and accomplish your goals and overcome obstacles. Alternatively, it may mean that you are working on finding yourself and in getting to the core of things.

Sculpture

To see a sculpture in your dream, indicates that you are refusing to accept things as they really are. You are afraid that you are not presenting yourself in a positive light or image.

Sea

To see the sea in your dream, represents your unconscious and your transition between your unconscious and conscious. It also often represents your emotions. The dream may also be a pun on your understanding and perception of a situation. "I see" or perhaps there is something you need to "see" more clearly. Alternatively, the dream may indicate a need to reassure yourself or offer reassurance to someone.

Sea Gulls

To see sea gulls in your dream, is a pun on "see go". The dream may indicate that there is something that you need to let or see go.

Sea Horse

To see a sea horse in your dream, signifies the power of your unconscious. It may also indicate a new perspective or different outlook in life. If the sea horse is invisible, then it suggests that there is an emotional issue that you are not acknowledging or recognizing. You may need to gain a new perspective or a different outlook in life.

Sea Lion

*Please see Seal.

Sea Urchin

To see a sea urchin in your dream, symbolizes your weakness in a situation.

Seafood

To see or eat seafood in your dream, indicates recognition and a merging of your spirituality with your conscious being. You are acknowledging and fulfilling the needs of your unconscious. The dream may also be a pun on "seeing food" and thus the symbolism of "food" is also applicable.

*Please See Also Food.

Seal

To see a seal in your dream, indicates your playfulness and your ability to use and incorporate differing ideas and thoughts into a situation. Seals are a symbol of good luck, success, and spiritual understanding. It also signifies prosperity, faithful friends, and security in love. The dream symbol may also be a pun and indicate you need to put closure on some situation.

Séance

To see or be part of a séance in your dream, represents your intuition and awareness. It suggests that you need to have more insight into some situation. You need to look beyond what is in front of your and look at the big picture. You may be trying to assess hidden secrets and information within your unconscious.

Search

To dream that you are searching for something, signifies the need to find something that is missing or needed in your life. You may be searching for a solution to a problem.

Seashells

To see seashells in your dream, represents security and protection. You are not showing your true self or real feelings. In protecting yourself from getting hurt and as a result, you are emotionally closed off.

Seasick

To dream that you are seasick, represents emotions that are dragging you and weighing you down. You need to get rid of these feelings.

Seat Belt

To dream that you are wearing a seat belt in your dream, suggests that you need to work on controlling your emotions. Remain compose and do not fall apart in any situation.

To dream that you are having trouble putting on your seat belt, indicates that you are worried about what is ahead in your future.

Seaweed

To see seaweed in your dream, suggests that you need to rely on your intuition and trust your instincts.

Secret

To dream that you or someone has a secret, represents hidden power. It suggests that something needs to emerge from your unconscious.

Secretary

To see or dream that you are a secretary, indicates that you need to be more order and organization in your life. Don't be afraid to ask for help when you need it.

Security

To dream that you have a sense of security, suggests that you may be experiencing much insecurity in your waking life. The dream is compensating for your lack of security. You need to feel well-protected, both physically and emotionally.

Sedate

To dream that you are sedated, indicates your need/desire to avoid an issue or situation that is causing you emotional pain. Alternatively, you may be trying to avoid some upcoming responsibility or decision.

Seduction

To dream of seduction, is an expression of your sexual desires. Alternatively, you may be feeling lured into doing something you might not otherwise have done. You may be giving up your power of choice.

Seed

To see seeds in you dream, symbolizes fertility, heritage, and potential. It also represents the continuity of life. Alternatively, it relates to the human psyche and soul. An idea has been planted in your mind and new experiences are created.

Seizures

To dream that you a seizure, suggests that you need to have more control in your life.

Selling

To dream that you are selling something, signifies changes and your feelings toward these changes. You may be experiencing difficulties in letting go or parting with something.

Semen

Please see Sperm.

Seminar

To dream that you are attending a seminar, suggests that you are expanding your knowledge and understanding.

Senile

To dream that you are senile, indicates that you are letting your abilities go to waste. You need to put more effort into your work and projects.

Separation

To dream of a separation, represents a waking situation or relationship that is breaking apart. You may be experiencing separation anxiety. Alternatively, it indicates that you are feeling torn apart and divided. Your feelings are pulling you in opposite directions.

Serpent

To see a serpent in your dream, signifies high intellectual power, deception, and the balance of good and evil.

To see a winged serpent in your dream, denotes wisdom and that you've overcome negative ways.

Settle

To dream that you settle for something, indicates that you need to free yourself from the burdens and responsibilities you are faced with in your waking life. Add some joy, amusement, and relaxation to your life.

Sewer

To see a sewer in your dream, signifies putrid conditions and old relationships. It suggests that something needs to be cleaned up or immediately changed.

Sewing

To dream that you are sewing, suggests that you are trying to make amends with others. There may be a situation or relationship that needs to be repaired. Perhaps you are creating a new self-image and taking on a new attitude. Alternatively, it represents fertility, growth, and emotional maturity.

Sewing Machine

To see a sewing machine in your dream, denotes that economizing will help you through difficult times.

Sex

To dream about sex, refers to the psychological completion and the integration of contrasting aspects of the Self. You need to be more receptive and incorporate aspects of your dream sex partner into your own character. Alternatively and a more direct interpretation of the dream, may be your libido's way of telling you that it's been too long since you have had sex. It may indicate repressed sexual desires and your needs for physical and emotional love.

To dream about sex with someone other than your spouse or significant other, suggests dissatisfaction with the physical side of your relationship. On the other hand, it may be harmless fantasy. In such situations, you may find that you are less inhibited sexually and you can even bring that sense of adventure to your existing relationship.

To dream that you are having sex with an ex or someone who is not your current mate, denotes your reservations about embarking in a new relationship or situation. You may feel nervous about exposing yourself or currently feel a resurgence of those old emotions and feelings that you felt back when you and your ex were together. Believe it or not, it is not uncommon for people approaching their wedding to experience especially erotic adventures with partners other than their intended spouses. This may be due to the intensity of your sexual passion with your fiancé. It also relates to the new roles that you will be taking on and the uncertainty that that may bring.

If you are heterosexual and you dream that you are having sex with someone of the same sex, signifies not necessarily homosexual desire, but an expression of greater self love and acceptance. You need to be in better touch of your feminine or masculine side.

To dream that you are the opposite sex, suggests that you exhibit or need to incorporate those qualities of the opposite sex. Ask yourself, how do you feel being a man or a woman? In what ways can you incorporate those feelings into your waking life.

Sexuality

To dream about your own sexuality, signifies the secrets and meaning of life. You may be dealing with life issues of birth, marriage, and/or death. Alternatively, it suggests that you are concerned about losing your sex appeal.

Shack

To see a shack in your dream, represents your undeveloped self. You need to expand your Self. The dream may also be a pun on "shacking up".

Shadows

To see you own shadow in your dream, signifies an aspect of yourself which you have not acknowledged or recognized. It may be a quality about yourself or a part of you that you are rejecting or want to keep hidden. These qualities may not necessary be negative, but can be creative ones.

To see a shadowy figure in your dream, represents aspects of this figure which you have not acknowledged or incorporated into your own personality. Alternatively, it symbolizes the young, the helpless or the under-developed.

Shaking

To dream that you are shaking, suggests that you are getting rid of your old habits and former ways of thinking. You need to get rid of the old in order to welcome in the new and better. Shake things up a bit. Alternatively, shaking is symbolic of fear.

Shaman

To see a shaman in your dream, symbolizes a spiritual messenger or guide. The shaman is a variation of the "wise old man", an archetypal figure who represents superior knowledge, wisdom and insight.

Shampoo

To see or use shampoo in your dream, indicates that you need clear out your old attitudes and old ways of thinking. You may also need to take a different approach toward some situation or relationship. Alternatively, it represents self-growth and you desire to present a new image of yourself to others.

Shark

To see a shark in your dream, represents a person whom you see as greedy and unscrupulous. This person goes after what what he or she wants with no regards to the well-being and sensitivity of others. The shark may also be an aspect of your own personality which exhibit these qualities. Alternatively, you may be going through a difficult, painful, or unpleasant emotional period. The shark symbolizes feelings of anger, hostility, and fierceness. You may be an emotional threat to yourself or to others.

Sharpen

To sharpen an object in your dream, suggests that you need to flexible in your thinking. Sometimes you need to adapt or yield to the requests of others. Consider the overall picture instead of just thinking about yourself.

Shave

To dream that you are shaving, suggests that you are making a minor life-changing decision. Some aspect of your daily routine is being altered. Alternatively, it may represent your severe attitude or self-punishment.

To dream that someone is shaving your leg, represents a lost of your independence. You are relying on others to get you through some difficult times. You need to build up your self-confidence and self-esteem.

To see someone shaving in your dream, indicates that there is some conflict in your self-image. Perhaps what you portray or project does not match who you really are inside.

To dream that you are shaving your head, indicates a desire that you want to reveal more of yourself. If you leave some hair on your head, then it suggests that you are not completely prepared to let others see who you really are. You are afraid what people might think. The few clumps of your hair serves as some sort of safety net.

Shed

To see a shed in your dream, suggests that you are not utilizing your full abilities and skills. You are letting your potential go to waste.

Sheep

To see sheep in your dream, indicates that you lack initiative to venture out on your own. You feel uncreative and just conforming or going along with the flow.

Sheet Music

To see sheet music in your dream, represents sensuality and a desire for harmony, especially in some waking relationship.

Shell

To see a shell in your dream, signifies your inner desire to be sheltered, nourished and protected from life's problems.

Shelter

To see or dream that you are at a shelter, represents the difficulties and sense of helplessness that you are going through. You are seeking for some sort of security Alternatively, it suggests your fear of things that are different from you.

Shepherd

To see a shepherd in your dream, symbolizes the nurturing aspect of yourself. It represents guidance, direction, and unification.

Shield

To see a shield in your dream, symbolizes emotional and spiritual protection, as well as physical protection. You may be feeling vulnerable and are in need of comfort.

Ship

To see a ship in your dream, denotes that you are exploring aspects of your emotions and unconscious mind. The state and condition of the ship is indicative of your emotional state. If it is a cruise ship, then it suggests pleasant moods. If it is a warship, then you are experiencing feelings of aggression.

To dream that you are sailing the high seas in a ship, denotes that you are standing tall in times emotional turmoil.

To dream that a ship crashed or is sinking, suggests that some aspect of your life is out of control You are expressing some fear or uncertainly within your emotional state. You are afraid of losing something close to you because of certain difficulties.

Shipwreck

To see or dream that you are shipwrecked, suggests that you are experiencing some emotional conflict or are having difficulties in expressing your feelings. Additionally, you may not be ready to confront issues in your unconscious.

Shirt

To dream of a shirt, refers to your emotions or some emotional situation. The shirt you wear reveals your attitudes and level of consciousness about a particular situation.

To dream that you are giving a shirt to someone, may be a metaphor or "giving the shirt off your back" and refers to your self-sacrifice and generosity.

Shit

Please see also Feces or Defecate.

Shock

To dream that you receive a shock, represents a sudden awakening and new awareness.

Shoes

In general, shoes represent your approach to life. It suggests that you are well-grounded or that you are down to earth. It also represents your convictions about your beliefs. If you are changing your shoes, then it refers to your changing roles. You are taking a new approach to life. If your forget your shoes, then it suggests that you are leaving restraints behind you. You are are refusing to conform to some idea or attitude.

To see old and worn shoes in your dream, signifies that through diligence and hard work, you will find success. It may also mean that you have come to grips with accepting who you are.

To see new shoes in your dream, suggests that you are overconfident in your success. Alternatively you may be on a life path that is unfamiliar to you.

To dream that you are wearing inappropriate shoes for the activity at hand, denotes that your progress and path in life will be laborious and ill-prepared. It may also indicate that you are heading in the wrong direction and need to reevaluate your goals.

To dream that you are not wearing any shoes, signifies that you have a lack of confidence in yourself and low self-assurance. You may be dealing with issues concerning your self-identity. Thus if you dream that you lose your shoes, then it suggests that you may be searching for your identity and finding/exploring who you are.

To see baby shoes in your dream, symbolizes purity, innocence, vulnerability, tenderness and the desire for love. If you are planning to have or already have a baby, then it suggests that the baby will or has grounded you. After all, with a baby to tend to, you find yourself rooted at home most of the time and not being able to go out as much.

Shooting

To see a shooting in your dream, indicates that you have a set goal and know what you are aiming for in life. Your plans are right on target!

To dream that you shoot a person with a gun, denotes your aggressive feelings and hidden anger toward that particular person.

To dream that someone is shooting you with a gun, suggests that you are experiencing some confrontation in your waking life. You may feel victimized in some situation.

Shooting Star

To see a shooting star in your dream, is a sign of self-fulfillment and advancement. A shooting star is also symbolic of a new birth and changes in your life.

Shopping

To dream that you are shopping, indicates your needs and desires. Consider what you are shopping for and what needs you are try to fulfill. In particular, to dream that you are shopping for food and groceries, signifies your hidden attempt to buy the attention of others.

Shopping Cart

To see or use a shopping cart in your dream, indicates that you are reaping the rewards and benefits of your hard work. If the shopping cart is empty, then it suggests that you are coming up empty in some endeavor or plan.

Shore

To see the shore in your dream, suggests that your emotional needs are satisfied and any inner turmoil has been resolved. It also symbolizes a place where the conscious mind meets the unconscious.

Shorts

To dream that you are wearing shorts, indicates that you readiness to be more open and expose yourself. Alternatively, it refers to your youthful image and playful attitude.. The dream may also be a metaphor suggesting that you are selling yourself short.

Shot

To dream that you are shot, represents a form of self-punishment that you may be unconsciously imposing on yourself. You may have done something that you are ashamed of or are not proud of. If you are shot and come back as a different person, then it indicates that you to start fresh. You want to wipe the past away and literally become a new person.

Please also see Injection or Syringe.

Shoulders

To see your shoulders in your dream, symbolizes strength, responsibility and burdens. It indicates that you feel that you have had too much responsibility to bear and is overburdened by circumstances in your life. Alternatively, shoulders represents support and your ability to nurture others.

Shovel

To see a shovel in your dream, suggests that you are seeking your self-identity, knowledge, insight, and inner intellect. You are on a quest for a new understanding of your waking life and true Self. Alternatively, you may be trying too hard in finding the truth to a problem.

Shower

To dream that you are taking a shower in clear, fresh water, denotes spiritual or physical renewal or the need to wash a burden out of your life. It is also symbolic of forgiveness.

To dream that you are taking a shower in muddy, dirty water, signifies misfortune and minor losses.

To dream that you (or someone) is showering with their clothes on, suggests that even though you (or someone) change your outer appearances, it does not change who you are on the inside. Alternatively, your dream may indicate that you are unwilling to let your guard down. You are still keeping up a protective barrier between you and others.

Shrimp

To see or eat shrimp in your dream, suggests that you are feeling overpowered and insignificant. You feel like you want to hide from the world and be left alone for awhile.

Shrine

To see or make a shrine in your dream, indicates that you are putting too much of your energy into one element of your life.

Shrink

To dream that you are shrinking, suggests that you lack self-confidence and self-esteem. You may also feel embarrassed or unimportant in some situation. Perhaps you feel that you have been overlooked by others. Alternatively, the dream may refer to a time were you were young and small and thus symbolic of your childhood.

To see others shrink in your dream, indicates their insignificance. This may also be a pun on a psychologist and your need to consult one.

To see objects shrinking in your dream, indicates that they are not as important as they once were.

Sibling

To see your sibling in your dream, indicates unresolved issues with your sibling. Consider their actions in your dream and how it may be a reflection of your own self and your character.

To see someone else's sibling(s) in you dream, represents a quality or characteristic of that sibling that you need to incorporate and acknowledge within yourself.

Sick

To dream that you or others are sick, denotes discordance and trouble in your life. It may also signal a part of yourself that needs to be healed, either physically or mentally. Perhaps you are wallowing in your own self-pity. You need to quit feeling sorry for yourself.

Please see also Illness.

Sickle

To see a sickle in your dream, is symbolic of your labor and hard work. The symbol may also be a pun on "sicko".

Sidewalk

To dream that you are walking on a sidewalk, your steady progress and direction in life. You may be moving on to new walks of life. If the sidewalk is cracked, then it signifies minor and temporary setbacks that are keeping you from getting to your destination. Your dream may suggest that you need to alter your course and make some changes in your life.

Sideways

To dream that you are traveling or walking sideways, suggests that you need to be more straightforward in your approach in life. Be more direct.

Sign

To see a sign in your dream, indicates that you need assistance You need some direction and guidance in your life. Pay attention to what the sign says and what it is pointing you to do.

Signature

To see your signature in your dream, represents your agreement and acceptance for a particular condition or situation. You are taking charge and responsibility. It is also an indication of your seal of approval.

Silk

To see or feel silk in your dream, represents luxury, smoothness, and softness.

To dream that you are wearing silk, suggests prestige. You will never lack the necessities of life.

Silo

To see a silo in your dream, suggests that you need to save your money. Perhaps you are wasting your money on frivolous things and need to think about saving up.

Silver

To see silver in your dream, symbolizes the moon, intuition and the feminine aspects of yourself.

Singer

To see a famous singer in your dream, represents harmony and some divine influence or vibrations. It indicates glorification of the human spirit. Consider also your general impression of this singer and how those specific qualities may be triggered by someone or some situation in your waking life.

Singing

To sing in your dream, represents happiness, harmony and joy in some situation or relationship. You are uplifting others with your positive attitude and cheerful disposition. Singing is a way to celebrate, communicate and express your feelings.

To hear someone sing in your dream, signifies emotional and spiritual fulfillment. You are changing your mood and experiencing a more positive outlook in life.

Sink

To see a sink in your dream. represents your feelings and how you control your emotions. You may need to cleanse yourself of past feelings and start fresh. Consider also the common phrase "everything but the kitchen sink" which refers to a situation where you have almost everything that you can possible want or need. The symbol may also be a pun on "sinking" or drowning.

Sinking

To dream that you or something is sinking, suggests that you are feeling overwhelmed and that someone or something is pulling your down. You may be experiencing lowered self-esteem and confidence. Alternatively, some important and significant stage in your life may be coming to an end. Consider what is sinking and its significance.

Please see also Drowning.

Sirens

To hear sirens in your dream, signifies a situation or problem that is giving you much stress. The sirens may serve to get your attention and focus on the problem at hand.

Sister

To see your sister in your dream, symbolizes some aspect of your relationship with her, whether it one of sibling rivalry, caring, protectiveness, etc. Your sister may draw attention to your family role and sense of belonging. It may also serve to remind you that someone in your waking life has characteristics similar to your sister. Alternatively, your sister may be a metaphor and actually refer to a nun. In this case, she may represent spiritual issues.

If you do not have a sister and dream that you have one, then it signifies some qualities that you need to activate or acknowledge within your own self. Pay attention to the actions and behavior of your dream sister.

Sister-In-Law

To see your sister-in-law in your dream, represents characteristics in her that you find within your own self. Consider also your waking relationship with her. If you are arguing with your sister-in-law, then it suggests that you are refusing to acknowledge the fact that you two may share similar qualities.

Sitting

To dream that you are sitting, indicates your indecision and not knowing what you want to do with yourself in the near future. It may also suggest that you are just being idle and doing nothing.

Size

To dream about the size of something, represents the importance we attach to objects and person. It also relates to the degree of power you are exerting and the power others have on you. According to Freudian school of thought, the size of an object, signifies the size of someone's penis, perhaps your own or your lover.

Skateboard

To see or ride a skateboard in your dream, indicates that you have the gift of making any difficult situation look easy. You carry yourself with style and great composure in the hardest of situations . Alternatively, the dream signifies your free and fun-loving side.

Skating

To dream that are skating, symbolizes your ability to maintain a balance in your life. You are utilizing your own energy, determination, and will to progress through your life's path and working toward your goal.

To dream that you are skating on ice, indicates satisfaction with current project. Consider also the phrase "skating on thin ice" to suggest that you may be on the verge of overstepping your boundaries in some situation.

Skeleton

To see a skeleton in your dream, represents something that is not fully developed. You may still in be the planning stages of some situation or project. Alternatively, it may suggest that you need to get to the bottom of some matter. You need to stand up for yourself and your rights.

To see someone depicted as a skeleton, signifies that your relationship with them is long dead.

Sketch

To see or draw a sketch of yourself in your dream, suggests that you need to view a situation from a different perspective. The dream may also be a pun on "drawing out" or recognizing some aspect of yourself.

Skiing

To dream that you are skiing, suggests that you are pushing yourself and putting your mental and/or physical ability to the test. You are your own fiercest competitor.

Skillet

Please see <u>Pan</u>.

Skin

To dream of your skin, represents protection or shield of your inner self. It serves as a physical boundary and how close you let others get to you. Alternatively, it may indicate that you are being to superficial or shallow.

To dream that your skin is covered with rashes or other skin deformity, signifies your fear in facing a harsh reality. This may also be a pun to indicate that you are making a rash decision.

Skinless

To dream that you or someone else is skinless, suggests that you are having difficulties in sensing your emotional and psychological world. You are experiencing anxieties about how you are being perceived by others. You need to look beyond the superficial and find the sensitive truth about yourself and about others.

Skipping

To dream that you are skipping, suggests your need to be more light-hearted. You may need to take a friendlier approach toward a situation. Alternatively, the dream may indicate that you have skipped something important.

Skirts

To dream that you are wearing a skirt, represents the signals that you are conveying or sending out.

Skull

To see a skull in your dream, symbolizes danger, evil and death. Alternatively, it represents the secrets of the mind. You may be keeping things hidden.

Skunk

To see a skunk in your dream, suggests that you may be driving people away or turning people off. Alternatively, it indicates that all is calm about a certain situation but you do not necessarily like it or agree with it.

Sky

To look up at the clear blue sky in your dream, denotes peace and freedom of expression. If the sky is cloudy and overcast, then it foretells of sadness and trouble.

Skydiving

To dream that you are skydiving, represents your high ideals. Sometimes you may need to compromise these ideals and be more realistic of your expectations.

Skyscraper

To see a skyscraper in your dream, represents your high ideals, creativity and imagination. You always aim high at whatever you do. It also suggests that you have great foresight.

Skywriting

To see skywriting in your dream, represents a spiritual message. It signifies a connection and union between the spiritual realm and the physical realm. You are looking for some reassurance.

Slap

To dream that you are slapped, indicates carelessness. You either feel unappreciated or betrayed.

To dream that you slap someone, suggests that you are harboring some deep anger and repressed rage.

Slaughterhouse

To see or dream that you are in a slaughterhouse, suggests that you may need to compromise an aspect of yourself in order to move ahead.

Slave

To dream that you are a slave, suggests that you are not taking charge of your own life.

Slavery

To dream about slavery, indicates that you re not utilizing your power. You are putting power in another's hand and allowing them to make choices and decide for you. Alternatively, you are experiencing a lack of autonomy and independence.

Sled

To see a sled in your dream, signifies childishness.

To dream that you are sledding, represents your fun-loving personality and open-minded perspectives on life.

Sledgehammer

To see or use a sledgehammer in your dream, suggests that you need to break down the walls that you have created around you.

Sleeping

To dream that you are sleeping, denotes peace of mind. Alternatively, it may also mean that you are ignorant and not fully aware of the conditions and circumstances around you. If you are sleeping with a stranger, suggests that you are avoiding some issue or situation that is being symbolized by the stranger. Perhaps you are refusing to recognize a negative aspect of yourself.

To see others sleeping, is often a reflection of yourself and your own unconscious mind. It is indicative of how you may not be alert or informed about a particular situation.

Sleeping may also be synonymous with death in that it beckons renewal and new beginnings.

Sleeping Bag

To see a sleeping bag in your dream, represents warmth and protection. You are expressing a desire to slowly explore the realm of your unconscious.

Slide

To dream that you or somebody is on a slide, indicates that you are experiencing some instability in your waking life. You may have lost your grip on a situation or relationship.

Slime

To see or feel slime in your dream, represents your inability to place your trust in somebody

Slip

To dream that you slip on something, signifies that you are forcing yourself to do things that you do not really want to do.

To dream that you are wearing only a slip, suggests that you are trying not to be like everyone else and finding your own way. You have the courage to live by your own beliefs. Alternatively, it indicates that you are revealing a part of yourself that was once unknown.

Slippers

To see or wear slippers in your dream, suggests that you are feeling sluggish and/or insecure. You feel that you do not have a strong foothold in some situation. Alternatively, it represents domesticity, ease, comfort, and/or relaxation. This dream symbol may mean that you need to relax. Or you are relaxing too much and are being lazy.

Slot Machine

To see or play a slot machine in your dream, suggests that you need to be more careful with your spending. Alternatively, you need to allocate your time and energy to something more productive.

Sloth

To see a sloth in your dream, indicates your passivity in a situation. You need to assert yourself and make your presence known. The sloth is also symbolic of gentleness, laziness or lack of ambition.

Slow Motion

To dream that you are moving in slow motion, signifies that you are presently going through a hard time and experiencing great stress in your waking life.

Slugs

To see slugs in your dream, indicates that you are progressing through life in a slow, steady, and persistent manner. You may be moving painfully slowly toward a goal.

To dream that slugs are coming out from inside your body, suggests that you are having difficulties expressing some aspect of your emotion. Consider where in your body are the slugs coming out from.

Slums

To dream that you live in the slums, indicates deteriorating thoughts and crumbling ideals. You are caught in your negative thinking.

Small

To dream that someone or something is smaller than usual, represents feelings of insignificance, helplessness and unworthiness. Alternatively, you may be literally trying to "knock" this person down to size. Perhaps it suggests that you or someone in your life has an inflated ego and need to be taught a lesson.

To dream that you are small and everyone is normal sized, suggests that you are suffering from low self-esteem and/or a sense of helplessness. Perhaps you are being overlooked.

Smell

To smell something in your dream, indicates your past experiences and feelings with that particular smell. Your dream is trying to convey a feeling by associating it with a familiar smell or scent. Alternatively, the scent may be part of your real environment which you have incorporated into your dream.

Smile

To dream that you or others are smiling, signifies that you are pleased with your achievements and approve of the decisions you have made. You will be rewarded for the good things you've done for others. Alternatively, you may be seeking for something or someone that will make you happy.

Smog

To see smog in your dream, indicates your negative emotions. You may be feeling upset and fearful of a situation or relationship. Alternatively, it suggests that you have not clearly understood a situation to make an informed decision.

Smoke

To see smoke in your dream, signifies that some trouble will be entering your life. You are suffering from confusion and anxiety. You are not seeing things clearly.

Smoke Stacks

To see a smoke stack in your dream, suggests that there is something rising out of your unconscious and into your awareness. It also indicates that there is a situation that requires your immediate attention before it gets out of hand. Alternatively, it symbolizes industry and hard work. A smoke stack can be seen as a phallic symbol and may refer to sexual release.

Smoking

To dream that you are smoking, indicates that you are trying to shield yourself and others against your emotions. You have trouble letting others in.

Smuggling

To dream that you are smuggling something, indicates that you are trying to claim what should be rightfully yours. You may be feeling locked out or denied of something. Consider what you are smuggling for additional significance.

Snails

To see a snail in your dream, suggests that you are being overly sensitive. You may feel inhibited but desire to be more outgoing and energetic. Alternatively, it suggests that you are making steady progress toward a goal. You need to go at your own pace.

Snake

To see a snake or be bitten by one in your dream, signifies hidden fears and worries that are threatening you. Your dream may be alerting you to something in your waking life that you are not aware of or that has not yet surfaced. The snake may also be seen as phallic and thus symbolize dangerous and forbidden sexuality. The snake may also refer to a person around you who is callous, ruthless, and can't be trusted. As a positive symbol, snakes represent transformation, knowledge and wisdom. It is indicative of self-renewal and positive changes.

See The Meaning In Action: "Two Snakes, "Snakes Everywhere!", "Raining Snakes" & "Snakes Jumping At Me"

Sneakers

To see or wear sneakers in your dream, suggests that you are approaching through life with ease and little obstacles. It also denotes comfort and satisfaction with yourself and who you are. Alternatively, the dream indicates that you lead an active life and is always on the go.

Sneeze

To dream that you sneeze, indicates a life of ease and joy.

Sniper

To dream that you are a sniper or are being attacked by one, represents hidden aggression that you need to acknowledge. You need to express your anger in a more controlled and healthy manner.

Snorkeling

To dream that you are snorkeling, suggests that you are exploring your emotions and trying to understand why you feel the way you do about certain things. It may also indicate that you are looking back at past emotions and what you can learn from those experiences.

Snow

To see snow in your dream, signifies your inhibitions, repressed/unexpressed emotions and feelings of frigidity. You need to release and express these emotions and inhibitions. You may also be feeling indifferent, alone and neglected. If the snow is melting then it suggests that you are acknowledging and releasing those emotions you have repressed. You are overcoming your fears and obstacles.

To see dirty snow in your dream, refers to a loss in innocence, impurity and uncleanness. Some aspect of yourself or situation has been tainted.

To dream that you are watching the snow fall, represents a clean start and a fresh, new perspective. It is indicative of spiritual peace and tranquility.

To dream that you are playing in the snow, indicates that you need to set some time for fun and relaxation.

To dream that you find something in the snow, suggests that you are exploring and accessing your unused potential, abilities, and talents. You have uncovered some hidden talent and ability within yourself. It may also indicate forgiving yourself or others.

Snowboarding

To dream that you or someone is snowboarding indicates that you are overcoming your fears. You are utilizing your skills.

Snowflake

To see a snowflake in your dream, represents purity and perfection.

Snowman

To see a snowman in your dream, suggests that you are emotionally cold or frigid. Perhaps you have been a little cold-hearted and insensitive. Alternatively, it is symbolic of playfulness and time of togetherness.

Snowstorm

Please See Blizzard.

Soap

To see soap in your dream, indicates that you need to wash away some of your emotions or past memories. You may also be feeling emotionally dirty or guilty and are trying to wash away the shame. Perhaps you need to confess something.

Soaring

To dream that you are soaring through the air, symbolizes freedom from restrictions. You may have escaped or gotten out from a burdening situation or relationship.

Please see also Common Dreams: Flying.

Soccer

To dream that you are playing soccer, suggests that you are suppressing your sexuality and/or aggression and expressing it in a more socially acceptable manner. From a Freudian perspective, sports, in general, serve as a disguise for attitudes about sex as a aggressive act. Hence soccer can be seen as a pun for "sock her". Alternatively, the game of soccer may refer to how you function and run your life when confronted with challenges. It is symbolic of your competency, integrity, strengths and weaknesses.

Socks

To dream that you are only wearing socks, indicates your warmth and your flexibility of understanding. You tend to yield to other's wishes.

To see a single sock in your dream, may be a pun for hitting someone or being hit. Alternatively, you may have been hit with some surprising information or news.

Sofa

Please See Couch.

Softball

To dream that you are playing or watching softball, indicates that you need to go back to you basic beliefs. Also, you need to stay within your own limits and capabilities. Alternatively, softball can symbolize relationship and how the masculine aspects (shape of the bat) are in opposition to the feminine aspects (ball).

Soil

To see or be in contact with soil in your dream, symbolizes growth and fertility. It also represents a solid foundation for life. You need to approach your goals with practicality.

Soldier

To see a soldier in your dream, signifies your staunch attitudes and how you may impose your opinions and feelings on others. Alternatively, you may be preparing yourself do battle over an issue and defend your values and opinions.

Son

To see your son in your dream, signifies your ideal, hopes, potential, and the youthful part of yourself. On the other hand, to see your son in your dream might not have any significance and is simply mirroring your waking life. The dream may also be a pun on "sun".

If you don't have a son and dream that you are searching for him, represents the undeveloped masculine aspect of your own self. You need to acknowledge the youth and child in you.

Songs

To hear or write songs in your dream, indicates that you are looking at things from a spiritual viewpoint. Your future path is a happy one with good health and much wealth. Consider the words to the song that you are dreaming about for additional messages.

Soot

To see soot in your dream, symbolizes immortality. In particular, if you are covered in soot, then it signifies your unconscious and the negative aspects of yourself. It may be parts of yourself that you fear or are ashamed of.

Sorcerer

To see or dream that you are a sorcerer, represents your talents, inner strengths, and creative ability. Your mind is squarely set on achieving your goals.

Sores

To dream that you have sores on your body, suggests that you are keeping in some negative emotions and attitudes that need to be released and expressed. Consider the symbolism of the body area where the sores are located. Perhaps the dream is an indication that you are still feeling sore and resentful about some situation or relationship.

Sorority

To dream that you are joining or in a sorority, signifies personal growth and social changes that you are experiencing in your life. You need to expand your awareness and knowledge. If you are in a sorority in your waking life, then the dream is a reflection of the waking relationship. The dream is also symbolic of the bounds of sisterhood and togetherness.

Soul

To dream that you have a lack of soul or no soul, suggests that you are feeling spiritually lost. You need to find yourself and what will make you feel whole as a person.

To dream that your soul is leaving your body, represents your feelings of self-guilt. You may have compromised your own beliefs and values. Perhaps you are feeling numb or out of touch with those around you. You need to change some vital part of your waking life in order to feel fully alive and whole again.

Soup

Similarly to food, to dream about soup, represents emotional hunger or nourishment. In addition, it also signifies comfort and healing. Consider the contents inside the soup and its symbolism.

South

To dream of the direction south, indicates life, expectations, and questions. Alternatively, it may symbolize love, passion and warmth. Or it is an indication that a plan has gone awry.

South America

To dream about South America, suggests that you are trying to resolve some conflict or conquer the obstacles in your life. It also refers to spontaneity.

Spa

To dream that you are at a spa, suggests that you need to take time out and pamper yourself. Perhaps you need to come clean and wash away old secrets, pains, or guilt. It is time to let your emotions out and begin the healing process. Start fresh.

Space

To see or dream that you are in space, represents exploration. You are an independent thinker.

Spaceship

To see a spaceship in your dream, symbolizes your creative mind. It denotes a spiritual journey of self-development and self-awareness. You may need to take a different perspective, no matter how bizarre or unusual it may be.

**See The Meaning In Action: "Spaceship In The Old West" & "End Of The World"*

Spades

To see the ace of spades in your dream, symbolizes spontaneity, mischievous, and/or heartlessness. It also represents authority and extreme competitiveness. You are afraid of losing.

Spaghetti

To see or eat spaghetti in your dream, indicates that you are feeling entangled in some messy relationship. Perhaps you are not sure how to end a relationship or situation. You may find yourself in an uncomfortable position.

Spanking

To dream that you are spanking someone, suggests that you need to work on your childish rage and tantrums.

Sparrow

To see a sparrow in your dream, represents inner dignity. Never underestimate the small or those that do not appear powerful.

Spear

To dream that you are throwing spear, indicates that you are thrusting forth your will and power into a situation at hand. It is a statement of your strength and commitment.

Spectacles

Please See Eyeglasses.

Speech

To give a speech in your dream, indicates that you need to vocalize your feelings and thoughts. You need to communicate something important and/or urgent. Alternatively, it may highlight your fear and nervousness of speaking in public.

To hear a speech in your dream, suggests that your inner feelings are being made conscious to those around you. Consider what is said in the speech. If you hear a politician give a speech, then it represents egotism and deceit.

Speeding

To dream that you are speeding, indicates that you are feeling compelled and driven to complete something. As a result, you may be pushing people away. You may also be moving too fast in some relationship or situation.

Sperm

To see sperm in your dream, symbolizes masculinity and/or fertility. It also indicates the potential for growth and development.

Sphinx

To see a sphinx in your dream, signifies fear of the unknown.

Spice

To dream of spice, suggests your need for variety in your life. You need to look at a situation/relationship from a different perspective/angle.

Spiders

To see a spider in your dream, indicates that you are feeling like an outsider in some situation. Or that you may want to keep your distance and stay away from an alluring and tempting situation. The spider is also symbolic of feminine power. Alternatively, a spider may refer to a powerful force protecting you against your self-destructive behavior. If you kill a spider, it symbolizes misfortune and general bad luck.

To see a spider spinning a web in your dream, signifies that you will be rewarded for your hard work. You will soon find yourself promoted in your job or recognized for your achievement in a difficult task. Spiders are a symbol of creativity due to the intricate webs they spin. On a negative note, spiders may indicate a feeling of being entangled or trapped in a sticky or clingy relationship. It represents some ensnaring and controlling force. You may feel that someone or some situation is sucking the life right out of you.

To see a spider climbing up a wall in your dream, denotes that your desires will be soon be realized.

To dream that you are bitten by a spider, represents a conflict with your mother or some dominant female figure in your life. The dream may be a metaphor for a devouring mother or the feminine power to possess and entrap. Perhaps you are feeling trapped by some relationship.

See The Meaning In Action: "Noisy Spider".

Spill

To dream that you spill something on someone, represents your carelessness and inconsideration for the feelings of others. You may be offending and upsetting others.

To dream that you spill some food, is an indication that you need to eliminate that food from your diet.

Spindle

To see a spindle in your dream, represents life and longevity. It suggests that history repeats itself and whatever comes around goes around.

Spine

To dream about yours or someone else's spine, represents your support system and responsibilities. You need to keep your head high even in difficult times.

Spiral

To see a spiral in your dream, indicates that some situation in your waking life is spilling out of control with end. Alternatively, it may mean your creative power and new ideas.

Spirits

To dream that you are talking to an unknown spirit, forewarns that someone is trying to deceive you.

Generally if the spirit is known and welcomed it is a sign of great good luck and/or good fortune in business affairs.

Spit

To spit in your dream, signifies an aspect of yourself that you need to get rid of. Alternatively, spitting may represent anger and contempt.

Splash

To dream that you are being splashed by water, represents your need to be revitalized and more expressive.

Spleen

To dream about your spleen, signifies your need to express your anger or sadness. It may also mean that you need to lighten up and show your humorous side.

Splinter

To dream that you have a splinter, suggests that you are letting petty and trivial things upset you. As a result you are hindering your progress. Try not to take other's opinions and remarks personally.

Sponge

To see or use a sponge in your dream, suggests that you easily absorb new knowledge and information. The dream may also be a metaphor indicating that you are "sponging off someone". You are being too dependent and need to find your own path.

Spoon

To see a spoon in your dream, indicates that you may need to give/receive nourishment. It may also mean that you feel you or someone is being given special treatment.

Sports

To dream that you are playing a sport, signifies the learning of rules, talents, and the achieving of your goals. It also highlights the importance of cooperation, harmony, and teamwork. Alternatively, it represents your attitudes about sex as an aggressive act.

To dream that you are watching a sports competition, represents two opposing viewpoints or conflicting opinions.

Spring

To dream of the season of spring, signifies new beginnings and creative endeavors. It is also a symbol for virility and fruitfulness.

To see a water spring, symbolizes your emotional energy and expressiveness. You have the tendency to make your feelings and opinions known. You may also have the ability to draw on your inner resources.

Sprinklers

To see sprinklers in your dream, indicates enlightenment. You have been able to shed some light on a situation or relationship. It also represents rejuvenation and cleansing. Those emotional wounds are beginning to heal.

Spy

To dream that you are a spy, indicates your mistrust of others and your tendencies to be in everyone's business and affairs. Perhaps you have recently stumbled upon some information that was not meant for your eyes.

To dream that someone is spying on you, represents your impulsive behavior. This dream may also serve as a warning that you are being watched, investigated, or evaluated.

Square

To see a square in your dream, denotes your need for more stability. It may also represent strength and solidity. Alternatively, you may be feeling limited in wanting to express yourself.

Squeeze

To dream that you are squeezing something, suggests that you need to make more space for other things. You need to stop dwelling on your past emotions and clear them away. Alternatively, it may mean that you are putting the "squeeze' on somebody. You or someone may be feeling pressured or stressed. The dream may also be a pun on your "main squeeze" or your mate. What is your dream trying to tell you about the relationship.

Squid

To see a squid in your dream, suggests that unconsciously you are feeling threatened. Your judgment may also be clouded. Perhaps you are not seeing things too clearly at the moment. Alternatively, it symbolizes greed. It is always about what you want.

To dream that you are eating squid, indicates that you are feeling self-conscious and worried how others perceive you. You may be finding it easier to isolate yourself instead of risking judgment from others.

Squirrel

To see squirrels running around, signifies that you are involved in a loveless or pointless relationship or an unprofitable business project. Squirrels also refers to the act of hoarding. It could either mean that you need to reserve something or it could indicate that you are retaining too much and need to learn to let go.

To dream that you are trying to run over squirrels with a lawn mower, suggests that you are trying to change your beliefs or alter your ideas in order to conform to others. You are seeking some form of acceptance.

To dream that you are feeding a squirrel, denotes comfort through hard work, diligence and prudence.

To see squirrels in a tree, forewarns that you will be faced with an embarrassing situation.

Stab

To dream that you have been stabbed, signifies your struggle with power. You may be experiencing feelings of inadequacy and defensiveness. Alternatively, you may be feeling betrayed as the popular phrase goes, "being stabbed in the back".

To dream that you stab someone, indicates your fear of betrayal and your untrusting nature. You may be too much on the defensive.

Stadium

To see or dream that you are in a stadium, represents your determination to succeed and achieve your goals. You need to be more active, aggressive, and bold.

Stag

To see a stag in your dream, represents grace and agility. You will elevate to a position of much status. You will feel spiritually uplifted.

Stage

To dream that you are on a stage, represents your behavior, manipulation of and relationships with others. It is telling of your interactions with society. There is a saying that goes, "All the world is your stage" and thus may refer to your desire to be the center of attention. Consider how your stage performance parallels a waking situation.

To dream that you are on a side stage, reflects your introverted personality. This dream may indicate your need to be more confident and self-assured.

Stain

To see a stain in your dream, indicates a superficial and reversible mistake in your life. Consider and analyze the substance and color of the stain and the location of the stain itself.

Stained Glass

To see stained glass in your dream, signifies spiritual healing and enlightenment. You are seeking guidance from a higher source. Consider also what color predominates and determine how you need to incorporate the symbolism of that color into your Self.

Staircase

To see a staircase in your dream, symbolizes change and transformation.

Stairs

To dream that you are walking up a flight of stairs, indicates that you are achieving a higher level of understanding. You are making progress into your spiritual/emotional/material journey. It also represents material and thoughts that are coming to the surface.

To dream that you are walking down a flight of stairs, represents your repressed thoughts. It suggests that you are going into your unconscious. It also refers to setbacks that you will experience in your life. If you are afraid of going down the stairs, then it suggests that you are afraid to confront your repressed emotions and thoughts. Is there something from your past that you are not acknowledging.

To see spiral or winding stairs, signify growth and/or rebirth.

See The Meaning In Action: "Up The Staircase"

Stallion

To see a stallion in your dream, symbolizes power, strength, courage, and independence. If you are riding the stallion then it signifies that you will or have attained these virtues.

Stalk

To dream that you are being stalked, indicates difficulties and problems which you are not confronting. Your avoidance of these problems is not making them go away. If you are being stalked in real life, then this fear may be carried over into your dream state.

To dream that you are a stalker, represents your shadow and the negative part of your Self. It is symbolic of a bad habit which you have unsuccessfully tried to break.

Please See Also Common Dreams: Chase Dreams.

Stamps

To see stamps in your dream, represents a need for communication. Consider what is depicted on the stamp and the amount. The symbol may also be a pun on stamping your feet. And thus you need to show more fortitude and confidence.

To see a stamp collection in your dream, signifies issues and concerns with money and/or security.

Standing

To dream that you are standing, suggests that you are asserting yourself and making your thoughts/feelings known. It also indicates that you are proud of yourself.

Staples

To see staples in your dream, indicates that you need to organize your life and keep things in order. Learn to sort our your feelings and express them. The dream may also be pun on the essentials and regular aspects of your life.

Starfish

To see a starfish in your dream, suggests a period of healing and regeneration. Alternatively, indicates that you have many options to weigh and decisions to make.

Staring

To dream that you are staring at something or someone, indicates that you need to take a much closer look at some situation or relationship. Perhaps you need to approach a situation from another perspective or viewpoint. Alternatively, it represents your passivity. You need to start taking action.

To dream that someone is staring at you, suggests that you are hoping someone would look your way more often. It may also represent anxiety or pride.

Star Of David

To see the Star Of David in your dream, represents the merging power of love and creativity. It also signifies the union of heaven and earth.

Stars

To see stars in your dream, symbolize high ideals, spirit, fate and luck. It also signifies your desire for fame and fortune.

Starvation

To dream about starvation, indicates that you are lacking in some mental or emotional area of your life. You may be ignoring or avoiding an important family/emotional issue. Starvation dreams are not uncommon in individuals who are dieting or who have an eating disorder.

Static

To feel static in your dream, depicts your magnetic personality and how you are able to draw things to you.

Station Wagon

To see or drive a station wagon in your dream, refers to your family and issues surrounding your family.

To dream that you are unable to roll up the windows of your station wagon, represents your anxieties about being able to protect and provide for your family. You are showing some hesitation and reservation about the direction that you are taking in life or the path that you have chosen.

Statue

To see people you know as statues in your dream, symbolizes a lack of communication with that person and that the relationship is inflexible. On a more positive note, it may represent someone you idealize and admire.

To dream that you are a statue, signifies that your true self is out of touch with reality.

Statue Of Liberty

To see the Statue of Liberty in your dream, signifies personal and/or cultural freedom. You have found your own independence and are learning to stand on your own. It is also a symbol of free enterprise and patriotism.

Stealing

To dream that you are stealing, denotes that you are deprived and where the stealing takes place (at home, the office, at school....) is indicative of your neediness. Alternatively, it may signify unrealized and unfulfilled goals. You may have set your goals too high.

Steam

To see or hear steam in your dream, denotes your emotional state regarding an issue or situation. It may indicate that you are headstrong and read to proceed forth on an issue. It may also indicate that you are angry with someone or something.

Steel

To see steel in your dream, symbolizes toughness and strength. The dream may also be a pun on stealing.

Steer

To see a steer in your dream, indicates a need for sexual contact or masculine energy. The steer may also be symbolic of several deities and gods. This symbol may also be a pun on "steering" in the right direction.

Please See <u>Bull.</u>

Steps

To see steps in your dream, represents your efforts in achieving your goals, ambition and material gains. The dream may be telling you to take things one thing at a time. Or that you need to take a chance and take that first step toward your goals/dreams.

Sticker

To see stickers in your dream, suggests your tendency to hold on and cling to your childhood. Also pay attention to what is depicted on the sticker; that may offer you a clue to what particular aspect of yourself you are not letting go of.

Stigmata

To dream that you or someone have stigmata, refers to the sacrifices you made and the difficulties you endured. Time will heal the pain. Alternatively, it symbolizes your passion and the intensity of what you believe in.

Stiletto

To see or wear stilettos in your dream, signifies sexuality and domination.

Stillborn

To dream of a stillborn, denotes your lost of trust in someone or something. In may also represent innocence that is lost.

Stilts

To dream that you are walking on stilts, indicates that you are feeling insecure. A situation or relationship is unstable. You are doing your best trying to balance various aspects of your life.

To dream that you fall off a pair of stilts, suggests that you should not put your trust in one person.

Stitch

To dream that you have stitches, represents your responsibility in keeping/holding a situation or relationship together. You may fear that this situation/relationship is falling apart and needs to be mended. Consider also the symbolism of where the stitches are on the body for additional clues.

To dream that you are stitching, indicates that you need to take extra care in adding your personal care and special touch to some situation.

Stock Market

To dream about the stock market, represents the ups and downs of your life. It also refers to the risks that you have been willing to take.

Stockings

To wear stocking in your dream, represents your sense of understanding. You are well-grounded and have the support of those around you.

To see some put on stockings, relates to some sexual situation.

To see a Christmas stocking, symbolizes a need for recognition and acknowledgement. On the other hand you need to be more giving.

Stomach

To see your own stomach in your dream, suggests the beginning of new changes in your life. The dream may highlight your difficulties with accepting these changes. It is also indicative of how you can no longer tolerate or put up with a particular situation, relationship, or person. The stomach is often seen as the center of emotions.

Stones

To see stones in your dream, symbolizes strength, unity, and unyielding beliefs. Consider the common phrase "etched in stone" which suggest permanence and unchanging attitudes. Some stones also carry sacred and magical meanings. Alternatively, stones may relate to issues of moral judgment and/or guilt.

To dream that you are carrying a bag of stones, refers to your inner strength and fortitude that you have yet to unleash and reveal to others.

To see rough stones in your dream, represents your quest in recognizing and developing your self-identity. Part of this quest is to become aware of your unconscious and suppressed thoughts.

For various cultures, stones have spiritual significance. Consider the Black Stone of Mecca which is believed by Muslims to allow for direct communication with God. For the Irish, the Blarney Stone is seen as a gift of eloquence.

Stop Sign

To see a stop sign in your dream, suggests that you need to stop what you are doing and think about the situation before moving forward. You need to proceed with care and caution. Alternatively, it signifies barriers and difficulties on our path.

To dream that you run a stop sign, indicates that you do not consider the consequences of your action. It may refer to your reckless habits.

Stoplight

To see a stoplight in your dream, suggests that you feel you are being held back from pursuing your goals. You may also feel pressure to succeed or else be left behind. If the stoplight is green, then it indicates that you have been given a seal of approval to follow whatever path you have chosen or whatever decision you have made.

Store

To dream of grocery or convenience store, suggests that you are emotionally and mentally strained. Alternatively, you may be brainstorming for new ideas or looking for the various choices out there for you.

Stork

To see a stork in your dream, symbolizes a new birth and/or fertility. The birth may be a fruition of some idea.

Storm

To see a storm in your dream, signifies overwhelming struggle, shock, devastating loss and catastrophe in your personal affairs. The storm also represents unexpressed fears or emotions, such as anger, rage, turmoil, etc. On a more positive note, the storm signifies the rising of spirit within.

To dream that you take cover in a storm, foretells that whatever disturbance or problems is occurring in your life will quickly blow over. Consider also the phrase "weather the storm", which suggests your ability and strength to withstand whatever comes.

Stove

To see a stove in your dream, suggests a developing awareness.

Straddle

To dream that you are straddling something, suggests that you are undecided about some issue or choice. You remain uncommitted to any one side for fear of alienating or distancing yourself from the other side.

Stranded

To dream that you are stranded, represents your feelings of isolation and loneliness. You are seeking for someone to help and rescue you from your situation.

Stranger

To see a stranger in your dream, signifies a part of yourself that is repressed and hidden. Alternatively, it symbolizes the archetypal dream helper who is trying to offer some insight and advice.

Strangle

To dream that you or someone else is being strangled, denotes that you are repressing or denying a vital aspect of your expression.

Straw

To see or use a straw in your dream, indicates that you may have been taking some things for granted. Pay more attention to the people around you. You will find that you will build stronger and more meaningful bounds with them.

To dream that you are buying straws, suggests that you are trying to buy your way into a situation or relationship.

Strawberry

To see or eat strawberries in your dream, signifies your sensual desires and temptation. Strawberries is often associated with feminine qualities and female sexuality. Alternatively, to see strawberries in your dream indicates that your ideas and goals are soon realized.

Stream

To see a stream in your dream, signifies that you will come upon a flow of fresh and profound ideas.

To see a frozen stream in your dream, indicates that your emotions have grown cold and hardened. This may reflect your hurt feelings which you need to confront and deal with.

Street

To see a street in your dream, symbolizes your life's path. The condition of the street reflects how much control you have over the direction of your life. Is there a name on the street which can offer some significance or hints to the meaning of the dream.

To see side streets, refers to a need to explore and return to more traditional ways. It may also suggest and alternative way of life.

*Please see also Road

Stress

To dream that you are under stress, is a reflection of the stress that you are experiencing in your waking life that has been carried over into your dream state. Even in your sleep, you may be unable to relax. The dream may call attention to setbacks, obstacles, self-doubts, criticism that you are facing in some waking situation or relationship. You need to take some leisure time off.

Stretch Marks

To see or dream that you have stretch marks, suggests that you are overextending yourself to others and are not paying enough attention to your own needs. You need to learn that you cannot be everything to everybody. You may be experiencing some emotional imbalance and tension. Alternatively, it represents a sense of failure or that others see you as unattractive.

Stretcher

To dream that you are lying on a stretcher, indicates your need to be rescued in some situation or relationship. Perhaps you need to take time out and confront your emotional demons.

To see a stretcher in your dream, suggests that trouble lies ahead of you in the near future.

Strike

To dream that you are going on strike, suggests that you are feeling under-appreciated. Perhaps you feel that you are being forced to do something that you don't really want to.

String

To see strings in your dream, represents binding, cohesion, and joining. It may relate to the strength of your involvement to a project, situation, or relationship. You may have concerns about holding some relationship together. Alternatively, the dream may indicate your need to use your position and leverage to get what you want.

To dream that you are tying a string, indicates something you have forgotten to do.

Stripes

To see stripes in your dream, suggests that you are making a bold and daring statement. Horizontal stripes represent your directness and straightforwardness, while vertical stripes indicate that you are a non-conformist. In particular, black and white vertical stripes signify your limited way of thinking and close-mindedness.

Stripping

To dream that you are stripping, indicates repression of your personal and physical desires. You are yearning for greater self-expression.

Stroke

To dream that you have a stroke, indicates your inability to function in certain situation of your waking life. You may be dealing with issues of acceptance/rejection and approval/disapproval.

To see someone suffering from a stroke, suggests your own repressed fears. Consider how aspects of that person has been repressed within your own self.

Structure

To see Asian-style structures in your dream, represents feelings that are foreign to you, particularly if you are not of Asian descent.

Studying

To dream that you are studying, signifies that you intellect and knowledge will catapult you into a path of success and wealth.

Stuck

To dream that you are stuck, represents helplessness and feeling of being unable to escape from life's problems/stress. You have lost confidence in yourself and in your ability to move ahead in your life. Your lack of clear goals and low self-esteem may be a common cause for such dreams.

Stuffed Animal

To see a stuffed animal in your dream, represents an immature attitude. You may be trying to escape from your daily responsibilities and problems. Alternatively, it may indicate your need to relax and be less serious. You need to allow your mind and body to rejuvenate.

To dream that a stuffed animal is choking you, indicates that something that was originally emotionally comforting is now giving you much stress. You are feeling emotionally restricted and unable to communicate how you feel especially in matters of the heart.

Stutter

To dream that you stutter, indicates your inability to make yourself heard or express yourself clearly. You may be trying to hide and conceal how you really feel.

Styrofoam

To see Styrofoam in your dream, indicates that you are undergoing some form of transition in your life. In particular to see a Styrofoam cup in your dream, suggests that you are feeling somewhat insecure or instable in a relationship.

Stumble

Please See Trip.

Submarine

To see a submarine in your dream, indicates that you are cautiously exploring your emotions and examining your unconscious feelings. You still remain guarded about certain emotional issues. Alternatively, the submarine indicates that you need to adapt a different perspective and understanding. You may need to get down to the core of some situation or problem.

Subway

To dream that you are in the subway, denotes that you are reaching your goal via unconscious methods. You may be exploring hidden aspects of yourself. Alternatively, it suggests that you are making a hasty decision.

Sucking

To dream that you are sucking on something, indicates that you need emotional nurturance. You are expressing a desire to escape from your daily responsibilities. Alternatively, it may represent low self-esteem and your feelings of inferiority. The dream may also be a metaphor for "sucking up" to someone.

To dream that someone is sucking on you, suggests that you are feeling drained, physically and/or emotionally. You feel that you are too much of a giver in a situation or relationship.

Suffocating

To dream that you are suffocating, signifies that you are feeling smothered or oppressed by some situation/relationship. Something or someone is holding your back. You are experiencing stress and tension.

Sugar

To see or eat sugar in your dream, signifies that pleasures and enjoyment that you are denying yourself in your life. You need to indulge yourself sometimes and forget about the consequences.

To see a sugar cube in your dream, suggests that you need to lighten up and quit being so serious.

Sugar Cane

To dream that you are eating sugar cane, is a good omen signaling vitality in health and prestige in your social circle.

Suicide

To dream that you commit suicide, denotes that conditions in your life is so frustrating that you are no longer willing to cope with a situation or relationship in the same way as you did in the past. Alternatively, you may be unable to overcome feelings of guilt and thus turning the aggression on yourself. On a more positive note, it may suggest that you are saying good-bye to one aspect of yourself or character that your have been carrying around.

To see someone commit suicide in you dream, highlights your concerns for that person. Also consider what characteristics and qualities in that person you may be trying to "kill" and annihilate in your own self. Perhaps you hope that you are not like that person in some way and are making attempts to get rid of those traits within your own self.

Suit

To dream that you are wearing a suit, indicate that you want to be acknowledged and recognized for our abilities and skills. You do now want your power to go unnoticed.

Suitcase

To see a suitcase in your dream, indicates that you are a very together person. You keep attitudes and behavior in check. Alternatively, it is symbolic of a much needed vacation or break. You need some changes in your life.

Sulfur

To see sulfur in your dream, represents a higher level of reasoning. You need to trust your intuitive side as well as your rational side.

Summer

To dream about summer, represents growth, knowledge and maturity. You are showing tolerance and expanding your realm of understanding .

Sun

To see the sun in your dream, symbolizes peace of mind, enlightenment, tranquility, fortune, goodwill, and insight. It also represents radiant energy. It is a good omen to have the sun shining in your dream.

Sunburn

To dream that you have a sunburn, indicates that there is an emotional situation or problem that you can no longer avoid. There is some urgent matter that is literally burning through to your soul and demands your immediate attention.

Sundial

To see a sundial in your dream, indicates that something in your waking life is not quite real. You may be trying to live up to unrealistic expectations or goals.

Sunflower

To see a sunflower in your dream, symbolizes warmth, abundance, longevity, and prosperity. The sunflower also serves to point you in the right direction and is a source of spiritual guidance. Even through difficult times, you will persevere. Alternatively, the sunflower may denote haughtiness. You may be deceived by the false appearance of others.

Sunglasses

To dream that you are wearing sunglasses, indicates your poor perception. You tend to see the dark or negative side of things. Perhaps you don't want to see or be seen.

Sunrise

To see the sunrise in your dream, represents new beginnings, renewal of life and energy, and fulfillment of your goals and purpose. It may also denote that you are about to embark on a new adventure in your personal life.

Sunset

To see the sunset in your dream, indicates the end of a cycle or condition. It is a period of rest, renewal, and evaluation.

Sunshine

To dream of sunshine, indicates that you are experiencing some sort of emotional or situational breakthrough. You are headed on the right track.

Suntan

To dream that you have a suntan, signifies the shadow aspect of yourself. It represents your primal instincts and natural senses. It is also indicative of hard work and owning up to your responsibilities.

To dream that someone else has a suntan, suggests that you not acknowledging a quality or aspect of that person within your own self.

Superhero

To dream that you are a superhero, represents your above-average talents, ideas, and other hidden abilities that you may not realize you possessed.

The Supremes

To see the Supremes in your dream, signifies your achievements. The Supremes may also be a metaphor for being supreme or being at the top of some situation or circumstance.

Surfboard

To see or ride a surfboard in your dream, suggests that you are going with the flow of things. You have giving in to the existing rhythm and is just there for the ride. The dream may trying to tell you that you need to take more initiative in where you want to go and what you want to do.

Surfing

To dream that you are surfing, indicates the ups and downs of some emotional situation or relationship. You may feel overwhelmed. One minute you can be in control of your emotions and the next minute you are not.

Surgery

To dream that you or someone else is undergoing surgery, signifies the opening of the Self and/or the need for emotional healing. You need to "cut out" or eliminate something from your life. Alternatively, you are feeling the influence of some authority figure. A more literal interpretation of this dream may reflect your concerns about upcoming surgery or about your health.

Surprise

To dream that you are pleasantly surprised, indicates that you are opened in acknowledging and confronting your unconscious feelings.

To dream that you are unpleasantly surprised, suggests fear of the unexpected and unknown. You are not wanting to face your feelings.

Surrender

To dream that you surrender, suggests that you need to rid yourself of past emotions and habits.

Suspended

To dream that you are suspended from school, indicates that you are feeling disconnected. You may be questioning your identity and who you are. Perhaps you are questioning your future. Alternatively, it refers to feelings of guilt and shame from your actions. You need to clear your conscience.

Swab

To see or use a swab in your dream, represents your need for healing and/or cleansing.

Swallow

To dream that you swallow something, indicates that you are holding back your feelings or words. You may feel unable to express your anger.

To see a swallow in your dream, symbolizes renewal and fresh beginnings.

Swamp

To see a swamp in your dream, symbolizes aspects of yourself that are repressed and dark. You may be feeling insecure. The dream may also be a pun on feeling swamped from work, a relationship, or other emotional burden.

To dream that you are walking through a swampy area, foretells that you will be find yourself in an adverse situation. Disappointments in love may also be implied from this symbol. You will suffer much displeasure from unwise conduct of those around you. On a less negative note, walking through a swamp, denotes that you will experience prosperity and pleasure, but through dangerous and intriguing means.

Swan

To see a swan in a lake or pond, is a good omen, signaling a future of prestige and wealth. Swans are symbolic of grace, beauty, and dignity.

Swastika

To see the swastika in your dream, symbolizes hatred, evil, cruelty, and destruction. It is commonly associated with the Nazis.

Swearing

To dream that you are swearing, suggests that you need to stop allowing others to harass you. Others see you as someone who they can easily take advantage of.

To hear others swear in your dream, indicates that you have overlooked an urgent matter or situation. Someone may even need to be rescued from some unusual circumstances. It may be your job to protect them.

Sweat

To dream that you are sweating, suggests that you are experiencing some overwhelming anxiety, stress, fear, or nervousness in your life. This dream may serve to remind you that in order to achieve success, you need to endure the struggle and efforts that go along with success. Alternatively, it may signify a kind of cleansing or ridding of bad karma. You may be going through an emotional cool-off period.

Sweater

To see or wear a sweater in your dream, symbolizes your continuing connection and strong ties with your family and home life. Alternatively, it represents a kind of innocence, immaturity, and/or naive thinking.

To dream that you are knitting a sweater, symbolizes your creativity. It may also indicate that you need practice patience.

Sweeping

To dream that you are sweeping, implies that you are clearing your mind of emotional and mental clutter. You are taking a new stance and have a fresh attitude toward life. Alternatively, you may be ignoring some important facts or going against what you gut and intuition is saying.

Sweet Potato

To see or eat a sweet potato in you dream, suggests that your libido is stronger than the person that you are with or vice versa. You need to try and compromise aspects of yourself in order to make the relationship comfortable and satisfying for both.

Sweets

To see or eat sweets in you dream, represents indulgence, sensuality, and some forbidden pleasure. Perhaps you have been depriving yourself of some joy or pleasure. Alternatively, it may symbolize your rewards. This dream symbol may also be a metaphor for your sweetie or the special someone in your life.

Swimming

To dream that you are swimming, suggests that you are exploring aspects of your unconscious mind and emotions. The dream may be a sign that you are seeking some sort of emotional support. It is a common dream image for people going through therapy.

To dream that you are swimming underwater, suggests that you are completely submerged in your own feelings. You are forcing yourself to deal with your emotional difficulties.

Swing

To dream that you are on a swing, represents an expression of great satisfaction and freedom. It also symbolizes cycles and movement. Alternatively, it signifies a desire for sexual variety.

To see a swing set in your dream, indicates memories from childhood. You may feel a need to escape from your current responsibilities and relax.

To dream that you are swinging, suggests that you are going back and forth in some situation and need to make up your mind.

Sword

To dream that you are wielding a sword, represents your ambition, competitive nature decisiveness and will power.. You seek to hold a position of prestige, authority, and distinction. Alternatively, the sword can be seen as a phallic symbol and thus represent masculine power.

Symbol

To see an unknown symbol in your dream, indicates your ambivalence, confusion, or ignorance in a situation. Consider what the symbol resembles for additional significance.

Symphony

To dream that you are attending a symphony, represents harmony and cooperation in a situation or relationship. The dream may serve as a form of inspiration and renewal. You are feeling emotionally and mentally uplifted.

Syringe

To see a syringe in your dream, signifies that you need to inject more enthusiasm, fun, or determination into your life. Consider also the contents of the syringe and how it would effect you.

From a Freudian perspective, the needle and its contents represents the penis and intercourse.

Please see also Injection.

Syrup

To see syrup in your dream, symbolizes sentimentality and nostalgia. Alternatively, you may have found yourself in a sticky situation.

T

To see the letter T in your dream, represents your stubbornness and your refusal to change your attitudes and opinions.

Table

To see a table in your dream, represents social unity and the potential for a meeting or gathering. It refers to your social and family connections. If the table is broken or not functional, then it suggests some dissension in a group. Perhaps there is something you cannot hold inside any longer and need to bring it out in the open.

To dream that you are setting the table, suggests that you laying the groundwork for a plan or personal matter. It also implies confidence.

To see a round table in your dream, indicates evenness, sharing, cooperation and equal rights and opportunities for all. It may also symbolize honesty, loyalty, and chivalry.

To dream that you are lying on a table, indicates your need for nourishment and relaxation. It relates to health concerns and anxieties about your well-being.

To dream that a table is walking or moving by itself, signifies that you will go through a series of new changes in your life as a way to relieve yourself from some dissatisfaction.

Tablecloth

To see a soiled tablecloth in your dream, signifies disobedience and quarreling.

Tacks

To see tacks in your dream, symbolizes annoyances in your life causing you to be very confrontational and quarrelsome.

To dream that you are pushing or driving a tack, signifies that you will overcome your rivals.

Tadpoles

To see tadpoles in your dream, denotes that your uncertainty in some business endeavor will give you much anxiety and worry.

Tail

To see only the tail of an animal in your dream, signifies annoyances and complications in situations where pleasure was surely to be expected.

To dream that you have grown a tail of an animal, forewarns that your evil and manipulative ways will catch up with you, giving you much distress and trouble.

To dream that you cut of the tail of an animal, symbolizes that you will suffer misfortune as a result of you careless ways.

Tailor

To see a tailor in your dream, forewarns that there will be trouble and much arguments before a journey.

To dream that a tailor is taking your measurements, signifies that you will get into an quarrelling match over a disagreement.

Talisman

To dream that you are wearing a talisman, signifies pleasant friends and living the good life.

To dream that you lover gives you a talisman, denotes that you will marry successful.

Talking

To dream that you are talking does not have any significance unless it is unusual or bizarre. Consider also if what you say evoke strong feelings or behavioral reactions.

To hear others talking loudly in your dream, signifies that you will be accused of not minding your own business and butting into everybody else's affairs.

Tall

To dream that you are taller than someone, indicates that you may be looking down on that person. You may feel that you are now above him or her. Alternatively, it represents authority and pride.

To dream that others are taller than you, suggests that you may have a tendency to overlook things. Perhaps you feel that a higher power is always looking over you and judging your actions.

Tallow

To see tallow in your dream, signifies that love and wealth will vanish quickly if you are not cautions and continue to carry on your careless way.

Tambourine

To see or play a tambourine in your dream, foretells that you will have much pleasure and enjoyment from an event that is soon to occur.

Tank

To see a tank filled with water in your dream, signifies prosperity and satisfaction with the current state of your life.

To see a tank truck in your dream, suggests that you are willing to find protection via destructive means. The way you are expressing your anger and feelings my be hurtful and volatile.

Tannery

To see a tannery in your dream, forewarns that you will catch some contagious disease.

To dream that you are a tanner, signifies that you have to engage in some work which is not what you want to do, but must continue to work for the livelihood of those dependant on you.

To dream that you are buying leather goods from the tannery, foretells that you will make little friends on your path to success and to the top of the social ladder.

Tape

To see or use tape in your dream, signifies unprofitable work and fruitless endeavors.

Tapestry

To see tapestry in your dream, signifies luxurious living and pleasurable surroundings.

To see torn and ragged tapestries, signifies that you will lack resources to satisfy your needs and desires.

To dream that the walls of your rooms are covered in tapestry, signifies that you will marry someone who is wealthy and high in position.

Tapeworm

To have or see a tapeworm in your dream, forewarns of poor health and little pleasure.

Tar

To see tar in your dream, signifies your dependency on something or someone. You need to be more self-reliant. Tar is also symbolic of the unconscious and the negative aspect of the Self.

Tarantula

To see a tarantula in your dream, represents your dark and sinister side.

Target

To dream that you are a target, forewarns that your reputation is in danger as a consequence of the jealousies of people around you.

Tarot Cards

To dream of a tarot reading, indicates your current situation and state of mind. You are open to exploring your unconscious thoughts and feelings. Pay attention to what the Tarot Cards revealed. Consider the following general meanings of the four Tarot suits: The Wands represent fire, inspiration, spirituality, action, initiative, and the Psyche. The suit of the Swords signify air, determination, strength, faith, and conquering of fear. The Cups symbolize water, emotions, purity, and your outlook toward life and the future. Finally, the Pentacles denote finances, social influence, worldly knowledge, and your connection with nature and earth.

Tassels

To see tassels in your dream, foretells that you will attain and reach your goals and ambitions.

Tattoo

To dream that you have tattoos, signifies that some urgent and difficult business will call you away from your home for an extended period of time. It may also signal a new stage in your life.

To see tattoos on others in your dream, denotes that you will be the object of jealousy.

To dream that you are getting a tattoo with a friend, represents your deep bond and long-lasting, solid friendship.

To dream that you are a tattoo artist, signifies that your strange life style will alienate your friends and family.

Taxes

To dream that you are paying taxes, signifies that you will succeed in overcoming your adversaries and destroy those evil influences.

To dream that you are unable to pay taxes, signifies misfortune and ill-conceived undertakings.

Tea

To dream that you are making or drinking tea, represents satisfaction and contentment in your life. You are taking your time with regards to some relationship or situation.

Teacher

To see your teacher (past or present) in your dream, suggests that you are seeking some advice, guidance, or knowledge. You are heading into a new path in life and ready to learn by example or from a past experience. Consider your own personal experiences with that particular teacher. What subject was taught? Alternatively, it may relate to issues with authority and seeking approval. You may going through a situation in your waking life where you feel that you are being treated like a student or in which you feel you are being put to a test.

Please see also <u>School</u>.

Teacups

To see teacups in your dream, signifies pleasantries and joyous affairs.

To dream that you break a teacup, signifies that sudden trouble will interfere with your pleasure and good fortune.

Teal

Please See <u>Duck</u> or See <u>Dream Themes: Colors.</u>

Teakettle

To see a teakettle in your dream, foretells of sudden distressful news.

Tear Gas

To come in contact with tear gas in your dream, suggests that you are feeling suffocated and smothered by some relationship. You need to cleanse yourself and get rid of past pain,

Tears

To dream that you are in tears, signifies that a healing of some sort is taking place in your life. It may also forewarns that will be stricken with some calamity.

To dream that others are in tears, signifies that your sorrow will concern your friends.

To see a teardrop in your dream, represents previous wisdom you have learned and remembered.

Teasing

To dream that you are being teased, signifies that you will win the favor of a wealthy person.

To dream that you are teasing another person, foretells of success in business and that you will be surrounded by cheerful and friendly people.

Teddy Bear

To see or receive a teddy bear in your dream, suggests a regression to an earlier state. It symbolizes lost security, comfort, companionship and implies that you need to be reassured and taken care of. You may be reminiscing about early childhood memories. Alternatively, a teddy bear signifies an immature relationship.

Teenager

If you are beyond your adolescence and you dream that you are a teenager, then it may suggest that you have been acting immaturely. An aspect of yourself may still need some developing in order to achieve a goal or fulfillment. Alternatively, you may be struggling for your independence and autonomy.

Teeth

To dream that you have rotten or decaying teeth, forewarns that your health and/or business is in jeopardy. You may have uttered some false or foul words and those words are coming back to haunt you.

To dream that you are brushing your teeth, signifies your level of confidence, struggles and aggressiveness. You need to look out for yourself and your own interest.

*For an in depth analysis, click on Common Dreams: Teeth

Telegram

To dream that you receive a telegram, foretells of bad news, deceit, and unpleasantness.

To dream that you send a telegram, signifies bitter separation or estrangement from a person nearby.

Telekinesis

To dream that you are telekinetic, represents a higher level of awareness and consciousness. You are not utilizing your full potential and need to start putting your stored energy levels and mental abilities to use. In other words, your dream may imply that you need to put your thoughts into action. For some, dreams of telekinetic powers may indicate your latent paranormal abilities.

Telepathy

To dream that you have telepathy, signifies a personal and highly spiritual message from your unconscious. Your telepathic abilities suggests that you need to pay more attention to what people are telling you and trying to convey to you.

Telephone

To see or hear a telephone in your dream, signifies a message from your unconscious or some sort of telepathic communication. You may be forced to confront issues which you have tried to avoid.

To dream that you do not want to answer the ringing telephone, indicates lack of communication. There is a situation or relationship that you are tying to keep at a distance.

To dream that you have trouble hearing over the telephone, signifies that you are the center of some malicious gossip.

To dream that you are having a telephone conversation with someone your know, signifies an issue that you need to confront with that person. This issue may have to do with letting go some part of yourself.

See The Meaning In Action: "Can't Make Phone Call"

Telescope

To see a telescope in your dream, suggests that you need to take a closer look at some situation. It may also indicate that you are going through a period of uncertain changes.

To dream that you are looking through a telescope at the stars and planets, signifies pleasurable but costly journeys.

Television

To dream that you are watching television, represents your brain, mind and its flowing thoughts. It shows how you are receiving, integrating, and expressing your ideas/thoughts. The programs you dream of watching is an objective view of the things that are in your mind.

See The Meaning In Action: "Roswell" & "TV Dream"

Tempest

To dream that you are caught in a tempest, signifies trouble and the indifference of friends.

See Storm or Cyclones.

Temple

To see a temple in your dream, represents your spiritual thinking, meditation and growth. It is also symbolic of your physical body and the attention you give it.

Temptation

To dream of temptations, signifies that an envious person will try to turn your friends against you and cause you much problems.

Tenant

To dream that you are a tenant, signifies that your new projects will be a failure and as a result you will suffer some loss.

To dream that a tenant pays you money, signifies that you will be successful in you undertaking.

Tennis

To dream that you are playing tennis, represents changes and the need to actively assert yourself. You may be feeling the need to prove yourself time and time again. Alternatively, you may be unable to commit to a situation or decision. You are literally going back and forth between two choices.

Since one of the score in tennis is denoted as "love", then the game of tennis may be a metaphor for a romantic relationship or a courtship.

Tent

To dream that you are in a tent, signifies of a refreshing, but temporary change in your daily routine. It may also mean instability and insecurity in your current situation.

To see a torn tent in your dream, denotes trouble for you.

To see a bunch of tents in your dream, signifies that you will go on a journey with unpleasant companions

Termite

To see termites in your dream, signifies a temporary increase in fortune over a short period of time.

Terrarium

To see a terrarium in your dream, indicates that you are keeping aspects of yourself a secret and protecting yourself from others. Alternatively, the terrarium, symbolizes fertility, creativity, and the birth of new ideas.

Terror

To dream that you are in terror, represents your lost of trust in others.

Terrorist

To see or dream that you are a terrorist, suggests that your frustrations is giving pay to your violent tendencies. You are feeling disempowered.

Test

Please see Common Dreams: Exam.

Testicles

To see testicles in your dream, symbolize raw energy, power, fertility or sexual drive. The dream may refer to anxiety about your sexual prowess. Alternatively, it indicates that you will need a lot of nerve to achieve some task.

Testify

To dream that you are testifying in your dream, represents the truth or what you believe is true.

Thanks

To dream that you are thanking someone, indicates that you are acknowledging and accepting some aspect of that person within your own self.

Thanksgiving

To dream about Thanksgiving, represents togetherness, family reunions, festivities, and your sense of community. The dream is a reflection on your life and the connections that you have made. Alternatively, this dream may be a metaphor indicating that you need to thank somebody. You may be feeling indebted to someone. Consider also your own associations and traditions with Thanksgiving.

Thatch

To dream that you thatch a roof with a perishable material, signifies gloomy surroundings and much discomfort.

Thaw

To see ice thawing in your dream, signifies that a problem that has once given your much worry will soon give you profit and pleasure.

To see the ground thawing after a long freeze, signifies a prosperous future.

Theater

To dream that you are in a theater, signifies that you will derive much pleasure from new companionships. Consider also how the performance parallels to situations in your waking life. Observe how the characters relate to you and how they may represent an aspect of yourself. You may be taking on a new role.

To dream that you are laughing and/or applauding in a theater, indicates that you tend to choose pleasure and instant gratification over working on future goals.

To dream that the theater is on fire, signifies that any new projects you take on will be risky.

Theme Park

Please See Amusement Park.

Thermometer

To read a thermometer in your dream, denotes unsatisfactory business deals and domestic strife.

To see a broken thermometer in your dream, forewarns of illness.

To see the mercury in the thermometer rising, signifies that you will be able to ward off bad luck in your business. To see it falling, denotes that you will be greatly distressed in your business.

Thief

To dream that you are a thief, suggests that you are afraid of losing what you already have. Perhaps you are feeling that you are undeserving of the things you already have. Alternatively, you may be overstepping your boundaries in some situation or relationship.

To dream that you are a witness to a theft, indicates that others are wasting and stealing your time, energy, and ideas.

Thigh

To see your thigh in your dream, symbolizes stamina and endurance. It refers to your ability to perform and do things.

To dream that you are admiring your thigh, signifies your adventurous and daring nature, but you need to be careful with your conduct.

Thimble

To use a thimble in your dream, signifies that you need to tend to the needs of others instead of thinking of your own self-pleasures.

To dream that you lose a thimble, foretells poverty and trouble.

To receive or buy a new thimble, signifies that you will make new friendships that will bring you much joy.

Thirst

To dream that you are thirsty, denotes that you are taking on too much than you can handle and you are reaching for goals that are beyond your reach. If you quench your thirst, then you will achieve your wishes and desires.

Thistle

To see thistle in your dream, represents your need to feel protected. You may be putting up an emotional barrier around you and pushing the people around you away.

Thorns

To see thorns in your dream, signifies dissatisfaction and evil forces that will work to hinder your advancement to the top. You need to put up your defenses. Alternatively, you may be sacrificing your own well-being for others.

Thread

To see thread in your dream, signifies that your road to fortune will be a complicated one. You will need to bind together and strengthen commitments and relationships.

To see broken threads in your dream, forewarns that you will suffer a loss due to the faithlessness of friends.

Threaten

To dream that you threaten others, denotes that you need to assert and stand up for yourself in your waking life.

To dream that you are being threatened, signifies that you have some internalized fear of inadequacy which needs to be addressed.

Threshing

To dream that you are threshing grain, signifies advancement in business and joy amongst family.

Throat

To see your throat in your dream, symbolizes the ability to express yourself and communicate your thoughts/ideas.

To dream that you have a sore throat, suggests that you are having problems saying what you really think. You may feel threatened when you express yourself. Alternatively, your dream may be telling you that you need to swallow your pride.

To see a nice and graceful throat in your dream, foretells of an advancement in your position.

Throne

To dream that you are sitting on a throne, signifies a rapid rise to fame and fortune.

To see others on a throne in your dream, denotes that you will succeed to wealth through the assistance of others.

Thumb

To see a thumb in your dream, indicates that you need to get a grip on things. It is symbolic of power and ability,

To dream that you have no thumbs, denotes poverty and loneliness.

To dream that you have an abnormally large thumb, signifies a rapid rise to success.

To dream that your thumb has a very long nail, denotes that you will be lured by into evil by seeking strange illicit pleasures.

Thunder

To hear thunder in your dream, signifies a violent eruption of anger and aggression. Alternatively, it is an indication that you need to pay attention and learn an important life lesson. .

To experience the incessant pounding of thunder in your dream, signifies great losses and disappointments.

Tick

To see or be bitten by a tick in your dream, suggests that a relationship or situation is sucking all the energy out of you. Ask yourself what in your life is causing you much exhaustion.

Ticket

To see a ticket in your dream, signifies the start of a new endeavor. You have decided on your path and goals in life.

To dream that you lose a ticket, denotes confusion and ambiguity in the direction of your life.

Tickle

To dream that you are being tickled, signifies non-stop worries and sickness.

To dream that you are tickling others, denotes that your weakness and foolishness will hinder you to have any true enjoyment in life.

Ticks

To see ticks in your dream, indicates that something is slowly draining the energy and strength out of you. A relationship, your job, or someone is sucking the life and energy out of you. The dream may also be a pun on being "ticked off" and thus represent your feelings of being annoyed or irritated.

Tidal Wave

To see a tidal wave in your dream, represents an overwhelming emotional issue that demands attention. You may have been keeping your feelings and negative emotions bottled up inside.

To dream that you can create a tidal wave with your mind, is analogous to your ability to control your emotions and keep them in line.

Tie

To see or wear a tie in your dream, represents your obligations and relational bonds. The dream may also be a pun on feeling tied down to a situation or relationship.

Tiger

To see a tiger in your dream, represents power and your ability to exert it in various situations. The dream may also indicate that you to take more of a leadership role. Alternatively, the tiger represents female sexuality, aggression, and seduction.

To dream that you are attacked by a tiger, symbolizes repressed feelings or emotions that frighten you.

To see a caged tiger in your dream, suggests that your repressed feelings/emotions are on the verge of surfacing.

Tightrope

To dream that you are walking on a tightrope, indicates that you are in a very precarious situation. You need to proceed carefully and weigh all the pros and cons of your decisions.

Tights

To dream that you are wearing tights, suggests that you are feeling at ease in exposing aspects of your Self.

Timber

To see timber in your dream, symbolizes prosperity and tranquility.

Time

To dream about time, indicates your fears of not being able to cope with the pressures and stresses of everyday life.

To dream that you do not have enough time, signifies stress, anxiety and fear. You may feel that time is running out in a business or personal matter.

Time Travel

To dream about time travel, indicates your wish to escape from your present reality. You want to go back into the past or jump forward to the future to a period where your hopes are realized. This type also represents your romantic nature or your desire to romanticize everything.

Tin

To see tin in your dream, represents mental and intellectual expansion. You are broadening your mind and opening yourself to new experiences.

Tipsy

To dream that you are tipsy, signifies your carefree nature and jovial disposition.

To see others tipsy in your dream, denotes that you need to be careful in who you associate yourself with. Their actions may reflect on your own character.

Tiptoe

To dream that you are tiptoeing, highlights your grace and poise in a situation or circumstance. It symbolizes your careful understanding of the smaller and minor details in your life. Alternatively, it may indicate your reservation and hesitance in pursuing toward some path.

Tired

To dream that you are tired, suggests that you are feeling emotionally drained and stressed. Dreams about being tired usually reflect how you really feel in your waking state.

Tires

To see tires in your dream, symbolizes that you are dwelling too much in the past and need to move on toward the future. It also refers to your emotional health and how it carries you from one situation to another.

To see or dream that you have a flat tire, indicates that you are feeling weary and emotionally drained. Your goals are temporarily hindered and as a result, you are unable to progress forward.

Toads

To see toads in your dream, suggests that you are trying to hide your true Self. Let the beauty from within shine through.

To kill a toad in your dream, signifies that you will be criticized for your decision.

Toaster

To see a toaster in your dream, suggests that you are quick witted and quick-thinking. It may also refer to your continuous flow of ideas.

Tobacco

To dream that you are smoking tobacco, signifies kind friendships.

To see tobacco growing in your dream, foretells successful enterprises and business, but failure in love.

Tocsin

To hear a tocsin being sounded in your dream, signifies that you will win over an argument.

Toddy

To see a toddy in your dream, signifies an interesting turn of events that will soon change your way of life.

Toes

To see your toes in your dream, represents the way you move and walk through life with such grace and poise (or there lack of). It also signify your path in life. Alternatively, toes may also represent the minor detail of life and how you deal with them.

To dream that your toe nails are growing, symbolize an extension of your understanding in a particular matter.

To dream that you lose or gain a toe(s), suggests that you lack determination and energy needed to move forward in some situation.

To dream that you hurt your toe or that there is a corn or abrasion on it, signifies that you are feeling anxiety about moving forward with something.

To dream that someone is kissing your toe, indicates that they are trying to reassure and reaffirm your progress forward.

Toilet

To see a toilet in your dream, symbolizes a release of emotions or getting rid of something in your life that is useless.

To see a clogged toilet in your dream, signifies that you are holding in and keeping your feelings to yourself. Your emotions have been pent up too long.

To see an overflowing toilet in your dream, denotes your desires to fully express your emotions.

Tomatoes

To see tomatoes in your dream, symbolizes domestic happiness and harmony.

To dream that you are eating tomatoes, foretells of good health.

Tomb

To see tombs on your dream, signifies aspects of yourself which you have kept hidden and buried away.

To dream that you see your own tomb, denotes that you are about to venture into parts of your personality which have been forgotten or have died.

Tongue

To see your own tongue in your dream, signifies the things you say and express. You may have said too much or you may need to express yourself.

To dream that you rip someone else's tongue out, indicates that you are extremely upset with something that this person has said, but you have not been able to fully express your anger. Because you tend to keep your emotions inside, it is finding expression in your dreams in a violent way.

Tonsils

To see your tonsils in your dream, suggests that you are ready to share an aspect of yourself.

Tools

To see or use tools in your dream, represents your self-expression, skills and abilities. You are using the resources that are available to you. Perhaps you need to create and move toward a different direction. Alternatively, it suggests that a situation or relationship is in need of some damage control or attention. According to the Freudian school of thought, tools are symbols of the penis and thus tools being used are symbolic of intercourse.

Toothbrush

To see or use a toothbrush in your dream, suggests that you are feeling defensive about any criticism directed towards you. You are putting up a shield or barrier to protect yourself from potential hurt. Alternatively, it may mean that you are preoccupied with your appearance and worry about how others perceive you.

Toothless

To dream that you are toothless, signifies your inability to reach your goals and advance toward your interests. Gloom and ill health will be part of your setbacks.

To see others toothless in your dream, denotes that your rivals are attempting to bring down your good name. Their attempts will be in vain.

Toothpicks

To see toothpicks in your dream, suggests that you are too picky. It also indicates that you needlessly dwell on minor flaws, faults, and other small issues.

To dream that you are using a toothpick, denotes your role in the downfall of a friend.

Top

To see or spin a top in your dream, represents idleness. You are wasting your time away on frivolous pleasures.

To dream that you are on top, signifies your aspirations and ideals. You are seeking higher understanding and knowledge.

Topaz

To see a topaz in your dream, signifies calmness and relaxation. You need to restore balance in your life.

Topless

To dream that you are topless, signifies your way of showing and exhibiting love. You may be inviting love toward your direction.

Torch

To see torches in your dream, symbolizes much pleasantries and a great outlook in business.

To dream that you are carrying a lit torch, signifies success in love.

Tornado

To see a tornado in your dream, suggests that you are experiencing some extreme emotional outbursts and temper tantrums. Is there a situation or relationship in your life that may be potentially destructive?

To dream that you are in a tornado, signifies that you are feeling overwhelmed and out of control. You will be met with a series of disappointments for the next week or so. Your plans will be filled with complications.

To see several tornadoes in your dream, represent people around you who are prone to violent outbursts and shifting mood swings. It may also symbolize a volatile situation or relationship.

**See The Meaning In Action: "_Tornado_"

Torrent

To see a torrent in your dream, signifies unexpected trouble.

Torso

To notice yours or someone else's torso in your dream, represents an emphasis on your feeling and emotions. It also symbolizes pride and confidence.

Tortoise

To see a tortoise in your dream, suggests that you need to take some chances in order to get ahead in life. The opportunities for advancement are opened to you, but you need to take the next step.

Torture

To dream that you are being tortured, indicates that you are feeling victimized or helpless in some relationship or situation. Alternatively, you may be exhibiting some sadomasochistic desires.

To dream that you are torturing others or see others being tortured, suggests that you are punishing yourself for your own negative or bad habits. You are projecting yourself onto the person or animal being tortured. Consider the symbolism of who is being tortured. Alternatively, the dream may indicate repressed feelings of revenge which you are not able to act on in your waking life.

Touching

To dream that you are touching someone or something, indicates that you are trying to communicate your feelings and your need for contact. You may also be trying to evaluate a situation or gather information about our surroundings.

To dream that you are being touched, represents your closeness and/or relationship with a particular person. It may also mean that you are connected with an aspect of yourself. Or you may be feeling emotional and sensitive.

Toupee

Please see _Hairpiece._

Tourist

To see tourist in your dream, signifies insecurity in love and unfinished tasks.

To dream that you are a tourist, denotes that you will go on a short and pleasant trip.

Tourniquet

To dream that you are using a tourniquet, indicates that you are feeling drained. You need to concentrate your energy on our strengths and now your weaknesses.

Towel

To see or use a towel in your dream, suggests that you need to deal with your emotions in order to move forward in your life. You need to find some sort of a resolution. Alternatively, it represents completion, a fresh start and new transition.

Tower

To see a tower in your dream, signifies high hopes and aspirations. If you are looking down from a tower, then it suggests your perceived superiority over others. Your ego may also be inflated.

To see a water tower in your dream, suggests that you are keeping your emotions inside. You may be unable to express your feelings, especially feelings of love. Alternatively, it indicates a false sense of security.

To dream that you are climbing a tower, denotes you quest for spirituality and unconscious ideas that may be surfacing.

Toy Box

To see a toy box in your dream, indicates that you are putting your childish ways behind you. Alternatively, the dream may represent your need to sort out unresolved issues from your childhood.

Toys

To see toys in your dream, symbolizes childhood, domestic joy and harmony. You may be searching for the comfort and security of home. It also represents playful attitudes and your childish ways.

To see others playing with toys, foretells of a happy and successful marriage.

To dream that you are giving away toys, denotes that you will not be recognized for your good deeds.

Track

To dream that you are tracking something or someone, suggests that you need to get in touch with some aspect of yourself. The dream may be a pun for some goal, person, or ideals which you have lost track of.

To dream that you are being tracked, indicates that you need to be more careful and stand up for yourself. You need to be on your guard and on the defensive.

Tractor

To see or ride a tractor in your dream, represents your resourcefulness and ingenuity.

Trade

To dream that you are trading, denotes mediocre success in business.

Traffic

To dream that you are in traffic, signifies frustrations in life and that things are not going as smoothly as you would like it to. You feel stuck at where you are in life.

Tragedy

To dream of a tragedy, forewarns of misunderstandings and disappointments.

Trailer

To see a trailer in your dream, suggests that you are feeling overburdened. You are carry more weight on your shoulders than you need to. The dream may also indicate that you are more of a follower than a leader.

Trailer Home

To dream that you live in a trailer home, suggests that you are feeling insignificant and undervalued. On the other hand, it may mean that you have a flexible self-image. You are able to adapt to any situation or circumstance.

Train

To see a train in your dream, represents conformity and go along with what everyone else is doing. You have the need to do things in an orderly and sequential manner. In particular, if you see a freight train, then it refers to the burdens and problems that you are hauling around.

To dream that you are on a train, is symbolic of your life's journey and suggests that you are on the right track in life and headed for the right direction. Alternatively, you have a tendency to worry needlessly over a situation that will prove to work out in the end.

To see or dream that you are in a train wreck, suggests chaos. The path to goals are not going according to the way you planned it out. Or you may be lacking self-confidence and having doubt in your ability to reach your goals.

To dream that you are the engineer, signifies that you are in complete control of a particular situation in your waking life.

To dream that you miss a train, denotes missed opportunities or nearly escaping your death.

Training

To dream that you are training for something, suggests that you are lacking self-confidence and are having anxieties about your ability. The dream may also reflect a desire to change your status or position in life.

Traitor

To dream that you are or accused of being a traitor, signifies unfavorable situations and little pleasure for you.

To see a traitor in your dream, denotes that you rivals are doing their best to distress you.

Trampoline

To dream that you are jumping on a trampoline, represents your resilience and your ability to bounce back from difficult and emotional times.

To see a trampoline in your dream, symbolizes the ups and downs of life.

Trance

To dream that you are in a trance, suggests that you need to look within yourself. Explore your emotions and open yourself up to others.

Transmission

To dream that you are repairing a transmission, suggests that you need to pace yourself and learn to adjust to your surroundings and situations. Perhaps you are going to fast or moving to slowly.

Transplant

To dream that you have an organ transplant, suggest that an aspect of yourself is worn out. You are seeking a fresh start and new beginning.

Transsexual

To dream that you are transsexual, symbolizes your anxieties or ambivalence about masculine/feminine roles or passive/aggressive behavior. You may be reluctant in dealing with these issues. If you are considering or awaiting transsexual surgery, then the dream may represent your anxieties and fears about the surgery, recovery, and life after surgery.

To see a transsexual in your dream, indicates that the masculine and feminine aspects of your Self has been damaged. You may be unwilling to confront your shadow self.

Transformation

To dream that you are undergoing a transformation, indicates a need for change or a deviation from your usual routine. It also suggests your expanded awareness and a deep-level personality development.

Please see also Metamorphosis.

Trap

To dream that you are setting a trap, signifies that you will use sneaky and sly methods to carry out your plans.

To dream that you caught an animal in a trap. denotes success in your chosen career.

To see an empty trap in your dream, signifies failure in business and illness in the family.

To dream that you are caught in a trap, denotes that you feel confined and restricted in a job, career, health, or a personal relationship. It may also mean that you will be outwitted by your rivals.

Trapeze

To see a trapeze act in your dream, signifies a carefree attitude toward life. You may want to escape from your daily responsibilities and take some time to relax.

To dream that you are swinging on a trapeze, signifies a desire or wish for sexual variety/adventure.

Traveling

To dream that you are traveling, signifies the journey toward your life goals and a journey through life in general. that you enjoy what you do and find much pleasure in it.

To dream that you are traveling through an unknown area, denotes the lurking of your rivals.

To dream that you are traveling in a car filled with people, signifies that you will make new and fun friends and exciting adventures.

To dream that you are traveling in a car by yourself, signifies troubling matters ahead for you.

Tray

To see trays in your dream, signifies you senseless spending.

Treasure Chest

To see a treasure chest in your dream, represents your hidden talents. It also represents a sense of security and belonging. You are content with where you are in a situation or relationship.

To dream that you are looking though the treasure chest, suggests that you are trying to recapture something valuable from your past.

Treasures

To dream that you find treasures, signifies that you have unveiled some hidden skill or talent. You will also receive an expected helping hand in your road to success.

To dream that you lose treasures, denotes bad luck in business and the revolving door of friends that has passed through your life.

Tree House

To see or dream that you are in a tree house, indicates that you are trying to escape from your waking problems. You are blocking off the harsh reality of daily life.

To dream that you are building a tree house, suggests that you are working hard to realize your hopes and goals. The dream is about self-development and maximizing your own potential.

Trees

To see lush green trees in your dream, symbolizes new hopes, growth and desires. It also implies strength and stability. You are concentrating on your own self-development and individuation.

To dream that you are climbing a tree, signifies that you will achieve your career goals and reach those high places in society. The degree of difficulty to which you climb the tree will measure the speed of your achievement of these goals

To dream that you cut down a tree, signifies that you are wasting your energy, time, and money on foolish pursuits.

To see a falling tree in your dream, indicates that you are off balance and out of sync. You are off track and headed in the wrong direction.

**See The Meaning In Action: "Scissors In The Forest"

Trenches

To see trenches in your dream, signifies that you need to be cautious with any strangers for you are threatened with loss and treachery.

Trespass

To dream that you are trespassing, suggests that you are forcing your beliefs on others. It may also mean that you are being overly attentive and need to give someone their breathing room.

Trial

To dream that you are on trial, indicates that you need to be more accepting of yourself and less judgmental on others.

Triangle

To see triangles in your dream, symbolizes aspirations, potential and truth. It is also a symbol of spirituality: the body, mind, and spirit. Alternatively, it may refer to a love triangle in your waking life.

Trickster

To see a trickster in your dream, signifies deceit or a cruel and cynical side of your own character.

Tricycle

To see a tricycle in your dream, indicates an ease of tension in your life. It may also symbolize simplicity and a carefree nature.

Trident

To see or use a trident in your dream, symbolizes the God of the Sea. Because of the relation to the sea, you may want to consider the symbolism of water and the ocean. Alternatively, It is also indicative of your creative energies and sensitivity.

Trip

To dream that you trip on something, indicates that something is out of order with your life. Things are not going as smoothly as your want as you are faced with minor obstacles.

To dream that you are going on a trip, suggests that you are in need of a change of scenery. You are feeling overworked and need to take time out for yourself for some fun and relaxation.

Tripe

To dream that you are eating tripe, foretells that you will be met with disappointment in some important matters.

To see tripe in your dream, signifies sickness and lurking danger.

Triplets

To see triplets in your dream, signifies that you will be met with success in situations where you assumed failure was expected.

For a man to dream that his lover is having triplets, signifies that a menacing dispute will come to a pleasant and amicable end.

For a woman to dream that she is giving birth to triplets, symbolizes that she will succeed in business and wealth, but fail in love.

To hear or see crying triplets in your dream, signifies a hasty reconciliation to a disagreement.

Tripod

To see a tripod in your dream, represents stability and swiftness.

Troll

To see a troll in your dream, suggests that you have an inferior self-image about yourself. It may also indicate that you are belittling yourself or others. The troll in your dream may represent someone in your waking life who you need to avoid.

Please See Also Dwarf.

Trophy

To see a trophy in your dream, denotes that you will reap part of the fortune or pleasure from the endeavors of others.

To dream that you are giving away a trophy, denotes questionable pleasure and doubtful fortune.

Trousers

To see trousers in your dream, signifies temptation and that you will be lured into dishonorable activity.

To dream that you put on your trousers the wrong way, signifies your gravitation for oddness and peculiarity.

Trout

To see a trout in your dream, symbolizes increasing prosperity.

To dream that you are eating trout, signifies your cheerful attitude towards life.

To dream that you catch a trout, signifies pleasure. If it falls back into the water, then your happiness will be short-lived.

Trowel

To see a trowel in your dream, represents the spreading of kindness and affection.

Truck

To see a truck in your dream, implies that you are overworked. You may be taking on too many tasks and responsibilities and are weighing you down. On a side note, pregnant women often dream of trucks or driving trucks. This may be a metaphor of the load they are are carrying or an expression of their changing bodies.

Truck Stop

To dream that you are at a truck stop, suggests that you need to reenergize and recharge yourself. You need to take some rest.

Trumpet

To see a trumpet in your dream, signifies a sudden new preoccupation that has taken over part of your time.

To dream that you are blowing a trumpet, denotes that you will achieve your desires. Or it may simply be a way for your subconscious to get your attention.

Trunk

To see a trunk in your dream, represents old memories, ideals, hopes, and old emotions. It may indications issues and feelings that you have not dealt with.

To see the trunk of a car in your dream, signifies a pleasant journey.

To see the trunk of a tree, signifies your inner sense of well being and personality. If the trunk is thick and large, then it denotes that you are a strong, rugged and durable person. If the trunk is thin and narrow, then it suggests that you are a highly sensitive person.

Trust

To dream about trust, symbolizes self-acceptance. You need to work on integrating aspects of yourself.

T-Shirt

To see or wear a T-shirt in your dream, suggests that you need to take it easy and relax.

Tsunami

To see a tsunami in your dream, represents that you are being overwhelmed by some repressed feelings or unconscious material that is rising up to the surface. You are experiencing some unhappiness and emotional instability in some waking situation.

Tug Of War

To dream that you are playing tug of war, suggests that you need to balance various aspects of your personality. You need to learn to compromise.

Tulips

To see tulips in your dream, indicates fresh new beginnings. You are loving life! Tulips are also symbolic of faith, charity, and hope. Consider it to also be a pun "two lips". Perhaps it is hinting to a kiss?

Tumor

To dream that you or someone has a tumor, suggests that some repressed memory or feeling remains unsettled and is threatening to emerge into your consciousness. You need to confront these issues. Consider where in the body is this tumor is located for additional symbolism.

Tumble

To dream that you are tumbling, signifies carelessness.

To see others tumbling, denotes that the negligence of others will mean your gain and profit.

Tunnel

To see a tunnel in your dream, represents the vagina, womb, and birth. Thus it may refer to a need for security and nurturance.

To dream that you are going through a tunnel, suggests that you are exploring aspects of your unconscious. You are opening yourself to a brand new awareness. Alternatively, it indicates your limited perspective.

To see the light at the end of a tunnel, symbolizes hope.

Turban

To see or dream that you are wearing a turban, suggests that you are feeling confined by what society considers normal.

Turf

To see green turf in your dream, signifies an interesting new affair that will occupy your mind.

Turkey

To see a turkey in your dream, indicates that you have been foolish. You are not thinking clearly. Alternatively, it may represent Thanksgiving and thus, a time of togetherness and family,

To see sick or dead turkeys in your dream, denotes an attack to your pride.

To see a flying turkey in your dream, foretells of a rapid rise from obscurity to a position of prominence.

To dream that you hunt turkeys, signifies that you will acquire wealth through dishonest means.

Turnips

To see or eat turnips in your dream, indicates that you will overcome your current problems. It is symbolic of compassion, wealth, or a bright outlook.

Turquoise

To see turquoise in your dream, symbolizes good luck and fortune. It is said that the turquoise gemstone wards off evil. Additionally, it possess healing energy and acts to unify forces between the spirits of the earth and the air.

As a color, turquoise is symbolic of healing power and natural energy. It is often associated with the sun, fire, and male power.

Turtle

To see turtles in your dream, suggests that you will make slow but steady progress. You need to slow down and pace yourself. Alternatively, it indicates that you are sheltering yourself from the realities of life.

To dream that you are being chased by a turtle, indicates that you are hiding behind a facade instead of confronting the things that are bothering you.

Tuxedo

To see or wear a tuxedo in your dream, represents culture, sophistication, and/or grace. It refers to a cultivated passion or to your desires for the finer things in life. Alternatively, it suggests that you want to amount to something in your life. You want to make a name for yourself and establish your reputation.

Tweezers

To see tweezers in your dream, denotes the uncomfortable situation that you have been subjected to by your companions has caused you much discontentment and unhappiness.

Twigs

To see twigs in your dream, represents small or minor growth that is occurring in your life.

Twilight

To see the twilight in your dream, signifies an end to old conditions and situations.

Twine

To see twine in your dream, forewarns of complications in your business which will be difficult to resolve.

Twins

To see twins in your dream, signifies ambivalence, dualities and opposites. It also represents security in business, faithfulness, and contentment with life. It may also mean that you are either in harmony with or in conflict between ideas and decisions.

To see twins fighting in your dream, represents a conflict between the opposites of your psyche. One twin signifies emergence of unconscious material and suppressed feelings, while the other twin represents the conscious mind. There is some situation that you are not confronting.

Typewriter

To see a typewriter in your dream, indicates that you need to open the lines of communication with someone in your life.

Typing

To dream that you are typing, signifies your difficulties in verbally expressing your thoughts.

Typhoid

To dream that you have typhoid, signifies that you need to be cautious of your surroundings and be on alert for rivals meant to do you harm.

U

U-Turn

To make a u-turn in your dream, indicates that you are altering the course of your life. You are changing directions and starting on a different path. It may also mean that you have made a wrong decision or choice.

To see a no u-turn sign, suggests that you cannot take back what has already been done. There is no turning back on the choices you made.

UFO

To see a UFO in your dream, signifies your desires to find your spiritual purpose in life. Alternatively, it indicates that you are feeling alienated from those around you. The dream may also be a metaphor suggesting that you are a little "spacey" or have "spaced out" attitude. You need to be more grounded and come back to reality.

Please see also Spaceship.

Ugly

To dream you or others are ugly, signifies aspects of yourself that disgust and repulses you. These may be feelings you have rejected or repressed.

Ulcer

To see an ulcer in your dream, signifies withdrawal from or loss of friends and loved ones.

Umbilical Cord

To see an umbilical cord in your dream, represents your lack of individuality. You may be expressing some anxiety about being on your own and/or supporting yourself.

To dream that you are cutting an umbilical cord, indicates that you need to be self-sufficient and stand on your own two feet. You need to pull yourself back up and get back into the swing of things.

Umbrella

To see an umbrella in your dream, suggests that you are putting up a shield against your emotions and trying to avoid dealing with them. It is also symbolic of emotional security. If the umbrella is leaking, then it indicates that you are unprepared in facing your problems.

To dream that you cannot open you umbrella and it is raining, then it suggests that you are open to confronting your own feelings and letting your emotions come to the surface.

Uncle

To see an uncle in your dream, represents some aspect of your family heritage and traits. It may also symbolize new ideas and emerging awareness.

Unemployed

To dream that you are unemployed, represents your lack of self-worth or lack of inspiration. You may feel that you are going no where in life.

Underground

To dream that you live underground, symbolizes loss of fortune and reputation and the desire for greater security and peace of mind. You may be pushing thoughts and issues into your subconscious mind.

To dream that you are riding in an underground railway, signifies anxiety and distress arising from a peculiar activity.

Undertaker

To see an undertaker or dream that you are one, represents your need to take charge of your life and the responsibilities that come with it.

Underwater

To dream that you are underwater, suggests that you are feeling overcome with emotions and are in need of greater control in your life. You may be in over your head regarding some situation.

To dream that you are breathing underwater, represents a retreat back into the womb. You want to return to a state where you were dependent and free from responsibilities. Perhaps you are feeling helpless, unable to fulfill your own needs and caring for yourself. Alternatively, you may be submerged in your emotions.

Underwear

To dream that you are in your underwear, signifies a situation that has created a loss of respect for you. Alternatively, it symbolizes some aspect of yourself that is private. If you feel ashamed of being seen in your underwear, then it indicates your hesitance in revealing your true feelings, attitudes, and other hidden habits/ideas.

To dream that someone is in their underwear, signifies an embarrassing and inexplicable situation. Alternatively, you may see that person for who he/she really is.

To see dirty or torn underwear, suggests that you are not comfortable in your own skin and have feelings of inadequacy. You may possess negative and critical feelings about yourself. You may also feel uncomfortable about your sexuality.

*Please see also Panties.

Undress

To dream that you are undressing, denotes scandalous behavior and possible separation from a loved one.

To see someone undress, signifies bad luck and loss of love and money.

To dream that someone is undressing you, signifies dangerous flirtations and stolen pleasures.

Unfortunate

To dream that you are unfortunate, signifies a turn of good luck will come your way.

To dream that another is unfortunate, signifies failure for this person.

Unicorn

To see a unicorn in your dream, symbolizes high ideals, hope and insight in a current situation. It also symbolizes power, gentleness, and purity. Alternatively, it may represent your one-sided views.

Unicycle

To dream that you are riding a unicycle, signifies that you are in total control of a situation and exercising authority in both personal and business matters.

Uniform

To see a person in uniform, indicates that you may be conforming too much and living in too much of a regimented manner. Also, you may need to fit in and stop going against the crowd.

To see people in strange uniforms, signifies disruption.

University

*Please See College.

U. S. Mail Box

To see a U.S. Mail Box in your dream, foretells that you may be asked to participate in illegal activity.

To dream that you are mailing a letter, signifies your accountability in a matter or problem at hand.

U. S. Visa

To dream that you are granted a US visa, represents how you feel about the United States and what it stands for to you. For example, if, for you, the US stands for freedom, then being granted a visa from the US may parallel a life situation in which you experience some new found freedom. You may be going through a period of self-exploration.

Unknown

To see an unknown person in your dream, signifies a part of yourself that is repressed and hidden. Alternatively, it symbolizes the archetypal dream helper who is trying to offer some insight and advice.

Up

To dream of being or moving up, suggests that you are emerging from some depressing or negative situation. You may be feeling high or euphoric. The dream may also compensate for your waking feelings of sadness. Alternatively, it signifies that your ego is inflated.

According to Jung, some material or repressed thoughts may be emerging from your unconscious.

Uproot

To see uprooted plants in your dream, indicates that you are out of balance. You may be feeling disconnected or distant from others. It could represent broken family connections or failed attempts in reestablishing familial ties.

Upside Down

To dream that you are upside down, suggests that there is some situation or problem in your waking life that you need to straighten you. It may also mean that your initial assumptions were completely opposite of what you thought.

Uranus

To see Uranus in your dream, represents originality, independence, freedom, and individualism. You are rebellious and unconventional in your thinking. It is also an indication of the unexpected.

Urinal

To see a urinal in your dream, signifies disorder in your personal relationships.

Urination

To see urine in your dream, signifies feelings you have rejected.

To dream that you are urinating, symbolizes a cleansing and release of negative or repressed emotions. Urination is symbolic of having or lacking basic control in your life.

To dream that you are urinating in public, symbolizes a lack of privacy in your affairs or your need to make a public apology or confession.

Urn

To see an urn in your dream, represents feelings that have burned out or that you are feeling burnt out and exhausted. It also symbolizes the past.

Utensils

To see utensils in your dream, indicates innovation. It also signifies your willingness to help others and lend a hand.

V

Vacation

To dream that you are on vacation, indicates that you need a break to recharge your energies and revitalize yourself. You need to break out of your daily routine and do something different. Alternatively, it represents your achievements. You are giving yourself a pat on the back and feel deserving of a reward for your hard work.

Vaccination

To dream of getting a vaccination, suggests that you need to overcome your vulnerability. It may also signify that you are susceptible to the charms of a person of the opposite sex.

To dream of seeing others get vaccinated, signifies disappointments in love and business.

Vacuum

To see a vacuum in your dream, suggests feelings of emptiness. You may be experiencing a void in your life. Alternatively, you may need to clean up your act and your attitude.

To dream that you are vacuuming, signifies a loss of control.

Vagina

To see your vagina in your dream, suggests issues with your femininity and you sexual needs/urges.

Vagrant

To dream that you are a vagrant, denotes that you are trying to escape from the confines of social expectations. It may also indicate your current condition of poverty and misery.

To speak and give to the vagrant, symbolizes your generosity and are surrounded by valuable friends.

**See The Meaning In Action: "A Vagrant Is Chasing Me"*

Valentine

To dream that you are sending valentines, indicates your need to express more love and affection.

To dream that you are receiving a valentine, represents your likeability, compassion and good-hearted nature.

To see a box of valentines, signifies that an old lover may come back into the picture.

Valley

To dream of a valley, signifies positive change resulting in happiness and peace.

Vampire

To see a vampire in your dream, symbolizes seduction and sensuality, as well as fear and death. The vampire represents contrasting images of civilized nobility and aggression/ferocity. It may depict someone in your waking life whose charm may ultimately prove harmful. Deep down inside you know that this person is bad for you, yet you are still drawn to it. Vampires also sometimes relate to decisions about sex and losing your virginity. Alternatively, to see a vampire suggests that you are feeling physically or emotionally drained. The vampire may also be symbolic for someone who is addicted to drugs or someone in an obsessive relationship.

To dream that you are a vampire, signifies that you are sucking in the life energy of others for your own selfish benefit.

**See The Meaning In Action: "Fighting Vampires & Alluring Vampires"*

Van

To see or drive a van in your dream, symbolizes convenience and/or practicality. Consider the load that you are carrying and what you can handle. Don't stress yourself out.

Vanilla

To taste or smell vanilla in your dream, indicates a welcoming experience or inviting situation.

Vanish

Please see <u>Disappear</u>.

Varnishing

To dream that you are varnishing furniture, signifies your victory over the battle but failure in the war.

To dream that you see someone varnishing furniture, denotes loss and threat of danger.

Vase

To dream that you receive a vase as a gift, signifies attainment of your heart's desires. You are open to criticism or suggestions.

Vat

To see a vat in your dream, denotes sorrow, grief, and unfaithfulness.

Vatican

To see the Vatican in your dream, denotes unexpected gain due to the action of others.

To see the Vatican deserted and in ruins, signifies loss of friend and lack of support.

Vault

To see a vault in your dream, forewarns that you should guard your own wealth against those who may steal or cheat. Symbolically, vaults represent your inner storehouse of psychological potential. You are at a time where you need to start using your inner reserves of skill an energy and quit continuing to lock and store them away.

To see an open vault, forewarns that you should not flaunt your wealth to everyone.

To see a burial vault in your dream, signifies a personal sadness and/or loss of someone close to you.

VCR

To see a VCR in your dream, suggests that something needs to be or has been carefully documented. There may have been something that you have overlooked. It refers to memories and lessons of the past and the insights you can gain from it. The dream may also be calling attention to the impression you leave behind and what others may think of you.

Vegetables

To see vegetables in your dream, signifies your need for spiritual nourishment. It may also foretell that you are lacking in that nutrient.

To see withered vegetables in your dream, denotes sadness.

Vehicle

To dream that you are riding in a vehicle (car, boat, trains, etc.), denotes that you are in control of your life or that others are exerting power over you depending on who is in the driver's seat.

To dream that you are thrown from a vehicle, symbolizes hasty and unpleasant news.

Veil

To dream that you or someone is wearing a veil, represents something that you wish to hide or conceal. Things may not be what it appears to be.

Vein

To see your vein in your dream, signifies that you are shielded from slander.

To dream that your veins are bleeding, foretells that you will experience great and inescapable sorrow.

To dream that your veins are swollen, signifies your hastiness in placing trust.

Velvet

To dream that you are wearing velvet, signifies distinction and honor. It also represents you sensuality and emotions.

Veneer

To dream that you are veneering, signifies your deception toward friends.

Venom

To come in contact with venom in your dream, represents pent-up anger and hostility you may be expressing or experiencing from others. Your feelings of hate are beginning to show through. The dream is also indicative of a lack of self-esteem, lack of self-love, or insecurities you have.

Ventriloquist

To see a ventriloquist in your dream, symbolizes deception and some treasonable issue effecting you in a negative way.

To dream that you are a ventriloquist, signifies dishonorable conduct and deception towards people who trust you. There is a part of yourself that you are not revealing.

Venus

To see Venus in your dream, symbolizes love, desire, fertility, beauty, and femininity.

Veranda

To dream of being on a veranda, signifies success in a matter which is giving you anxiety.

Verdict

To hear a verdict in your dream, indicates that you are afraid of the truth. You may also fear being judged and criticized for your actions.

Vermin

To see vermin crawling in your dream, signifies sickness and trouble. You may also be faced with many disappointments and obstacles.

Vertigo

To dream that you have vertigo, symbolizes gloominess and loss in domestic happiness.

Vessels

To see vessels in your dream, symbolizes labor and activity.

Vest

To dream that you are wearing a vest, represents compassion for others.

Veterinarian

To see a veterinarian in your dream, indicates that you need to tame your instinctive behavior and unconscious self such that it will be more acceptable in your waking life.

Victim

To dream that you are a victim, forewarns that you will be oppressed and overpowered by your enemies. Such dreams suggest that you feeling powerless and helpless in a situation in your waking life.

To dream that you victimize others, foretells wealth via dishonorable means.

Video Camera

To dream that you are using a video camera, suggests that you need to be more objective in your decisions. Focus on the task at hand and try not to let your emotions cloud your judgment.

To dream that someone is using a video camera, indicates that you are reflecting back on your past and old memories. You may be trying to learn from previous mistakes or relive the good and bad times.

Video Game

To dream that you are playing a video game, represents your ability to manipulate others into doing what you want them to do. Alternatively, it suggests that you are trying to escape and not confront the stress and problems in your real life. Consider the type of video game for additional insights.

To see or dream that you are a character in a video game, suggests that you are feeling controlled and manipulated by others. You feel that you have no control over your actions or are not taking responsibility for them.

Village

To dream that you are in a village, represents restrictions. It may also indicate that you are unsophisticated, but well-balanced. Alternatively, it signifies community, simplicity, and tradition.

Vines

To see vines in your dream, represents your ambitious thoughts or ideas. It may also indicate your clinginess to others.

To see grape vines in your dream, symbolizes rewards, prosperity, and spirituality.

Vinegar

To see or drink vinegar in your dream, suggests that you are feeling sour about some situation. It may denote a relationship that has gone sour. You are worried about something.

Vineyard

To see a vineyard in your dream, represents the fruits of your labor and your life experiences.

Violated

To feel or dream that you have been violated, represents feelings of being oppressed by others or by situations in your life. You feel that you cannot change the path that your life is taking on. Try not to blame yourself for circumstances that are beyond your control.

Violence

To see violence in your dream, indicates unexpressed anger or rage. You need more discipline in your life. The dream may also reflect repressed memories of child abuse.

Violets

To see violets in your dream, signifies joy and possible marital bliss.

Violin

To see or hear a violin in your dream, symbolizes peace and harmony in the family.

To play a violin in your dream, denotes honor and foretells that you will be a recipient of lavish gifts.

To see a broken violin in your dream, signifies separation, sadness, and bereavement.

Viper

To see a viper in your dream, foretells that your tranquility is being threatened.

Virgin

To dream that you are a virgin, symbolizes purity and potential. In particular, for a married woman to dream that she is a virgin, signifies past regrets and remorse and a bleak future.

Virgin Mary

To see the Virgin Mary in your dream, signifies spiritual harmony and/or ideal motherhood. Alternatively, the Virgin Mary represents a repressed fear of sexuality or difficulties in relationships.

Vise

To see or use a vise in your dream, suggests that you are feeling confined and restricted. You feel that you cannot fully express yourself.

Vision

To dream that your vision is obstructed, signifies that you are having difficulties and errors in judgment.

To see strange visions in your dream, denotes misfortune and illness.

Visitor

To have a visitor in your dream, signifies good news will reach you. It also foretells of new conditions or changes.

To see a darkly dressed visitor, forewarns of illness or accidents that might befall on you or someone you know.

Vitamins

To see or take a vitamin in your dream, indicates that you need to strengthen your willpower. You may also need to stand up for yourself. Alternatively, it may point to you waking eating habits and the need for you to add certain nutrients to your diet.

Voiceless

To dream that you are voiceless, represents a lost of identity and a lack of personal power. You are unable to speak up and stand up for yourself.

Voices

To hear pleasing and calm voices in your dream, signifies pleasant reunions and reconciliation.

To hear angry and high-pitched voices in your dream, denotes disappointments and unfavorable situations.

To hear voices that is barely audible, denotes that you need to listen more carefully and pay attention to your inner needs.

For a mother to dream that she hears the voice of her child, signifies lingering misery and grief.

Volcano

To see a volcano in your dream, denotes violent disputes or repressed thoughts. Your emotions are about to "erupt". Your honesty and fair character may also be threatened or attacked.

Volleyball

To dream that you are playing volleyball, represents your indecisiveness and your inability to make commitments. Alternatively, it indicates the importance of cooperation and teamwork. You need to learn to rely on others instead of doing everything yourself.

Volunteer

To dream that you volunteer for something or are a volunteer, represents the value of helping others in need. It also implies charity and your willingness to offer your assistance.

Vomiting

To dream that you are vomiting, indicates that you need to reject or discard an aspect of your life that is revolting. There are some emotions or concepts that you need to confront and then let go.

To see others vomiting in your dream, signifies false pretenses of people who try to take advantage of you.

Voodoo

To dream that you are practicing voodoo, suggests that you are unconsciously trying ward off surrounding negative energy.

To see a voodoo doll in your dream, represents a primitive and shadowy aspect of yourself.

Vote

To dream that you are casting a vote, suggests that you are speaking your min and letting your voice be heard.

Voucher

To see a voucher in your dream, foretells of schemes against you that may affect your fortunes.

To dream that you sign a voucher, denotes that you have the aid of confidence of those around you.

Voyage

To dream that you are making a voyage in your dream, foretells of an inheritance.

To dream of a disastrous voyage, symbolizes incompetence and false loves.

Voyeurism

To dream that you are a voyeur, suggests that you are afraid of your own desires and fantasies. Your are afraid of getting close to some relationship or situation.

Vultures

To see vultures in your dream, suggests that your past experiences is providing you invaluable insight into a current situation or problem.

W

Wading

To dream of wading in clear water, signifies a wonderful love affair and good luck in your undertakings.

To dream of wading in muddy water, signifies bad luck, illness, violence or loss of love and money.

Wadding

To dream of using wadding in the loading of a rifle, foretells that you need to arm yourself against the hostile actions and words of others.

To dream of using wadding in the filling of artistic work, indicates that your creativity will be greatly rewarded.

Wafers

For a young lady to dream of eating wafers, indicates that she is too picky in her search for male companionship.

For a young lady to dream a cooking wafers, signifies a long and happy marriage with the man of her choosing.

For a man to see wafers in his dream, signifies general good fortune.

Wager

To dream that you won a wager, signifies good fortune coming your way.

To dream that you lost a wager, signifies misfortune and losses.

To dream that you are making a wager, denotes dishonesty.

Wages

To dream that you are paying out wages, signifies your dissatisfaction over a particular issue.

To dream that you are receiving wages, symbolizes an omen of good fortune for your business.

Wagon

To see a wagon in your dream, is symbolic of difficulties. It also signifies your thrifty nature and your unwillingness to take risks.

To see an empty and abandoned wagon, signifies loss and dissatisfaction.

Wagtail

To see a wagtail in your dream, foretells that you will be a victim of unpleasant gossip resulting in some sort of loss.

Waif

To dream that you take in and care for a waif, signifies an increase in your business affairs.

To see several waifs in you dream, symbolizes that your sorrows will increase tenfold.

Wail

To hear a wail in your dream, foretells fearful news and sorrow.

Waist

To see a large full waist, signifies a pleasing and comfortable life.

To see a small petite waist, signifies success in business and educational pursuits.

To dream of an unhealthy, emaciated waist, signifies failure in business and educational pursuits.

Waiter/Waitress

To dream that you are a waiter or waitress, indicates that you are catering to the demands of others instead of your own. You feel that you are waiting on somebody hand and foot and are not being appreciated.

Waiting

To dream that you are waiting, is indicative of issues of power/control and feelings of dependence/independence, especially in a relationship. Consider how you feel in the dream while you were waiting. Alternatively, it may denote your expectations and anxieties about some unknown situation or result. You are ready to take action.

Wake

To dream that you attend a wake of a friend or loved one, foretells that you will hear sad news.

To see a friend attending a wake, forewarns that that friend is in grave danger.

To dream that you are waking up in your dream, indicates that something is missing or lacking in your life. There is an aspect of your life that you are not utilizing to its fullest potential. You are not recognizing your abilities.

Walking

To dream that you are walking with ease, represents the way you are moving through life and progress toward your goals. Consider your destination.

To dream that you have difficulties walking, indicates that you are reluctant and hesitant in proceeding forward in some situation. You may also be trying to distance yourself from certain life experiences. The difficulty in walking is a reflection of your current situation and the obstacles that you are experiencing.

To dream that you are walking at night, signifies discontent and struggle for contentment.

Walking Stick

To see a walking stick in your dream, indicates that you are jumping commitments too quickly and will suffer as a result.

To see yourself using a walking stick in your dream, signifies your dependence on others for advice.

Wallet

To see a wallet in your dream, symbolizes financial resources or self-identification.

To dream that your wallet has been stolen, indicates that someone may be trying to take advantage of you.

To dream that you lost your wallet, suggests that you need to be more cautious and careful about your spending and finances. You need to be more responsible with your money.

Wallpaper

To dream that you or someone else is hanging up wallpaper, signifies that you are putting up a barrier or some sort of shield between yourself and others. It also suggest that you are covering something up - a secret of sorts. Alternatively, it may mean something that needs beautifying.

To dream that you are peeling or stripping off wallpaper, denotes that you are beginning to let your guard down or breaking down a barrier that you have kept between you and others. It also indicates that you are revealing aspects of yourself that have been kept well hidden.

The color and pattern of the wallpaper will offer clues as what kind of barrier, secret, or feeling is being represented by the wallpaper.

Walls

To see a wall in your dream, signifies limitations. obstacles and boundaries. There is a barrier obstructing your progress. You may have been accustomed to your old habits and way of thinking.

To dream that you jump over a wall, suggests that you will overcome tough obstacles and succeed.

To dream that you demolish or break down a wall, indicates that you are breaking through obstacles and overcoming your limitations. If you see a wall crumble, then it suggests that you have easily risen above your problems and overcame your barriers.

To dream that you are building a wall, represents a bad relationship or some childhood trauma. It also suggest that you have accepted your limitations.

To dream that you are hiding behind a wall, suggests that you ashamed in acknowledging your connections.

To dream that you are being thrown or shot through a wall, literally means that you need to breakdown those walls that you have put up around you. You need to venture out and explore.

Walnut

To see walnuts in your dream, symbolizes that much mental activity is being expended towards a task at hand. Walnuts also represent joy and abundance.

To dream that you crack a walnut, foretells that your expectations will collapse.

Walrus

To see a walrus in your dream, signifies protection and your display of dominance in some situation or relationship. You are always on the lookout for anybody who is trying to out-maneuver, out-rank, or out-wit you. Alternatively, the walrus may represent your thick-skin and how you do not let the comments/criticism of others get to you.

For Eskimos and Native Americans in the North, the walrus symbolizes supernatural ability and powers.

Waltz

To see a waltz in your dream, foretells that you will have pleasant relations with a cheerful and exciting person.

To dream that you are waltzing, denotes that you are the object of much admiration.

Wand

To see a wand in your dream, symbolizes the power of love. It also represents your will and good heartedness.

Wander

To dream that you are wandering, suggests that you are searching and looking for some direction in your life. You are lacking motivation. Alternatively, it represents a transformation.

Want

To dream that you are in want, denotes misfortune, sorrow and adversity.

War

To dream of a war, signifies disorder and chaos in your personal affairs. You also be experiencing some internal conflict or emotional struggle. You are feeling torn between aspects of yourself. Perhaps the dream may indicate that you are being overly aggressive or you are not being assertive enough.

**See The Meaning In Action: "_Drafted Into War_"*

Wardrobe

To dream of your wardrobe, signifies that your fortune will be endangered by your attempts to appear richer than you are.

To dream that you have a small wardrobe, foretells that you will seek association with strangers.

Warehouse

To see a warehouse in your dream, represents stored energy or hidden resources. They also refer to memories. You may also be putting your ambitions and goals on hold.

To see an empty warehouse, indicates that you inner resources have been depleted. You need to take some time off to restore your energy and replenish your resources.

Warrant

To dream that a warrant is being served on you, denotes that you will involved with some important matters which will lead to uneasiness.

To dream that a warrant is served on someone else, signifies misunderstandings and quarrel.

Warrior

To see or dream that you are a warrior, represents life's challenges and your ability to confront them.

Warts

To dream that you or someone have a wart, suggests that you need to learn to acknowledge the beauty in you. The dream indicates that you may be self-punishing yourself and unwilling to forgive yourself.

Washboard

To see or use a washboard in your dream, signifies embarrassment. You may be feeling emotionally and/or physically drained.

To see a broken washboard, signifies grief and disgrace as a result of living on the fast lane.

Wash Bowl

To see a wash bowl in your dream, denotes a new interest resulting in much joy and contentment will occupy your time.

To dream that you are washing your face and/or hands in a wash bowl, signifies that you will be consumed with passion for someone close to you.

To see a broken wash bowl in your dream, signifies small pleasure for you while giving pain to others.

Washer Woman

To see a washer woman in your dream, signifies infidelity and/or a peculiar adventure.

Washing

To dream that you are washing yourself, signifies that you are proud of your social life and personal endeavors. You may even receive some fame and prestige. Alternatively, it may symbolize the cleansing away of unhappy experiences or emotions in your life.

To dream that you are washing your feet, signifies that you will be changing your line of work and undertake a more fruitful venture.

To dream that you are washing your car, foretells that you illness and troubles will soon pass.

Washing Machine

To see or use a washing machine in your dream, suggests that you need to resolve past issues and old problems in order to make a clean start for yourself.

Wasp

To see a wasp in you dream, signifies angry thoughts and feelings.

To dream that you are stung by a wasp, symbolizes growing envy and hatred towards you.

To dream that you kill a wasp, signifies your fearlessness to ward off your enemies and maintain your ethics and rights.

Watch

To see or wear a watch in your dream, suggests that you need to be more carefree and spontaneous. You are feeling limited and constrained.

To see a broken watch in your dream, indicates that you are unsure of your own feelings or how to express yourself. You are experiencing an emotional standstill.

Watching

To dream that you are watching something, represents you lack of initiative to take any action. It may also symbolize your neutrality in some situation.

Water

To see water in your dream, symbolizes your unconscious and your emotional state of mind. Water is the living essence of the psyche and the flow of life energy. It is also symbolic of spirituality, knowledge, healing and refreshment. To dream that water is boiling, suggests that you are expressing some emotional turmoil. It also may mean that feelings from your unconscious are surfacing and ready to be acknowledged.

To see calm, clear water in your dream, signifies that you are in tune with your spirituality. It denotes serenity, peace of mind, and rejuvenation.

To see muddy or dirty water in your dream, indicates that you are wallowing in your negative emotions. You may need to devote some time to clarify your mind and find internal peace. Alternatively, it suggests that your thinking/judgment is unclear and clouded. If you are immersed in muddy water, then it indicates that you are in over your head in a situation and are overwhelmed by your emotions.

To dream that water is rising up in your house, signifies your struggles and overwhelming emotions.

To hear running water in your dream, denotes meditation, reflection and pondering of your thoughts and emotions.

To dream that you are walking on water, suggests that you have supreme and ultimate control over your emotions. It may also suggest that you need to "stay on top" of your emotions and not let them explode out of hand. Alternatively, it is symbolic of faith in yourself.

Water Carrier

To see a water carrier in your dream, signifies favorable prospects in fortune and love.

To dream that you are a water carrier, foretells that you will rise above your current position.

Water Lily

To see a water lily in your dream, signifies grief, sorrow, and bereavement.

Water Skiing

To dream that you are water skiing, represents an uplift in your spirituality and increase in your self-confidence. It also indicates feelings of peacefulness and freedom.

Waterbed

To see a waterbed in our dream, suggests that have come to accept and recognizing your emotions. You are slowly acknowledging aspects of your unconscious. It also represents a rise in your unconscious and repressed energy, particularly issues dealing with sexuality, fear, aggression, etc.

Waterfall

To see a waterfall in your dream, is symbolic of letting go. You are releasing all those pent up emotions and negative feelings. The dream may also represent your goals and desires. In particular, if the waterfall is clear, then it represents revitalization and renewal.

To dream that you are at the bottom of the waterfall, suggests that you are feeling emotionally overwhelmed. You are experiencing difficulties in coping with your feelings.

Watermelon

To see a watermelon in you dream, represents emotions of love, desire, lust, and fiery passion. Pregnant women or women on the verge of their menstrual cycle often dream of such fruits, as watermelons. Alternatively, watermelons may be associated with summertime ease, leisure, and relaxation.

Watermill

To see a watermill in your dream, suggests that you need to keep your options open and utilize the resources that is available to you. You also need to proceed at a steady pace in realizing your goals. The dream is one of motivation and renewal.

Waterslide

To dream that you are on or see a waterslide, suggests that you are being swept away by your emotions. You are slowly exploring the realm of your unconscious. Alternatively, the dream suggests that you are going with the flow of things without any objections or resistance.

Waves

To see clear, calm waves in your dream, signifies a calming of emotions. It may also signal an important decision to be made.

To hear waves crashing in your dream, indicates tenderness and relaxation. It also brings about feelings of sensuality and sexuality.

To dream that you are caught in a tidal wave, signifies the strength of your emotions, perhaps accompanied by tears that you are holding back in your waking life.

To see muddy, violent waves in your dream, signifies that a fatal error was made in an important decision.

Waving

To dream that you are waving to someone, signifies your connection to that person. You are trying to get their recognition, acknowledgement, or attention. Additionally, you need to incorporate certain aspects of that person into your own self. The dream may also signify your need to develop deeper and closer friendship ties.

Wax

To see wax in your dream indicates that there is too much activity going on in your life. You may need to slow down and take a breather. Alternatively, it may symbolize the passage of time that has long passed.

To see dripping wax in your dream, represents your hidden passionate emotions.

Way

To dream that you lose your way, signifies the threat of failure in your endeavors.

Weak

To dream that you are weak, refers to your feelings of inadequacy. You need to be more firm and forceful. Stand up for yourself.

Wealth

To dream that you are wealthy, signifies vitality and zest leading to your success.

To see others wealthy, denotes that your friends will be supportive in your times of need.

Weapons

To see or hold a weapon in your dream, indicates a need to defend and protect yourself emotionally and/or physically. You are experiencing some conflict in your waking life. Alternatively, it suggests a fear of sexuality.

Weasel

To see a weasel in your dream, represents your lack of trust in others. It may also mean that you are acting or being decietful.

Weather

To dream about the weather, signifies your emotional state of mind. Stormy or windy weather implies conflict and aggression. Rain and hail represents depression and sadness. And rainbows and sunshine signifies hope and happiness.

To dream that you are reading the weather report, foretells that you will move from your current resident.

Weather Vane

To see a weather vane in your dream, indicates unpredictability and versatility. You may feel that you are going around in circles. The dream may also be a pun on being vain or doing something in vain.

Weaving

To dream that you are weaving something, suggests that you are trying to piece together some information. You need to look at the picture as a whole.

Web

To see a web in your dream, represents your desire to control everything around you. Alternatively, it suggests that you are being held back from fully expressing yourself. You feel trapped. The dream may also symbolize your network of acquaintances and associates.

Wedding

To see a wedding in your dream, symbolizes a new beginning or transition in your current life. Dreams involving weddings are generally negative and highlight some anxiety or fear. It often refers to feelings of bitterness, sorrow, or death.

Alternatively, wedding dreams reflect your issues about commitment and independence.

To dream that you are getting married to your current spouse again, represents your wedded bliss and happiness. It highlights your strong commitment to each other. It may also signify a new phase (such as parenthood) that you are entering in your life.

To dream that you are planning your own wedding to someone you never met, is a metaphor symbolizing the union of your masculine and feminine side. It represents a transitional phase where you are seeking some sort of balance between your aggressive side and emotional side.

Please see also Marriage. See The Meaning In Action: "Black Wedding"

Wedding Clothes

To see wedding clothes in your dream, signifies new friends and pleasurable undertakings.

To see soiled wedding clothes in your dream, signifies a falling-out with an admirable person.

Wedding Ring

To see your own wedding ring, signifies protection from pain and hurt.

To see a wedding ring on another's hand, signifies your unfaithfulness, which may lead to illicit behavior.

Wedge

To see a wedge in your dream, means trouble and possible separation from loved ones.

Wedlock

To dream that you are forced into wedlock, foretells that you will be forced into a disagreeable situation.

To dream that you are dissatisfied with your wedlock, foretells tendencies toward illicit behavior.

Weeds

To dream that you are weeding, suggests that you need to rid yourself of the negativity in your life in order to move on and grow as a person. It is time to release past grudges and build on future relationships.

To see weeds in your dream, signifies that you may have to get rid of some old ideas or negative thoughts in your mind. It is symbolic of neglect. Weeds can also represent friendships or relationships that have gone awry.

Weeping

To dream that you are weeping, signifies bad news and disruption in the family.

To see others weeping in your dream, symbolizes pleasant reunion after periods of saddened estrangements.

Weevil

To see a weevil in your dream, signifies business losses or falseness in love.

Weight

To dream of your own weight, represents your self-worth, self-esteem, influence or power or persuasion. It is also indicative of the burdens you carry in life. Alternatively, it may represent your preoccupation with your physical shape and appearance. The dream may also be a pun for "wait".

To dream that you are losing weight, indicates that you are no longer being weighed down. It is as if something has been lifted off your shoulders.

To dream that you are overweight or that you are gaining weight, suggests that you are feeling over-burdened and pressured. You may be carrying too many responsibilities.

To dream that you are underweight, implies that you need to work harder at something. You may also be way out of your league in some situation.

Well

To see a well in your dream, refers to your willingness to share.

Welcome

To dream that you receive a warm welcome into any society or situation, foretells that you will be distinguished amongst your social circle.

Werewolf

To see a werewolf in your dream, indicates that something in your life is not what it seems. It is symbolic of fear, repressed anger, and uncontrollable violence.

To dream that you are a werewolf, suggests that some aspects of your personality are hurtful and even dangerous to your own well-being. You are headed down an undesirable path. Alternatively, it refers to your repressed instincts.

West

To dream of going west, represents fulfillment, opportunities, and growth. Alternatively, it may symbolize an ending of something, death, or old age.

Wet

To dream that you are wet, suggests that you are drenched in emotions. It also signifies spirituality.

Wet Nurse

To see a wet nurse in your dream, foretells that you will be widowed.

To dream that you are a wet nurse, signifies dependence on your own labors.

Wet Suit

To see or wear a wet suit in your dream, suggests that you are slowly and safely exploring your inner feelings and emotions. You may at a point where you are comfortable in acknowledging your vulnerabilities and feelings.

Whale

To see a whale in your dream, represents your intuition and awareness. You are in tuned to your sense of spirituality. Alternatively, it indicates a relationship or business project that is too enormous to handle.

Wheat

To see a field of wheat in your dream, signifies success in your goals.

To see large grains of wheat, symbolizes prosperity and opened doors in your endeavors.

Wheelbarrow

To see or use a wheelbarrow in your dream, represents hard work, labor, and difficulties. It also symbolizes your body and the way that you are moving about through life.

Wheelchair

To see or dream that you are in a wheelchair, suggests that you need to stand on your own two feet and stop depending on others. Perhaps you are feeling helpless. Alternatively, it indicates that you are literally letting others push you around. You need to start standing up for yourself.

If someone is able-bodied in real life, but you dream that they are in a wheelchair, then it suggests that he/she is in need of your help. They may be afraid to ask you directly and have been dropping hints which your unconscious may have picked up on.

Wheels

To see rotating wheels in your dream, signifies completion or continuation of a familiar situation. Your life and daily routine is become to repetitious. Be more spontaneous.

Whip

To see a whip in your dream, symbolizes punishment and an abusive situation. It also represents unhappiness, unfortunate circumstances and to a certain degree, shame and guilt. Alternatively, it may indicate that you need to exercise more control over your life. You need to have more discipline.

To dream that you are whipping an assailant, signifies that through your perseverance and courage, you will experience wealth and honor, despite of any opposition.

Whipping Boy

To see a whipping boy in your dream, suggests that you are doing damage to yourself. Your reckless behavior and activities will lead you to a road of self-destruction. You need to find your Self, who you are, and think about what you want to do with your life.

Whirlpool

To see a whirlpool in your dream, signifies great and imminent danger in your business affairs and disgrace to your reputation.

Whirlwind

To dream that you are in the path of a whirlwind, signifies changes which may lead to loss, chaos and scandal. You are being pulled unwillingly into a facing your repressed thoughts.

Whisky

To see whisky in bottles, symbolizes your alertness, carefulness and protective nature.

To dream that you are drinking whisky, suggests that your selfishness will cost you your friends. Alternatively, it represents your lack of self-confidence. You are trying to escape the responsibilities of your everyday life.

Whispering

To dream of whispering, signifies malicious and disturbing gossip surrounding you.

Whistle

To hear a whistle in your dream, signifies shocking news that will alter your plans.

To dream that you are whistling, signifies joy and pleasure.

White Moth

To see a white moth in your dream, forewarns of sickness and possibly death of a loved one.

Whitewash

To dream that you are whitewashing, indicates an attempt to change your old ways and habits. It also suggests that you are only pretending to change and trying to cover up your flaws.

Whore

Please See Prostitute.

Widow

To dream that you are a widow, represents loneliness. You may be feeling isolated and/or abandoned.

Wife

To see your wife in your dream, signifies discord and unresolved issues.

Wig

To dream that you are wearing a wig, symbolizes deception, false impressions and falsehood. You may be taking on other people's ideas and opinions and trying to pass them off as your own. You are not being true to your own beliefs. You need to start thinking for yourself.

To dream that you lose a wig, indicates that you have completely lost your mind.

Wilderness

To dream that you are running through the wilderness, suggests that you are uninhibited and free. You feel that there are no restrictions to hold you back.

Willow

To see a willow tree in your dream, symbolizes mourning and sadness.

Wilted

To dream that something is wilted, suggests that you are feeling physically and/or emotionally drained. You may be feeling depressed. Alternatively, the dream indicates that you are not utilizing your full potential. You may be wasting away your talents.

Win

To dream that you win at something, signifies triumph and success. You have much confidence and belief in yourself. All your self-doubts have subsided.

Wind

To dream of blowing winds, symbolizes your life force, energy, and vigor. It reflects changes in your life.

To dream of strong or gusty winds, represents turmoil and trouble for you. You are experiencing much stress in some waking situation.

Windchimes

To see or hear windchimes in your dream, symbolizes harmony and tranquility. It may also represent memories or the passage of time.

Windmill

To see a functional windmill in your dream, represents the power of the mind. It is also indicative of your emotional state of mind.

To see an idle or broken windmill, signifies unexpected obstacles.

Window

To see windows in your dream, signifies bright hopes, vast possibilities and insight.

To dream that you are looking out the window, signifies your outlook on life, your consciousness, point of view, awareness, and intuition. You may be reflecting on a decision and seeking guidance. If you are looking in the window, then it indicates that you are doing some soul searching and looking within yourself.

To see shut windows in your dream, signifies desertion and abandonment.

To see shattered and broken windows, denotes misery and disloyalty.

To see a tinted window in your dream, represents you need for privacy and your ways of getting it. You are keeping aspects of yourself hidden or that you want to remain ambiguous.

See The Meaning In Action: "Online Encounter"

Window Washer

To see a window washer in your dream, represents your ability to clarify a situation and shed some perspective on an issue.

Wine

To dream of drinking wine, refers to festivity, celebration, and companionship.

To dream that you are breaking wine bottles, signifies overindulgence in your desires and passion.

Wine Cellar

To see a wine cellar in your dream, signifies great pleasure and good times.

Wine Glass

To see a wine glass in your dream, symbolizes trouble and shocking disappointments.

Wings

To dream that you have wings, indicates your sweet, angelic quality. You may be in need of some protection from life's stresses and problems. Or you may be trying to escape from a difficult situation.

To see the wings of birds, denotes that you have overcome your struggle to attain wealth and honor.

Please see Common Dream Themes: Flying

Winter

To dream of winter, signifies ill-health, depression. and misfortune. For others, it may symbolize a favorite time of the year signaling the holiday season of fun and frolic.

Wire

To see a wire in your dream, symbolizes your short but frequent journeys.

To see old or rusty wire in your dream, signifies your bad temper.

Wish

To dream that you are making a wish, indicates that there is something that you are longing for and missing in your life. What do you hope to accomplish in the future.

Witch

To see a witch in your dream, represents evil, destructive, and dangerous feminine forces. It may point to your negative ideas of the feminine and your experiences with heartless women. Alternatively, a witch is symbolic of goodness, power and enchantment.

Witchcraft

To dream about witchcraft, suggests that something or someone is manipulating you and your surroundings.

Wizard

To see a wizard in your dream, suggests that you are trying to hone your skills and exercise your power.

Woke

Please See Awaken.

Wolf

To see a wolf in your dream, symbolizes beauty, solitude, mystery, self-confidence and pride. You are able to keep your composure in a variety of social situations and can blend in with any situation with ease and grace. You are a loner by choice. Negatively, it represents hostility and aggression. It may also reflect an uncontrollable force or situation in your life. In particular, if the wolf is white, then it signifies valor and victory. You have the ability to see the light even in your darkest hours.

To dream that you kill a wolf, indicates betrayal and secrets revealed.

Woman

To see a woman in your dream, represents nurturance, passivity, caring nature, and love. It refers to your own female aspects or may also represent your mother. Alternatively, it may indicate temptation and guilt. If you know the woman, then it may symbolize the concerns and feelings you have about her.

To see an old woman in your dream, indicates aging and growing old.

To see a group of women talking in your dream, refers to some gossip.

To see a pregnant women in your dream, symbolizes abundant wealth.

Wood

To dream of wood, suggests that you are feeling dead inside and emotionless. You may be behaving automatically and just going along with the flow. Or you may be acting out without fully thinking things through.

To dream that you are carving or shaping a piece of wood, indicates a power-giving, creative act/gesture. Alternatively, the wood may also symbolize spirituality and vital energy.

Wooden Shoe

To see a wooden shoe in your dream, signifies solitude and unfaithfulness.

Wood Pile

To see a wood pile in your dream, signifies unsatisfactory business and misunderstandings in love.

Woodpecker

To see a woodpecker in your dream, indicates that there is something in you waking life which you have overlooked. The woodpecker also symbolizes industry and diligence.

Woods

To see the woods in your dream, represents life, fertility, rejuvenation, and spring. Alternatively, it symbolizes the unknown and unconscious. You need to be more open-minded to discovering your potential and instinctual nature.

To dream that you are walking through the woods, signifies your return to an aspect of yourself that is innocent and spiritual.

To dream that you are lost in the woods, indicates that you are starting a new phase in your life. You are expressing some anxiety about leaving behind the familiar and what you know.

To see dried up, dying woods in your dream, suggests that there is a situation in your life that has not yet been resolved. You may also be overwhelmed with a problem or issue.

Wool

To see wool in your dream, symbolizes warmth and coziness. You are seeking protection from loved ones.

Work

To dream that you are at work, indicates that you are experiencing some anxiety about a current project or task. The dream may also be telling you that you need to "get back to work". Perhaps you have been slacking and need to pick up the pace.

To dream that you are at your former or past work, suggests that there is an old lesson that you need to learn and apply to your current situation.

To dream that you are hard at work, signifies success and merit. Alternatively, it may suggest anxieties about a current task or project. You may need to "get back to work" and stop procrastinating.

Workman

To see workmen in your dream, signifies that you need to work on yourself and explore your mind.

Workshop

To see a workshop in you dream, represents the development of your skills. You are trying to understand your Self and find out who you are.

World

To dream that it is the end of the world, suggests that you are under a tremendous level of stress. You may be feeling vulnerable or helpless in some situation.

To dream that you are saving the world, signifies confidence in your abilities and belief in yourself. You do not let others question your intelligence or your abilities and generally have a good perspective on life and what your goals are. Don't let someone or something prevent you from progressing forward.

**See The Meaning In Action: "End Of The World"*

Worm

To see a worm in your dream, represents weakness and general negativity. You have a very low opinion of yourself or of someone in your life.

To dream that the worm is crawling on your body, indicates that you feel someone around you is taking advantage of your and feeding off your kind heartedness.

Wound

To see a wound in your dream, is symbolic of grief, anger, and distress. You are looking to be healed.

Wreath

To see a wreath in your dream, signifies opportunities and enrichment.

To see a withered wreath in your dream, symbolizes sickness and wounded love.

Wreck

To see a wreck in your dream, represents obstacles and barriers toward your goals. You feel that you are being held back or that you are not making any progress.

Wrestling

To dream that you are wrestling, signifies that your are grappling with a problem in your personal or professional life. You are dealing with ideas and habits that need to be brought back into control.

Wrinkle

To see a wrinkle in your dream, represents your feelings of getting older or wiser. It also represents the things you have learned from your past experiences.

Wrist

To notice your wrist in your dream, represents your ability to bring about fun/excitement and productivity at the same time. You are able to grab the attention of others and get them involved.

Writing

To dream that you are writing, signifies some sort of communication with someone or with your conscious mind. It also denotes a mistake that you have made.

X

To dream of a treasure map marked a big X , indicates that your goals are in sight and you will soon be greatly rewarded.

X-Ray

To dream that you are being x-rayed, denotes that you are being deceived by a person or situation. It is time for you to look beneath the surface of this person or situation. On the other hand, you may have sought yourself through a problem or issue that has been troubling you

Xylophone

To dream of seeing a xylophone, foretells you will achieve your greatest ambitions with recognition and honor.

Y

To see the letter Y in your dream, indicates some decisions that you need to make. It may represent a fork in the road or path you need to choose. The letter Y may also be a pun on "why". You need to start questioning things.

Yacht

To see a yacht in your dream, symbolizes wealth, pleasure, and luxury. You are worry-free and pursuing a life of ease. It may also indicate your desire to devote more time to recreational pursuits. You need to take it easy for a while.

Yak

To see a yak in your dream, represents your uniqueness and dependability. The yak may also be pun on yakking too much. Maybe you should stop talking and listen more.

Yam

To see yams in your dream, signifies memories of family gatherings and celebration.

Yankee

To dream of being called a Yankee in your dreams, foretells that your lover could be less than true.

To call someone else a Yankee in your dreams, foretells that your plans will go accordingly without a hitch.

To see Yankees in your dream, signifies happiness, possible gains and loyalty to your duty and promise.

Yard

To see a neat and well-kept yard, reflects your ability to maintain and organize aspects of your outside life, such as work and your social activities.

To see a messy and un-kept yard, denotes that aspects of your life are out of your control.

Yard Sale

To hold or be at a yard sale in your dream, indicates that you are recycling past experiences and finding use for your old skills and ideas. You are learning from your past and making productive use of the lessons you have learned.

Yard Stick

To see a yard stick in your dream. foretells much anxiety over your business and/or personal affairs.

Yarn

To see yarn in your dream, symbolizes your connections and creativity. It may also mean that you are stuck in a rut and going about your daily life in the same old pattern. If the yarn is tangled and knotted yarn, then it signifies emotional distress or confusion you may have with a situation.

Yawning

To dream that you or someone is yawning in your dream, suggests that you need to be emotionally and intellectually stimulated. Your are lacking energy and vitality in your life.

Yearn

To dream that you are being yearned for, indicates that you will soon be greeted with a proposal for marriage.

To dream that you yearn for someone, foretells that you will find joy and contentment with your present love.

Yeast

To see yeast in your dream, indicates a spiritual quest. You may need to do some soul searching and/or self-improvement. Alternatively, yeast is symbolic of your renewed energy or increased enthusiasm for an idea/project.

Yelling

To dream that you or someone is yelling, represents repressed anger that need to be expressed.

Yeti

To see a yeti in your dream, suggests that you need to learn to find balance between your reasonable, rational side and your emotional, instinctual nature.

Yellow Bird

To see a yellow bird in your dream, foretells good luck in financial affairs, but not so good in affairs of the heart.

To see a yellow bird land on your, denotes misfortune.

To see a dead or sick yellow bird, foretells disaster in your affairs.

Yew Tree

To see a yew tree in your dream, symbolizes mourning and death.

Yield

To dream that you yield to another in your decision-making, denotes your willingness to sacrifice your authority to secure peace in the family.

To dream that others yield to you, denotes an enhancement in your present business position.

Yoga

To dream that you are performing, symbolizes calmness and control of mind and body. You have great self-discipline.

Yogurt

To see or eat yogurt in your dream, suggests that you need to learn to behave appropriately for the different situations and circumstances you find yourself in.

Yoke

To see a yoke in your dream, signifies your unwillingness to conform to the customs and wishes of others..

To dream that you are yoking an oxen, indicates that your advice and counsel will be accepted by a friend or family member.

To dream that you fail to yoke an oxen, indicates your worry for someone in your life.

Young

To see young people in your dream, symbolizes an end to your worries and a fresh outlook on life will be gained. It may also represent the younger aspect of yourself.

To dream that you are young again, symbolizes your failed attempts to rectify past mistakes and lost opportunities.

Yourself

To see yourself in your dream, is a reflection of how you act and behave in your waking life.

Yule Log

To see a Yule log in your dream, signifies a positive turn of events in the coming year.

To dream of burning a Yule log, warns that you should not set your sights too high.

Printed in the United States
65512LVS00005B/41